Reading Under the Covers

To Murray Hunt,
neighbor and friend,
Elizabeth

To my parents, who gave me life, and to my children—my dearest friends—who have loved me and been with me unfailingly.

Contents

Prologue 1

Chapter 1	Puritan Child in New England 7	
Chapter 2	Visiting Hitler's Germany in 1938 27	
Chapter 3	Introduction to Segregation. 38	
Chapter 4	Marriage, Childbirth, Abusive Husband 47	
Chapter 5	Divorce and Descent into Breakdown 70	
Chapter 6	A Cornell Freshman at 33 87	
Chapter 7	Political Awakening and Prison 99	
Chapter 8	Back to Square One—A Single Mother Again 109	
Chapter 9	From Hippie Mother to Professor's Wife 116	
Chapter 10	Culture Shock and Adventure in Ankara, Turkey 129	
Chapter 11	Guest Lecturer in Izmir, Turkey 146	
Chapter 12	Troubled Years 166	
Chapter 13	The *est* Training and Transformation 187	
Chapter 14	Dreams of Being an *est* Trainer 198	
Chapter 15	LSD, Awakening and Hawai'i 215	
Chapter 16	Supporting *est* of India 226	
Chapter 17	"It Will Happen by Christmas"—The Holiday Project 241	

Chapter 18	The Last Man	252
Chapter 19	Mrs. Santa Claus: Another Year of The Holiday Project	262
Chapter 20	Expect the Unexpected	268
Chapter 21	The Prodigal Returns	283
Epilogue		291

Acknowledgments

This book is in partial fulfillment of a debt to all those out of my past who had greater faith in me than I had in myself, to the teachers who made me realize how much was possible: Gladys Jubb, Gordon Pyper, Knight Biggerstaff, George McT. Kahin, Clarence Shute, Bill Lauroesch, Leo Zeff, and Werner Erhard.

A special acknowledgment is due to Kenneth Ireland, who worked with me as editor and without whose encouragement I might never have completed the book.

There are many others who aided and abetted in various ways: Laurence Platt who shared with me his experience of Werner to add to my picture of the man, Fran Alexander who read the whole manuscript and gave me line-by-line criticism, Priscilla Williams who gave me professional commentary, Byron Callas who read and read and read and gave me honest feedback, Joan Jackson who made sure the commas were in the right places and Michael Sells, whose book, *Mystical Languages of Unsaying* kept drawing me back to its pages. Mort Weinstein coached me in looking for a title and Rich Wiersba gave me computer assistance. Also, Tim Batchelder gave me a much-needed place to use as a retreat when I needed solitude for writing.

Then there were those readers who, not knowing me well, served as representatives of a public readership: Jean Mehren, Barth Marshall, Harriett Hunter, Dr. Jane Curry, Xav DuBois, Jake Goldenflame, Micki Goldberg. To Sheila Babbie and Carolyn Goto my thanks for continuing to remind me that I had promised them a book.

My daughters, Marta and Rebecca, and son Jerry gave me feedback on family events that may or may not have been accurately represented in my writing and it was Marta who gave me the title that seemed to fit my life.

My thanks to Randy McNamara who told me how to start the process of examining a life.

And, finally, I will always be grateful to Martin and Esther Russell for encouraging me on this path.

Prologue

Mother was barely recognizable under the network of wires and tubes. Her sparse gray hair was, in some spots, plastered to her head and, in others, spread out like a broken halo on the pillow. Her hands, still on the white sheet covering her frail body, were a life map of veins and bones thinly concealed by the delicate parchment of skin covering them. I stood at her bedside, tears slipping down my cheeks.

As if sensing my presence she opened her eyes, and reached a hand out to me. At 91, nearing death, Mother began a conversation we'd never had. She asked me, "Has it mattered that I have lived? Has my being alive made any difference? What's the point of it all?"

At first I fumbled for an answer, but then said, "Both Paul and I are grateful to you for giving us life." Knowing this was not what she wanted to hear, I realized that these were questions I couldn't answer for her, that she would have to find her own answers or go without finding them.

As I sat holding her hand, she seemed distraught, as if there were something she needed to say but couldn't. I waited and watched her struggle. When she spoke, her words were almost inaudible. "There's something I think you've wanted me to say, ever since you were a child. It's no easier today than it has ever been but I don't want to die without saying it." There was a pause during which tears collected in her eyes and began slipping, almost reluctantly, down her cheeks. Then she pulled me toward her, motioning for me to come closer so she could speak in my ear. In a voice barely more than a whisper, she haltingly said, "I love you, my little girl."

I had waited fifty years to hear those words. My mother had never said them to me before. I was sobbing as I put my head next to hers on the pillow. In an instant, the past—all the anger, the hurt, the things I hated in growing up—had disappeared. There was nothing left but my love for her and hers for me. She squeezed my hand and closed her eyes. Mother died a week later, having given me the greatest gift she could possibly have given.

In my life there have been times of joy, times of pain, but underlying most of it has been a pervasive loneliness which, I suspect, does not distinguish me from most of my fellow humans. During much of my life I was searching although, had you asked, I couldn't have told you for what I was searching. Perhaps it was for love, for an end to loneliness (which even my marriages didn't end), for someone to listen, perhaps for answers to questions like my mother's.

Sometimes that search seemed futile but I was always aware of an elusive something just out of my grasp, something that every once in a while revealed itself momentarily and kept me searching. It was like a secret not quite hidden, that hints at something beyond. I had been aware of that secret from early childhood, when I looked up at the stars or into a flower and wondered how I was related to them. As a child I wanted someone to explain that to me but my questions were always dismissed. The routine of everyday life pushed the wonder into the background for days at a time but it was always there, ready to be awakened by the call of a bird, the sight of a squirrel, the scent of lilacs on a spring breeze, the sound of music.

Later in life I had a professor who used myths and allegories to communicate difficult ideas, as if he knew that explaining would be only that—an explanation—while alluding to the ideas without trying to explain might allow us to discover them for ourselves. I knew then that I hadn't tried to tell anyone about my secret because I knew that I couldn't tell what it meant to me, and I was afraid of being ridiculed.

The search had its origin in the mind and heart of a lonely but rebellious little girl who wondered but could not or would not accept the answers supplied by parents and church. From looking up at the sky at night and from listening to my Great Uncle Will read history, I knew I was part of something larger but when I spoke of it to my parents, they said I was being silly and that when I grew up I would understand. I stopped talking to them but kept the experience of wonder close to my heart.

It was assumed that I would live my life repeating the pattern of my mother, and her mother before her, whose family had been in Connecticut since 1639. I spent the first sixteen years of my life trying, albeit reluctantly, to adapt to the way my parents and church taught me it was supposed to be. As a New England Puritan, I was part of a conversation that had been going on, in this country, for almost three centuries. I was being trained to suppress my feelings. Puritanism lived as a deliberate attempt to subdue nature and circumvent life. Growing up, it was the air I breathed and, as an adult, I realized that the training had been effective. I had learned to distrust feelings and, even today, express them only rarely. I looked at my mother's life, at how circumscribed it had been, and knew, with certainty, that I would not repeat that pattern. I had questions that parents and church wouldn't answer and I couldn't accept that they were questions I shouldn't be asking.

My mother spanked me until I was in junior high school and told me I would never go to heaven behaving as I did. I remember her watching me, always watching me, as if to catch me doing something wrong. During these years I kept my sense of wonder well hidden but it didn't die. And I had heroes—my father who was my champion against Mother, my brother who, until I was nine, was my role model. Uncle Will gave me a sense of being part of history by reading to me and by sharing with me the family genealogy, which showed me the centuries of people to whom I was related. Gramma Goodell always loved me and let me know it, as did Auntie Bea, my father's sister, and Aunt Ella, Momma's sister, who was my "Auntie Mame."

I went to school because it was the next thing to do and because my friends went. The best part of school was recess. I learned to read early, however, which I was not supposed to do. My mother called it "a sinful indulgence and a waste of time." But books let me escape into a world where people had adventures and lived lives totally different from my own. For many years I read by flashlight under the covers in my bed. In spite of remembering almost nothing of my school years, I must have learned what I needed to learn because I succeeded in moving from elementary school to junior high and then graduating from high school with honors.

After high school there was a summer of travel and a school year in North Carolina. In those months I experienced a freedom I'd never known but marriage two years later, to an abusive husband, threw me back into a struggle for the survival, not only of my sense of wonder but of my physical and emotional well being. That struggle ended in divorce and in my finding a way back into the books that were my salvation.

The sense of being part of history, that was born with Uncle Will, was confirmed when, as a 33-year-old student browsing in the Cornell Library, I took one book after another off the shelves and began reading. Suddenly there was an easing of the loneliness as I realized that my questions were part of a conversation that had been going on for centuries, and that I too was now engaged in that conversation even if, at the time, only as a listener. It was a corroboration of that sense of wonder I'd had as a little girl, and it kept me studying in spite of all the blocks that seemed to get in the way.

The path of the search has been through the everydayness of my life where that wonder, that elusive something, shows up at unexpected times. As a child sitting on the breakwater with my father, I had a sense of being related to the ocean, to the sky, to the birds that landed beside us on the rocks. The birds looked as if they were wondering about us. But usually I said nothing, I just wondered, for I had already learned that it was not safe to share my wondering. As a Freshman at Cornell I was in awe when, looking through a microscope, I saw that the cell from a rose petal looked identical to the cell from a piece of skin from my finger. It was as I had expected from the start—I was related to the rose!

Years later, when I put my hand on the railing of the cellar stairs of our hundred-year-old house in New England, and felt the satiny finish, I wondered how it got so smooth. Then I realized it was from the hundreds of people who, over the years, had slid their hands down that rail as I was doing. In that moment I was present to every generation of people who had lived in that house, to all of us who had ever used that railing. In that same house, looking at the freezer which we had filled with garden produce, at the end of summer, I suddenly felt a kinship with the chipmunks and squirrels in our backyard whom I had observed storing up acorns for the winter.

Although I am an ordinary woman, I haven't lived an ordinary life. In a time when conventional wisdom dictates that we think ahead and plan, my life seems to have been governed by impulse or, as I prefer to say, by gut instinct or intuition. At the age of ten I took my hidden savings, secretly bought a ticket to a symphony concert and went by myself to the next town, not telling anybody I was going for fear they wouldn't let me. Later I threw over the man who had been my lifelong friend and married a man who abused me then, after a divorce, remarried that abusive husband. Again divorced, I married a professor three weeks after we met. Later still, I sold all our worldly possessions to go to India for six months as a volunteer. And, to be honest, I must own up to the times I acted without forethought in provoking a boss into firing me.

I used to wonder what accidents of history had conspired to assemble the pieces of my life in such a way that I turned out as I have. I wondered how different my adult life would have been had I not gone to Europe in 1938 when Hitler began annexing Germany's neighbors or had not gone to school in North Carolina at a time when segregation was the rule or if I had married the boy next door instead of that stranger who came to town and swept me up in a passion I'd never known.

The only thing that can be told about a life is a story, and telling that story is like recounting a series of incidents, more or less related to one another. Today, as I approach the end of my life, I know that I am someone other than that series of incidents. On rare occasions, Elizabeth disappears and there is nothing but an awareness of being at one with the whole of things and a momentary end to the loneliness and the separateness. If that is perplexing to read, take comfort in knowing that it was perplexing to write. My writing is an attempt to catch hold of that elusive something that hints at a waiting secret.

This story spans the major part of the 20th century and is a journey through my life. It takes into account that all the challenges faced have contributed to the person I am today but only hinted at who I really am. I invite you to come with me on this journey—a journey shaped not only by the accidents of history but also by the moments of wondering, of being in the presence of that elusive something—a journey nearing its end but not over yet.

1

Puritan Child in New England

Paul and Celia Goodell didn't know that the child about to be born was the girl they both wanted. They were elated when our neighbor, who was assisting at the home birth, announced on that June 16th morning, "It's a girl!"

The year was 1920. It was the eighth year of Woodrow Wilson's presidency, the year women won the right to vote and the year Babe Ruth hit fifty-four home runs. A loaf of bread cost twelve cents, a gallon of gas thirteen, and you could buy a house for less than a thousand dollars. Prohibition spawned speakeasies as fast as saloons closed, but not in Stratford, Connecticut, where the "blue laws," a remnant of strict Puritan rule, were still on the books.

My brother, Paul Jr. was eight years old when I was born and was the most important person in my life those early years. He had curly brown hair, a pointy nose and a twinkle in his eyes, as if he knew something I didn't. Momma called him "wiry" which I decided meant skinny. I adored him and as soon as I was old enough to keep up, I followed him everywhere.

My father was straight and tall and he was always tan from working outdoors. His hair was dark brown and thin and he had a pug nose. He used his hands a lot when he talked. On the pinky finger of his left hand he wore a gold signet ring, but he didn't wear a wedding ring. He wore glasses and they got thicker as he got older. He had one of the first cars in Stratford—a Lambert. When we came to a big hill we all had to get out so Daddy could turn the car around. He said that the car could get up the hill only in reverse gear. I remember fussing and being told to be quiet when he had to change a tire, which he seemed to do every time we went out.

Momma was short, coming up only to Dad's shoulder. Her hair was light brown almost until the end of her life. Her weekly wash and set must always have included a touchup though she didn't tell us. She had what was politely called an "overbite" and when she eventually got false teeth her face changed and was flatter. She looked so different I pulled away from her until Daddy told me I might hurt her feelings. She was also fat and always on a diet except that she dieted only at the table. She nibbled and tasted while fixing meals, and when she cleared the table after dinner, she ate leftovers from the plates.

My father had been on the architectural team that designed the pediment on the top of Grand Central Station in New York. By the time I was born, however, he'd stopped drawing because his vision had failed, and he had a job as Director of Public Works for the town of Stratford. Some years later he bought a Standard Oil franchise and built a combination gas station and General Electric appliance store right in the center of town.

Daddy's Uncle Ted had given my parents our house, at 86 Warwick Avenue, as a wedding gift. It was a small house, set between a large one with lots of trimming (my mother called it "gingerbread") and a three-story house on the other side. Ours was shingled on the second story, with stucco on the first, and had a wide porch on two sides. A driveway led past the house to a garage fifty feet behind. The coal man put a chute through a cellar window next to the driveway and poured coal down into the bin. I can still remember the roaring, crashing sound and the clouds of black dust. In back of the garage there was a fenced-in area with a hen house where Momma sent me in the morning to look for eggs.

The front door of our house had narrow glass windows on either side and opened to a hall going to the kitchen. The only thing in that hall was the telephone, which had a crank to ring the operator. Momma used to say, after giving the operator the number, "Now don't you listen, Mabel, do you hear?" It was bad enough, she said, that any of the other four families on our line could listen in. I learned, early in life, that the telephone was for emergencies only—to call the doctor, to call the fire department, or for Momma to call my friend's mother if I was late coming home to dinner. It was never used for "idle chatter" and, many years later when I had children of my own, I harangued them about spending hours on the phone.

Our parlor had a fireplace, but it usually had make-believe flowers in it. We didn't use that room except on Christmas or when the minister came to call. Dad used to say jokingly that we should have one of those velvet ropes at the entrance to the parlor—the kind you see in museums that warn people not to enter. But on Christmas morning the parlor was a fairyland. Momma and Daddy always trimmed the tree after I'd gone to bed and, when Paulie and I came down, it was all lighted up, glistening with tinsel and surrounded by packages that held secret treasures. Every Christmas I got a new doll and every Christmas I dreamed about being a real mommy.

Christ Church was the Episcopal Church to which my family had belonged for generations and was the church in which I was christened Elizabeth Wood Goodell. Christmas Eve services at Christ Church were special. Closing my eyes I can see myself soberly walking down the aisle toward a huge Christmas tree, clutching a candle in one hand and a present for baby Jesus in the other, being careful not to drop the candle and to put the present for baby Jesus in the crèche. Then I went back to the pew and knelt for a few minutes before we all began to sing Christmas carols. On the way out of church I was given a little box of hard candies to take home. In those early years, God was closer to me than my father. I could tell Him all the bad things I had done and how lonely I was because He knew already. Mother had told me I could have no secrets from Him. When my mother came to tuck me in at night, we said the Lord's Prayer together and then she would add, "You think God cannot see you when you are under the covers but you are wrong. God sees everything, knows everything—even what you are thinking. To go to heaven when you die, you need to be good." Many nights I went to sleep wondering what that meant. Dying was some mysterious thing that most people seemed afraid of. The only dying I knew about was when our canary went to sleep and didn't wake up. His dying bothered me only when we put him in a hole in the ground and threw dirt on him. What would happen when he woke up? Then I wondered, where or what was heaven? Where would I go if not to heaven? I had heard about a place called hell but that was no more real for me than heaven. I had lots of questions about things like that but when I asked the Sunday-school teacher she said questioning was the greatest sin of all, so I stopped asking. She said that if we had faith we could just accept those things we didn't understand but then she didn't answer when I asked her what faith was.

Paulie and I spent three summers together on Grandpa D'Lea's farm in Great Barrington, Massachusetts. (Grandpa D'Lea wasn't really my Grandpa but all the adults in my life were Grandpa or Grandma, or Auntie or Uncle.) Paulie taught me to ride bareback on the work horses and to jump from the barn's second story into hay on the ground floor. I remember squatting close to watch him milk the cows and giggling when he squirted milk into my mouth. When he had finished milking he let me help him carry the full pail to the milk cooling house, a small stone building with a stream running through it. It was icy cold in the milk house even on hot days. I loved picnics with my brother on the Green River in Great Barrington. Sometimes we left the picnic basket on the bank, took off our shoes and jumped from rock to rock in the stream. At the farm we had big breakfasts—bacon and eggs, heavy cream on strawberries and thick slices of bread just out of the oven with fresh butter. I can smell that kitchen today just by closing my eyes. Paulie was patient and gentle. At home he took me to the beach and helped me collect shells and stones and ribbons of seaweed. He taught me to swim and dive and row a boat. With his encouragement I dove from the high board at the yacht club before I was ten.

Stratford is at the mouth of the Housatonic River where it flows into Long Island Sound. Daddy always had a boat and I learned to love the water when I was still quite young. Daddy and I could be sure of being alone if we took the skiff and rowed out to the breakwater, at the mouth of the river, to picnic and fish. We sat together on the jetty for hours with a line in the water, waiting quietly for a bite. With the picnic basket, the water, the sun, and my father, I had everything I needed to be happy. We didn't talk much. Being there with him was enough. Sometimes I would lie back, watch the sea gulls, and wonder what it would be like to fly. For a few minutes it was as if I were not confined to that little body but was out there with the gulls, flying like a bird. These days passed much too quickly. Once in a while Daddy and I would take his cabin cruiser out into Long Island Sound and trawl for blue fish and, if it was calm enough, drop anchor and swim from the boat. I loved it when we did that and I loved that it had to be Daddy's and my secret. We both knew Mother would have a fit if she knew I was jumping off the boat to swim in the middle of Long Island Sound. Sometimes at night I would go with Daddy to watch as he speared eels from the porch of the Pootatuck Yacht Club. I didn't know why he did that because we didn't eat the eels but when I asked him he said there was no particular reason, it was just the challenge. When we were both in trouble with Momma, Daddy and I would walk the beach together. I loved hopping from one rock to another along the shore near the lighthouse and looking for shells and stones at the water's edge. If I were barefoot I would marvel at the way the water filled my footprints as soon as I took the next step. Sometimes at night I looked at the sky and wondered how many stars there were, how far away they were and how long it would take to get to them. In those quiet times I felt as if I were part of something bigger than myself, but beyond wondering I did not question except to ask myself if I was the only one who wondered. Did Uncle Will wonder or did he know? Sometime I would ask him.

From the time I was small I remember loving Momma's perfume. She always wore *Evening in Paris*, spraying cologne behind her ears, especially on Sunday. We didn't have a shower in our house and bathing was a Saturday night ritual, getting ready for church on Sunday. When my brother got older he took more baths, and I remember my mother sputtering at him about wasting water and about what she called his "vanity." That was a word she used a lot, particularly if she caught me looking in a mirror or putting ribbons in my hair. There were few mirrors in our house and no pictures on the walls. I wasn't quite sure how mirrors and pictures were related but they must have been because Momma had very strong opinions about people "fancying up their houses with pictures."

Momma spanked me often. I always hated it and rarely understood why I was being spanked. When I wanted to feel sorry for myself I would go into my room, shut the door, climb up on a chair in front of my dresser mirror and look at the big red swelling on my backside, the mark made by the hairbrush she used. That hairbrush was part of a matching set of brush, comb, hand mirror and hair receiver, all silver trimmed and sitting on her bureau on one of the lace doilies she had everywhere. I hated that hairbrush and sometimes would go into Momma's room and think about throwing it out the window or smashing it on the floor but I knew that if I got caught Momma would wallop me with something even worse than the hairbrush. Most of the time I refused to cry when she spanked me. She would tell my father about my not crying and he'd say, with admiration in his voice, "She's a spunky little thing." If I crawled quietly into Momma's bed in the night, without waking her, she would embrace me and I'd feel loved. I might stay there for hours, cuddled up against her soft warm body but, if she woke up, she would scold me and send me back to my bed. For that brief time I felt she loved me but when she woke up and scolded me I decided I must have been mistaken.

Many summers Daddy took me to Barnum & Bailey Ringling Brothers circus in Bridgeport. We saw elephants and tigers and a man swallowing fire and the fattest lady in the world. My favorite of the whole circus was the trapeze acts. I held my breath and sometimes even closed my eyes when someone jumped until Daddy told me it was okay, they'd been caught. In the back yard I had a swing with a trapeze and rings hanging from an ancient oak tree, and tried performing some of the feats that I'd seen—hanging by my knees, or by one arm, pulling myself up and over on the rings. Sometimes hanging by my knees I would pick up horse chestnuts that had dropped to the ground in the back yard. Daddy said they weren't for eating but I just liked to hold them in my hand and rub their smooth surface. I may have been four or five when I planted a horse chestnut in our backyard, watering it, watching it, and being disappointed when a tree didn't show up the next week. I gave up watering it and forgot it until many years later when my father pointed out that we had a new tree growing in the backyard, right by the fence, and I realized it must have come from that horse chestnut I planted when I was a little girl. Daddy had mowed around it for years waiting to see if it was something more than a weed. My questions about horse chestnuts, like all others, were turned away by my mother. "You ask too many questions," she would say. I stopped asking. Sometimes I would save up my questions until I got to Gramma's house because Gramma and Uncle Will always had time for me and my questions. Usually Uncle Will also had time for a game of *Chinese Checkers*.

Gramma was my Daddy's mother, Mary Palmer Goodell, who lived on Broad Street with her two brothers, Uncle Ted and Uncle Will. Daddy's sister, Auntie Bea, lived on the second floor of that house with Uncle Herb and their son, Herbie. Auntie Bea was eight years younger than Daddy. He told me she walked with a limp because she had polio when she was twelve and was left with one leg shorter than the other. Herbie was Auntie Bea's only child. Four months apart in age, Herbie and I were like brother and sister and grew up together. I wished that Auntie Bea was my mother. When I got old enough to go places by myself, I would ride my bike over to see Gramma and Auntie Bea. They always gave me hugs and kisses. I could ask Auntie Bea questions and she gave me real answers. I could talk to her when I felt like running away and she would listen and then send me home. One time I asked her why Momma was so mean to me and she responded, "Your mother probably shouldn't have had you. She is too old to be raising a little girl. And besides, she is going through 'the change.' But don't feel bad, it has nothing to do with you. It's really how she feels about herself." Though I didn't know what "the change" was, I knew that Auntie Bea understood and was trying to comfort me. When she moved to Hartford some years later, I felt as if she had abandoned me.

Sometimes Auntie Bea and Gramma played *Mah-Jongg* and they promised to teach me when I was older. Gram had graduated from Mount Holyoke at a time when few women attained that level of education. Both Uncle Ted and Uncle Will were Yale graduates. Daddy's father, Clarence, died when my father was sixteen so he had to leave school and go to work. Although he took correspondence courses to learn architecture, he hadn't studied since then and didn't seem to think education was important.

When Gramma Goodell's father died, he left her and her brothers a substantial sum of money. With some of that money Uncle Ted built the Warwick Avenue house. The rest of his money, they said with raised eyebrows, he had given to a "friend," which was as much as was ever said. It was a time when intimacy between men was not even discussed much less condoned. Uncle Will was said to have used his money to buy a gold mine that never yielded gold. Gramma alone managed her inheritance in such a way that she was able to support herself and her brothers in their old age.

I loved my Gramma Goodell. I like to remember her as she was one evening when I was perhaps four. The adults were playing bridge at her house. Her deep purple dress had a high lace collar with bones that made it stand up. She wore a cameo brooch on a heavy gold chain and lots of rings and bracelets. A mass of white hair was piled high on her head. In it was a jeweled tortoise-shell comb and silver hairpins threatening to fall out. Her hands were so soft that I loved it when she smiled at me and patted my cheek.

Uncle Will was the smartest person alive and I wanted to be just like him when I grew up. He was tall and his clothes always seemed too big for him. What hair he had was white and he usually had little pieces of tissue paper on his face where, he said, he had cut himself shaving. It seemed as if most of the day Uncle Will sat in his rocking chair by the big bay window, reading. Sometimes I tiptoed into the room and sat quietly on the little stool beside his chair. In a few minutes he would begin to stroke the top of my head, then start reading aloud. I rarely understood what he was reading but it didn't matter. I loved the sound of his voice and his hand on my head. He would sometimes pause in his reading to smile down into my eyes and make me feel important. Afterward, he might tell me a story to explain what he had been reading. He always talked to me as if I were a real person instead of a little girl.

Momma's mother was sick for years and died when I was four or five. Momma said her father, Grandpa Wells, was an "ornery old man." She said he had been superintendent of Stratford schools but that he drank heavily on Saturday nights, beat his wife and the children when he came home, but always went to church on Sunday. When I was little, he walked down to our house almost every day from Oronoque where he lived with my mother's brother. Momma said Grandpa would still be alive if he hadn't been hit by a truck one day while walking to our house. He was 95. Momma had six siblings and was usually not talking with one or another of them. By the time she died, she had alienated all those still alive. I suspect I have lots of cousins whose names I don't even know.

Momma loved to tell the story about how she and Daddy got married. She said he started courting her when he was only fourteen years old and she, at twenty-two, looked at him with contempt. He was her family's newspaper delivery boy and used to put flowers and messages in their papers. She ignored him for years but he persisted. By the time she was 28, and still unmarried, he had grown up and looked more interesting. They were married in Stratford in 1908. Because he was younger, she was sure that she would set the rules for the marriage and, for the most part, she did. Momma called Daddy "Mr. Goodell" except when she was angry and called him by his first name. He called her "Mrs. Goodell" unless he was impatient with her, in which case he spoke sharply, calling her "Ceal." Writing of this made me remember that Paulie had always called me "Liz," my father called me "Betty," and my mother called me by name only when she was angry and then it was "E-lizabeth!" People in town called me "Paul's daughter," or "Little Paul's sister." It was as if they didn't know my name. As a child I never wanted it any other way—I reveled in being Paul's daughter and little Paul's sister—but later on I decided it was the Pauls who ran the world, not the little girls whose names people couldn't remember.

When I think back to dinner at home, I see us sitting in silence except when someone asked for the gravy or potatoes to be passed. My father sat at one end of the long, oval mahogany table, my brother and I on either side, and my mother sat at the end near the kitchen. Behind her was a long sideboard with a mirror all along the back and on it was a set of cruets—one with vinegar and one with oil. Momma said they were for when guests came but we almost never had guests for dinner. Momma wouldn't let me leave the table until my plate was clean. I hated her for making me stay there, sometimes even missing "Amos and Andy" on the radio. I pushed lima beans around on my plate hoping they might disappear. When I discovered that I could take one bean at a time and swallow it, like a pill with a drink of water, it worked as long as no one noticed what I was doing. Momma boiled vegetables with fat salt pork added, she said, for flavor. When the vegetables were mushy and colorless, she drained off the water and added a huge chunk of butter, salt and pepper. Dad said he ate the vegetables only so he could have dessert. Momma baked great pies and cakes. She used her chocolate cake—famous at Christ Church fairs—to console me when I had a hurt or a disappointment, for being brave at the doctor's or to reward me for getting A's in school. (I still eat chocolate to console or reward myself.)

After dinner at night, Daddy would sometimes lean back in his chair, smoke a cigar, read the paper and then doze off. I can still hear Momma saying to him, "Paul Goodell! You shouldn't be sleeping after a big meal. Get out of that chair, put your hat on and go take a walk." Dad would always get up, put his hat on and go out.

One Sunday, when Momma was away, Daddy and I went to the movies. It was only because she was away that we could go to the movies on Sunday. (Daddy followed the Sunday rules only when Momma was around to make him.) We saw *Lost Horizons* and then decided to splurge and see another movie. Whatever it was, it was so bad that when we came out Daddy said, "We should have stopped while we were ahead—*Lost Horizons* was wonderful!" I grinned at him and said, conspiratorially, "We could go back and see it again." And we did.

I grew up wondering where all the rules came from but when I was old enough to read about Puritanism I decided that must have been the influence that kept us from having any fun on Sunday. (I once read that Puritans were people who were constantly worried that someone, somewhere, was having fun.) Sunday was a day of quiet, church and a special dinner. In early 17th century Connecticut, the Sabbath was strictly regulated by Puritan law. There could be no card playing, no radio, no movies, no playing of any musical instruments not mentioned in the Bible, no smoking or drinking of spirits. Many of these restrictions were still observed in our home when I was growing up. There was also a prohibition against unnecessary work, but that didn't seem to relieve my mother of the need to prepare a big dinner. As I grew older I saw that the Puritan influence, plus the work ethic and Victorian morality were all at work in our home and in my life.

Saturday afternoons from the time I was six, I went to the Stratford Theater. Sometimes Paulie would walk with me but, after finding a seat for me, he would go and sit in the back row with his girlfriend. The movie cost only ten cents, and sometimes I would stay from noon to five because we could see a second show if we wanted. We got previews of coming attractions, a cartoon, a newsreel, a regular movie and a chapter of a serial. It was the serial that made me not want to miss a Saturday. In the "Perils of Pauline," those perils were so real I often hid my face in my hands, only occasionally peeking out between my fingers to see if the train had run over Pauline and if the villain was still there. The show always ended leaving us wondering, so we would have to come back the next week to find out. Even though I was so scared I didn't want to leave the theater, I couldn't wait to get back the next week to see what happened to Pauline. Some times it was dark when I left the theater and Momma had told me that the bogey man waited behind bushes after dark so when I left the theater I ran home as fast as I could.

The one exception to the Saturday matinee was when there was a Yale football game in New Haven. On those days, Daddy and I would carry folding canvas chairs to the corner of East Broadway so we could sit and watch cars going by. I had a Yale banner and waved it until I was exhausted. Once each season Daddy drove my brother and me up to a game. Even though New Haven was only fifteen miles away, it was a big trip then. We took a picnic basket, a gallon of lemonade, heavy lap robes and a cushion for me. I felt very grownup going to the game with Daddy and Paulie. At one of those games I saw the famous Albie

Booth score three touchdowns, winning the game for Yale. Daddy said Albie was one of the best players Yale ever had.

I loved the first snow of winter—putting on galoshes, mittens and my knitted hat, then running out to play. I would tilt my head back so I could get snow flakes in my mouth and then laugh because they didn't stay snowflakes in my mouth but just disappeared. If there was a heavy snow at night, Momma would let me run out first thing in the morning to collect a big bowl of fresh snow and we'd eat it with maple syrup drizzled over it. As soon as there was enough snow, we'd make a snowman in the front yard. When I was small, my brother rolled up big snow balls for the snowman's body and let me put the coal buttons up the front. When I was older, Daddy helped me make the snowman and sometimes our neighbor, Don Campbell, would wander over to help me. Before the snow had all left the yard, the first crocus peeked up out of the ground and then, not too long afterward, there were daffodils everywhere. I wondered how they knew it was time to come up but knew better than to ask.

On winter weekends, Daddy and I would go skating at Brewster Pond or take sleds to Academy Hill. We slid down together on my Flexible Flyer sled and then Daddy would pull me back up the hill. We did this until we were shivering and then went into Aunt Ella's for hot cider and to warm up. Aunt Ella was Momma's sister, who lived in a big house on Academy Hill.

Aunt Ella was so different from my mother it was hard to think of them as sisters. While Momma rarely smiled, Aunt Ella was always smiling and usually had a cigarette dangling from a fancy holder in her mouth. Where our house was always neat and we never had company—even though we had Wedgewood china that Momma said was for company—Aunt Ella's seemed always filled with people, music and lots of activity. Momma didn't want hired help because, she said, "I can do it better myself," while Aunt Ella had lots of servants and was as friendly with them as she was with us children. Our house seemed kind of empty and quiet compared to Aunt Ella's, which seemed almost alive. Her house had two ballrooms, each with a full wall of mirror so that the reflections made the rooms look even larger than they were. It seemed as if Aunt Ella and Uncle Walter were always having parties—those rooms filled with flowers, music, people dancing. Sometimes if there was going to be a party, Aunt Ella would invite me to sleep over, giving me little things to do so I could feel part of the excitement of getting ready. Then, when the party actually started, Aunt Ella would bring me in for a few minutes, let me be a part of it, then hug me and send me back to bed.

Uncle Walter's library had books from floor to ceiling, except on one wall where there was a big stone fireplace. In the winter there'd always be a fire on the hearth. I used to like to sit in front of that fire and stare into the flames, dreaming. On the third floor there was a playroom across the back of the house. It had a rocking horse almost as big as those at the park, cradles with dolls that looked like real babies, a pile of blocks almost as tall as I was, and a carpet so soft that sometimes I would just lie there looking out at the great big trees in the yard. One of those trees had a crook in a lower branch where I liked to climb and sit, wondering what it would be like to live in that house and be my Aunt Ella with her bright clothes, jewelry, red fingernails, and that cigarette holder in her mouth. Aunt Ella could see me in the tree when she was lying in her bedroom hammock and sometimes she blew a kiss to me. Aunt Ella seemed to like me just the way I was.

I started Center School at five but had to repeat first grade because I was sick a lot. When I started back to school my friends were in second grade. At first I felt left out but it didn't take long to make new friends. Every morning I left home with two pennies in my pocket, went past the school, and stopped at the candy store between Center School and the theater. Standing on my toes I could see in the candy bins and look over everything before deciding. But, even after all that looking, I always bought the same thing—Squirrel Nut Twins, inch-long caramel candies with chopped nuts in them, each wrapped in a piece of waxed paper twisted at the ends. These were two for a penny and with my other penny I bought a long string of licorice.

When I was in the second grade, Momma was driving home from town one day and saw me walking from school with a little colored girl friend who lived farther down East Broadway, where most colored people lived. Mother rolled down the car window and shouted at me, "Elizabeth! Get in the car this minute!" Then she took me home and spanked me while scolding me. "You know you are not supposed to play with 'coloreds.' There are enough children of your own kind to play with. Now don't make me have to tell you that again!" I knew my mother was wrong about my friend but also knew that she wouldn't listen to me had I tried to tell her why she was wrong.

I liked to read but soon learned to hide any books I brought home. My mother had finished high school but her disapproval of my reading seemed to be one of those accidents of history. For Puritans the only acceptable books were the Bible and school books, and Momma regarded even the latter with suspicion. If she saw me reading a story book, she'd say, "If you haven't anything better to do than that, I'll find something better for you to do." (Uncle Walter had so many books in his library, he must not have thought reading was wrong.) In our home there were only two or three books, other than a dictionary, and they were on a high shelf in the parlor, supposedly out of my reach. Today I suspect that those books came from Uncle Ted when he had the house built. Both Ted and Will were well-read. Surely they weren't books read by my parents. Sometimes when I was home alone, I'd get a step stool and climb up so I could reach one and take it down for a quick peek. The titles intrigued me. I understood little of what I read but just enough to know that Momma would spank me if she caught me reading it. It had language not used in our home. My favorite books were the *Bobbsey Twins* and *Nancy Drew* mysteries and books that made me cry, like *Little Women*. The only time I remember my mother buying a book was when a man came to the door selling the *World Book Encyclopedia*.

I also liked to write and started keeping a journal but, when I discovered my mother going through my room one day, I threw the journal away. After that I didn't keep anything I wrote for more than a day or two because I had no place at home to keep it where my mother couldn't find it. Sometimes at night she would come into my room, without knocking, as if to catch me at something I wasn't supposed to be doing, like reading, with a flashlight, under the covers. But if there were clothes on the floor or over the back of a chair she would pick them up, put them away, and then lecture me about cleanliness being next to godliness.

One summer, when Momma was away, I coaxed my father into letting me have a haircut like Paulie's. I had always wanted to look like my brother and, besides, my mother seemed to like Paulie better than me, so maybe if I looked more like a boy, she'd like me better. I was thin and straight and, with my short hair, looked as much like a boy as a girl could. By that time, however, Paulie was in his senior year in high school, president of his class, captain of the basketball team, and had a girlfriend who seemed to have taken my place. And he seemed to have changed. He didn't want me following him around, as I had ever since I could walk. He would teach me things when it suited him, but by the time I was nine or ten he seemed more interested in his high school friends. He had been my favorite person from the beginning, and I was hurt and resentful. I think that must have been when I began being a pest and looking for ways to get him in trouble with Momma. One night when he was having a party, I was sitting on the stairs peeking between the banister rails. One of his friends took a toothpick from the table, speared one of my goldfish and ate it. I covered my mouth to keep from screaming, ran to my room and the next morning told Momma. She scolded Paul and made him buy me a new goldfish. Another morning I came down to breakfast innocently holding up a condom I had found when snooping in Paul's bureau drawer, and asked Momma what it was. She turned red, snatched it from me and, pulling Paul by the arm, went upstairs. I could hear the bedroom door slam and the sound of voices but never did find out what she said to him nor, for many years, what the thing was that I had found.

I'm not sure when I first experienced loneliness but when I first acknowledged it was at the age of nine when my brother ceased being my adored playmate and I was sure my mother didn't love me because of the things she said to me, like: "Why don't you behave yourself? Why don't you listen to what you're told? What's the matter with you anyway?" Having no answers to her questions I began to feel not only that she disliked me but that she must be right, there must be something wrong with me. Mother's judgment was reinforced by my regular church attendance. For many years, every Sunday, I repeated the words from my Common Prayer book: "I am not worthy to so much as gather up the crumbs from under thy table, Oh Lord." I was so sure I would never be any better that one summer day when I was nine I swam out to a rock my father had told me would be covered with water at high tide. It was quite a way from shore and I was tired when I reached it but after I climbed up on it and the sun began to warm me, I wavered a little in my intention to stay there and let the water cover me too. By the time the water came up to my shoulders I had changed my mind, swam off the rock and headed for shore, not certain I could make it, but desperately wanting to.

I stirred up trouble between my parents. Their quarrels were mostly about me. Momma spanked me often and I usually complained to Daddy who said spanking wasn't necessary. Momma's response was always, "I'm the one bringing her up. If it was up to you, she'd do anything she wanted." One time Daddy took my side in an argument I was having with Momma about the privacy of my room. We were in the kitchen before breakfast. Daddy was dressing for work and came through the kitchen in his under shorts and dressing gown. I was crying. Momma was yelling. Daddy tried to intervene, "Now, Mother, Betty's room should be her own. Everybody needs a place of their own, a place for some privacy. At least let's talk about it quietly."

Mother's response was, "This is none of your business! Stay out of it! You're as bad as she is!" Then she added, "Go get the newspaper! That boy threw it way out in the driveway again." As my father left the kitchen, Mother slammed the door and locked it behind him. When he came back, she told him to stay out there. He tried reasoning with her, tried banging on the door and nothing worked. She kept him locked out of the house in his dressing gown and shorts all morning.

Dad, in his usual stoic fashion, accepted that she would let him back in when her mood changed and not a moment sooner. He spent the morning rearranging his tools on the garage wall.

I remember thinking, as a little girl, that if Momma died, Daddy would marry me. As I grew up I knew that wouldn't happen but I never missed an opportunity to create trouble between them or do things that would endear me to Daddy. I learned to do all the things he enjoyed and Momma didn't—playing tennis, boating, fishing, swimming—and I would often spend the better part of a weekend with him while Momma stayed home, cleaning or ironing.

My mother made sure I had all kinds of lessons—dancing lessons, swimming lessons, riding lessons, piano lessons, voice lessons, figure skating lessons and elocution lessons. I can still hear myself repeating, "How now, brown cow?" and, "The rain in Spain..." The one thing not included in the social graces my mother thought I should have was an appreciation of art. We never went to art museums or exhibits. We had no art on the walls of our home, at least not until my father, in his seventies, began painting by numbers and hanging his paintings on the walls. There were groups to which I belonged—the Girl Scouts, the Children of the American Revolution, the Order of Rainbow for Girls. Although I enjoyed most of this activity, I secretly railed against having my mother so organize my life. I knew she thought of it as the way to prepare me for the good marriage she anticipated for me. Not only did Mother choose what I should eat each day and most of what I should do, but she also chose what I should wear. We took the train into New York City to shop and came home with bundles of clothes, most of which she had picked out for me. She told me I must always wear gloves and a hat for shopping or going to church. She told me about being polite to old people, and writing thank-you notes but she never taught me to cook. She said she didn't want me making a mess of her kitchen.

Momma didn't talk to me about sex except to warn me that I should never let a boy pull my pants down and then, on the occasion of my first menstruation, saying, "That's something you have to put up with for being a woman. When you get married you'll find out there's something worse than that you have to put up with." It was many years before I realized what a sad commentary that was on her life and how much it had affected mine.

I loved music, but radios didn't reproduce music well when I was growing up. Daddy used to sing *My Blue Heaven* while shaving, and Momma whistled with the canary when she was working in the kitchen, but that was about all the music we had at home. One summer when I was ten we went to a concert at Seaside

Park in Bridgeport. Listening to the music I was spellbound, so the next week I took money saved from my allowance and secretly bought a ticket for a fall performance of the Philadelphia Symphony Orchestra at the new Klein Memorial Auditorium in Bridgeport. I didn't tell anyone I was going because I was sure they would say I couldn't. I took a bus alone into Bridgeport, then found I had a ticket to a seat in the front row. When the music began I was swept away. It was as if all my questions didn't matter. It was like the experience I had in church when the organ music crescendoed and I felt something I was unable to name. The music enveloped me and erased everything from my mind. When the concert was over I didn't want to leave the auditorium. From that time on I was a regular concert-goer, saving my allowance and doing whatever it took to get a seat right up front.

I had been taking piano lessons since I was six or seven. Although I loved it when my playing began to sound like music, I hated it when Momma made me play for her friends. I knew I made mistakes, knew the guests heard them and it seemed that only Momma didn't hear the mistakes or to her they made no difference. Only later did I realize that she never scolded me after one of those performances, even when I made mistakes. She must have been pleased at the way I was learning. At the beginning of Junior High I began voice lessons and joined the Drama Society at school. I blush even today remembering the night I stood on stage in front of an auditorium full of people, a painfully thin thirteen-year-old singing *Night and Day*, looking not at all like a torch singer. Then one time Momma insisted that Daddy attend a recital. I was singing a solo, *The Flight of the Swallows*—a song totally inappropriate for a youngster—when I saw Daddy in the audience and read the truth on his face. It was my last recital for many years.

The church was central in my life for several years after my first communion at age twelve. I sang in the choir, worked on the altar guild, and attended Young People's Fellowship meetings on Sunday evenings. My father didn't go to church at all and called himself an "unbeliever." He said it was all hypocrisy—that people could get drunk on Saturday night, beat up their families, then go to church Sunday morning and get absolved of guilt. I didn't know what he meant but from the tone of his voice I knew he was not kidding and wondered if he was referring to my Grandpa Wells.

Each year, as Easter approached, I spent Good Friday afternoon in church, kneeling and weeping. Jesus' death on the cross was very real for me then and it gave me an outlet for the tears I didn't shed at home. I lived through it every

Good Friday for years, wondering why it was so real for me and wondering what it meant. At such times and for a few moments during communion each week I lost the sense of being inadequate, imperfect and alone.

There was something magnificent about this high church in which I was raised, even though my mother objected to the "pomp" as she called it. But that magnificence was at odds with the words of prayer that made me feel unworthy, sinful, even though I wondered how I could be so sinful at such an early age. When I asked about that, I was told there was something called "original sin" with which we were all born, but that made no sense to me at all so I stopped asking. Later I learned that the church taught that people were born sinful, incapable of doing good until regenerated by divine grace, but it still made no sense to me so I put it away with the other things the church had taught and I had rejected.

If my religious experience had been only the indefinable something I felt during communion, all would have been well, but there were things about Christian doctrine which became increasingly difficult for me as I grew up. With the awakening of sexual feelings, I was reminded to be on guard against "temptations of the flesh." Before I had an interest in boys there were those hints of something feeling good when I touched myself, hints that there was something strangely wonderful happening in my body, yet I was sure that was what the church meant by "temptations of the flesh." It seemed that the activities of my body were bad and so were some of the activities of my mind.

I was constantly reminded that it was a sin to doubt but could not get rid of some of the questions: "If ours is a loving God, how is it He made me with this body, these feelings which I'm now told are bad? How is it He has given me a mind which is not supposed to question? How is it these church people seem to know how it is? Who told them they could say what Jesus meant?"

At seventeen, the problems I was having came together in a focus on the words I was saying in church Sunday mornings, "I believe..." and all that followed in the Apostles' Creed, for I knew I no longer believed. There was no one I could talk to about it. Auntie Bea had moved away and Gramma Goodell still seemed to believe, so one day I simply stopped going to church. Mother started to make a fuss but Dad immediately took my side and told her it was my choice, not hers.

In giving up the church I also gave up the experience of wonder and awe provided by the music, the ritual and communion, an experience which, at least for an hour or two, relieved the loneliness that had come to characterize my life. Without the church, that loneliness became more pronounced. There was an emptiness where the church had been and I grieved, but also knew the choice had been mine.

One winter when I was in high school, Mother and Dad went to Florida on an exploratory visit, to see if they might like to spend winters down there. They left my mother's friend, Auntie Grace Cargill, in charge of me and the house. As soon as my friends heard that my folks were out of town, they decided my house was the place for a party. Though I'd never had a party of my own before, I thought it was a good idea and on the first Saturday night Mother and Dad were gone, my friends took over the house. By ten o'clock it was a raucous affair—loud music blaring from the radio, kids drinking beer even though all of them were under age, the parlor rug rolled up for dancing, boys in the kitchen opening refrigerator and cupboards to see what they could find, having devoured all the prepared refreshments. It was out of control, but I didn't know what to do. Chubby, our rat terrier, was yapping until I was ready to strangle him. Then somebody dropped a can of beer on the coffee table and broke the glass top. I began to cry. One of the boys decided to go upstairs to the bathroom. When he opened the bathroom door, he found Auntie Grace in the bathtub, with her radio on full volume to protect her from the racket downstairs. She saw him and screamed. He slammed the door and came running downstairs looking as if he'd seen a ghost. In a few minutes Auntie Grace came down in her dressing gown and quietly suggested that everyone leave, that the party was over. I was relieved. When she saw the mess, she threatened to call my mother in Florida, then relented, told me to go to bed, saying we'd clean it up the next day. In the morning we surveyed the damage, cleaned up the mess, and I had the glass replaced on the coffee table. She never did tell my parents.

My mother's obsession with making me "good" made me doubt that I could ever be good, but I survived by being rebellious, by doing things she didn't want me to do. With my "I'll show her" attitude, I fought her all the way, although I learned to be covert about it. I pretended to conform and believe what my adults told me. But the downside of that pretense was that whenever I was doing something I knew she wouldn't approve of, I felt guilty. Even today I have difficulty just having fun without feeling guilty for not being productive.

Mother resented Dad's control of finances. He allocated funds, paid the bills and never shared information about his income or what he had in the bank. We always seemed to have enough money, enough so that I wasn't even aware of the Great Depression until I read, sometime later, that for millions of Americans it seemed like the end of the world—with one in four people out of work, schools not opening, people staying in bed to save fuel and calories. During these years, when others were suffering, Dad traded in his car for a new one every couple of years, bought an orange grove in Florida and hired an overseer to take care of it. Today I'm a little uncomfortable about this but at the time I just enjoyed it. I had a generous allowance and Mother and I were always free to buy clothes. He said, "You and Mother just go enjoy yourselves shopping and put it on the charge account. I'll worry about paying the bills." But his word was law in money matters. I remember him standing by Mother one day while she signed over to him a check she had just received in the mail. "Why can't I keep this, Paul? It isn't much and it's really my money—the check is made to me. Why do I have to give it to you?" Dad's reply left no room for argument, "You get everything you need, dear. I take good care of you. Just sign your name." And he did take care of us. I believed Dad's assurance that I didn't need to worry about money. He assumed, I guess, that I would go from his home to a husband's home where that husband would take care of me in the same way.

In High School I did good work and got good grades but it was easy and not challenging. I got into sports and wrote for the high school's *Clarion*. The only person who kept alive my interest in learning was Gladys Jubb, my history teacher who also directed the debating society. I loved going to the library for the research that enabled me to build a good argument and then win a debate. Of the students in my high school class, some were from old New England families, some from newly arrived immigrant families, and a very few from colored families rich enough to move to Stratford. My mother's attitude suggested that some of my friends were more okay than others and it depended on who their parents were, or what the color of their skin was, rather than how nice they were.

We couldn't shop for clothes in Leavitt's in Bridgeport because colored people shopped there and Mother wouldn't try on a dress if there was a chance that one of "them" might have tried it on before her. Underlying all this was Mother's conviction that we were the "real" Americans because our family had been in this country for three centuries. All the others, when she considered them at all, she considered outsiders. "We don't have anything to do with them," she would say, "They're *riff raff* (or, *micks, kikes, wops, niggers*)." When my father heard her, he would say, "You don't want to pay much attention to the names your Mother calls people. She doesn't mean it." I knew that the labels were insulting and as I grew up I became uncomfortable, feeling cowardly for not speaking up. I listened to her, didn't agree with her about my friends but I seldom dared be honest with her because she was so sure she was right and that I was too young to know anything. I didn't know the word "prejudice" until much later. My mother wouldn't have considered herself prejudiced even if she had been familiar with the term—that's just the way it was for her, that's what these people were.

My mother's primary concern was to see me married to a nice boy from a "good family" which meant that they had been in Stratford as long as our family, had money, belonged to Christ Episcopal Church, the Mill River Country Club, and the Sons or Daughters of the American Revolution—social status accrued by having descended from someone who had fought in the Revolutionary War.

On my sixteenth birthday I got my driver's license and Dad let me drive his Buick. He had tried to teach me to drive but when, pulling into the driveway, I hit the house, he gave up and turned me over to a professional driving instructor. On my seventeenth birthday Dad gave me a car, a black Chevy coupe with a rumble seat, and I felt quite grown up. The sense of freedom that a car gave me has never diminished, but in high school it was also a way to make friends because I was one of the few who had cars.

I was slow to mature socially but I loved to dance. My brother was often coerced into taking me to the more important functions, such as proms. I was embarrassed by having my brother as an escort but Mother would not hear of me staying home on such occasions. There was a great ballroom in Bridgeport to which all the name bands came—Benny Goodman, Guy Lombardo, Glen Miller, Artie Shaw. I can still see people in evening dress and the revolving mirrored ball lighting the dance floor and remember wishing, as I danced with Paulie, that I were dancing with someone who would look at me as Ralph Walker was looking at Mary Peck.

Now my mother had new questions: "Why don't the boys like you? What's the matter with you? Why aren't the boys flocking around you as they were around me when I was in high school?" These were questions I was asking myself. Some of the girls in high school had steady boy friends and others had dates every weekend. I was part of a group that regularly went out together but I had no special boy. My mother's questions bothered me but I no longer had anyone to whom to turn. Auntie Bea was gone and, as much as I loved Aunt Ella and wanted to emulate her, she wasn't one of whom to ask serious questions. She could tell me what dress to wear, how to fix my hair and what lipstick to wear—to my mother's horror—but she wasn't one to whom I could pour out the yearnings of my soul.

It seemed as if my parents weren't eager for me to grow up. It was as if they were trying to protect me until they could pass on their responsibility to a husband. They thought it unnecessary and, perhaps, even undesirable for a girl to go to college (this despite Dad's mother having been educated). My brother had been given two years at a junior college to learn accounting and so, even though I had won a Scholarship-Leadership award and a mathematics scholarship to Tufts,

I was registered for nurse's training in the fall term at Presbyterian Hospital in New York.

In the spring of 1938 my father had told me he wanted to give me a trip for a graduation present as he had my brother. Paul had chosen to go on a Caribbean cruise but I had a more daring request and tentatively suggested that I would like to go to Europe. Dad didn't laugh at me or ridicule my request. He actually said he would look into it. At the end of the school year, Dad announced that his graduation present to me would be a summer in Europe. I could scarcely believe it but it was what I said I wanted. It meant leaving before my birthday and before graduation ceremonies but that seemed of little consequence. I was thrilled and excited but also a little frightened. Europe seemed a long, long way from Stratford.

2

Visiting Hitler's Germany in 1938

We crossed the Atlantic on the *Rotterdam*, a Holland-America Line ship. I had always loved being on the water and the trip across the Atlantic was an undreamed-of joy. The North Atlantic was rough in June but, for me, that added to the thrill of being on a ship that seemed to be a city block long.

Dad had made my travel arrangements through the Students International Travel Association in New York and I was in a group of twenty-five students. Dad had persuaded some friends of his to let their daughter go on the trip so that I would have someone I knew.

Most of the passengers were sick the entire ten days. At times Clyde Mitchell, our tour guide, Bart Curtis, a Harvard sophomore, and myself were the only people from our group in the dining room. In addition to great meals, there was coffee and snacks between breakfast and lunch, tea and snacks between lunch and dinner, and drinks with snacks late in the evening. I wondered what my mother would have thought had she seen me drinking a whiskey sour at midnight.

Bart Curtis quickly became a friend whom I enjoyed listening to, even though I understood little of what he talked about. As we went along through the trip he told me interesting things about places we visited. He seemed to know more than Clyde. The first night I walked around the ship with Bart but the second night I met Bep Smits, a young Dutch steward. Bep befriended me when he saw me standing alone at the prow with the wind blowing in my face. As I looked out at the sea and up at the stars, I was again caught in wonder. He came and just stood beside me for a few minutes, as if he too wondered. Then he said that I must like the sea as much as he did. From that night on we spent many evenings on deck after others had gone below. Sometimes we went aft and stood staring down into the ship's wake. I told him it was tempting to me, making me want to jump in. Then he put his arm around my waist and hugged me close. My first instinct was to pull away but I realized that I liked that arm around me and the way my body responded to his touch.

Sometimes when we were walking on deck I felt awkward, worrying about whether our walking was synchronized—should I be taking longer steps to keep up with him or should he take shorter steps to adjust to me. As soon as I noticed that I was worrying about it, it seemed silly and I let it go but, writing this, I notice that I still do this when walking with a man.

Bep spoke enough English so that we could talk about his growing up and mine. We talked about everything—boys and girls dating, about our parents, about what I was going to do in Europe. He wanted to know how it was that boys and girls were travelling together and why we were going to Europe at this time. His speaking was the first time I'd had any hint of trouble in Europe. Our newspapers at home had said there was nothing to the "war scare" in Europe. I was sure that must be the case or my father would not have let me take the trip.

The cabins were stuffy and filled with the smell of sickness, so I asked Bep if he could find me a place to sleep on deck, away from the wind. After my first night on deck, Bep frequently slept alongside me, each of us wrapped in blankets on deck chairs. One night he ventured to reach over and take my hand in his. I liked that and gently squeezed his hand to let him know I did. Usually he stayed with me until early morning, when he had to get back to his cabin before he was missed. Falling asleep those nights, in the clear cold air and the sound of the ship cutting through the water, all I could think of was freedom. I'd never had this kind of a relationship with a boy and wouldn't be having it then if my parents had known.

On calm days our tour group had orientation meetings giving us some common-sense suggestions and teaching us a few simple phrases we might find useful in the countries in which we'd be travelling. Although we had received detailed information about all this after signing up, the tour company wanted to give us a chance to ask questions and learn pronunciation. I particularly remember three German phrases we were given: *Grüs Gott* which we were to use in greeting people, *Vo ist der bahnhof?* (Where is the train station?) and *Vo ist die toilette?* (Where is the toilet?)

It was suggested that we dress modestly. Shorts were okay, as long as they were not too short, but sleeveless blouses and halters were not a good idea. In Italy we would be expected to cover our heads whenever going into a cathedral, so it would be wise to bring a scarf for that purpose.

As we approached Rotterdam I felt a little sad at having to say goodbye to my young Dutch friend but my anticipation of what was coming was so great that I was abrupt with my thanks and goodbye. Today I wonder that I could have been so unfeeling. After all, we had spent ten nights together on deck, had some wonderful talks, learned a lot about each other and here I was just sort of brushing him off. I did give him my address so that we could stay in touch but I never heard from him.

Having picked up our bicycles, which were waiting for us in Rotterdam, we settled in for the night at a youth hostel. Our tour leader, twenty-five year old Clyde Mitchell, from Albuquerque, New Mexico—tall, blond, muscular and very good looking—told us what to expect the next day. He would set the pace for the group. If we were really unable to keep up with the cycling we could take the train, but he encouraged us to give it a fair try. My first glimpse of Holland was dazzling. As far as I could see there were flowers. Flowers everywhere, clean streets and a country so flat it was if I could see into tomorrow. On that first day we rode fifty miles and at the end of the day I was sure it was a mistake to have come. I had never ridden more than a few blocks to the library in Stratford and was not prepared. That night I ached so much that I cried until exhaustion and sleep took over. After a few days, however, I began to feel invigorated by the exercise and knew I would be okay. Some days we rode almost a hundred miles and some days we packed up our bikes and took the train.

We bicycled fifteen hundred miles that summer. Our route took us from Holland through Belgium and into Germany. From Germany we went down to Italy, then to Austria, back through Switzerland and then into France, leaving from LeHavre for the return trip. I was amazed at how many cultures existed side by side. I had read about it, but to experience it was quite different. In a few hours we could be with a different group of people, hear a different language, see different architecture. We visited cathedrals and museums, we rode in gondolas, we went to the Folies Bergére. We did all the things tourists do and, by staying in youth hostels, we met other young people from all over Europe.

Everything that happened that summer of 1938, however, was eclipsed by the experience of being in Adolph Hitler's Germany. His was a seen presence, his portrait hung everywhere—in shops, homes, public buildings; it was a felt presence in the actions and reactions of people we met. When we entered bake shops and proudly offered the greeting *Grüs Gott* as we had learned on shipboard, a shopkeeper would draw back, utter *Nein, nein* then raise his right hand a little above his shoulders, in a kind of salute, and respond, *Heil Hitler!* (So much for our shipboard language classes.)

People stopped whatever they were doing when the stiff young men in uniforms with swastikas on the sleeves came by. "Who are they," I wondered, "and why do people seem afraid of them?" Most of them appeared to be not much older than we. When we asked, the most we could get was, "They are the Hitler *Jugend* of the National Socialist Party."

Bart said these young men had been recruited at a very early age. He said there were eight million German children in the *Jungvolk* and they graduated into the Hitler *Jugend* at the age of fourteen. Then they were indoctrinated into "National Socialistic Principles" which included "Racial Science," teaching that the Germans were a master race and Jews were inferior and responsible for everything that was wrong. Bart said he'd heard that children said *Heil Hitler* anywhere from fifty to one hundred and fifty times a day—on leaving home, greeting a friend, in school, to storekeepers, the postman. On returning home, if the parent's first words were not *Heil Hitler,* they were guilty of a punishable offense, could be, and sometimes were, denounced by their own child.

But we were kids from America, kids who had heard little about Hitler and who wanted our visit in Germany to be about song fests, beer gardens, pastry shops, beautiful scenery and warm hospitable people. We talked about Hitler some but none of us wanted to spoil the summer. Those unfriendly young men seemed like wooden soldiers. At first we were surprised that they seemed not interested in attractive young female tourists but then decided that there must be something wrong with them. Among ourselves, at night, we talked a little about it but tried to pretend that the unease we felt was the product of our own imaginations. We sang as we rode our bikes, swapped life stories on rest breaks, gloried in the baths at Wiesbaden. We ate hearty German food and drank beer. We must have visited just about every pastry shop we saw. The pastries and beer were incomparable and none of us, in our late teens and early twenties, gave a thought to our weight.

The morning after we arrived at the Heidelberg Youth Hostel we heard that Hitler was to speak that afternoon and the activity in the town seemed to make it something we didn't want to miss. Clyde asked the hostel manager if it would be okay for us to go watch and was told we could go as long as we stood back out of the way because we were obviously not German. So, at two o'clock we followed the crowd to the field where Hitler was to speak, lingering in the back so as not to appear too curious. In addition to the Nazi Youth, there were the storekeepers we had met, and most of the people we had seen on the streets. It seemed as if everybody in town was there—attendance was obviously not optional. There was an eerie quality to the gathering. We knew the city to be a center of learning yet everywhere there were those tall, stiff, unsmiling men in uniform, marching with an exaggerated step that made them seem like mechanical toys and then there were people in doorways, peeking out of curtained windows.

Hitler's speech was interrupted frequently with salutes and cries of *Sieg Heil!* There were those, like the Nazi Youth, who shouted with fanatic fervor and raised their right arm toward the sky, then there were those whose *Sieg Heil* was uttered as if they were reluctant but felt they had no choice. Their hands were raised only partly up. They seemed quiet and subdued except when it was time to utter that *Sieg Heil.* These were the people we had seen in shops, on the streets—older people who looked as if they were obeying rules which had been imposed on them, rules they hadn't had a voice in making. There was fear on some of the faces but excitement and anticipation on many more.

Although we were far from the platform, I could see Hitler and hear him clearly. As I listened to him, even without understanding the words, his tone of voice, the expression on his face and the fevered response of the Nazi Youth made me uncomfortable. Bart, who spoke German, said there was a slogan that seemed to be repeated during the speech, at signals from the stage: "One People, One Reich, One Fuehrer."

I could no longer avoid the feeling that something was wrong. At that time I just wished I knew more about what was happening. I didn't understand the tension and knew only that there was fear, suspicion, fanaticism, hostility and many things were *verboten*. But how was it that we knew nothing about this before coming? Surely my father wouldn't have let me come had he thought there was any danger. It was as if Americans were oblivious to what was happening here. No one seemed to know anything about it.

Most of our group came away from the rally quiet and shaken. When we got back to the youth hostel, we questioned the manager who shook his head and indicated clearly that he would not discuss it with us. The only thing he told us was that there had been about 15,000 people at the rally. Bart reported a little about the speech although he seemed reluctant to talk out loud, almost as if he were afraid the walls had ears. He told us Hitler said that, with his *Jugend,* he could make a new world. Hitler was training the German youth to be violent, dominating and brutal. They would have no intellectual training because "knowledge would ruin them." We talked among ourselves until late that night. Clyde tried to reassure us but it was clear that he was as worried as the rest of us.

Having been warned, on shipboard, about modesty in dress, we checked each other mornings before leaving the hostel. When one of the girls, a dark-haired girl, showed up wearing a halter top, we reminded her of that warning. Her response was, "I'll wear anything I like!" Later, while we were riding our bikes in the countryside, a uniformed man on a motorcycle passed us slowly, shouted *Verboten*, then struck a whip across the back of the girl wearing the halter top. We were shocked. The girl was furious and protested that no one could tell her what to wear and what not to wear. Clyde looked to see if the whip lash needed attention and then pointed out that her headstrong attitude might get her into more trouble if she weren't careful.

For the first time that summer I felt, personally, the fear that was present and wondered what the weeks ahead might hold. I didn't have long to wonder. One night I ate some fruit soup that didn't digest and spent the night vomiting. I knew I would be unable to leave with the group in the morning. Clyde spoke with the innkeeper (we were staying at a small inn that night instead of a youth hostel) and arranged for me to stay an extra day and then take a bus to catch up. The town was in a military area and though the innkeeper had agreed to my remaining behind, he said I would have to stay at the inn and would not be free to wander outside. The fear I had been experiencing grew but I knew I had no choice.

When our group left, the innkeeper escorted me to a basement room, where there was a chair, a table and a toilet, but no windows. He told me I would have to stay there until evening. With nothing to read I walked around the room, listening to the sounds of marching and guns being fired while my apprehension grew. I didn't know what was happening. It sounded as if military exercises were being conducted but there was no one to ask. The innkeeper brought lunch down to me and seemed genuinely apologetic but his manner only heightened my anxiety. It was clear that he'd rather not have me there and I imagined that if I were discovered there would be consequences for him. By the time I finished lunch I had worked myself up into a real fright. The conversation in my head had taken over and I was imagining all sorts of consequences of being discovered, consequences for me as well as for the innkeeper. I began to wonder if I would ever rejoin our group, what I would do if I couldn't, and how I would contact the American Embassy if that became necessary. Toward evening my host invited me upstairs, served a generous meal with great courtesy and escorted me to my room for the night.

In spite of the traumatic day, or perhaps because of it, I slept very well and woke looking forward to leaving. The innkeeper served me breakfast, then took me to the bus station and put me aboard a bus that would take me to the group's rendezvous point. The scenery out the bus window was beautiful and by the time I had reached the end of my trip I had calmed down. It was a relief to see those familiar faces, and the unpleasantness of the day before was temporarily forgotten.

By the time our travels took us to the beer garden in Munich, it was as if the uniformed, boot-stomping young men belonged to a different world. It was in Munich that I first acquired a taste for Heineken—which is still my favorite beer—and where I first noticed the attention that Clyde Mitchell was paying to me. With a few glasses of beer I was considerably less inhibited than usual and I'm sure I flirted with him.

In Garmisch-Partenkirchen, a little south of Munich and the site of the 1936 winter Olympics, women on their knees scrubbed front steps and sidewalks every morning. I had never seen anyone do that but neither had I ever seen a place as clean. It made me want to settle down and stay. These were the warm, hospitable people I had expected to see in Germany. I ate sauerbraten and drank beer and listened to music. I climbed part way up Mount Zugspitze, learned a little German and promised myself I would come back one day. I think Clyde was impressed when I tried to climb Zugspitze because I was the only girl who attempted that. He told me how great I was.

Then the fear returned. As we were leaving Germany the train stopped at the border and a group of uniformed men boarded as if they owned the train. They yanked some people out of their seats and almost threw them off the train. They didn't take the passengers' luggage. There was a box car on a side track and it looked as if the passengers were being pushed into that car. These men were very rough and the people being removed obviously didn't want to go. I couldn't understand what was happening. I wanted to protest but could tell from the demeanor of other passengers, as well as the fierce expressions on the faces of the uniformed men, that any such protest would not only be useless but might also be dangerous.

Hearing the news in 1946, after the end of the war, I realized that I might have witnessed the beginning of the incarceration of Jews. The people we had seen being removed had probably been Jews trying to flee the country, although this was early for the mass exodus. They didn't need their luggage because they were probably destined for a concentration camp. After I learned what might have been happening, the scene haunted my dreams for months. That small, ordinary-looking man I had seen on the stage at Heidelberg was responsible for changing the course of history and sending millions of people to their death.

After we were safely out of Germany, one member of our group showed us a souvenir he had smuggled out. He wouldn't say where or how he'd gotten it but it was a Hitler Youth dagger, with *Blut und Ehre* (blood and honor) engraved on the blade.

In Holland and Germany the youth hostels at which we had stayed were comfortable and clean but Clyde told us the youth hostels in Italy did not meet the tour company's standards so we would be housed in little *pensions* with which the company had an arrangement.

We saw all the tourist sights in Italy, but most of the Italian wonders were wasted on me. I had little appreciation of the magnificent works of art. This was an area of my development that my mother had neglected, perhaps because of her background. We didn't have art in our house. I watched pilgrims in St. Peter's Square, feeling a little smug because I thought I had outgrown religion, but with that thought came a wistful longing as I remembered the sound of the organ, the flowers and candles, and kneeling at the altar to receive communion.

In Italy we were as unaware of the threat of war as we had been in America, but in Austria it was very evident. Hitler had just annexed Austria. Although Vienna was beautiful, the music was stilled, the people were subdued. The Nazi presence was everywhere and the effect was chilling. Our visit was brief and guarded. The first time I saw the movie, *The Sound of Music*, I cried because I knew it could easily have been happening when we were there.

In spite of Hitler's presence there were light moments. One morning I was riding my bicycle down a mountainside in Switzerland, glorying in the day and the fact that the day's ride was all downhill. I was going faster than was safe and knew it. What I didn't know was that just around the next curve would be a man coming out of a side road, on a bike loaded with eggs he was taking to market. I squeezed the hand brakes, my front wheel brakes took hold abruptly but not in time to avoid a collision. The man and his eggs and I made a messy heap in the road. No one was hurt and the bikes suffered only minimal damage but ten flats of eggs were splattered on the road and all over us. I apologized and indicated I would pay for the eggs. Even though we lacked a common language, we laughed together as we cleaned up the mess. I paid the farmer for the eggs by reaching in my pocket and holding out all the cash I had. He helped himself, then we waved to each other and rode on.

In Paris, Bart exclaimed about how wonderful it was to be on the Left Bank where Ernest Hemingway and Gertrude Stein and other writers had talked and drunk. Another day we went out to the magnificent Palace of Versailles and wandered through the gardens and the building as if in a dream. There was nothing like this in New England. When we went to the Folies Bergére, I couldn't help wondering what my mother would say if she knew about the show I was seeing. My Dad would have loved it!

The Atlantic was calm on our return voyage from LeHavre. Often Clyde and I would walk the deck at night after the evening program was over and most of the others had retired to their cabins. I enjoyed being out with him after hours because I felt special at having been singled out and getting so much attention but, at the same time, I was fearful that this might be leading to that "something" my mother had warned me about. After all, Clyde was twenty-five and seemed very self assured.

One evening at dinner, the captain announced that there would be a demonstration of hypnosis as part of the evening's entertainment and invited us all to attend. I was curious, never having seen anyone hypnotized, and sat in the front row. The captain, who also seemed to be the hypnotist, looked around the audience, pointed to four or five people farther back, then pointed at me. We were all asked to join him on the stage. He told us what would be happening.

"You are to keep your eyes on this watch I'm swinging. You will feel sleepier and sleepier and then you will no longer be aware of me or the watch. When that happens I will give you commands which you will obey. I will not ask you to do anything harmful to yourself or others. You can trust me so don't let that worry you. When the demonstration is over I will clap my hands three times, and you will open your eyes and be here. You will feel refreshed, as if you'd had a nap, but you'll remember nothing of what happened while you were under hypnosis."

I was excited to be taking part and did exactly as I was told. It was only seconds before my eyes closed and the watch disappeared. It also seemed only a matter of seconds before I opened my eyes again, although they told me later that it had been fifteen minutes.

"How do you feel, young lady?" "Fine, but no different. I think nothing must have happened. Perhaps I'm not a good hypnotic subject." The captain laughed, as did the audience. "Oh really? Did you come in wearing your sweater backwards?" I looked down and saw that the cardigan I was wearing was open up the back instead of the front.

My parents drove down to meet the ship when it docked in New York. By the end of the summer I had developed muscles from riding, was tanned and healthy looking and had a whole new confidence in myself. But we had been eating German pastries and drinking beer all summer and, trying to get into a dress for debarking, I was suddenly confronted with the results of my casual attitude about eating. I'd managed to get into a dress, but one look at my mother's face made me know it was a mistake.

Mother said, "What happened to you? You're a mess!" I knew I was home but her remark couldn't dampen my spirits or the confidence I had gained during the summer. Mother was Mother and I suspected she always would be.

Dad said, "That's not nice, Mother. Our little girl has been gone all summer." Then to me he said, "Glad to have you back looking all healthy and tanned."

Before Clyde and I had said goodbye to one another, he said he would be staying in New York for a month or so and would like to see me. I told him that my mother and I often came into the city to shop and he suggested that the next time I came in, I let him take me to dinner. A few days after getting home I called him and arranged to meet him after our next Saturday's shopping trip. Mother said I needed some new clothes, at least until I lost some of the weight I had gained during the summer. In the city I told her about Clyde's invitation and persuaded her to go back on an earlier train, saying I would have dinner with Clyde and take a later train. Surprisingly she didn't make a fuss. Perhaps it was because she thought he'd been taking care of us all summer and could be trusted or perhaps, unlikely, she thought I'd grown up enough to take care of myself.

Whatever the reason, one Saturday afternoon I was in Grand Central Station saying goodbye to Mother, who was laden down with bundles from our shopping, all except the new dress which she had insisted I wear "for going out to dinner with a young man," and I was promising to be home on the eleven o'clock train.

I was thrilled to be going to see Clyde again and, after a trip to the ladies room to check my hair and lipstick, I hailed a cab and gave the driver the address Clyde had given me. He greeted me with a quick hug, grabbed his coat and we were off to a restaurant. I don't remember where we went but only how handsome Clyde was and how grownup I felt. After a long, leisurely dinner spent talking about our summer, Clyde suggested we go back to his hotel for coffee. I still marvel at my naiveté. It wasn't long before I learned that "for coffee" was a ruse. His overtures frightened me, so I thanked him for dinner, made an excuse about needing to catch the last train and fled. I had felt free to flirt but when it came time to deliver on what my flirting might have suggested, I ran. Clyde seemed annoyed but also amused. I suspect he recognized that he was dealing not with a woman but with a girl pretending to be a woman.

I was standing in the lobby of Clyde's hotel when I realized I'd missed the last train and began to wonder where I would spend the night. I didn't have enough money for a room in Clyde's hotel so I asked one of the porters if he knew where

I could find a cheap place to spend the night. He gave me an address on a slip of paper. When I got there I was terrified. It was a flea bag of a hotel in a run-down neighborhood, but I didn't have much money and it was late, so it would have to do. I paid for the room in advance.

When I got to my room I locked the door and stacked furniture in front of it. Then I discovered a door to an adjoining room that was locked on the other side so I had to move some of the furniture from the hall door and put it in front of the other door. Lying down, fully clothed, I realized that I wasn't as grown up as I had thought. I hadn't even called home to let them know I wouldn't be coming until morning. Suddenly I was a scared little girl who wanted her mommy. Awake most of the night, I left the hotel at seven o'clock the next morning and caught the first train back home. My mother was waiting at the phone when I called from the station. She said, in a cold, threatening voice, "Your father will be up to get you. And you'd better have a good story!"

Dad warned me that Mom was steaming and suggested that I give her time to cool off before trying to explain what happened so all I said when I greeted her was, "I made a mistake in New York. I'm sorry I worried you. I'll tell you about it when I wake up but right now I'm going to take a bath and a nap." Mother seemed surprised but didn't object.

I can only imagine the explanation I must have invented about missing the train and staying at the YWCA but whatever the story, it prompted only an expression of worry and concern rather than the diatribe I'd expected. My disappointment may have been so evident that they didn't want to add to it.

It was the last time I heard from Clyde from Albuquerque.

3

Introduction to Segregation

Home from my escapade with Clyde I fully expected to be packing and going to New York to the Presbyterian Hospital but when I spoke to my mother about getting ready she said, almost casually, "Oh, yes, dear, we've been meaning to tell you. There's been a change of plans. I don't think you'd really like being a nurse. It's not a job for nice girls, it's mostly carrying bed pans and changing beds and things like that. While you were gone I talked with Mrs. Mitchell and found out that Pat is going to a school in North Carolina where they have a fine music program so I withdrew your registration at Presbyterian and signed you up for Salem instead. I'm sure you'll be much happier there and besides, you'll be with Pat."

I was astounded. I knew that I didn't have much choice. My father had been willing to pay for two years of nursing school, and I had agreed since there was nothing I really wanted to do, but now my mother had undercut even that decision without so much as asking me.

It seems as if I must have rebelled, but I can't remember doing so. Perhaps it was because I was so accustomed to having my mother make decisions for me, perhaps it was because I wanted to get away from home and it didn't matter much where I went, or perhaps it was because I knew the futility of protest. Mother managed my life and that's just the way it was. My brief taste of freedom during the summer was just that—a brief taste. I knew I was home again. So when she informed me of the decision to send me to Salem, I sighed and said, with tongue in cheek, "Okay, Momma, I'm sure you know what's best for me."

Salem was a small Moravian college, founded in 1772 and reputed to be the 13th oldest college in the country. The Moravians were members of the United Brethren religious sect in Germany, and the Moravian community in Winston-Salem was one of the earliest planned communities in the colonies. Salem was considered a liberal arts college, although most of the girls referred to it as a "finishing school." It provided a carefully insulated environment for its girls. There were no "people of color," no Jews, and, of course, no men. And it had rules, rules, rules—about where we could go, what we could do, with whom we could do it and when.

There were only three northern girls in Salem that year—Pat Mitchell, Pris Dean, and myself. Each of us roomed with a girl from the south. My roommate was Mary Beth Warren. The girls in our dormitory made fun of us from the north. They called us "Yankees" but the fun poking was done as if they expected us to enjoy it. After a few days, one of the more brazen girls on our floor stopped by our room, saw me dressing and laughingly said, "What a mess you are, girl! But it won't take us long to fix you up. A little makeup, a little curl in your hair, a little attention to your clothes and you'll be fine. Just you wait and see."

That evening, almost as if my silence signaled agreement, she and her friends started working on me—teaching me how to put on makeup, how to put curlers in my hair, showing me the high-heeled shoes I should buy and telling me to get a padded bra since I was so flat-chested. Suddenly I knew what the term "finishing school" meant. My mother had sent me here to be fixed up so I would become a lady and make that good marriage she wanted for me.

All this fixing was done in the evening because in the day, for classes, we were expected to dress in a subdued fashion and I wore loafers for getting around the campus. But when it came time for a tea or a dance or an evening at the symphony, my floor mates would supervise my dressing and make me up just before I went out so that I wouldn't be able to take the makeup off. I felt like a painted lady but it didn't matter because the only one who came to Salem as my guest was Dupuy Sears and I was sure he would approve of what the girls had done.

Dupuy was a cousin of one of the girls on our floor and she had first introduced us, saying, "I thought you two might like each other, so I've had Dupuy put on the approved list." This was the list of boys who had been checked into by the administration and deemed appropriate to be invited to teas and dances. Although I never thought of Dupuy as a boyfriend, he must have had some interest in being that because during the summer following my year at school, he drove north to pay us a visit and meet my parents. My mother thought he was lovely. "He has such good manners," she said. I realized she had immediately put him on her list of eligible young men.

I had been so fascinated by the shipboard demonstration of hypnosis that one evening, in an attempt to make friends with the girls on my floor at Salem, I experimented with my dorm mates. Having watched the Rotterdam's captain I felt sure I could do it. I invited several girls and asked for a volunteer. The volunteer and I sat in chairs facing each other and I took the medallion I had on a chain and waved it back and forth before her eyes while speaking in a low, persuasive tone. The girls circled around us watching, waiting for their turn. It seemed like no time at all before I heard laughter and opened my eyes to see the others standing around me guffawing. It took me a minute to realize what had happened. I had succeeded only in hypnotizing myself.

My roommate, Mary Beth, had problems which became mine when I moved in. She had never taken care of herself or her clothes—she had a Nanny at home—and seemed unwilling to take care of those things at Salem. When she ran out of clean clothes she started in on mine. The day I came back to the dorm to get ready for gym and found that she had taken my last set of clean gym clothes, I lost my temper and told her that if she thought having had a nanny entitled her to some special consideration here, she'd have to think again. I was not going to help her with her bath and I never wanted to come back to the room again and find that she had helped herself to my clean clothes. Mary Beth started to cry and I felt awful but knew that I meant what I had said.

The southern girls seemed to have a different orientation toward life than those of us from the north. Pris Dean and I often gossiped about them, wondering if men and clothes were all they ever thought about. Pat Mitchell and I had not been close on the European trip and, at Salem, that friendship still did not develop beyond being members of the small group of "Yankees." But we sometimes talked about our summer in Europe and Pris joined in because she had been an exchange student in France during high school. We were all interested in what was happening in Europe and there was still little news about that, at least at Salem. The other girls on our floor did not seem at all interested and would avoid us if they heard us talking. Actually there was almost no one on the campus who seemed interested and it was difficult for us to get any news.

I was unhappy at Salem and there were two major factors. One was that I hated my music program, another was that I was upset over the segregation, which I confronted on an almost daily basis. For the first month of school I had been closeted in a practice room for four hours a day with nothing to do but practice scales and fingering. My love of music was almost extinguished by the process. It was not at all what I had expected. I actually don't know what I expected but maybe I thought they could magically turn me into one of those concert pianists I'd heard at Klein Memorial. Also, when I got to Winston Salem I was met by the overt practice of discrimination. The college was in Old Salem, which was the colored section of the city, so we were not allowed off campus after four in the afternoon and were not allowed to use city buses. To go into town we were supposed to use taxis. In the city, there were separate restaurants, separate schools for colored children, separate drinking fountains, separate toilet facilities and colored people had to ride in the back of buses. The sharp lines of segregation were unsettling for me. In Stratford High School we had colored students and although we had our own social groups, we were in classes and sports together and respected each other.

I had known my mother was wrong about my friends, judging them by the color of their skin, but I had never confronted her because I knew she would say I was too young to know what I was talking about. I just went along, not agreeing with her but not openly contradicting her. Being at Salem, I realized that Mother was not alone in her discrimination and my attitude toward her changed. I guessed she couldn't be any other way than she was, but I didn't have to adopt her values or her attitudes about people. Pat and Pris shared this concern and once Pris said, when we were in my room, "I thought the Civil War was supposed to have settled all this."

After a month in Winston-Salem I knew it was not the place for me. One day I decided to leave and packed up my things. I told Pat I was leaving and she tried to dissuade me but I was sure I was right and that my father would understand. I sent him a telegram, saying I was leaving Salem and asking him to meet me at the Bridgeport station. It was a long train ride home, thinking about what I would say.

Dad was at the station but had no sympathy. He didn't even want to hear my reasons for leaving. He said, "For one thing I have paid tuition for the year and I'm not going to lose that money. And, your mother wants you to become a fine pianist and singer. Don't you realize what an opportunity this is?"

He listened to my pleas, with courtesy if not interest, then bought me a meal in the train station, kissed me on the cheek and put me on the next train back south. I was back in school before the administration noticed I was gone.

I was humiliated at having to return but soon learned about a "weekend permission" slip which promised to make life easier. The girls told me that if my parents signed such a slip, it would give me almost unlimited freedom on weekends. Mother and Dad, anxious only to have me stay at Salem, signed without having any idea of what it meant. I was allowed to leave campus on Friday after classes and not required to sign back in until Monday morning. I wondered if the administrators didn't care what I did on Saturday and Sunday, since it was then my parents' responsibility, or if they thought they could count on me as a "Salem girl." We all wore sweatshirts that said, "I represent Salem" on them and were frequently reminded that being a representative of Salem required us to be models of courtesy, obedience, and decorum. Whatever the rationale behind the weekend permission policy, it was a reprieve that made the rest of the year endurable.

I first went to Chapel Hill for a fraternity party to which I had been invited by the brother of a Salem girl and, at that party, met Ned Houston, a third-year University student. It was a beautiful evening and from that time on, I spent weekends away from Salem at Ned's fraternity house. There were always other girls visiting and, even though we were carefully chaperoned, I enjoyed the weekends. They bore little or no relation to weekends at Salem where we had stilted teas and occasional dances.

I enjoyed the relationship with Ned and was grateful to him for the discovery that I could have a normal, healthy, on-going relationship with a boy. He honored my reluctance to engage in intimate behavior and never pressed me. At Chapel Hill, we walked around the campus arm in arm, sat in groups in the lounges, drinking beer and discussing politics, religion and the courses people were taking. At this point I didn't have much to offer to the discussions but I enjoyed listening and sometimes participating in the speculation about what was happening in Europe. It was a relaxed, casual and intellectually stimulating environment at Chapel Hill and I could not help making comparisons with the environment at Salem, where every social gathering was strictly supervised and men visited the campus only on special occasions and had to be on an approved list before they were welcome.

We had dances at Salem, about once a month, but whenever I thought of telling my Stratford friends about them I would begin laughing to myself. Boys from the approved list were bussed to the campus on Saturday night and dropped at the gymnasium. These affairs seemed like the dance classes I remembered as a child with boys holding me at arm's length and me looking at my feet to be sure I didn't trip. The emphasis at Salem seemed to be on making sure body contact was minimal. During the evening, chaperones descended like hawks on any couple dancing too close. The boys were counted as they left the bus and were counted at the end of the evening as they got back on. On those nights there was also a room check before lights out. In spite of all that, once in a while a girl would manage to keep her young man with her for the night.

Many of Salem's programs were designed to develop our social graces. There were Sunday afternoon teas to which eligible young men could be invited for a chaperoned tea hour in the lounge. We introduced our guests to the college president, Dr. Rondthaler, his wife, our housemother and any other members of the faculty who dropped in for tea. Then we sat around, on uncomfortable straight chairs, sipping our tea and engaging in polite conversation about our studies.

In another of Salem's social programs, students were escorted to dinner and the symphony by prominent older men from the community. My escort was Theodore J. deYaure, a Persian rug dealer and philanthropist. He was probably fifty years old, obviously wealthy. I enjoyed those evenings and felt like Cinderella when my escort came for me in a chauffeur-driven Rolls Royce. The evenings were designed to teach us how to eat in fine restaurants and how to behave at the symphony. I was introduced to food I'd never had before—*escargot*, frog's legs and *caviar*. My escort quietly and gently made sure that I was using the right fork and that I didn't talk at the symphony. He needn't have worried about me at the symphony because I had learned symphony behavior many years before at Klein Memorial and when the music began, I was totally absorbed for the rest of the evening.

Mr. deYaure treated me as if he considered me a beautiful woman on a date. When he took me back to Salem he walked with me to the reception area and checked me in. Then he kissed my hand as he said goodnight and, for that instant, I was a woman. Before I left school, Mr. deYaure gave me a beautifully illustrated first edition of the English translation of the *Rubáiyát of Omar Khayyám*. He corresponded with me when I returned to Connecticut and came north to take me to the World's Fair when it was on Long Island. As always, I felt like a princess when I was with him and he appeared to enjoyed that as much as I did.

My roommate, Mary Beth, had invited me to her home for Thanksgiving. I was grateful for the invitation because otherwise I'd have been on the campus with the two or three others who weren't going home. At Mary Beth's home, however, I was aghast at the size of their household staff. There were servers, kitchen staff, butlers, upstairs maids, nannies for each of the children, downstairs maids, a chauffeur, a gardener and goodness knows how many others that I didn't even see. In Connecticut such a staff would have cost a small fortune but I suspected that was not the case here. Mary Beth said all their servants had been trained by their parents—this was the fourth generation of "nigras" to serve her family. My calculations told me that these families were in the same relation to each other as they had been before the Civil War, a war that did little to change their status. Mary Beth said there was a family bond—these people were part of her family and her parents took good care of them, providing medical care and good food. Her mother ministered to their children when they were sick.

The man standing at my elbow to see if I needed anything or to refill my water glass when it was only half empty was so polite and so gracious I scarcely knew how to act. It was as if we were in one of those high-priced restaurants you saw in the movies, yet this was Mary Beth's home. Once I dropped my napkin on the floor and when I reached down to pick it up, the manservant also reached for it, then smiled at me under the table and chided me gently, saying I should let him do that. There was something very appealing about that gracious style of living. A year or two later, when I saw *Gone With the Wind* it reminded me of Mary Beth's home.

I was confused because everyone at Mary Beth's seemed content in their roles but when, in Winston-Salem, I saw toilet facilities bearing signs, "For Whites Only," I realized the contentment had to have been purchased at the price of pride. I was going to add "self-respect" to that price but realized, as I was leaving Mary Beth's, that these people knew who they were and what they were doing. They had chosen to continue in their roles and suffered no loss of self-respect for that choice. I couldn't help wonder how it would be when their children grew up. But in town it was different. Many colored people looked angry and most looked poor. They were all in service jobs—sweeping sidewalks, loading trucks, washing windows and dishes.

On returning from our Thanksgiving holiday, I realized that Mary Beth was not likely to change. Her nanny had done everything for her since she was born and would continue to do so every time she went home, so we agreed to make a roommate change. By Christmas, Mary Beth had moved in with another southern girl and Pris Dean and I were living together.

Pris and I grew close in my year at Salem. We had long talks about life and parents and growing up. She was the first real girl friend I'd had since Janis Dow, on Warwick Avenue, and I thought we would be friends forever. But the year after I left Salem, Pris was diagnosed with multiple sclerosis. My first thoughts were purely selfish—it wasn't fair, she couldn't leave, I needed her. But then I went to see her and felt only love and compassion, wishing there were something I could do to ease her suffering. One day we were having lunch on trays in her room and she tried to lift a spoonful of soup to her mouth, but her arm and hand wouldn't cooperate. She gave up and looked at me with an embarrassed laugh. She had barely finished laughing when the hand holding the spoon lifted involuntarily and splashed its contents all over her face. She turned away from me and began to cry. I had to call on a strength I didn't know I had, to keep from crying with her.

I visited five or six times before she died and each time it became increasingly more difficult for both of us. Her deterioration was rapid, it embarrassed her, and she would break into tears when she was unable to do something. I never left her without crying on the way home. One day, as I was leaving, she kissed me and asked me not to come again. I wanted to object but, looking into her eyes, I was silenced. Shortly after that she died. It was my first experience of the death of someone I loved. At first I couldn't grasp it. How could she have died—she was only twenty years old! Then the aching loneliness returned.

My music program at Salem continued to be deadly. By Christmas I had not progressed beyond doing exercises, still confined in a piano practice room four hours a day. If this was what it took to become a concert pianist, and I suspected it was, then I knew I'd settle for going to listen at Klein Memorial. Before the end of my Christmas holiday I told my parents I was switching to the secretarial course in the new term. It was a one-year course and I knew I wouldn't be returning to Salem for a second year although, at that time, I didn't tell my folks. The secretarial program was supervised by Miss Wilmot, who was probably eighty years old, not more than five feet tall and a hundred pounds, with a wrinkled face, a sharp tongue and dark clothes that just seemed to hang from her shoulders to her ankles.

Sitting at the typewriter it felt as if I had simply traded one instrument for another. I spent hours learning the keyboard and being drilled in exercises to test that learning. But as I gained skill I did begin to feel a mastery that I'd never felt at the piano. Shorthand was like learning another language. It was fun and I became so adept that it has remained with me through my lifetime.

Until the summer in Europe I had never been particularly concerned with civil rights or any other social issues—they were not discussed in our house. But the summer in Europe had raised questions and the year in Winston-Salem raised more. My outrage at the whole system erupted one day in the spring when I was riding home from town on a bus, having broken the school rule about not riding buses. An older colored woman, laden with bags of groceries, boarded the bus. It was nearly full so she walked toward the back and stood in the aisle. I offered her my seat. She protested, I insisted and she sat down. The bus driver yelled at me, "You can't do that, Miss. She has to ride in the back of the bus." "I paid my fare and took this seat. If I now want to let someone else sit in it, I will do so!" The simple act of courtesy had become an issue. The bus driver glared at me but let it go. I suspect, now, that he knew I would get off the bus ahead of the old woman although, at the time, I thought he was showing me the deference often shown Salem girls. When I did leave the bus I saw the driver get up, go down the aisle, grab the woman by the arm, yank her out of the seat and push her to the back of the bus. I was appalled and realized that I had done her no favor. On another occasion the debating team from Salem met with the debating team from Winston-Salem Teachers' College, a school for colored women. I was delighted that we were going to do this but was humiliated when, at refreshment time after the debate, we were separated from the girls with whom we had just been debating. We had our refreshments on one side of the room and they had theirs on another. I didn't say anything because, by that time, I realized that the whole environment was structured this way and my classmates didn't see it because it was like the air they breathed.

At Salem I learned to dance, to eat in fine restaurants, to ride a horse and to pour tea. I learned how to put on makeup, how to dress for and behave at the symphony and how to introduce a young man to Dr. Rondthaler. I learned shorthand and typing. And I learned more than I wanted to know about bigotry and discrimination.

My parents couldn't have had an inkling of what would be the impact of my summer in Europe and my year in Winston Salem or they would never have supported either. Today, as I write, I am grateful for both experiences.

4

Marriage, Childbirth, Abusive Husband

When I saw Don Campbell in June of 1939 I knew something in our relationship had changed. He was no longer just the nice neighbor who always smiled at me when he went by our house. He was a big, gorgeous hunk! He had graduated from college, was going to Yale Law School in the fall and when he asked me to go to a movie with him, I felt like turning handstands.

Don had been president of the senior class and captain of the football team when I was in my first year at Stratford High School. He looked like a football player—six foot two, and weighing over two hundred pounds. He had dark hair with just a hint of a wave, which he tried to tame. He had a square chin, brown eyes flecked with green, perfect teeth and a smile that made his whole face light up. While most of my classmates had sighed and swooned at the sight of him, to me he had always been the next-door neighbor with whom I grew up, the neighbor who sometimes stopped to help me build a snowman or hollow out a tunnel through the snow. He always seemed like another brother to me but suddenly that image changed.

After that first movie we were inseparable. We spent evenings at the country club, we played tennis, we tried out all the new restaurants and went to the symphony. We swam and sailed and walked on the beach. His parents took us to New Haven to the opening of plays at the Schubert Theater. I remember dancing with him and thinking back to the times in high school when I envied Mary Peck for the way Ralph Walker had looked at her when they were dancing. Don looked at me that way now, as if he were lucky to have me for a girlfriend. When we were dancing I never needed to worry about my feet—he led with a certainty that made me feel light and graceful. He was strong but also gentle. I was in love!

He was a thoroughly nice guy and made me feel as if I were someone special. Both sets of parents were delighted. Don and I had grown up together, went to the same church, his parents and mine were friends. My mother and I started my hope chest. I picked out the pattern for my sterling flatware and Mother was adding the beautiful linens she knew I'd need. All girls my age were supposed to prepare for marriage by buying, or being gifted with, sterling flatware and fine linens for setting a beautiful table. My hope chest was cedar lined and every time I opened it, the scent started me dreaming about what it would be like when Don and I were married because, from the end of the summer of 1939, I was sure we would be. It just seemed right, like the next step in a plan.

There was only one thing wrong. I always dreaded the end of an evening, when Don would drive off and find a place to park. With the first kiss he changed from the nice social companion of the evening into a stranger—his mouth and hands grasping, his body tense and insistent. Often at this point I would plead tiredness or an early morning ahead. When I did, he would pull away, start up the car and take me home in silence.

At nineteen my friends said there were "fast" girls who were popular with boys because they "went all the way," and, for me, that was forbidden until marriage. My mother and I had no discussion of sex other than what she said to me the first time I menstruated. That warning made it seem like something to be avoided as long as possible. But I was confused because I liked intimacy. I remembered being with Ned at Chapel Hill, enjoying being held and kissed but getting nervous and withdrawing when he began fondling my breasts. Ned sensed my discomfort, had immediately withdrawn his hand and laughed gently at his "little Puritan girl."

With Don I thought my mother might be right because he frightened me. I was pretty sure his insistence was leading up to that to which my mother had alluded in our talk. I never thought about telling him truthfully that his behavior frightened me. My response to Don was to withdraw and, at those times, the loneliness returned and I wondered if it would always be that way. We had been seeing each other almost every day but, at the end of the summer, Don went off to Yale and I went to work at General Electric, Bridgeport, in a clerical job, earning fourteen dollars a week. In the fall we saw each other only on weekends when he came home but I so enjoyed being with him, I was able to convince myself that if we married he might be less urgent or I might be less afraid, so when he asked I accepted. We were going to announce our engagement on Christmas but in late November I met Gerry Quigley.

During my year at Salem, my folks had built a new house in Lordship, a waterfront section of Stratford, and one day Mrs. Stevens, a neighbor, called and asked me for dinner that evening. "I have a new roomer, a young man named

Gerry Quigley, who has just come down, from New Hampshire, to work at Chance Vought Aircraft. He seems not to know anybody and he's about your age. I thought it would be nice if you met him and then perhaps could introduce him to some of your friends." I accepted the invitation.

I sat across the table from Gerry and the first time my eyes met his, something happened that had never happened before—I had strange, unfamiliar stirrings in my body. I scarcely noticed what I was eating and, instead of helping Mrs. Stevens acquaint Gerry with Stratford, I seemed tongue tied. She tried to keep up a conversation but Gerry appeared totally disinterested, and I was aware only of confusion. What was this? It had never happened with Don and I was sure I loved him. Somehow we got through the evening and Gerry offered to walk me across the street to my house. Half way across he took my hand.

"When can I see you again?" he asked as we reached the house. "I don't know," I said, blushing and hesitating. "Call me." I broke away and rushed into the house. I closed the door and leaned against it as I thought of what I had said, and of Don. I had told Gerry to call, suggesting that I might be willing to see him again. Worse than that, I knew I wanted to see him again. Whatever it was that I had been feeling that evening I had never felt with Don.

Reason and good judgment seemed to fly out the window. Gerry wasn't what I considered handsome. He had blondish-red curly hair, a nose that was too long and an adolescent-like complexion with spots on his face. He was shorter than Don, about five foot eleven, but from having worked in the paper mill in his home town, he had unusually developed shoulders, wrists and hands.

Thoughts of Don seemed like unwelcome intrusions, making me feel guilty as I remembered the weeks we'd spent together and my promise to marry him. By the middle of December it was clear that Don and I would not be announcing our engagement. I had severed our relationship with so little consideration for his feelings that I am embarrassed to recall it. My infatuation with Gerry had taken over. Where Don was gentle and courteous, Gerry was rough and rude. When Don wanted sex, I withdrew and he drove me home. With Gerry it was quite different. My fear of sex had not diminished and he was furious every time I pulled away from him. I saw Don only once after we split up and I felt more guilt than anything else. He acted just as he had on those nights when I pleaded tiredness and he took me home. Kissing me goodbye on the cheek he said, "If this is the way you want it, good luck." I cried as he left.

Mother and Dad were dismayed. They had been looking forward to having Don as a son-in-law. They had known him all his life, he was a charming, stable guy with a promising future as a lawyer. What little they knew about Gerry only contributed to their dismay—he was Catholic, with a French-Canadian mother and an Irish father who had disappeared before Gerry was born. My mother had little tolerance even for Congregationalists or Methodists but none for Catholics, and a child born out of wedlock was something not even discussed in our family.

My mother was also disturbed because, with Gerry, I seemed to be in constant turmoil. Rarely did I come in from a date that I was not in tears. I no longer saw any of my school friends. Gerry didn't want to socialize and when I spoke of doing something that left him out, he would accuse me of trying to "cheat on him." Much of the time he acted as if he disliked me, and the confidence I had gained in the year away from home, and in my relationship with Don, began to fade. It was not long before I was making comparisons between Gerry and Don and thinking of the good times I had before meeting Gerry. One night I made the mistake of saying just that, as we were driving down Stratford Road on the way home.

"Don and I used to do things with our friends, things I'd like to do with you too, but…"

He interrupted with, "If you were so crazy about Don why'd you get rid of him? You could probably get him back if you tried. Why don't you try?" His voice rose to a crescendo of fury. "As a matter of fact, why don't you try right now? Go ahead and try right now!"

He slowed the car down, reached across me, opened the passenger door and pushed me. Before I realized what had happened I was tumbling out of the car onto the shoulder of the road. He raced the engine and was gone. I got up, dusted myself off, and walked the few remaining miles home, unhurt but stunned and crying. My mind was a whirl of thoughts. What had I done? What a mess I was making of my life. I knew I had regressed in my relationship with Gerry. I no longer liked the person I was becoming. I thought about Don but knew I could not tell him what was happening. Reaching the house I tried to let myself in quietly to avoid questions but my mother was waiting.

"What happened to you, young lady?" she demanded. "Oh, I fell," I lied. "I don't believe you but neither do I expect you to tell me the truth. I bet it has something to do with that young man of yours. He's no good!" She paused but when I failed to respond she went on, "Go on upstairs and get yourself cleaned up and into bed. You have to go to work in the morning."

Crying in the shower I wished I could talk to my mother. I knew she didn't like Gerry, and I wouldn't have known what to say. I was sure whatever I said would prompt an, "I told you so," and that would have ended it. I ached with loneliness and wished for Auntie Bea who was no longer there for me. Writing this, I realized that I might have telephoned her except that, in our home, the phone was used only for emergencies and certainly not for talking at length about personal problems. Auntie Bea would have known what I should do. From the time I was a little girl, she was the one who listened to my complaints about my mother without taking sides. She was the only one in whom I had been able to confide. When she died, three years after I met Gerry, I was bereft.

My evenings with Don had been filled with dancing, the theater, going somewhere with his parents and then, perhaps, driving down to the beach to park for a little while before going home. Sometimes we would walk on the beach, hand in hand, without talking, then go back to the car. I liked it when he put his arms around me but when he became more aggressive I got frightened and withdrew. Don always seemed disappointed but took me home without saying anything. With Gerry, dates were stormy and passionate. A date was only finding someplace to park—usually a wooded or secluded spot—and "making out." Frequently I went home in tears because he was furious with me for having refused him. I continued to refuse for months but Gerry was adamant and kept telling me that if I really loved him I would show it.

Our first sexual intercourse was accompanied by pain (my mother had been right), massive guilt and fear of pregnancy. Then I knew we had to marry—that's just the way it was. There was no allowance, in my family or in our community, for sex outside of marriage. When Gerry gave me a diamond for Christmas in 1940, Mother and Dad said they would not give their permission for us to marry. But I felt I had no choice and reminded them that I would be twenty-one the next June and could elope, so they could not actually stop us.

One morning in May, my father came down to breakfast and said, "Betty, we're not being mean with you, we're just afraid you won't be happy with Gerry, but if you are intent on getting married, then do it here. Don't elope. Your mother and I will give you a nice little wedding at home." My parents knew that, as a Catholic, Gerry would not be married in our Episcopal Church. I was relieved and thanked my father. I had wanted a real wedding.

Gerry had grown up in a small mill town in New Hampshire, living in one of those fragile houses that hung out over the edge of the Ashuelot River, houses without central heating, electricity or plumbing. His mother, Phoebe, had been given a home by her bachelor brother but he kept her and the child cloistered, hidden from the community. Gerry's mother told me she used to bring him home from school in the middle of the day to change his clothes and clean him up so that he was always immaculate. It was as if she thought she could scrub away the sin of his having been born out of wedlock. She would not let him have a bike and he rode a tricycle until he was ten, finally lashing out at his mother and Uncle Joe because the other kids made fun of him. He had not been allowed near the water to learn to swim so one day he jumped off a ledge into a nearby pond, stayed afloat and learned on his own.

His mother was treated like a second-class member of the family and it should have given me an idea of what to expect in my marriage. She kept house for her brother, Joseph. At mealtimes she served him and his friends, who sat at the dining room table while she ate in the kitchen, standing up with her plate on the shelf which was part of the kitchen stove, at the ready for the call of the men. By the time I met her she was completely cowed, timid and almost afraid to speak, except on the rare occasions when she let her brother know that she wanted an oil stove, instead of a wood-burning one, and town water, instead of water from the well.

Gerald Francis Quigley and I were married on June 14, 1941, in my parents' house in Lordship. The fireplace wall was banked with flowers, the baby grand piano my parents had given me for my 21st birthday stood in one corner of the living room, the dinette table was set up with punch and cookies. The door to the porch was open, letting in the fragrant salt breeze from Long Island Sound. Dad's study had been converted to a showplace for wedding gifts, for although the wedding was small—"For immediate family" the invitation said—my family had many friends in Stratford and there were many wedding gifts. My Uncle Will's wedding gift was a three-dollar gold piece that had been minted in the year of his birth, 1857, and had never been circulated. I have kept that coin all my life, with the intention of passing it on to one of my children when I die.

The living room was crowded. Gerry's mother, Phoebe, her brother Joe, and sister, Carrie, had come down from New Hampshire for the wedding. Gram, Uncle Will, and Uncle Ted were there, as was Aunt Ella and her family. Auntie Bea had come down from Hartford for the occasion. Everyone in the room looked uncomfortable, Gerry's family visibly ill at ease. His mother and her sister would whisper together but otherwise did not engage in conversation. My parents were meeting them for the first time and made a heroic effort to be hospitable, but it didn't work. It was not a joyous affair.

Even as I heard myself repeating the vows after the minister, I knew I had misgivings but still felt I had no choice. I was promising to stay with this man until the end of our lives and I couldn't imagine that I would do so.

Gerry had decided to wear a white suit and I was carrying a huge bouquet of daisies and baby's breath. When the minister pronounced us man and wife and told Gerry he could kiss the bride, he did. The yellow centers of the daisies in my bouquet rubbed off on his jacket as we embraced. He looked down at the front of his jacket and snarled at me, "Look what those damned daisies of yours did to my suit!"

Somewhere deep inside me a laugh threatened to erupt but I knew it wouldn't do and, instead, I switched to feeling sorry for myself that those were the first words he spoke as my husband. Then I heard Gerry's mother gasp and looked over to see her covering her mouth as if she too had wanted to laugh. I knew then that I would get along with Phoebe.

We were going to Virginia Beach for our honeymoon and had reservations at a hotel in New York for the first night. We left the house at four o'clock, midst the throwing of rice. Gerry was cursing about the rice in his hair and on his suit and, backing out of the driveway, he hit the telephone pole near the corner of the drive. His cursing took on new color. The trip from Stratford to New York City was characterized by Gerry's outbursts—swearing at a too-slow driver, then gunning the engine, passing, and pulling in front of him so close I was amazed that there wasn't an accident. He had trouble finding his way to the hotel, cursed at the map, then at me, then at my father for reserving rooms at a hotel so hard to find and, finally, waving off the porter who wanted to help with our luggage, saying, loudly enough for everyone around to hear, that the only thing they wanted was a tip and he'd be damned if he'd tip them for something we could do ourselves.

Our accommodations were appropriately bridal—my father had made the reservation—but as I changed into my new lace nightie I discovered, with horror, that I was menstruating. I didn't know how it could have happened but was afraid to tell Gerry for fear of what he would think.

"You planned it this way, didn't you!" he accused me, when he heard. "I didn't! What a horrible thing to say!" I didn't try to explain. I knew it would be futile. It was a miserable night with me on my side of the bed and Gerry on his. The next day we drove on down to Virginia Beach but it didn't get any better. The beach and weather were glorious, our room had a magnificent view, but it was all wasted on us. For three days we fought, over everything and nothing, having food brought in because my face was swollen from crying. The enormity of my mistake was becoming apparent. We canceled the remainder of the two weeks and drove back to Connecticut.

We had rented a flat at Myrtle Beach in Milford and furnished it before the wedding, so it was waiting for us when we arrived home two days later. On the drive north we talked about what had happened, and by the time we reached

Myrtle Beach we had agreed to let the past be the past and start over. Our first night at home was more like the wedding night I had dreamed about. Gerry bought a bottle of champagne and we sat on the bed, drank toasts to each other and to the marriage and then made passionate love, which was not at all as my mother had said it would be.

Our apartment was one block from Myrtle Beach and I had visions of Gerry and me walking on the beach. We had a porch that ran across the front and around the side of the apartment, a small living room with a fireplace, a large kitchen with a breakfast nook, a small extra room in back of the kitchen and a bedroom that looked out onto the side porch. If the bedroom windows were open, we could smell the salt air, hear the sound of waves and, sometimes, a fog horn. I liked the apartment and its location near the beach and began to be hopeful about our future.

But then, two days after we returned from Virginia Beach, I was on a step ladder hanging curtains in the spare room off the kitchen when Gerry came in demanding to know what I was doing. I don't remember my retort but given the annoyance I was feeling at his barked question I suspect it was a smart remark. The next thing I knew he had hit me—a sort of back-handed blow to the side of my body—the ladder tipped over and I was on the floor in a heap. Marriage hadn't altered Gerry's behavior but seemed to give him even greater license for his violence. One Saturday afternoon my parents dropped in for a visit. I felt I had no option but to let them in and when I opened the door they saw me with a face red and swollen from crying and what would be a black eye. Gerry came in from the back of the apartment and was surly in his greeting. All of us pretended that nothing was wrong but I knew what they were thinking. My mother's look said, "This shouldn't have surprised you. It doesn't surprise me." What they really said was, "We were just going by and decided to drop in, but obviously it isn't a good time for a visit so we'll come again another time." Since they lived a town away, they weren't "just going by" and we all knew it. They never dropped in again.

A few months later, when my father told me that Don had joined the Royal Canadian Airforce, the news glanced off like something I might have read in the newspaper. Then I learned that he had been killed in action over Europe. I didn't want to hear it and, at first, couldn't believe it. By the time I let it in, I was overwhelmed with guilt and sadness, momentarily thinking of what might have been, but by that time my problems with Gerry took precedence over everything else in my life. It was many years before I allowed the grief over Don's death, and the enormity of what I had done, to come to the surface. His parents never spoke to me again.

For our first Thanksgiving Gerry had invited some of his co-workers to join us for dinner. Although we had beautiful pots and pans given to us as wedding gifts, neither of us knew how to use them. By that time, however, I had mastered the art of cooking hamburgers and decided to try a turkey. When I brought the bird home from the store it looked just as my mother's turkeys always did when she put them in the oven. I rubbed the bird with butter and sprinkled salt and pepper on it, then put it in the pan and into the oven.

Our guests arrived early to listen to the football game and we were sitting in the living room having drinks and eating peanuts when there was an explosion. Gerry and I ran to the kitchen. The oven door had blown open and our turkey was splattered all over the inside of the oven. The stench was terrible. In 1941 turkeys didn't come from the store ready to go in the oven, they had to be cleaned. We took our guests out to dinner. And Gerry was not angry or upset with me. In fact he thought it was funny and that night he was particularly tender with me because he knew I felt like such a failure.

When I told Mother what had happened, she laughed then explained that first she had to clean the turkey, by reaching inside the bird and pulling out all the entrails, then filling the cavity with stuffing. She offered me her recipe for stuffing but I found the prospect of cleaning the turkey so repulsive, I vowed I'd never again try to roast a turkey. But that vow was short lived and I prepared many turkey dinners through my life.

On Sunday, December 7th, we were having a late breakfast and listening to the radio when we heard the announcer say that Pearl Harbor had been attacked. We were stunned and unbelieving. How could such a thing have happened?

I realized how fully my life was now defined by the parameters of our marriage. I knew that World War II had something to do with Hitler and what I had seen in Germany in the summer of 1938, and that Don had been killed fighting in it, but other than that, the war was happening far away and had little significance for me. I still remember thinking—what does this pronouncement mean to us? When Gerry's draft number was called, he reported but was deferred because of his health—he had debilitating migraine headaches and flat feet—and because he was working in an essential industry. I confess to having mixed reactions about his deferment. Somewhere deep inside me I had hoped he might be called up. My brother had been drafted and would go to the Pacific. One night, when I was alone, I cried because I was afraid I'd never see him again and though we hadn't been close in recent years, he was still the big brother whom I'd adored through childhood.

Gerry was earning good money at Chance Vought so, instead of suffering hardships as many people were, we were able to buy a house, for which we paid four thousand dollars, in Long Hill, a suburban development north of Bridgeport. We were issued food rationing stamps, and instead of butter we bought oleo margarine in white pound-sized chunks which we softened and mixed with yellow food coloring to make it look like butter. For me, the war was only about the way it affected my life. My developing social consciousness had gone underground.

One of the ways the war affected me was that I was moved into a job in the payroll department of General Electric, a job vacated by a man who had been drafted, a job that almost tripled my salary. I was trained by IBM personnel to do board wiring and to perform alphabetical and numerical sorting operations with data processors, and I enjoyed the challenge of learning something new. At the end of that year, I was given what was considered a promotion into the job of secretary to General Electric's Advertising Manager, Ferrol C. Stevens. Although America's entry into the war had changed the employment situation for women, it hadn't changed men's expectations of them. In the advertising department job I was expected to serve coffee, water plants, perform housekeeping tasks in my boss's office and, sometimes, even pick up his dry cleaning for him. It was also expected that I would not object if one of the men in the department tried to sneak a kiss or a pinch. Office parties were the worst because most of the men drank and seemed to think that the occasion gave them special privileges. I knew that if I were rude, or rebuffed such overtures, it would show up in the attitude rating on my employee review.

Gerry and I began to make friends in our Long Hill neighborhood and I was optimistic about our marriage, but we had been there only a few months when that optimism was shattered. One Saturday afternoon I went to visit a neighbor down the street and came home two hours late. In the living room the upholstery on the couch and chairs had been slashed and the stuffing was sticking out. One chair was overturned. The contents of the corner cupboard, where I had arranged our crystal and china wedding gifts, were thrown all over the room and there was broken glass and china everywhere. In the kitchen there were broken dishes, and a bottle of catsup had been slammed on the counter so hard it exploded and there was catsup on the ceiling and walls. Gerry was sitting in his leather chair, the torrent over, waiting for my reaction. He looked at me sullenly as if the mess had been my doing. On the kitchen counter I saw the knife he had used and, picking it up, ran toward him. He stood up, twisted my arm, and took the knife from me as easily as he might have from a child. Only later did I recognize my foolishness.

I doubt that I would have used the knife, but if Gerry had wanted to turn it on me he could easily have done so. The damage was done. Although I was furious, all I could do was clean up the mess.

Gerry's headaches were increasingly frequent and crippling in their severity. Some evenings he would come home from work blind with pain and go immediately to bed. I massaged his back and neck and changed ice packs until the headache passed or erupted, as it generally did, in a violent nose bleed or vomiting. At such times I felt enormous compassion for him but the relationship continued to be stormy.

When friends invited us to do things with them his response was much the same as it had been before we were married. "I'm not going. If you want to go you can go by yourself." If I took him at his word and went alone, he was furious when I returned. If I made an issue of it and coerced him into going I always regretted it because he would be unpleasant the whole time. The option of staying home with him, making an effort to understand and work it out together simply did not occur to me. I was sure he was wrong and made it a point to see that friends and neighbors knew that also.

In February of 1943 I discovered I was pregnant. Despite our problems, we were both delighted. We had been married almost two years and had begun to wonder why it hadn't happened sooner. As my pregnancy advanced, our life together became quieter. I enjoyed the changes in my body. For the first time in our marriage Gerry offered help around the house. My health was good and I had lots of energy. I transformed the extra bedroom into a nursery—painting walls and ceiling, stenciling bunny rabbits on the walls, making curtains, braiding rugs. Our child would have its own room as soon as it came home from the hospital. Those who knew told me that the child should have its own room so that it would learn at the beginning of life that it was, and always would be, alone.

We moved the piano from Lordship to our house and I began playing again. Often after dinner Gerry would ask me to play and sit listening, with his eyes closed, for as long as I was willing to play. When Gerry was reading, I knit sweaters, booties and little hats. There were months of contentment. Sometimes Gerry would go in and stand in the middle of the nursery, looking around as if he could not believe what was happening. I knew how he felt at those times—I, too, was having difficulty believing what was happening, even as I felt that new life moving within my body. I could never persuade him, however, to put his hand on my abdomen and feel that movement.

Janis was born on November 21st, in the middle of a blackout. Because the country was at war, at night we drew dark shades down to the window sills, and if we went out in the car we put little eyelid-like things over the headlights to keep the light low and down. The drive to the hospital was slow and difficult, and labor was even more so. I had never read anything about the birth process and I had no idea of what was coming. Then, when the first major contraction caught me, it was like, "Ohhhh, my God! What's this? I didn't bargain for this!" As the contractions came closer, I began to writhe and cry out. Then, every time a contraction began, the nurse put a mask over my face. The only thing the mask seemed to do was release my inhibitions so that I could really scream, and scream I did. I thought I must be dying, the pain was so excruciating. That birth was my initiation into adulthood. I had never known pain like that and I knew there would never again be anything to whine about, that nothing would ever approach that level of pain. I came out of it a different person. Gerry was standing by my bed saying that it was a girl and that she weighed almost nine pounds. He was disappointed that the baby had not been a boy. I was delighted. I had wanted a girl and even knew I would name her Janis, after my childhood Warwick Avenue friend.

As soon as the baby was born she was whisked away from me to a nursery, where she was kept for twelve hours and given sweetened water from a bottle. They said it was customary to do that until my milk came in. I had wanted to nurse my baby but by the time they brought her to me she had learned to use a bottle and would not take my breast. The nurses said it was wartime and they couldn't take the time required to teach a baby to nurse. It wasn't until my fourth child was born that I discovered that a healthy baby doesn't have to be taught to nurse. But in that era, mothers were encouraged to use formulas and bottles. I was disappointed and, to make it worse, my breasts felt as if they would burst while I waited for the milk to dry up.

By the second day after she was born, Janis had contracted impetigo and was confined to the hospital nursery for the remainder of her first week of life. Her little legs and arms were tied to the corners of the bassinet. In addition to suffering with the impetigo, she was fed only every four hours. It was believed that a baby would benefit by being on a rigid feeding schedule. The rationale was that discipline had to start early—you couldn't let them have their own way—so in the hospital I lay listening to the crying in the nursery, sure that one of those crying was Janis.

Even after I got home I had little contact with the baby because my mother had hired a nurse. At that time people thought new mothers needed two weeks of bed rest and would know nothing about caring for a baby, so needed to be trained. The nurse said that the baby must not be fed more than once every four hours and must never be picked up in between feedings. Sometimes I listened to her cry for what seemed hours before the nurse would give her a bottle. Nurse also said that new babies needed a certain amount of crying to develop their lungs. The nurses seemed to know, my mother seemed to know, and everybody assumed I knew nothing. Yet, instinctively, I did know that something was wrong with all this. I didn't protest because the nurses were professionals who should know, and I had no reason to believe that I knew how to make good judgments. As soon as the nurse left, however, so did the schedule and the rigidity. I rocked the baby, sang to her, fed her when she was hungry, and loved being a mother. In my murmurings to her I poured out all the love and longing for which I had no other outlet. The only thing I didn't like about caring for the new baby was the mess she made in her diaper each morning but I soon found a way to deal with that. By laying her on her back on the changing table, I could play with her until I noticed a grimace on her face. Then I'd hold up her little legs and put a Kleenex under her bottom. After that I rarely had to change a messy diaper.

As I began reading books about child raising, I realized that my mother had not read any such books. I began to understand some of her raising of me. She had nothing to guide her but her own experience. With an invalid mother and a father who regularly beat up his children, she really didn't have any role models.

It didn't take Gerry long to let go of his disappointment that this was not the son he wanted. Each night when he came home from work he would go straight through the house to the nursery and stand by the bassinet cooing and making faces at the baby. It was several weeks before he would pick her up or hold her but he seemed to marvel at this little bit of humanity that he and I had produced. When Janis was only a few weeks old she began having difficulty breathing. One night she had a spasm and turned purple. I looked at her, panicked and ran to the telephone. Gerry picked her up by the feet and whacked her backside to get her breathing again. Then we took her to the hospital where they said she had a vitamin deficiency, gave her a shot and sent us all home. I sat in the rocking chair by her bassinet all that night waking every time she moved, knowing that Gerry's quick action had probably saved her life.

When Janis was less than seven months old, I discovered I was pregnant again—in spite of the diaphragm. I was distressed and kept my pregnancy a secret as long as I could. I was sure both Gerry and my mother would consider it my fault. When I could no longer hide it, I got the expected response, "How could you let this happen?" The calm was over. Gerry's headaches grew worse. I was overwhelmed by the prospect of another baby. But the months flew by and once again we were racing through the middle of the night to the hospital. My second girl child was born on the 13th of March, 1945, with no less struggle than I'd had bringing Janis into the world.

When they first brought the baby to me I was sure they had made a mistake. She was wrinkled and red and had black hair that grew all the way down to her eyes. I refused to take her and wanted Gerry to come and straighten it out, but he had left the hospital after dropping me and didn't return until visiting hours the next night. I cried most of the day. Gerry was inconsolable that his second child was also a girl. He held me responsible and would have nothing to do with the new baby. I was embarrassed and dismayed by our rejection of the baby. Because I wouldn't take her and feed her, she was kept in the nursery and then, by the third day of life, she had contracted the impetigo which plagued that hospital's nursery. By the time we were ready to go home, I was ashamed of my initial reaction and couldn't wait to hold her, love her and make up for lost time. Only much later did I learn of the importance of that immediate post-natal period and realize that my first two children had been deprived of one of the most nurturing experiences of a lifetime.

I named this new child Priscilla, after my Salem roommate and friend, but as soon as Janis began talking about her sister, "Priscilla" became "Jill" and has been Jill ever since. In a few weeks her black hair fell out and was replaced with soft blonde fuzz which soon turned into curls. She became a startlingly beautiful child.

My third pregnancy followed even more closely than the second had followed the first. I couldn't believe it was happening. I did not want another baby, I didn't think I could cope with another baby, but I could see no alternative. My brother Paul had just returned from military service in the Pacific and had been given the name of a New York doctor who performed abortions, which were then illegal. Paul offered to take me to New York and I hesitated only briefly because everyone in the family—my father, my mother, my husband and my brother—thought it was a good idea and I thought it might be the answer. We drove to New York together but our visit to that abortionist's office was all I needed to convince me that it was a mistake. The place was in a back alley, up a flight of outside stairs, and was filthy. The doctor himself looked more like a gangster than a doctor. I was horrified and ashamed of even having entertained the idea. I told Paul that I would not submit myself to that man and wanted to go home. My brother was furious and refused to speak during the two-hour ride home.

This was when I realized that I had lost my brother to the war, even though he had come home alive. He'd been in an advanced echelon in the Pacific islands, had gone in ahead of the troops to scout for their disembarkation. He said he wasn't allowed to carry a gun, only a knife, so that when he killed somebody he wouldn't make a noise. And, he said, he did kill somebody—lots of somebodies. He also contracted malaria and lost most of his hair. He was twenty-nine when he enlisted, thirty-three looking more like fifty when he came home—the smile was gone, as was the twinkle in his eyes. This brother was not the one who had gone to war. This brother acted as if aborting a child was purely a matter of convenience, of expediency.

The son Gerry wanted was born on Saturday, May 11, 1946, almost as if affirming the decision not to abort. He was born rapidly and with such ease that I knew something had been wrong with the first two deliveries, but I didn't understand what that something was until ten years later when preparing for the birth of my fourth child. At that time I learned that in my first two deliveries, my body had responded by initiating the "flight or fight" syndrome, a totally disastrous way to respond. Only by understanding and cooperating with the process could one avoid that agony. We had our little boy and Gerry was elated. He passed out cigars, he glowed. And of course the baby was named for him, Gerald Francis Quigley, Jr.

Shortly after Jerry was born, Janis came down with rheumatic fever. She was confined to bed and had to be kept quiet, so my mother took the little ones for a few weeks. Each day a visiting nurse would come in and help me change Janis's bed and bathe her. We kept the shades drawn in her room so that she would not be excited by anything she saw going on outside. Every night in bed I cried quietly, wondering what I had done wrong. Janis was very seriously ill and I couldn't even think about what I would do if I lost her, but after a few weeks of bed rest she came back.

Three babies in two and a half years, coupled with Janis's rheumatic fever was almost too much. Jill and Jerry were still in diapers and I spent two hours every morning washing diapers and hanging them out on the line. I was also sterilizing bottles and preparing formula for Jerry. By the end of the summer I was exhausted and turned to my mother. She offered to stay with the children so Gerry and I could get away for a few days. I gratefully accepted her offer.

Gerry and I drove up through New Hampshire to Lake Winnepesaukee and found a lovely little inn outside of Wolfboro. It looked like the perfect place to spend a few days resting. Just being out of the routine was rest enough in itself and I tried not to think of how Mother might be coping. The first evening we were there, the hotel management hosted a cocktail hour and, after having a couple of glasses of wine and listening to a conversation between two guests about the exclusivity of the hotel, I told Gerry what I had overheard. He told me it was excluding Jews that made it so nice and I lashed into him about discrimination. He tried to hush me but I'd had enough to drink so that my diatribe drew the attention of the other guests. Management shortened the cocktail hour, and my tirade, by announcing dinner. Gerry looked as if he could have eaten *me* for dinner but we joined the others in the dining room, then went up to our room without speaking. In the morning we came down, had breakfast and began planning for the day. As we were on our second cup of coffee, the waiter brought us a note asking us to please stop at the desk on our way out of the dining room. When we did, we saw that our bags had been packed and brought down to the desk for us. We had been invited to cut short our stay and leave.

Gerry was furious with me and I told him he was as bad as they were. We gave up the idea of vacation and drove home, scarcely speaking to each other on the drive back. I was actually ashamed of myself but wouldn't admit it to him. Mother started to ask why we had come back early but one look at Gerry's face changed her mind. She gathered up her things and left. That night I cried myself to sleep.

Shortly after our return we accepted an invitation to a birthday party for our neighbor across the street. By eleven o'clock, even though we had been drinking and nibbling all evening, they still had not cut the birthday cake nor given Al his presents.

Gerry found me talking with Al's wife and whispered in my ear, "We're going home." I moved away from Nora and spoke quietly to him, "Gerry, they haven't even cut the cake yet. We have to stay for that. It's only eleven o'clock." "I'm going home. And I advise you to come with me." "Oh, please," I started, then changed my mind and snapped, "Fine! Go if you want but I'm not going with you. I'm staying until they cut the cake and sing Happy Birthday to Al." I hated being ordered by Gerry but much of the time I did as he wanted, to avoid unpleasantness. Once in a while I got fed up and this was one of those times.

Gerry stormed out without saying a word to his host or hostess. Nora looked at me and shook her head. She understood. All of our neighbors knew Gerry. The party went on. They cut the cake and opened the champagne at midnight and Al spent an hour opening gifts. It was close to two when people left. I said good night and walked across the street to our house. Gerry was waiting for me. I remember only that he called me a slut and I lashed out at him as never before, telling him he had been rude to our neighbors, that he was a boor, that I'd had it with his behavior. I was still ranting when I went into the bathroom to brush my teeth. As I leaned over the sink he grabbed me by the neck. I have never been sure that he meant to hurt me as much as he did, but after a few minutes everything went black and I fell to the floor.

When Alice Fox came over for coffee the next morning I told her what had happened and she was horrified, but when Gerry returned and said he was sorry, I let it go because I knew I had provoked him. Instead of facing the truth about him, I apologized when he beat me up or tore up the house, and always found excuses for what he did.

Alice and Cliff Fox were our next-door neighbors. He was in a middle management position at General Electric, a small, slender man with dark hair greying in the sideburns. He was a nice guy but always in Alice's shadow, even literally, because she was considerably bigger than he was. Alice was always on a diet but came to our house every morning for coffee and doughnuts. We talked while I washed diapers and sterilized bottles. The babies were usually down for morning naps by the time she came. The youngest one was always asleep in a carriage on the small porch off the kitchen with Smitty, our Dalmatian, in his watch dog role, sleeping near or under the carriage. As the children got bigger they would sometimes be in the fenced-in area of the backyard where they had a sand box and outdoor toys. The door from the dining room led out to the yard so Alice and I could listen for any untoward noise and avert eruptions before they got too serious.

My marriage to Gerry didn't stand a chance after the children were born because they were more important to me than he was. Had our relationship been a real partnership perhaps that wouldn't have happened, but as it was, the children provided me with an outlet for the love I had to give, the love I wasn't able to give my husband. During the years when the three children were small, my life centered around them totally. I washed their diapers, made their clothes, prepared formulas, played with them. Holding a child in my arms was the most deeply satisfying experience I'd ever had. I used to stand at the kitchen window and watch them playing together in the backyard. Jan was the bossy one (she still is), Jill a scrapper, and little Jerry seemed always to be the one whom the girls manipulated. I noticed and reveled in their differences.

By spring of 1947 Gerry and I were both ready to acknowledge that our marriage was not working. Each was sure the problem was with the other, and that made it impossible to correct. His headaches were so frequent and severe that our lives seemed to revolve around them. And I had begun having respiratory attacks which the doctor said was asthma. Gerry was sure that getting away from the influence of my parents would solve everything. After the children were born I had begun listening to Mother's outspoken criticism of Gerry. So that spring we began looking for property to buy in New Hampshire where we could, perhaps, run a guest house. I was less sure that a change of location would help but was willing to try anything.

In late summer we found an old Georgian house on the main street in Northfield, Massachusetts, just south of the New Hampshire line. It had twelve rooms and was perfect for what we wanted to do, except that it had no plumbing or electricity and the central heat was a coal furnace supplying hot air only through one large floor register in the downstairs hall. Getting that house to a level that would serve our purpose was a huge project but I was excited by the opportunity it represented and looked on it as a challenge. We bought the house and through the fall and winter of 1947–1948 the children and I lived in two rooms, while I supervised the remodeling. In one of our two rooms we set up a temporary housekeeping room with a Franklin stove for heating and cooking, a large galvanized tub for bathing, a table and chairs for meals and an assortment of rocking chairs, two of which had been Gram's and Will's. In the other room we put two large beds. When Gerry came home for the weekend, we put the three children crossways in one bed and used the other for ourselves. The arrangement was not conducive to either privacy or intimacy, but it served the purpose for sleeping.

It was a winter of working with carpenters, electricians, plumbers and painters. The kitchen had a large black slate sink with a pump at one end, a wood-burning stove, an old wooden ice box and a floor that slanted down toward the porch. We modernized it without destroying its country flavor. We also installed two bathrooms—one on the second floor and one on the first to take the place of the three-holer we had been using in the shed. We restored the fireplace that had been closed off in the dining room. It was a creative process and I thoroughly enjoyed it. The weeks were wonderful. I worked on the house, the children played and laughed, and came crawling into my bed in the mornings. We even had pillow fights. But as Fridays approached I would be apprehensive, never knowing what the weekend would bring. Sometimes Gerry came with gifts, sometimes he took me skiing, sometimes we spent an evening just sitting in front of the fire together. But more often he came home tired and irritable and at those times we all knew the safest thing to do was to stay out of his way. I began to wish he wouldn't come home at all.

By the summer of 1948 we were ready for the tourist trade and hung out our sign, "Samuel Lane House—Guests." We had found the name of Samuel Lane, first owner of the house, in records in the attic. The house had been built in the late 1800s on his retirement from being a sea captain. In the attic we also found a swing suspended from the peak beam by long wooden arms. When someone was swinging you could hear the sound throughout the house. Sometimes, at the end of a day, the children and I would go up into the attic, taking turns on the swing and poking through old boxes that had been stored there for over half a century.

Right after Memorial Day guests started coming. We had five rooms to rent and the house was full most nights that summer. Our guests were impressed with the house and I delighted in showing them around. I prepared a continental breakfast each morning, and spent the rest of the day cleaning up, changing beds and washing sheets. The children thought it was fun having different people staying with us each night and they behaved beautifully. The tourist business held up well through the October viewing of foliage. In the second weekend of October the riotous color brought the most tourists we had seen all summer but after that they stopped coming. While we were busy with tourists, Gerry came home less often and there was less tension. But when the season ended I once again began to dread the weekends. My asthma worsened. I used an inhaler regularly but gradually the attacks became serious enough to require hospitalization. Dr. Gamble warned me that an attack might come in the night sometime when help was beyond reach and that would be it. Always on Monday I was fine again and sure that the attacks were over. If Gerry let us know that he was not coming home for a weekend, I kept right on being fine. It was clear that the attacks were related to my dread of his coming home.

While in Northfield I developed a friendship with Henry and Marjorie Prescott, a friendship that became one of the most important in my life. Henry was a brilliant scientist who appreciated music and had sound equipment that made listening almost as good as being in Klein Memorial. Often they invited me over for a glass of wine and an evening of music. Henry and Midge were good listeners and I often called on them when my responsibilities or my troubles seemed too much. One time Henry took me to the hospital when I had an asthma attack in the middle of the night. And they were always impartial. Henry admired and respected Gerry's ability and offered friendship without passing judgment on our marriage or on either of us.

Martha Lopez and her family were also good friends. Martha sang in the choir of the Trinitarian Congregational Church and I began attending church with her. She told me that going to church with her would be a good way to make friends in the community. Martha was a lovely woman with a slight build, dark blonde hair and the voice of an angel. She was also tender, thoughtful and kind.

Her husband, Manuel, was a dairy farmer with a fierce temper which he aimed at everyone except Martha. As the months went by, Martha became more concerned about me. She knew that I was unhappy in my marriage and that it was affecting my health. One Sunday, as we were leaving church, she spoke to the minister, Mr. Rivers.

The next Saturday Mr. Rivers and Dr. Gamble came to call on Gerry and me. After a few minutes of admiring the work we had done on the house and greeting the children, Dr. Gamble spoke to Gerry and me. He was very direct. He said that my health was deteriorating, that more and more often I was being taken to the hospital with acute attacks of asthma. He also said that, from the timing of the attacks, they seemed to be related to our marriage. He said we should look seriously at what to do about it, adding that it would be tragic if the three children were left motherless. Mr. Rivers conceded that it was always difficult for him to accept divorce but that there were times when that might be the best solution.

Gerry was furious. He told them to get out and mind their own business. Although I was embarrassed, I knew how he felt. I thought the two men had a lot of nerve. I had never heard of a doctor or a minister taking such liberties. I was angry with Martha, feeling that she had betrayed my confidence, although when I was honest with myself, I knew that confiding in her was a plea for help. I had been denying that there was anything seriously wrong because I couldn't, or wouldn't, let my parents know. They had told me from the beginning that my marriage was a mistake and I wasn't about to let my mother have the satisfaction of saying, "You made your bed, now lie in it." This is what I was sure she would say if she knew what was happening, but today I know I did her a disservice. She did care for me and was probably genuinely concerned. The visit did make me think. I had not really contemplated divorce. There had never been one in our family and it was not an option I had seriously considered. That night Gerry and I talked and agreed that the weekly separation seemed only to make matters worse. We would think about getting back together in Connecticut, near Gerry's work, now in Windsor Locks.

In the spring of 1949 two women from New York stopped and asked if we would be interested in selling the house. They said they had been guests the previous summer, and had fallen in love with the place. They made us an offer that meant a hundred and fifty percent return on our investment. Although I had grown to love the old house and was pleased when people admired the work we had done, it seemed like the answer to our problem. We accepted their offer, sold the Samuel Lane House, and moved to West Hartford late that spring. By this time Gerry was earning a good salary working with Charlie Kaman in the helicopter manufacturing company they had started in a quonset hut at Bradley Field. (That business had turned into a multi-million dollar corporation, Kaman Aircraft, by the time of Gerry's death in 1972.)

In late summer, two of Gerry's co-workers came to live with us. A sudden downturn in business had made the company ask people to work temporarily for stock instead of salaries. Gerry had savings and refused to work until he could be paid, but the two men were settling for stock. Norm Stewart and Milt Krause had families in towns some distance away and Gerry offered them a place to stay during the week until they began getting paid again. I was surprised that Charlie Kaman didn't fire him at the time, but later Henry Prescott told me that Gerry could get away with that because he was the leading engineer at the factory and they didn't want to lose him. Henry said that, in the industry, Gerry was considered the brains behind Kaman and the company.

Because he wasn't working, Gerry was at home most of the time for several months. It was the first time he had been around the children for long periods and he clearly didn't like it. He avoided them as much as possible and told me to keep them quiet and away from him. We had a playroom in the basement and when he was home the children had to be down there, or out in the yard, or up in their bedrooms. He didn't want them making noise and he wanted them to do what they were told without giving him any "back talk."

Norm was as considerate as Gerry was thoughtless. Gerry woke up in the morning grumpy, always finding something wrong with breakfast, but Norm sang in the shower, came down in time to help get breakfast ready and was appreciative of everything I did. Gerry and I rarely talked, except when we were fighting, but Norm and I sometimes sat around the dining room table talking for hours after the children were in bed and Gerry was reading in the living room. With Norm I satisfied, if only briefly, my longing to be heard, to communicate fully with another human being. Gerry resented our closeness, was sure we were having an affair, and the marriage deteriorated even further. Although Norm and I were very close, the relationship never went beyond friendship—he also was married.

After Gerry went back to work, he wanted the children fed and in bed before he got home. It didn't always happen. I remember Jan looking out the window as his car pulled in and reporting, "Oh, Daddy looks like he's in a bad mood," and scampering to her room. Sometimes I gave them dinner early and let them play in the basement while Gerry and I had dinner and then I put them to bed.

Gerry's mother came to visit us once in West Hartford. I got along well with Phoebe and my difficulties with Gerry never spilled over into my relationship with her. She had no illusions about his disposition. One evening the three of us were sitting in the living room reading. Gerry was in his rocking chair with an engineering book in his hands, Phoebe and I were on the couch—I with a book and Phoebe with a newspaper.

"Do you have to make so damned much noise?" Gerry snapped at his mother, alluding to the sound of the pages turning. She put the paper down and sat without doing anything for the next hour until she went to bed. I wanted to berate him for being so rude but knew that would make Phoebe even more uncomfortable than she was already. I went up with her to see if there was anything she wanted before going to sleep but she urged me to go back down to be with him.

I felt closest to Gerry when I was playing the piano. Sometimes after dinner he would ask me to play for him and then keep urging me to continue. He seemed not to mind my occasional wrong notes and would sit rocking for hours with his eyes closed as I played. Sometimes, at the end of such an evening, he would approach me with tenderness, but I had begun to suspect that tenderness. I knew that it meant he wanted sex and the tenderness would be gone by the time he was through, leaving me unsatisfied. Only at the very beginning of our marriage had he made an effort to see that sex was enjoyable for me. I was lonelier in this marriage than I had ever been before in my life.

Gerry was always hard on Jill. She was spunky and when he spanked her, which he did often, she would give him a fierce look but would never cry or say she was sorry for whatever she had done. In watching their interaction I was reminded of my response to my mother when I was a little girl. I would never cry out when she spanked me. I wasn't going to give her the satisfaction of knowing that it hurt. One day I was in the kitchen and heard Gerry's voice upstairs. "You will cry, you little bitch. I'll spank you until you do!"

I raced upstairs to find him, with Jill across his knees, spanking her viciously. I tried to intervene but he waved me away and I knew, from the look on his face, that he would tolerate no interference. Stopping for a moment, he lifted her up so that her face was near his. She was not crying. "Damn you," he said, but before he could put her down across his lap again she spit in his face. That did it. With one hand he hit her so hard I was sure he must have broken something, then he threw her down on the bed and put a pillow over her head.

The other children had come upstairs. Little Jerry was standing in the doorway, with terror in his eyes. Janis, who was almost six, came screaming into the room. "Let her go, Daddy, let her go!" Jan and I tugged at his arm, crying and pleading. Finally reason took over and he stood up, glared at us and left the room. That day I knew it was over. That was his final act of abusiveness. There was no hesitation, no wondering. It was all in the past. I knew I would leave him.

I began making plans, calling Mother and Dad to be sure they would put us up until I found a job and a place to live, calling movers for estimates and to schedule the move. I did all this while the children were napping so they wouldn't tell their father. I quietly suggested to Milt and Norm that they find another place to live. They had both witnessed Gerry's brutishness and I knew neither of them would betray my plans. It was Norm who made me aware that the connection I had with him was what was missing with Gerry and it was that kind of connection that made a marriage. Norm actually gave me the courage to leave.

One morning, a month later, I spoke to Gerry as he was going out the door for work. "We'll not be here when you come home tonight, Gerry. I'm taking the children and leaving."

It was evident he didn't believe me. He just went to the garage, started his car and drove off to work. We packed our bags and the movers came and took my furniture (the piano and the antique rocking chairs) to storage.

Mother had driven up to West Hartford to get us and we left, quietly, in the middle of the day. She was caring and helpful and, on the drive back to Stratford, chatted with the children, allowing me time with my thoughts. We went home to Lordship, and when I saw the house tears welled up in my eyes and I experienced a kind of peace. The next day, after eight years of marriage, I filed suit for divorce. I had known, from the beginning, that the marriage wasn't what I dreamed marriage could be. I had ignored my parents' advice and lied to them over the years so they wouldn't know how bad it was. My relief at being away from Gerry was tempered only by my sense of failure. Where did I go wrong, what could I have done?

5

Divorce and Descent into Breakdown

"What do you think you're doing?" It was several days after we left before Gerry called me at my parents' house. "I told you the other morning, Gerry. We've left, for good. And yesterday I filed for divorce." "Well I hope you can find some way of supporting yourself because you won't get a nickel out of me!" The phone slammed down.

When Gerry's lawyer told him that he would have to contribute to support of the children and he offered thirty dollars a week, I felt lucky to get anything. Thirty dollars sounded like enough but it was not, even in 1949. I accepted without seeking legal counsel or even talking with my father about it. Knowing his distaste for lawyers and litigation, I figured he'd probably tell me to take what I could get.

It had been six years since I'd worked at General Electric and now I had three children. Where could I work? What could I do? Who would take care of the children? Suddenly, in spite of Gerry's abusiveness, this divorce seemed like not such a good idea. Throughout December Gerry phoned me, telling me how sorry I'd be, reminding me of the marriage vow I had taken. Then a letter from his attorney demanded that I sign papers giving Gerry custody of the children "in the event of your commitment to a mental institution." Though I understood the words in the letter, I couldn't fathom his purpose in writing it. I did know how angry Gerry could get when he didn't get his way and that frightened me. The text of that letter haunted me every night as I waited for sleep. Even though I thought of it as emotional manipulation, I also knew I had entertained the idea of suicide many times in my life and that must mean something about my stability.

Living with four extra people was difficult for my folks. We had descended very suddenly on my mother, who never had overnight guests. The Laurel Street house, which they had built in 1938, had two bedrooms and a bath on the second floor and a den and half bath on the first floor. The children slept in the second bedroom and I slept on a rollaway bed in the downstairs den. The crowding added to my mother's distress over mine being the first divorce in the family. I knew she was shamed by it even while trying to be compassionate. I once overheard her talking to a friend, saying, "I never thought I'd see it happen in our family, and yes, it's hard having them all here, but what else could we do? She is our daughter."

It was easier on the children. They knew Gramma loved them, even though she used her hairbrush on them as she had on me. (I learned of this only much later, from my son Jerry.) Every afternoon she would treat them to sodas made from ice cream and the homemade root beer that was stored on a shelf over the basement stairs. They loved the wonderful desserts she made for them and delighted in hearing her whistle along with the canary. They were fascinated by television, which we'd not had at home. Being away from their father, and the tension and fear that had dominated our lives for years, had a calming effect.

But I was lost. Never having seriously contemplated divorce I was unable to think about what was next. My thoughts were about where I'd gone wrong, what I could have done that I didn't do. How could I have three children I so loved and yet acknowledge that the marriage had been a mistake? But loving those children seemed only to increase my sense of failure. They would be raised without a father. The holidays were difficult. Thanksgiving and Christmas had always been special holidays in our family and this year I couldn't wait to get through them. Mother and Dad tried to inject some holiday spirit but I could see no cause for celebration and couldn't get out of myself long enough to see that it was important for the children.

In early January I swallowed a bottle of iodine in a suicide attempt. It was a cry for help. Had I been more serious I could have walked down to the beach and into the water. Mother's neighbor found me and took me to the hospital to have my stomach pumped. Then she took me to the Episcopal priest, who told me that I had committed a mortal sin. He went on to say that if I divorced I would never be able to remarry unless I was willing to risk eternal damnation. That talk marked my final break with the Episcopal Church. I left angry, knowing that I didn't need him to make me feel guilty. I was feeling bad enough already.

One morning a few weeks later, Dad came down to breakfast and said, "I've been thinking about you and the children, dear. Wouldn't you be happier in Northfield? You seemed to enjoy living there and you made friends. Take my car and drive up. You can leave the children with us for a couple of days. Talk to some of your friends, see if you can find a job and a place to live. I'll help you financially until you get on your feet."

It was all I needed; I had been given a reprieve. With tears in my eyes, I thanked my father and squeezed his hand. That day I told the children where I was going and that I'd be back soon, then left them with my parents and drove north. The first person I sought out was Martha Lopez, feeling that she would probably be able to help me. We talked, she was delighted that I was thinking about returning to Northfield and offered to introduce me to her boss, Monroe Smith, who was the founder of Youth Argosy, a travel organization with an office in Northfield. We met, talked and before the end of the day I had a job. Then she took me to see a small house down the street from hers. It was perfect, it was available, and the rent was thirty dollars a month. By the time I got back to Stratford the next day, I had both a job and a place for us to live. I was elated. Mom and Dad were relieved.

I took out of storage the rocking chairs and a few boxes I had taken from West Hartford—leaving only the piano—packed up the children and left. By Feb. 15, 1950, we were in our new home on Beers Plain Road in Northfield, Massachusetts.

The house was charming, over a hundred years old, with white clapboards, a slate roof and neat green trim. Like most old New England houses, it was situated close to the road with a driveway that led back to a small barn. There was one bedroom on the first floor and two others upstairs under the eaves. It was heated by the wood stove in the kitchen and a pot-belly stove in the living room. The bathroom was just off the kitchen, the only place where pipes wouldn't freeze. I wasn't good at banking fires to burn through the night, however, and sometimes we would wake in the morning to find the fire out, the bathroom pipes frozen and the stockings I had washed the night before looking as if they could stand up on their own. At an auction, I bought a rubbed pine table and benches which we put at the end of the living room nearest the kitchen. The antique rocking chairs that had belonged to Gram and Uncle Will were near the stove. Janis, a very grownup six by this time, helped me hang pictures.

We always had a pot of soup simmering on the back of the wood stove and our Saturday night baked beans tasted like New England baked beans should. I looked forward to coming home from work, seeing the smoke spiraling out of the chimney and then stepping into the warm welcome of the little house. I felt that all was well with my world again. I was happy in my job, Jan was in first grade and the two younger children were cared for during the day by our next-door neighbor, who also made sure our fires were fed.

Monroe, founder of the American Youth Hostel movement, had started Youth Argosy to provide low-cost travel to Europe for teachers and students. Monroe was a short, stocky guy who wore jeans that looked as if they'd never been washed and had a mass of hair that never looked combed. I used to think the term "human dynamo" was coined for him. He rose early and worked until well after the rest of us had given up.

I started as a clerk but within a few months was promoted to a job as booking agent, responsible for bookings on ships and commercial planes as well as filling Youth Argosy's own chartered flights. Youth Argosy leased planes from Seaboard and Western and offered daily flights across the Atlantic, from the first of May through the end of September, at a fare dramatically lower than commercial rates. During this time Monroe invited me to attend, with him, a reception in Luxembourg hosted by Perla Mesta, who was then the U.S. Ambassador to Luxembourg. I couldn't attend because I had let my passport expire. (It has never expired since!) I knew Monroe had to be important to have been invited to the reception but I never knew what that importance was.

Working for him was at once inspiring and exhausting. During the height of the season we kept the office open day and night and would take turns being on the phones. We set up cots on the second floor so that when one of us was exhausted we could go upstairs, waken a replacement and then sleep for a few hours until wakened by the next person needing sleep. I had never felt so needed in a job and loved it. When I didn't get home at night, the children were cared for by my next-door neighbor or by Martha's teenage daughter.

Monroe was a charismatic figure. Some would have described him as a benevolent dictator. He charmed us into thinking that it was a privilege to work from eight in the morning until six, eight, midnight, however long it took to get the job done. Later I acknowledged that he wasn't paying us enough and he was skirting the law, but at the time I loved my work and him. He had a reputation for charming animals as well as those of us who worked for him. I've never forgotten the day a man arrived in town with a violent bull tethered in the back of a truck. The man spoke briefly to Monroe, "We can't do anything with this beast. Can you tame him or at least get him so we can handle him?" Monroe responded, "Take him into the barn." Then the man unloaded the animal, keeping him at arm's length with poles tied to the horns, and took him into the barn. Monroe went into the barn and after perhaps an hour, came out leading a docile bull by a light cord in his nose ring. I wouldn't have believed it if I hadn't seen it with my own eyes. But it was pretty much the same with us, we worked the hours we did without ever complaining.

In the spring of 1950, shortly after I began working for Youth Argosy, I met a friend of Monroe's, Russell Johnson, who worked for the American Friends Service Committee. He spoke about an upcoming conference on international relations, noted my interest, and invited me to attend. When I told him of my limited resources, he offered scholarships for myself and the children. The conference was held on the campus of Avon Old Farms School outside of Hartford, Connecticut. The beautiful old stone buildings of the school were monastic in their simplicity. The campus was closed to all but conferees that week. People from all over the world came and children were free to run about until the bell signaled meal or worship. The biggest challenge they confronted was getting acquainted without the use of a common language. My kids loved being there and responded by getting along better with each other than I had ever seen them do before.

Each morning there was a Quaker silent meeting on the central green of the campus. We gathered there in a huge circle and sat quietly for an hour. On the first morning, as the hour dragged, I began listening to conversations in my head. "When is somebody going to say something? It's been only ten minutes and I have to sit here for an hour? These all seem to be important people. Who am I to be in this august company?" But when everybody joined hands at the end, sat quietly for another minute or two, and then exchanged greetings, it was as if there were an electrical current running from hand to hand. When I turned to the persons on either side of me to shake hands, I had tears in my eyes without knowing why. I had never experienced anything like it. Thereafter I looked forward to each day's silent meeting. That hour provided me with a sense of being intimately related, not only to the others in the circle, but to something larger than all of us. It was like the wondering I did as a child looking at the night sky. It was another dimension to that secret.

Being with people from all over the world, I became aware of problems more important than the petty things with which I dealt on a day-to-day basis. The conference began to shift the focus of my life. The social consciousness, which had been born in 1938, was coming out of hiding. In the sessions after the morning circle, I learned about the American Friends Service Committee's work in relieving suffering and in addressing social problems such as the racism I had encountered in Germany and in North Carolina. There were also sessions on international economics, politics and finance. It was at one of those sessions that

I met A. J. Muste, an Episcopal priest who introduced people to the principles and practices of civil disobedience. Six years later, this would land me in jail in New York City for my refusal to participate in a federal civil defense drill.

It was also at this first Avon conference that I met Alex Wang, with whom I got another glimpse of what was possible in a relationship with a man. Alex was a scholar from China, invited to study in this country, who had just completed his doctoral work at Brown University and would be teaching there in the fall. He was a member of Brown's famous plasticity group and later gained international recognition. Alex told me that plasticity is the branch of mechanics concerned with how bodies behave under the actions of forces of various types. It is the basis for understanding planetary motion, the behavior of climate, of oceans, of natural materials as well as those forces encountered in the processes of engineering and technology. This helped me to understand Alex's interest in earthquakes. I sensed that he was an outstanding human being but he was so unassuming I had no idea of his greatness until years later, when I read his obituary.

We walked together from meetings to the dining room, sat with the children at lunch, talked at the edge of the pond while the children swam. It was clear that Alex liked being with us and I found him intelligent, open, caring, interesting and interested. The children and I had a rare and wonderful experience at Avon. There were families at the conference and all of us became one family. We were sorry to see the week come to an end. After that summer, Alex visited us occasionally in Northfield. For several summers we attended these conferences and at one of them I decided to join, and applied for membership in, The Society of Friends. What moved me was that intangible something I had felt in church at the altar rail but which, when I left the church, was no longer available to me. In Quaker meetings I had a place where I could have that experience without committing to any particular belief.

My work at Youth Argosy sometimes required that I travel with Monroe to meetings in major metropolitan areas. On one such occasion we were flying back from Montreal, in Monroe's Cessna. Monroe had permission from a local farmer to land in one of his open fields, where we first touched down. Immediately, however, Monroe accelerated and took off again. He knew we couldn't land, that something was wrong. "Betty," he said as we gained altitude, "look down and see if there's a wheel on the ground. I'm afraid we may have lost one on that go around." He tilted the plane to one side and there on the ground, a little way from where we had touched down, I saw the Cessna's wheel. When I told him,

Monroe paled and said, "Then hold your hats, ladies, I'm going to have to try an emergency landing."

Looking over, I saw the expression on his face and the way his hands were gripping the controls. He didn't want to make that emergency landing. We circled around and around. I became very tense. Mildred, a secretary from the office, began to weep softly in the back seat. Looking at the fuel gage, I saw that we were nearly out of gas and knew that Monroe would be forced into that emergency landing soon. Suddenly the engine began to sputter and cough and the waiting was over. I fully expected we were all going to die. In the space of a few minutes I went through being furious with Monroe, not believing what was happening, raging at the injustice of dying so young, fearing death, then experiencing a calm into which flowed the love for my children and my parents. By the time we crashed I was at peace with myself and the world.

The plane hit the ground and everything went black. Opening my eyes, I realized I was still alive. My first inclination was to laugh but then I looked over and saw that Monroe was unconscious, his head smashed against the plane's windshield, blood trickling down his face, and the laugh stopped in my throat. Mildred appeared shocked but unharmed. The plane had dived into the ground up to its wings. Monroe and I were smashed against the windshield. I unfastened my seat belt, climbed out of the plane and stumbled out toward the road for help. I didn't have to go far because the crash had brought people running from all over the neighborhood. The farmer, into whose planted field we had crashed, came running out, waving his arms and yelling.

After they had taken Monroe to a doctor, I asked someone to drive me to the office. There were protestations that I too should see the doctor but I said there were people to be notified, things to be done, and I was sure I didn't need a doctor. One of the neighbors helped me into his car and drove me down to the Youth Argosy office. I got out of the car, walked up on the front porch and rang the bell. Martha Lopez opened the door and said, in a shocked voice, "What happened to you?" I collapsed in a faint on the porch and then they took me to the doctor. I had only two small cuts, one on the bridge of my nose and the other on my forehead. Monroe had suffered a concussion, a nasty cut over his left eye and some facial lacerations. Mildred was unhurt but vocal about "never again setting foot in an airplane." We were very fortunate.

I had met Stanley Kisloski in 1950, through a Youth Argosy co-worker. Stanley was smiling, vigorous and open. He had the tanned and muscular body of a farmer. I was attracted by his enthusiasm and brashness. The first time we dated was the first time I'd had a "boilermaker" (a shot of whiskey followed by a glass of beer) and it was the first time I'd danced the Polish polka. It was also the first time I'd had sex with a man on a first date and the first time I'd experienced orgasm. After that evening we went out regularly. On Saturday nights we would *hupaj-siupaj* at the local Polish dance hall and make love in the car on the way home. Stanley was good fun, and a gentle lover, as considerate of me after the act as he had been before and during.

In early 1951 I met a Greenfield architect, with an experimental house design he wanted a chance to build. He said he could arrange it with a builder friend so that the mortgage payments would be the same as the modest rent I was paying on Beers Plain Road. With Dad still helping me financially we decided to go ahead and bought a piece of land on Pine Street, just a block from the Northfield School for Girls. By the end of that summer we were in our beautiful new home, relieved of the chores of heating and cooking with wood stoves and delighting in the comforts of a modern home. The house had a flat roof with a three-foot overhang and solar panels, designed to catch the sun in the winter and shield us from it in the summer. There were large thermal windows. Built on a concrete slab with radiant heating coils, we enjoyed such luxuries as running around bare foot, getting into a warm bathtub and sitting on a warm toilet seat in winter. This house was one of a very few experiments designed to show that solar heating could work in New England climates.

That fall, I began to hear unsettling rumors that Monroe was taking money from the company and that there was a legal question of our no-refund policy being in violation of Civil Aeronautics Board regulations. At first I couldn't believe this was true of Monroe. Then I was saddened, then angry. Several of us who worked for the organization talked to Monroe, asking him to refute the rumors or tell us what was happening. He evaded our questions and treated us as if we were children not old enough to understand. I was so intimidated that I didn't press for answers but my fear increased. This situation demanded answers, but Monroe was so powerful I just backed off.

By Spring of 1952 things had deteriorated even further. On one occasion, when the Federal Aeronautics Administration examiners were coming to see if we were complying with the nonprofit charter under which we were set up, Monroe called a staff meeting and gave us a list of files he wanted moved immediately from the office to the basement. Shocked and horrified by what this implied, the staff objected. Monroe did not argue with us, he just loaded boxes and moved the files himself. By this time most of us at Youth Argosy had come to believe that

Monroe's business practices were unethical, if not actually illegal, but he was absolutely certain that he was right and wouldn't listen to our protests.

The staff had been warned that if Monroe and Youth Argosy were in serious trouble, we could be held liable for the actions of the company if we didn't register a formal protest. Together we wrote a letter which we sent to the *New York Times* file, a public record, stating that we had objected, unsuccessfully, to what we considered questionable practices of the company. Some of us quit, hoping to paralyze the operation before the summer of 1952, and I was one of those. The company accountant, who was also my friend, told me I was crazy. "You never quit one job until you have another lined up," he said, "and particularly not with three children to support." But it was done and I'd left without a safety net.

Youth Argosy was eventually closed down and, although I felt very righteous, I still knew that it had made a huge contribution by forcing the major airlines into offering coach fares for the first time, making international travel available to a whole new class of passengers.

When I left Youth Argosy, Stanley Kisloski offered me a job. I protested that I knew nothing about farming but he laughed and said it wouldn't take him long to train me, and he was right. So, in the summer of 1952, I worked as a farm hand on the Kisloski produce farm in Gill. I worked in the fields from seven in the morning until dark, and ate the hearty meals Stanley's mother prepared in the middle of the day. I learned to drive the tractor, cultivate potatoes, hoe onions, pick tomatoes. I went home utterly exhausted each night, but with an enormous sense of well being.

Stanley knew farming and was a good businessman. I drove to Boston with him once when he was taking his produce to market and saw the way he interacted with buyers—pleasant, courteous, but firm about his prices. People buying from him seemed to know that they could depend on the quality of his produce and didn't argue. I never saw Stanley angry.

In August, Stanley asked me to marry him. He was not put off by the fact that I already had three children. I recognized a very decent, generous and kind man who knew how to have a good time—very different from my ex-husband. I liked him but knew I could not marry him. Not only did I think it was it too soon to remarry, but I knew that the qualities I liked in Stanley were not enough for the kind of relationship I suspected was possible. I wanted more from life than I thought I would have with Stanley. (I was always comparing him with Norm Stewart and Alex.)

By the end of the summer my body was tanned, lean, and strong, but my job was over and I was looking for another. My accountant friend from Youth Argosy suggested I apply to Mount Hermon School for Boys which was also in the Town of Gill. I did so and, at the beginning of September 1952, began working for Gordon Pyper, Dean of Admissions at Mount Hermon. Soon after starting work at Mount Hermon I ended my relationship with Stanley. I felt at home in the academic environment of Mt. Hermon and when Stanley joined me at school affairs I was uncomfortable with his rough exuberance and his casual use of English. His vocabulary and pronunciation, which had brought smiles to my face when we were working together on the farm, suddenly embarrassed me. With Stanley gone I realized how difficult it was to get along without a sex life. I knew I was divorced and sometimes thought of the analogy of amputation in which you get rid of the disease but also lose the limb.

Being a divorcee in a small town seemed to be an invitation to all manner of men—the oil delivery man, the plumber, my friend's husband. The first time one of them came knocking on the door at night I was mystified but courteously invited him in. The courtesy lasted only long enough to discover his purpose in knocking on my door.

During the next few weeks I had furtive relationships with a variety of men—including the architect who had designed our house—relationships that not only failed to satisfy my need but undermined my self respect. I was embarrassed and ashamed of my desperation and the ways I handled it. I was lonely and these relationships didn't do anything to relieve the loneliness, they only made me feel disgusted with myself. With the architect I saw that he had expectations and I felt an obligation, but the relationship only contributed to my self-disgust. My Puritanical upbringing made no allowance for such behavior.

One night I packed the children into the station wagon and headed for the Bernardston Inn in the next town, determined to find someone with whom I could talk or have a few drinks and a dance. I bedded the children down in the back of the car and they were all asleep by the time we got there so I cracked the window a bit for air, locked the doors and went into the Inn. It must have been eleven o'clock when someone came over to me and said, "Lady, do you have some kids waiting outside for you?"

I raced out the door and there they were, sitting on the steps of the Inn, crying. I was mortified and ashamed. It was the last time I went to the Bernardston Inn. Since then, whenever I read of a mother leaving children in the car I think of that time and relate to her with empathy.

Alex Wang began coming more frequently to Northfield on weekends. He was a stabilizing influence. Once he took us down for a weekend at a Brown University retreat on a lake. Ever since I was a little girl I had wondered about the universe when I looked up at the sky on starry nights, and I confessed to Alex that, although I felt a little silly asking about those things, I still wondered. He didn't laugh at me or act as if such wondering was only for children. Even though he was a scientist he said that, in spite of what we might come to know, there would always be mystery and that he shared my wonder about the universe. He talked, without being condescending, in ways I could understand. This was the first time since my childhood with Uncle Will that I felt free to ask the questions others said were nonsense. There was nothing I couldn't ask Alex and he always listened. He was gentle with me and respectful of my wondering. Alex's presence in our home was good for all of us. I found myself seeing the children through his eyes. His quiet ways were a great influence on the children who were always well behaved when he was visiting. He was patient and gentle and taught them games that involved cooperation instead of competition. When he took them fishing, they tied pieces of bread to the end of a string, with no hook, and got their pleasure out of watching the fish come to eat. He told us almost nothing about himself but seemed totally focussed on making us happy.

With Alex I experienced racism on a more personal level. The small town had little tolerance for outsiders—I was still referred to as "that city gal." One Sunday morning Alex, the children, and I went to the eleven o'clock service at the Trinitarian Church. As we sat waiting for the service to start, the woman in front of us, a neighbor of mine, leaned over to someone in the pew in front of her and in a loud stage whisper said, "I didn't know Mr. Quigley was Chinese." Emma Powell, with her snide remark, was betraying her racism as well as alluding to my divorced status. I was embarrassed, and squeezed Alex's hand where it lay on the pew between us. He turned toward me and smiled. He was accustomed to slights. He said that when he went to Brown to teach and began looking for a room, people would tell him, as soon as they saw he was Chinese, that the room had just been rented. He said people thought all Chinese belonged in laundries or restaurants. I was upset every time he recounted such an incident but he seemed amused by them. He said people who couldn't see beyond the color of his skin didn't have the power to hurt him and were only hurting themselves. He knew who he was. And he helped me to know who I was. With Alex I had a glimpse of another dimension possible in a relationship with a man. With him I was much less preoccupied with myself.

I took Alex home to Stratford only once. Mother was clearly offended when he put his face too close to the plate and when he belched loudly in appreciation of the meal. It taxed her to be hospitable. Later she told me that he had bad manners. Instead of getting upset with her, I remembered Alex talking to me about forgiveness and told her that what she thought were bad manners were just cultural differences. She seemed puzzled but let it go.

By late fall of 1952 I knew I was beginning to love Alex and was pretty sure he was in love with me. But he seemed remarkably restrained, as if there were something he wasn't telling me. We had the kind of communication for which I longed, but I knew that complete communication would include the sexual dimension and that was missing. One night when we talked until well after midnight, I took his hand and looked into his eyes, wanting him to say something. He pulled back and I turned away so he wouldn't see my tears. Realizing he had to give me some explanation, he told me that he loved me but was promised to a woman in China—a woman he had not met but to whom he had been betrothed by his parents when he was a child. I just sat there, trying to take it in. How could a man like Alex, a scientist, allow his life to be governed by such an antiquated custom? As he talked to me, I saw that part of it was the deep respect he had for his parents and his tradition. After he had told me, we sometimes talked all night to avoid the inevitable separation but suddenly another door had closed and, once again, I experienced that aching loneliness.

The move to Pine Street had created childcare problems—we no longer had the next-door neighbor who had been such a life saver when we first returned to Northfield. Little Jerry had just turned five and Jan was not yet eight. They still needed someone with them after school until I came home. The weekly forty dollars I earned went for food and other expenses, and Gerry's thirty had to cover childcare. We had a succession of caregivers.

First there was Mabel—patient, kind, and lethargic. I let her go when I came home from work one night to find one end of the long dining-area bench propped up on the rubbed pine table and the other end stuck out the window, serving as a slide down which the children were sliding on bed pillows. Mabel, seemingly oblivious, sat on the couch reading her *True Confessions* magazine.

Then there was Judy. She had a boy of seven and agreed to work for a modest sum in addition to a place to live. I gave up my room for her and Danny and moved into the small extra room. It looked like a solution until I came home from work one night to find her drunk. We had a long talk and made an agreement that I would take over as soon as I got home and that there would be no drinking until that time. One day my mother paid an unexpected visit, found Judy drunk at two o'clock in the afternoon and fired her. By the time I got home from work she had packed up and gone. I was furious with my mother, even though I knew she was right.

"Where's Judy?" I asked. Mother responded, "I came here and she was drunk and I fired her. You can't have her taking care of the children." I said, "Who gave you the right to fire my housekeeper? If you think that giving me money gives you the right to interfere in my life, you've got another think coming." Mother said, "I've driven four hours to come up to visit you and this is the reception I get?" "What kind of reception did you expect to get when you come into my house while I'm away, fire my housekeeper so that she's actually gone by the time I get home and I don't know where she is or how to get her back or anything. You have no idea how difficult it is to find childcare workers here." She said, "Oh, you're so ungrateful! We're always doing things for you and you are so ungrateful."

I was doing my damndest not to cry. All I could think of was, this is the last straw. Then I invited her to leave. "Now you've done your damage, you might as well go home."

She left and I didn't hear from her again for weeks. I wrote her a letter in which I said that if she thought that Dad giving me money meant that she could run my life, I'd find a way of getting along without that money. It was sheer bluff. I knew I couldn't get along without Dad's help. But Mother hung onto that letter and for years, every time she was mad at me, she would drag it out and quote from what I'd written, to remind me of how ungrateful I was.

One weekend, in an effort to mend this, I packed the children in the car and drove down to Stratford. My timing couldn't have been worse. That Saturday was the day my Mother was breaking up the home of Gram, Will and Ted and sending the old people off to institutions. My father didn't want to take part, so I talked with Mother to see if I could understand what she was doing. When I asked her why she thought it necessary to break up their home, she replied, "They can't keep on living the way they've been living. They are a danger to themselves. I've made all the arrangements so don't you try to interfere. If you're going to make a fuss, stay here with your father and the children."

I went along with Mother, hoping until the last minute that I could dissuade her. But when we reached Gram's house, it was evident that she had, indeed, made all the arrangements. There was a van in front of the house and two white-coated attendants from the state hospital were waiting for Mother to give the final word.

"Celia Wells, this is your doing; my son wouldn't have done this to me!" These were the last words I ever heard my grandmother speak. They were hurled at my mother as the attendants wrapped Gram in a straight jacket and took her from her home to the van. I was paralyzed. I knew I should be doing something but also knew that my mother would tolerate no interference. I stood by and watched, tears rolling uncontrolled down my cheeks.

Watching at the window, Uncle Will still wore his suit and tie, as he did every day. There was food on the tie and urine stains on his trousers but neither affected his dignity. It was the first time I had ever seen him look confused. He was shaking his head slowly from side to side as if unable to comprehend what was happening. Uncle Ted was openly weeping. I stood in the yard, not quite believing, not wanting to be a part of this terrible thing and being ashamed of myself for not speaking out.

Gram was to go to the State Hospital, a sort of dumping ground for old people and mental incompetents; Ted and Will were each to go to different nursing homes. The question of why it was necessary to take them out of their home and separate them has never been answered for me, even though I heard Mother's reasons for doing so.

Her decision to intervene in the lives of the old people was helped along by a couple of incidents and an opportunity. One day she learned that Will had traveled alone, by bus, to Chicago where he had been invited to speak. At that time he was the oldest living graduate of Yale and was frequently so honored. He never confided his plans for fear of having them thwarted; Mother usually learned about the trips after he was safely back and each time she told him firmly that he must decline any future invitations. He'd never before gone as far away as Chicago and I overheard her telling my father that it was the last time. Another day Gram was unable to get out of the bathtub, and after the two old men gave up trying to lift her, Ted called the Fire Department. I thought it was uproariously funny but Mother didn't. She said, "What will the neighbors think?" To my father she said, "They'll kill themselves one of these days." I'm still wondering why death was considered worse than being separated and robbed of dignity.

The opportunity came in the form of an offer, from the Catholic Church next door, to buy Gram's house. They wanted to convert it into a school. I've always suspected that while Mother believed she was breaking up the old folks for their own good, she was swayed by that offer.

Driving home to Northfield I felt utterly hopeless. Not only had I been unable to do anything for Gram, Ted and Will, but I seemed unable to do anything for myself. I had still found no one to care for the children. Then when we got home, there was a message from my next-door neighbor, saying, "I know you are up against it and you've got to have someone to be there for the children. I know a woman who is seventy years old but she thinks she can handle it. Why don't you give her a chance?"

And so I hired Edna. I had concerns about her stamina, but she seemed to need a job and a place to live as much as I needed help, so I agreed that we would give it a try. The trial turned out to be short. On the third Sunday that Edna was with us, she didn't come out of her room for breakfast. I asked Jillie to knock gently, then go in and waken her.

Jill ran back screaming, "Mommy, Edna's head is falling off the bed and her tongue is hanging out and she looks terrible!" Edna had suffered a stroke in the night. She died in the hospital a few days later.

I was once again feeling as if I couldn't make it. Edna's death was the last straw. The problem was no longer loneliness, it had become about survival. The constant parade of baby sitters, lack of money, worries about the children and the long days were getting to me. The children were just being children but at times it seemed as if they were trying to see how much mischief they could get into. I had bought a light fixture for the hall and had put it on the shelf in the closet. One of the kids climbed up on a chair, got the box off the shelf, then accidentally dropped it on the floor. Talking with me recently, Jerry said they figured that since it was already broken there was no point in not having some fun with it so they took turns jumping on it to smash it and were having a great time when I came home from work. For many years, I had righteously maintained that I had never spanked my children but, in that recent talk, Jerry disabused me of such a claim, saying that I frequently spanked Jill. He also said he had great admiration for me just being able to survive that time, that he remembered how much trouble the three of them were, how much mischief they got into.

It was a frantic time for me. I loved going to my job in the morning and dreaded coming home at night. There was always a mess to clean up, dinner to get ready, baths for the kids, laundry to be done, and always the kids fighting. I remember asking them to give me just one day without fighting but it never happened. During this period Gerry added to the strain. He would take the children on weekends for his visitation and not bring them back on Sunday night. I didn't know where they were or if something had happened to them. Sometimes they were with his mother in New Hampshire but I would find them only by driving up there. She had no phone. Other times he would leave them with friends and let me worry for two or three days before telling me where they were.

I went to bed most nights exhausted and discouraged and woke up wishing I hadn't awakened at all. Many nights I played the piano all night, unable to sleep. I remember playing Rachmaninoff's *Prelude,* banging on the keys so hard it was amazing the children could sleep. Sometimes after being awake all night I discovered I couldn't go to sleep the next night and then by the third night I was afraid to go to bed for fear of having another night of lying there with the thoughts that swirled in my head. I knew I was close to a breaking point but couldn't surrender to it. I had three children depending on me.

One night when Gerry failed to return with the children I set out walking and walked most of the night, to keep myself from going down to the river. That river seemed like the solution to my problems even though, in rational moments, I knew it was not a real option. I could not leave the children for Gerry to raise. On that night I must have walked ten miles on the Northfield-Winchester road, oblivious to the cars whizzing by. Under normal circumstances I wouldn't have dreamed of taking such a risk but that night it didn't occur to me to be afraid. I was captive to that voice in my head. It was as if I thought I could walk the thoughts away or, perhaps, that if I got tired enough they would stop. Gerry knew that not bringing the children back on time, or not letting me know where they were, would make me frantic. In the midst of this I remembered the letter Gerry's lawyer had written me and began to wonder if Gerry's actions might be deliberate. It looked as if he were trying to push me over the edge.

Then one early December morning in 1952, I woke up and quietly retreated into a corner of my mind. There is no other way to describe it. It was a conscious choice. The children came into my bedroom and it was as though they were strangers in whom I had no interest. Unable to rouse me or even get an answer to their questions, they ran to our next-door neighbor and asked her to come. She did and, after failing to get a response from me, called the doctor, who examined me and said he would take me to the hospital in Brattleboro. Marjorie Prescott, who had been my friend since our first years in Northfield, took the children.

Later, I realized that at any time while those children were pleading with me, I could have opened my eyes, spoken, and come back. I knew that, but I chose not to. It was very clearly a choice. But, by the time the doctor had come and taken me to the hospital, the choice was no longer mine. There had been a suspension of self consciousness, a suspension of identity, as if I had abdicated responsibility for my life. It was as if my mind had said, "You can only play around with me so much."

For three weeks I remained in a detached, peaceful state, being fed and bathed and exercised, but taking no interest in those operations or any others. I was in the world but not of it. I spent the days staring at the ceiling, as if the person inhabiting the body had gone on vacation. I heard voices but not what they were saying. My mother came to plead with me and though I felt her presence, I didn't acknowledge her. One of the few memories I had of those weeks was of noticing two flies copulating on the ceiling.

The morning before Christmas, Mother brought the children to the hospital. Although hospital rules forbade their visiting, the hospital administrator let Mother bring them up outside the room on the fire escape. The nurse turned my head toward the window. I saw three little noses pressed against the window and suddenly I came back. It was as if I were waking from a long nap. Without wondering about where I was or what had happened, I was wholly with them in the present moment. I wept and called out to them, grateful for being alive. They took me home that afternoon. Mother had trimmed a tree and baked cookies and, though I was weak from my time of inactivity, we had a Christmas like none I could remember.

The doctor ordered me to recuperate at home before returning to work. The children were on Christmas vacation from school and I spent my days loving them and observing them, almost as if I hadn't seen them for a long time. I watched Jerry trace the path of a raindrop down a window pane and then, the minute the rain stopped, rush out to splash in the new puddles, watched Jillie build the tallest building in the world with blocks in the corner of her room, saw Jan curled up in a chair with a book, completely oblivious to everything around her. They seemed totally focussed in the present, whereas I had always been thinking about what had been or what was going to be.

During my recovery I listened to the children, I learned from them. It was almost as if I'd never really seen them before. I allowed them to do things for themselves and to do things for me. They were considerate of me and there was much less of the usual fighting between them. It was as if their behavior prior to my breakdown had been a bid for attention at a time when all my attention was elsewhere. This was a time during which I discovered a new dimension of love and appreciation for those children. I had lost touch with that wondrous feeling I'd had when I first held them in my arms, but it was back. These three made my life worth living. I experienced a peacefulness I'd never known. I didn't realize it at the time but, looking back from the present, I know that this was the moment when thoughts of suicide and ending my life were laid to rest. I had made a choice for life.

6

A Cornell Freshman at 33

"Look, Mr. Pyper, this Tod Hunter is a really bright one!" He glanced at the paper in my hand, nodded, then looked up at me. "It does seem so, doesn't it." He paused. "You're a bright one too, Betty. How is it that you didn't go to college?"

This was the start of the conversation with Gordon Pyper that altered my life. After a few weeks rest I had gone back to work and discovered how much I liked my job and the man for whom I worked. Gordon Pyper was a man close to my father's age; more than my boss, he was a friend. He knew I was a single mother with three children, that I was struggling financially, that I had just returned to work after a collapse. He was concerned about me.

He noted the interest I showed in the bright boys whose tests I was grading at the time. I wanted to be sure that each boy applying was either accepted or was turned down in a way that left him still feeling good about himself. One day after my return I stood at Mr. Pyper's desk and handed him some admissions tests that I had been scoring, excitedly pointing out one from a student who was obviously a good candidate.

I was surprised by Mr. Pyper's question but answered, "My parents didn't think girls needed college. They sent me to a finishing school in North Carolina to study music and learn to be a lady." "Have you never wanted to go to college?" "I thought about it only when I was in history class in high school. I had a teacher who made it exciting and occasionally I wondered what it would be like to go to a great college like Cornell with teachers like Miss Jubb. But I never thought of it as a real possibility." "Do you still wonder what it would be like to be in college?" "Mr. Pyper!" I looked at him to see if he was joking. "I have three children, no husband and barely enough income for us to survive. I've stopped wondering about such things."

He paused for a minute, as if deciding, then said, "Close the door and sit down for a minute, Betty. I want to tell you a story."

I couldn't imagine what he wanted to tell me but did as he asked without questioning.

Then he started. "I grew up on a farm in Iowa, married at seventeen, had fathered two children before I was twenty. My wife died giving birth to our third. I was left with three children to raise and a job that had to be done in order to support them. I had quit school at sixteen, but one of my teachers knew about Mount Hermon and the work-study program here. He wrote a letter about me, and almost before I knew what was happening, I was on my way to Massachusetts, with my children. I completed high school here at Mount Hermon and went on to Brown University—all of this with my kids in tow. It can be done, Betty."

I was stunned. For a moment I couldn't speak. Could he be suggesting what I thought he was suggesting? I looked at him and saw him smile. A whole new world of possibility opened up for me when I realized Mr. Pyper's purpose in telling me his story. I didn't think about any of the complications—selling the house we'd only recently moved into, getting the money to move and live on—but simply grabbed at the opportunity. It was a gut reaction. When he opened that door I knew I was meant to go through it. Having survived my breakdown, I had absolute trust in the process.

The next day I took one of the admissions tests we gave the boys to get an IQ score. Mr. Pyper turned the test over to the college counselor and asked him to help me. So it was that in January of 1953 I was spending hours after the kids were in bed looking at college catalogs to see what I might want to study and where I wanted to go. Although Mr. Pyper had urged me to apply to Cornell, after I confessed that I had dreamed of going there, I thought I would have a better chance at one of the New England state universities, so I applied to all of them as well.

As part of the Cornell application I wrote a letter about why I wanted to go to college. The only thing I remember writing was that I believed there was a job for me to do in life and I would know what that job was when I was prepared to do it. My applications to the state universities were all turned down, the rejection letters almost the same: "We don't have enough room for the eighteen-year-old applicants, so aren't in a position to consider an older person." I was disappointed but also amused. I didn't think of myself, at thirty-three, as an "older person."

I shall never forget the surprise and elation I felt when my application to Cornell was accepted. Perhaps it was the letter, perhaps Mr. Pyper's recommendation, perhaps Cornell was looking for unusual cases. I never knew the why of it, but I was given scholarship assistance and told that if I could make it through the first year with a good record, I could count on substantial assistance for the succeeding years. I was as excited as I had been when my father told me I was going to Europe. It hardly seemed possible. I was going to Cornell! I didn't stop to think about the children and taking them out of their school. The only thought I had about them was how glad I was to be getting them away from their father.

Dad had rented a closed truck and we loaded it with as many of our things as it would hold. Much of the furniture in the Pine Street house looked as if it belonged there and we sold it with the house. The piano went to my Long Hill friend, Alice Fox, with the understanding that she would take care of it and give it back whenever I wanted it. All we took with us was our personal stuff, our bicycles, the antique rocking chairs and the cats.

The move to Ithaca was a comic adventure. Dad and I took turns driving, while the kids sang, "The Bear Came Over the Mountain," and "Old MacDonald Had a Farm," nibbled on crackers and fruit, and took turns napping on each other's shoulders. Our two cats were in boxes at the back end of the truck, so whenever we went up a hill, we had to stop and make sure none of the stuff had slid down and squashed the cats. The stuff had always slid down and the cats were always mewing, even though not squashed. And in between stops for the cats, there were frequent toilet stops for the children, more often than not alongside the road. I can still hear Jilly saying, "I won't do that!"

I was sure the trip had thoroughly traumatized the cats and when Blackie took off the day after we arrived I was not surprised. I decided he was heading back to Northfield and at that point could not really blame him. I too was wondering what I was doing in upstate New York, with three children, little money, no friends, no job and a scary future as a college student.

Home in Ithaca was a three-room second-floor furnished apartment on DuBois Road, on the outskirts of town, a quarter of a mile from the nearest neighbor. Dad, before returning to Connecticut, had bought an old Ford for me to use in commuting to the University. Our house belonged to Mr. Barnum, who told us what we could and couldn't do. There was a tiny man-made pond in the side yard and Mr. Barnum had a row boat in it. Looking at it I decided he must like to just sit in the boat, because there was hardly enough room to turn it around in the pond. One of the things he said we couldn't do was go anywhere near that boat. A swing hung from a big old tree near the pond and he said the kids could swing on that.

The girls shared the one bedroom, I slept in the living room and Jerry slept in the hall area by the stairwell outside the living room. The two younger children attended a one-room schoolhouse which accommodated grades one through four and Janis, who was in fifth grade, took the bus into town to a middle school. In the afternoon she looked after the younger kids until I got home and usually had something started for dinner.

As soon as we had settled into our new home we began attending Quaker Meeting on Sundays. I didn't want my children to have to unload a burden of beliefs when they grew up, and I knew those meetings made no demand for belief and gave us an hour of quiet each week in the middle of our chaotic lives. It was a time of living frugally, shopping for grocery bargains and buying clothes at second-hand clothing stores. It was also a time of social consciousness because of our association with the Friends. Birthday gifts were packed off for needy children in other countries.

Because of my friendship with Alex Wang I had elected to begin my work at Cornell in Asian Studies, and Professor Knight Biggerstaff, who was head of Cornell's China program, became my adviser. My first year included an Introduction to South Asia and a History of Western Civilization. In the South Asia course I had my first look into the history, culture, and languages of India, and satisfied my language requirement with Hindustani and Sanskrit. I exempted, by exam, the Freshman English requirement.

Working ten hours a week was part of my tuition agreement. My first job that fall was as research assistant to Professor George McT. Kahin, head of the Southeast Asia Program. In that job, I discovered the Cornell Library. I did research for Professor Kahin and then browsed. Looking back, I suspect that Professor Kahin was less interested in the research assignment he gave me than he was in having me discover the library and in that, he succeeded. In classes, whenever given the choice, I opted for a paper rather than a test so I could do my own research. It was my first exposure to a really fine library. Sometimes I would forget why I was there and just browse, picking up one book after another, thrilled by the realization that I was listening in on a conversation that had been going on for centuries and that, through my reading, I was a part of that conversation.

The first paper I wrote for my History of Western Civilization course, a class of 1,000 students, was a review of Thorstein Veblen's *Theory of the Leisure Class*. I read the book and then searched for contemporary reviews of it. I knew nothing about politics or economics but Veblen's thesis that the captains of industry should not be paid exhorbitant sums, but should get their reward by having made a contribution, was a thesis that had great appeal to me. It was much the same argument that our society seemed to make for paying teachers, but we didn't apply it in paying the executives who ran giant corporations.

Writing the Veblen paper was the most rewarding academic experience I'd ever had and when the paper came back with a grade of "95" on it, I cried. Then I thought it must be a mistake. When I finally accepted that it was my paper, and my "95," I was ready to do handstands. Mr. Pyper had been right—I *was* smart enough for college. But my reluctance at accepting that I'd earned a high grade was always the way it was. Whenever I wrote a paper or took an exam I was unsure of what I had done, yet more often than not they came back with high marks. I realized that something in me had not been expressed, didn't have the space to be expressed until I got into the Cornell environment. It was a kind of intellectual awakening and made me recall the times when, as a child, I listened with awe, if not understanding, to Uncle Will as he read philosophy and history to me.

The lecturer in my Western Civilization course was a brilliant man who made history live. At first I just listened, fascinated by what he was saying, but before long I realized that I wasn't taking notes, as everybody around me seemed to be doing. That was when I decided I'd better start using my shorthand, so for the balance of the course I took down whole lectures in shorthand and spent the nights transcribing them.

One of the things I read for this course was Carl Becker's *Freedom and Responsibility in the American Way of Life* which introduced me to the fundamental moral and social problems of a citizen in a democracy such as ours. At home it had seemed that my father thought the government was there to protect his interests alone and I recalled how upset he was when Franklin D. Roosevelt was elected and instituted such things as work programs for people who were suffering in the Great Depression. This was the first time I thought my father might have been wrong about something.

In addition to my work for Professor Kahin, I also worked in a secretarial pool in the Graduate School of Business and Public Administration. Most of my work was typing case studies and, like the work I did in the South Asia Program, it provided me with another avenue of learning. The professors for whom I typed were always willing to answer questions about their papers.

I was excited being at Cornell but it was not easy. I was carrying twelve hours of classes and between ten and fifteen hours of work. I usually got home just in time to help Janis finish preparing the dinner she had started. Serious studying could not begin until after the children were in bed, around nine o'clock. It was generally two or three o'clock in the morning before I finished and occasionally I would skip sleep, just shower and get breakfast before returning to the campus.

Initially I had planned on staying in the DuBois Road house for my entire stay at Cornell but by the end of the first year I realized we needed to be in town. There was too much commuting, and living where we did meant that we missed out on most of the evening activities at the University. Planning to return to Massachusetts for the summer, I paid two months rent at the beginning of May and told Mr. Barnum that we would not be returning in the fall. He was furious and the next day evicted us, literally putting all our stuff out on the front lawn. When I came home to three crying children and no place to sleep, I too was furious and railed at the landlord before setting out to find a place for us to stay. Later I realized that although he threw us out, he didn't give me back the two months' rent I had paid in advance. His actions were clearly illegal, but I had no money for attorney's fees. Friends from the Quaker Meeting took us in and helped us put our belongings in storage, but I knew that before leaving for the summer I had to find a place for us to live when we returned in the fall.

People had reservations about a female student who was a single mother with three children. I was turned down over and over again. Finally I learned that the old Episcopal rectory was going to be for rent. It was so run down, the new minister's wife refused to live in it and they had been renting it to an old couple, both of whom had died in recent months. I went to a meeting of the church deacons to make my application and it looked as if they too were going to turn me down. I looked around at that circle of faces and the tears that had been gathering began to slip down my cheeks. The deacons relented and let us have the house, with one condition—that the church could use the front parlor Sunday mornings for church school. I was elated, thanked them, and was finally able to look forward to the vacation.

Little Jerry was not returning to Northfield with us for the summer. He had been invited to visit friends in British Guiana, and before driving back to Massachusetts we took him to New York to put him on a plane to South America. We had spent many evenings talking about it because Jerry was only eight years old and I had misgivings about letting him go so far from home, but he pleaded and I finally gave in. The Hawleys were missionaries who had been visiting the Northfield School for a few months the previous year. They had a son about Jerry's age and when the two became friends, the Hawleys invited Jerry to come spend a year with them, saying he could go to school with their son.

I will always remember the day he left. It was a five-hour drive from Ithaca to New York City. I was excited for him and apprehensive. The girls were envious—they had not been invited. With his ticket cleared, luggage checked through and a seat assignment made, we all went into the Pan American lounge to await the boarding call. It could have been a half hour, or two hours, but it seemed like no time. I gave Jerry lots of last-minute advice, trying to ease the discomfort I was feeling. He was the only one who seemed not to have any doubts about what he was undertaking. The boarding call came and Jerry leapt from his seat and headed toward the gate. We all followed and stood with him in line until we reached the "Passengers Only" sign. Then there were hugs and kisses and tears and he disappeared among the other passengers.

The huge plane was out on the airstrip and the passengers had to cross a long stretch of asphalt to reach it. The girls and I had gone to the observation deck to watch. Suddenly Jan cried out, "There he is, Momma!" I looked to where she pointed and my eyes again filled with tears. There was my little boy, my baby, the youngest of the three, walking alone across the tarmac, apart from the crowd, looking up at the plane. Who knows what he was thinking. He wore khaki shorts, a navy T-shirt, argyle knee socks, a white jacket, and a khaki-colored jungle hat, which he insisted on wearing on the plane. His camera strap was slung over one shoulder and he carried a navy tote bag.

He looked so small. What had I been thinking of, to let him go off alone? I wanted to run after him, call him back, ask them to hold the plane, anything! But I didn't. Jan, who had "mothered" me since she was old enough to see that I had never grown up, turned to me, saw the tears and took my hand. "It's okay, Momma. He'll be okay."

And he was okay. He had an experience few youngsters are fortunate enough to have. He lived in British Guiana for three months, was introduced to a totally different culture and, as a bonus, had a camping trip up the Berbice River through the jungle, with Mr. Hawley and native guides. Although Jerry had been invited to stay for a year he was attacked by chiggers and, by the end of the summer, was covered with a rash and was miserably uncomfortable. Then, when school started, he confronted not only racial segregation in the classroom but the harsh discipline of the Catholic school and decided to come home.

Waiting for him at the airport, on his return, was even more traumatic than waiting for him to leave. When the plane on which he was supposed to arrive came in, he was not on it. It was hours before we learned that he had been bumped from the flight in Puerto Rico and was waiting there for the next plane to New York. I was ready to fly down after him but the airline assured me that he would be cared for. In the meantime the girls and I had to think about the night. We spent part of it sleeping in the car and then came back to the airport early so we would be there when the first plane came in. When he finally arrived, he was all smiles at his big adventure.

During the summer that Jerry was gone, the girls and I visited Mom and Dad, went to the Friends Avon conference and spent the remainder of the summer in Northfield, living and working with Martha and Manuel Lopez. I drove Manuel's tractor while we brought in hay for the winter. I learned how to back up the tractor with a trailer attached and how to corral a wayward cow. The latter I learned only because I was more afraid of Manuel than I was of the cow. The Lopezes were a real challenge to me because I loved Martha but was a little afraid of Manuel, who was like Gerry in many respects. But Martha loved him, was his partner and made excuses for him. They both milked the cows, both drove the tractor, both gathered in the hay. She had learned how to live with him and it seemed as if she was never compromised by giving in to his demands. It was a strenuous summer and I was glad when it was time to return to Ithaca.

The Episcopal rectory in Ithaca was a big, old, gray Victorian house in back of the church at the corner of Buffalo and Cayuga streets. The house needed a lot of work but I could overlook that because the rent was so low. When I saw the five bedrooms, a huge living room, dining room and kitchen plus a laundry room, I decided that renting out some of the rooms would help us financially, so the house became a sort of cooperative boarding house.

Del Barley was the first to move in. He was a professor at Ithaca College, about my age with a family in Germany. He and I became good friends. We often talked in the late evening, after we had finished studying. Mike and Larry were two young physical education students from the college, and Kathy was a music student, also at Ithaca College. Del and I met and discussed how to run the house, then had a meeting with the students to let them know what we were proposing. We suggested that breakfast and lunch be independent meals but, for dinner, each of us would take turns buying food and cooking for the whole "family" with me kicking in extra for the kids. The plan was agreed upon and dinner became a community affair. Because of the differing backgrounds of the people in the house, meals were varied and interesting. Del and I had also come up with some house rules which we ran by the students, rules about keeping the common rooms picked up and clean, dishes washed and put away, rules about loud radios, raucous behavior and overnight guests.

I was usually the one who told the guys to keep the radio down and I was the one who told Kathy that her boyfriend could come to visit but not spend the night. One morning when I came down to breakfast and learned that he had spent the night I told Kathy the next time there would be no warning. If there was a next time she would be out looking for another place to live. A couple of weeks later she tested me and was out by noon. Mike and Larry thought it was great. They laughed and kidded me about being tough.

That was the year that Janis began playing the saxophone and the rest of us agreed the only place she could practice was in the laundry room way at the back of the house. Also, living in town, Jan discovered Cornell's stables. Most afternoons after school she went to the campus where she brushed the animals, cleaned stalls and did whatever it took to be able to ride. She would come home dirty, disheveled and radiant. She loved the horses.

It was also the year that Jilly, now nine, began to assert her independence. She would take off after school on a bus and ride it to the end of the line, where someone would call and tell us to come to pick her up. She attended released-time classes in the Catholic church, unbeknownst to me, until the day the priest called to get permission for her to convert. I refused, but when I told her of my decision she said it was no big deal, that she had signed up for those classes mostly to get out of school.

As promised, Cornell gave me a full scholarship for my second year, which meant that my tuition was covered and I needed to earn only enough money to support myself and supplement Gerry's support of the kids. The scholarship was Ford money from the Southeast Asia program, so that year I began Southeast Asian studies in earnest. My work in this second year was with John Echols, another member of the Southeast Asia group. I worked with him on a dictionary. The name, *Bahasa Indonesia* was coined by the Indonesian Nationalists to denote the dialect of Malay that was spoken by the majority of people in Jakarta, the country's capital. The language came to symbolize national unity, in Indonesia's mid-twentieth century struggle for independence from the Dutch, and it became the official language of the Republic of Indonesia. Cornell had a contingent of graduate students in Indonesia and, with them, we were developing a *Bahasa Indonesia-English Dictionary*. It was a fascinating job and in order to make the most of it I enrolled in a *Bahasa* language-intensive class which met twelve hours a week.

In that sophomore year I had my first course in the Philosophy Department—a course in ethics. I was hooked. I went to see Knight Biggerstaff and told him I had found my major and it was philosophy. He laughed and told me I was behaving just like a sophomore, all of whom thought they wanted to major in philosophy. But that year I was being supported financially by the Southeast Asia program and knew that philosophy would have to wait. It was also the year I took botany, to satisfy the science requirement and was awed by the discovery that the cells from a piece of my skin looked just the same, under a microscope, as those from a rose petal or the wing of a fly. College was a series of moments of wonder and I never ceased being grateful to Gordon Pyper.

Alex Wang had been delighted when I was accepted at Cornell. We talked on the phone regularly and he came to visit a few times early that fall, but each time he did I was afraid it would be his last. In 1954 the United States was making it difficult for Chinese students. The United States had supported Chiang Kai-shek, and the hospitable climate in which Alex had been invited to America had changed to a climate of hostility. Alex was not as upset as I was. He said he had planned to go back soon anyway, because of his filial obligation to his aging parents and his marriage promise. Not long after his last visit I learned that he and the other Chinese scholars had been deported. I was distressed and angry because it seemed so clearly wrong. Alex had been invited here by our government, was teaching at Brown University and had nothing to do with China's revolution. I talked with my advisor, Knight Biggerstaff, who was head of the China program at Cornell but he told me there was nothing that could be done. All Chinese nationals in this country were being deported. My personal sense of loss was magnified by a sense of responsibility for my government's actions. Alex and I corresponded regularly over the years after he left, except for a brief time when our governments refused to allow the exchange of mail. Later, as his career developed, he began making international lecture tours and frequently included a visit with me on those tours.

In the late fall of my second year at Cornell, I had a surprise telephone call from Gerry Quigley who said he was in Ithaca on business. When I heard his voice on the phone I was stunned but, oddly, thrilled. He asked to see the kids and take me to dinner. I suggested he come over to the house and say hello to the children and we could then go out. It had been several years since I had seen him but, hanging up the phone, I noticed that I no longer harbored ill feelings and was actually looking forward to the evening.

He came to the house one afternoon and he and I were sitting in the living room when Jill and Jerry came home from school. Before I had a chance to speak, they nodded to him, obviously not recognizing him, and raced out to the kitchen for their after-school snack. His expression told me nothing, but I was mortified. I knew I should have stopped them the minute they came into the room and said something like, "Look who's here, kids! Say hello to your Dad." But I hadn't, and only Jan spoke when she came in. She greeted him with a quiet "Hello," gave me a look of perplexity, and then joined the others in the kitchen. When they came back, I did what I should have done before and there were a few awkward minutes as the children tried to figure out how to behave. It bothered them only briefly, however, and soon the two younger ones raced off to whatever it was they planned to do next. Janis, looking pensive, went to her room.

Gerry and I left early and had a pleasant dinner and evening. Before it was over I was sure we would remarry. The attraction that had drawn us together the first time was still there. Neither of us had remarried in the five years since the divorce, and my memory of the unpleasant times had dimmed. It was just as it had been in 1939, at Mrs. Stevens' house, when I sat across the table from him, had these weird stirrings in my body and gave up all rational behavior just to go with those feelings. I forgot Don, upset my parents and threw my own life into a turmoil. In Ithaca it was the same thing. Sitting across the table from Gerry in the restaurant, I looked into his eyes and all the memories of the past disappeared or were rationalized away. I could think of nothing but being with him.

As I was going to sleep that night after our dinner together, I wondered if I had taken leave of my senses. Here I was, with a life of my own, having found something I was good at and loved. People had trusted me, giving me a great opportunity to study at Cornell, and here I was about to throw it all away. Wasn't one round enough with this man? But my success at Cornell and my new-found pacifism convinced me that I could make it work. We were both more mature, he seemed somewhat subdued and he had said I could continue studying at the University of Connecticut. I felt strong and capable of handling any outcome that being together might produce. And, to be honest, I did think about Gerry's good job and being relieved of my financial responsibility. I persuaded myself that it would be good for the children to have a father although I don't understand how I could have, given his earlier treatment of Jill.

There was another element in the picture which I didn't recognize at the time. Alex Wang had just been deported from the United States. He had been a stabilizing factor in my life over the last few years. He knew everything about my life—my children, my financial struggle, my breakdown. He was the one person to whom I could tell anything without his making judgments. He just listened. I had only recently given up hope that his proposed marriage in China would somehow not happen. I finally had to accept that he and I were never going to be together and I was bereft. Only when he was gone did I realize how important a part of my life he had become.

Although Gerry had said, "We don't have to rush into this," we were married a few weeks later, in a non-denominational church on Buffalo Street. The children sat in the front pew, sober-faced and wondering. Jan was crying. She was old enough to remember how it had been and, I'm sure, must have felt betrayed.

Our first night together in Ithaca was almost as bad as our first night had been fourteen years earlier in New York. Gerry was allergic to almost everything, including cats, and shortly after we had gone to bed, he sat up as if he had been shot. Mike and Larry had taken an instant dislike to Gerry, thought I was making a mistake and disapproved of the hasty marriage. Partly as a joke and partly to foul up our first night back together they put our big black cat in the room, knowing that as soon as we were in bed, the cat would jump up and join us. Gerry's reaction shouldn't have surprised me. He leapt out of bed, threw the cat across the room and bellowed, "God damn it, what's this cat doing in the bed! What the hell is going on here!"

For a moment I thought, "Oh, no, what have I done!" I was throwing away a fully-funded education at Cornell and the future it promised. I was betraying the trust of both Cornell and Gordon Pyper. Reflecting on the ease with which I left Cornell I am reminded of the ease with which I left Don Campbell when Gerry appeared fifteen years earlier. I asked myself, "What happened to me when I was with this man? Why did I get myself back into this situation? What was I thinking?" And I had no answers.

7

Political Awakening and Prison

Once we were back in New England, Gerry reneged on his agreement that I could continue studying and insisted that I stay home with the kids. I was upset and angry, but determined to make this marriage work and do whatever it took, so I capitulated and postponed my return to school. Somewhere under the surface I vowed to make him suffer for that decision.

Our first home in Connecticut had the charm of an early colonial with wide-board floors and an enormous fireplace but it also had rats. We waged war on those rats until admitting defeat when one of them bit off the leg of the children's hamster who had dared put his foot out of the cage one night. Then we moved to Agawam, Massachusetts, where we rented a two-story frame house on top of a hill at the end of a cul-de-sac. The kids and I liked it the first time we saw it and Gerry didn't care where we lived as long as it was close to his work. The area around the house was wooded, and down the hill from the house was a small fieldstone cottage belonging to the property and rented out to Marjorie Fredericks, a reporter who wrote for a Springfield newspaper. Marjorie looked as if she belonged in the fieldstone cottage—she was all tweed and brogans. When she was walking about the property she even carried a fancy carved cane. An open, friendly face with a large mouth and wide eyes, coupled with her light brown hair and blue eyes made it seem as if she belonged in an English countryside.

Although Gerry hadn't attended that summer's Quaker conference with us, we returned from it so full of goodwill that once again I was certain I could make our marriage work. On the first night back, I made love to Gerry with such ardor that the next morning, he laughingly said, "Wow, I should send you to one of those conferences every week!" According to my calculations, that was the night my fourth child was conceived.

In the spring of 1956 I began flying lessons. I had always wondered what it would be like to fly, and Gerry having a small Ercoupe gave me the opportunity to learn. I did the course work and was certified as a student pilot on the 16th of

May. I had my first lesson in the air on June 8th. Between the 8th of June and the 12th of July I had logged eight hours and fifteen minutes of instruction. On the 13th, the instructor and I climbed into the plane, went around once with a near-perfect landing and were preparing to take off again when I turned to him.

"Why don't you get out and let me do it. I'm ready and I want to do it myself."

He hesitated, but when he saw I meant it, he climbed out. From the ground he gave me an okay signal and I took off. There had never been a thrill in my life that could compare with that moment. As I left the field and soared over Agawam I felt like queen of the world. It was as if I were alone up there with the clouds and blue sky, looking down on the meadows and fields and the Connecticut River, which looked like a little stream. It was as if I were somehow holding all that. Again, the amazing experience of being one with all that is, of being closer to that elusive secret I'd been pursuing all my life.

I was slightly more subdued in landing but no less confident. It's humbling to acknowledge my hubris in assuming that I had learned all I needed to know and could dismiss my instructor after less than eight and a half hours of instruction. It was one of those moments when I acted impulsively without thinking of possible consequences. But the instructor wrote in the log book, "Better than average performance," and I was sure that I had been right in letting him go. For several weeks I was flying on the ground as well as off. There was something about being up in the air by myself that put everything in perspective. I remember feeling as I had on my first visit to a planetarium and as I had with my father on the breakwater—filled with wonder.

Gerry had told me that early morning was the best time to fly, that the air was still and cool, the winds usually calm until afternoon. As many mornings as I could arrange it I was at the airport taking the Ercoupe out of the hangar, but on the 4th of August I had been unable to get to the field in the morning. Ignoring my better judgment and Gerry's advice, I decided to take the plane up for an hour in the early afternoon. It was a mistake.

The flight was beautiful but as I approached for landing, I was aware of a crosswind coming from my left. I was nervously trying to correct for its influence when I came alongside part of an old stadium structure that hadn't been torn down when the field was converted to an airport. The structure blocked the crosswind at that point and the plane dropped. From my training I knew I should hold the nose steady, accelerate and gradually pull up and go around again for another try but, obviously, I had not learned it well enough because I pulled the nose sharply up and the plane stalled out. It plummeted down, nose first, right into the tarmac, tearing up fifty feet of runway before finally coming to a halt beside a cornfield, with the plane standing on its nose, tail straight up in the air. For a few seconds it hovered, then settled back down on its wheels. Had it gone on over instead of falling back down, I might have been killed, because the plane had only a Plexiglas bubble over the cockpit.

Farm workers came running from the cornfield like ants, and other fliers, Gerry among them, came out of the hangars. One of them jumped up on the wing. "Are you hurt?" he said, "Do you need a doctor?"

I was stunned but able to respond, "No thanks, I seem to be okay, but look what I've done to the plane."

And that's what Gerry was doing—looking at what I had done to his plane. I don't know why he was at the airport at that time of day and can only surmise that he had come home from work early, saw my car gone, and suspected I might be at the airport. He didn't get there in time to stop me from going up but was there to see me fly his plane into the ground. Later I realized how devastating it was to him. The plane had been his baby, it was not insured, the cost of repair was prohibitive. Gerry kept it in the garage for years, eventually selling it for salvage. It was the end of flying, for both of us, for many years.

Aside from damage to the plane I knew I was pregnant and was most concerned for the other life in my body. But it was a hardy one, determined to be born and not shaken loose by a plane crash.

In late July I learned that A. J. Muste, the pacifist and Episcopal priest who had attended Avon with us for several years, had been arrested in New York for anti-war activity. A. J. was a gentle old man, very tall, white haired, saintly. He walked around the Avon campus talking to the children as if it were the most important thing he had to do. I had listened to him talk about Ghandi and the effectiveness of non-violent civil disobedience. I knew that was what he had been doing and couldn't believe they had put him in jail. I was massively upset and shared my feelings with the children who had come to know him at Avon. We talked about it and I told them there must be something terribly wrong with a system that would lock him up, that it was almost a sacrilege to lay a hand on him in violence as they had done.

For days I was raging with impotence, feeling helpless to do anything about this miscarriage of justice. Then I heard from Russ Johnson, the man who had first invited me to a Quaker conference, that there was to be a protest, in New York City—a protest against a national air raid drill. I talked with Gerry who seemed to understand how important it was to me and then I made plans to join the group. Gerry and our neighbor, Marjorie Fredericks, said they would take care of the kids while I was gone. I knew that Marjorie wanted the inside information on this for a story.

I had been objecting to air raid drills even before leaving Ithaca. The children were being told that pulling their skirts over their heads and crawling under desks would protect them in a nuclear attack. I talked to them and explained what nonsense that was. In Ithaca, I also walked in parades, carried banners, and wrote to the editor of the local paper. I believed the only purpose of the drills was to intimidate people so they would not object to the outrageous defense spending being proposed by the government.

On the last Friday in July 1956, twelve of us were arrested in Central Park for refusing to take cover during the drill. Again it was one of those ridiculous drills during which everybody was supposed to take cover in a doorway, as if that were any protection against a nuclear attack. There were several like myself for whom this was a first act of civil disobedience, but there were also those who earned a reputation protesting—among them Dorothy Day, Bayard Rustin and Ammon Hennacy, editor of *The Catholic Worker*. Being roughed up by the police and herded into a paddy wagon was a little scary but it also had the excitement of an adventure.

We were taken to night court and charged. The charge would have been a misdemeanor had it been only a New York drill but because it was a federal drill the charge was automatically a felony. The group lawyer got us out on bail within an hour but was not able to give us any idea of how long it might be before our case came to trial.

I had not told my folks about the demonstration and the first they knew of it was when, watching the eleven o'clock news, they saw me being arrested in New York City. Mother phoned me the next day to tell me how upset they were. "What are you trying to do to us? We saw you being pushed into a paddy wagon in New York last night. You should be ashamed of yourself! Don't you ever think about your parents?" She didn't wait for a response, but hung up and I didn't hear from them again for about two months.

They forgave me, however, when I called in October to report that I was pregnant and that they would have another grandchild in early April. They adored their grandchildren and were excited by the prospect of another, even though they had misgivings about this second marriage to Gerry. I was thrilled because I thought this baby might be the key to a successful marriage.

Soon after the first of the year I received notice that our trial had been scheduled for late February. I had almost forgotten about the trial and was not eager to go to New York but knew I had no choice. Once again our neighbor, the newspaper reporter, offered to take care of the children. She was interested in the trial and was reporting on it. I can still see the Springfield newspaper headline, "Agawam Pacifist to Stand Trial in New York."

In the courtroom, the judge asked each of us how we pled. All said, "Guilty." He then offered us the choice of paying a fine or going to jail. A few paid the fine but most of us elected to go to jail, as we had originally agreed to do. Dorothy Day, who was considered a saint by many New Yorkers, was not going to pay the fine nor was Bayard Rustin, a hero of mine who was deeply involved in the civil rights movement. Later, in 1963, Bayard was the organizing power of the March on Washington in which Martin Luther King made his, "I have a Dream" speech.

I thought it would make a much greater statement if I went to jail, but if I had known then what was to happen over the next few days, I would have paid the fine. As I entered my plea, the judge looked at me, recognized that I was in advanced pregnancy, and asked if I realized what I was doing. I said I did. The clerk of the court, a pleasant middle-aged man who seemed concerned, shook his head at me indicating I was making a mistake. But once again, I was so sure our position was right that I was determined to follow through. Today I'm chagrinned to realize that I felt condescending toward both the clerk and the judge. They seemed not to realize that we were using our right to demonstrate in order to save the people of our country from a government gone mad and that we would go to prison if that was the cost of such a demonstration. The judge sentenced me to three days in the Women's House of Detention in Greenwich Village. That sounded easy and I was sure it would be worth it to make my point. A few hours later I was not so sure but then it was too late.

Along with others who had been sentenced that day, I was herded into a room and told to remove my clothes and put them in a plastic bag. Then I was hosed down with a spray so powerful that it almost knocked me off my feet. The matron gave me a muslin johnny coat, a pair of muslin slippers, told me to put them on and have my picture taken. It was taken with me holding a number card in front of me. From that moment on I was addressed only by number, or as "girlie." Then the matron pointed and said, "Now go over there and get in that line."

I did as I was told and waited in line for probably half an hour. As I got closer to the front of the line I could see what was happening and began to panic. I asked the woman in line next to me what they were doing. She answered briefly,

"Checking for drugs." "Checking where?" Our clothes and purses had already been taken. "Body cavities."

Body cavities! My God! I was eight months pregnant. But certainly I would be exempted. No matter how callous they might have seemed at the first processing station, surely the doctor would not endanger my baby. Suddenly I felt an overwhelming helplessness—I'd had my name taken away from me and a number strapped on me, my clothes and purse had been taken away. I was terrified! As I got closer to the front of the line, I saw what was happening. A woman I assumed to be the doctor was examining all entering women and it was an examination of great intimacy—checking ears, hair, fingernails and finally rectum and vagina. When I was second in line I watched in horror as the doctor called the woman in front of me, had her climb onto the examining table and then, without changing the rubber gloves she was wearing, examined the woman. I suddenly realized that she was wearing the gloves to protect herself, not to protect from disease or infection the women she was examining. As my turn approached I was almost helpless with fear but suddenly it turned to anger.

When the doctor indicated that I was to get up on the table, I said "I'm about to have a baby. I don't want you to mess up me or that baby. You haven't changed those gloves since you started. Don't you dare touch me!" "Just get up on the table, girlie," she responded. "No, I won't run that risk with my baby."

"Guards!" she called, and suddenly there were two burly men picking me up as if I were a child, putting me on the table in front of the doctor, then holding me down while I cried out and struggled, unsuccessfully, to prevent the examination. When it was over I knew the meaning of rape. I was numb as I stumbled out of the examining room.

"This way, sister," another voice said. I was in tears as they led me down the hall, upstairs and into a cell. The heavy metal door clanged shut behind me. There were six beds in the room and a little glass and wire cage in the corner. A uniformed matron sat in the cage and nodded to me as I entered the room. Five women of various ages, sizes and races watched.

"Look what we got," laughed one of the women on the other side of the room. "Yeah," chimed in another. "What'd you do wrong, honey—jaywalk?" Wiping my eyes on the sleeve of my muslin coat, I replied, "No, I was in a demonstration." The tenor of the teasing changed. "What kinda demonstration?" "I refused to take part in a civil defense drill." "She's a Commie," one of them said. The others turned away.

There was no more light banter. Later I learned that being considered a Communist was the worst thing you could be in there and anyone committing an act of civil disobedience was considered a Communist.

It was four o'clock when I realized my family was unaware of what had happened. I asked to make a phone call but the matron just shrugged. I went to the door of our cell, opened the little peep door at eye level and called out, "I understand I'm entitled to a telephone call. Where can I make it?" "Just give us a little more lip, sister, and you won't need a phone call or anything else. Shut that door!" The guard sitting in the corridor had a gun on his lap. I backed into the room, shaking.

When night came I looked at the bed assigned me. The sheets were filthy, there was no pillow and only a single light cover. I was wondering where the bathroom was when one of the women emerged from a curtained-off area on one side of the room. I realized that must be it. I drew the curtain aside, went in and pulled it closed. There was a toilet with no seat, no lid, and a small sink with a cold water faucet. I used the toilet as quickly as I could, ran my hands under the cold water, wiped them on my johnny coat and left.

I crawled up on my bed, too tired to be bothered even by the dirty sheets. But the smells and the noises and my thoughts kept me awake. Finally exhaustion took over and I slept, but woke up suddenly. One of the prisoners was nudging me over to get into my bed and putting her hand over my mouth to keep me from making a noise. I made no noise, but managed to slide off the other side of the bed and run to the cubicle where the night matron sat.

Her voice cracked out like a whip at the other woman, "You over there, get back in your own bed. D'ya hear me?" This woman was my one ally in the cell. Then she said to me, "You'll have to watch out. You're the new girl in here and you're fair game for everybody in the room."

As soon as I understood what she meant it ended my sleep for the night. The experience was one long nightmare. I couldn't sleep for fear of being assaulted, the first meal offered had a cockroach floating in it and after that I couldn't eat. Each time I had to use the toilet, others in the room would pull the curtain open, stand around, making obscene remarks and guffawing. And I was cold all the time. The muslin johnny coat gave me no protection against the February winds that came in around the cell windows, and there was only a single light cotton blanket on my bed.

I would never have believed how rapidly one could be stripped of ordinary human dignity. Suddenly I found myself behind locked doors, having exchanged my name for a number, being treated as a member of a community that society considered to be discards or threats. The next morning, the matron said the doctor wanted to see me. An involuntary shudder went through my body. Two guards came to the door and took me to a room where another man, who claimed to be a doctor, said he was concerned about my baby and needed to check to see that it was all right. Again I protested that I didn't think it was such a good idea, that my own doctor had stopped doing internal examinations a month ago and I had just been examined the day before. But this time my objection didn't have the force of anger behind it. I was resigned to whatever was going to happen, knowing I had no power to change it. "Around here you don't get to say what's a good idea and what isn't," he answered. "Please…" I said, begging with my words and my eyes. It was useless. Once again I was lifted onto the table and held down while the doctor probed and poked and the guards watched. When it was over and the guards had taken me back to the cell, I climbed onto the bed and sobbed. My baby's life was being threatened every day in this place and I was helpless to do anything about it.

In the afternoon I was told that yet another doctor needed to check me. There was another set of attendants who also wanted a look. The place was full of sadists! I was numb and knew that resistance was futile. I was sure I would lose the baby. I had no comb or brush or toothbrush and when I saw my reflection in one of the windows I was shocked. Not only was I unkempt and dirty but there was a vacant, lost look on my face, a look of despair. I was no longer sure of anything except that the repeated examinations must have done irreparable harm to the baby. Late that afternoon, the matron told me they would probably transfer me to Bellevue because they thought I might be in labor and they did not want to be responsible if anything went wrong. "But they *would* be responsible, they *would* be!" I cried out, my fury momentarily overcoming the helplessness. "If anything's wrong it will be because of all the probing and poking they've done over the last couple of days." The matron shrugged.

That evening, the matron told me I had a telephone call and led me down the hall to a phone. It was A. J. Muste. "Betty, are you all right?" "I don't know, A. J. Am I ever going to get out?" "That's why I'm calling. You're being released tomorrow morning." "They said they were taking me to Bellevue. Is that where I'm going?" "No, Betty," he said patiently, gently, "you're being released, freed. You can go home tomorrow. We've filed an appeal. You will be released tomorrow morning." I couldn't speak. Nor was I sure I believed him, much as I wanted to. I mumbled, "Thank you," hung up the phone and let the matron take me back to the cell.

Early the next morning a guard came to the cell, called out my number, then led me down to a room where I was given my clothes and told to dress. I could scarcely believe what was happening, but dressed quickly. The woman in charge handed me a paper and told me to sign it. It was a paper relieving the Women's House of Detention of responsibility for anything that might happen to me after my release. I was sure they were going to be responsible for me losing my baby but realized I had no more choice about signing it than I'd had about anything else over the past two days. When I had signed, the matron gave me my purse, three dollars and some change. She opened the big metal door, pushed me out onto the front steps and closed the door behind me.

Suddenly out on the street, it was as if I didn't know what had happened or what was supposed to happen next. But then I realized I was out. For a few minutes, as I looked up at the sky and drew a breath of fresh air, I was overwhelmed by a sense of gratitude. The world looked beautiful—even the dirty streets of the city. I had survived and was alive and free. The money given me was insufficient for cab fare but enough for a phone call. I called my reporter friend on the Springfield paper. She made arrangements with a friend in the city who agreed to pick me up and get me safely on a train.

There was an unreal quality about that ride home and about everything that happened for the next week. The relief I had felt on being released was only temporary. I couldn't let go of the horror and was fearful of what might have happened to the baby. I had no appetite and didn't want to be touched, either by Gerry or the children. The thought of sex was so repugnant that I even slept in the guest room and turned away any overtures. I wasn't willing to run the risk of Gerry taking me in the middle of the night, as he often did. Even though I hated that, he seemed to think it was his right as a husband. I remembered that my father joked about having to chase Mother around the house in order to "have his way with her," so I figured the call must be the man's to make.

Gerry took me to the doctor who checked my vital signs, listened to the baby's heart and said we both seemed okay. He took a specimen from my vagina and a blood sample to check further. He said I was in a state of shock, that I was having mild contractions and might deliver prematurely but that the baby seemed all right. He suggested that Gerry take me home and put me to bed for a week of complete rest. After a day in bed the contractions stopped.

As soon as I was able, I began talking, to any group that would listen, about conditions in the prison. Except for my cell matron, who was kind in an environment that did not require kindness, the others I encountered seemed to be overt sadists, with license to play out their fantasies. I could see no way that people would fail to come out of such an institution worse than they went in. A letter I wrote about the experience was published in *Fellowship,* the magazine of the Fellowship of Reconciliation, Bayard Rustin's organization.

Marjorie Fredericks had covered the demonstration and my imprisonment for the Springfield newspaper, and when I recovered she had me make a written record of the whole experience so it would not be lost. There was no danger. Those days in New York are as vivid to me as I write, as they were in 1957. That demonstration marked the end of my anti-war activity until October in my 83rd year when I marched in demonstrations against the Iraq war. I'm still confronted by the arrogance that made me subject myself and my baby to that ordeal. At the time of sentencing I had a choice of paying the fine, but chose not to, and then laid all the responsibility for my miserable experience on the system. I've wondered many times since, why that experience? What was I to learn from it? What did I learn? As a child, "righteousness" was a virtue to be cultivated; today I'm afraid that righteousness has turned into my greatest enemy.

Later I learned that our appeal had been denied, and because this was a federal offense, I would have a felony on my permanent court record. For years I was embarrassed by the notation, on the back of my driver's license, that I was a felon. When, as a result of having been turned down for jury duty, I inquired about having that record expunged, I was told that it would cost $750 so I let it go. The record is a barrier to my being President of the United States, but somehow I don't worry about that.

8

Back to Square One—A Single Mother Again

Marjorie Fredericks had told a friend that I was looking for work I could do at home, and the friend said she knew of just the thing, that she would introduce me to Lawrence Dennis, who was looking for someone to type and mail his weekly newsletter, *The Appeal to Reason.* Soon I began working with Lawrence. My first impression of him was of a very large rumpled professor with hair growing every which way, including out of his ears, and eyes that always seemed slightly amused and a little sad. I was told that he was an economist who had been an American diplomat and a "behind-the-scenes" advisor to some of the more prominent congressional critics of the Roosevelt administration and that he had been ruined by the Sedition Trial of 1944. That trial took place during the war when I was so absorbed in housekeeping and childcare, I knew nothing about it and not much more about the war except for what I learned in my Western Civilization course at Cornell. Working with Lawrence at this point in my life made sense to me.

As soon as the children started school I also took a part-time job at the United Way in Springfield, in addition to my work for Lawrence. At the United Way I met a visiting nurse who asked if I had thought of having my baby at home. She said that since I'd delivered three babies without complications, the chances were pretty good I could have a fourth successfully without all the intervention hospitals provide. She suggested I shop for a doctor who would be willing to be with me while I delivered at home. Then she recommended a book, *Childbirth Without Fear,* by Grantley Dick Read, which I promptly bought and started reading.

Finding a doctor who would go along with the plan was not easy. Most obstetricians were not willing to merely support a patient, but wanted to be in charge. Finally I found a local family practitioner who, influenced by his wife and nurse, agreed to come to the house for support and to help only if I asked.

My nurse friend had told me what I needed to do to get ready, so as soon as I was over the trauma of the jail experience, I began preparing. I made up bed pads from newspapers wrapped in pieces of old sheet, gathered diapers, gowns, receiving blankets for the baby, wrapped everything in aluminum foil and put it in the oven to sterilize it.

From reading Grantley Dick Read, I learned that an easy birth, such as young Jerry's, could be planned for and achieved. I learned about the autonomic nervous system and the flight or fight syndrome that is activated by the first major contraction in labor. It was easy to recognize what happened in my first two experiences of childbirth. My fear had prompted me to fight a battle I couldn't win. I studied and practiced breathing techniques and relaxation. I was excited because this time I understood what was happening in my body and was confident that I could have some influence on it.

On April 9th, 1957, Martha was born. I called the doctor at about eight in the morning although the contractions had started a few hours earlier. The doctor had to use snowshoes to reach the top of our hill because there had been a blizzard during the night, it was still snowing and the road had not been plowed. An hour or so later his wife, who was also his nurse, showed up. Once again I made sure we had an understanding about the doctor's role. He was there on a standby basis, not to intervene unless I was clearly in trouble and called for his intervention. I was determined to have this baby my way.

As soon as Gerry saw the doctor and realized I was in labor, he got sick. He spent most of the day running back and forth between the living room couch and the downstairs bathroom. He was the doctor's first patient and was given a sedative. It had been eleven years since my last child was born. The labor was long and difficult, but at no time did it approach the agonizing experience with Jan and Jill. To the contrary, it provided me with what I think of today as the peak experience of my life.

In the second stage of labor there was only a vague awareness of my surroundings and the activity around me. My rational consciousness was almost suspended. I functioned instinctively. I was immersed in, and part of, creativity. With each contraction, I was the universe contracting and expanding. There was only the process, of which I was a part. It was as if I, for a brief moment, were the focal point at which the whole universe was expressing itself and, at the next moment I disappeared and there was nothing but that universe.

During this time there was a prolonged experience of that elusive something I'd been aware of all my life, a sort of uncovering that allowed it to be present in all its beauty and vulnerability. When the experience had concluded I noticed that the word "reverence" came to mind, though at the time I couldn't have described what I meant by "reverence." In retrospect I realize it was reverence for that brief glimpse I'd had of the universal, of the eternal. Since that day, the elusive something has been with me. It remains hidden when I seek it but comes unbidden frequently and when least expected.

When the baby finally arrived, she greeted the world with a great howl, without being spanked. The doctor was impressed that she needed no help in taking that first breath. Her second action was to start suckling. I took her immediately and put her to my breast, even before the doctor cut the umbilical cord. She ate her fill, then fell quietly asleep on my chest. The other three children had been in and out of the room during my labor and were present at the birth. Kneeling by the bedside they were awed by the experience and Jan had tears on her cheeks. "It was so beautiful, Momma."

I smiled at her. All I could say was, "Yes it was, darling, it was beautiful," even though that was so inadequate to describe what I had just been through. I named the new baby Martha Elizabeth as a tribute to my friendship with Martha Lopez. Gerry made no complaint about the sex of this child. He adored her from the first. After the birth, as I rested, consciousness sharpened and my feeling of individuality returned. I thought *about* what had been happening, but I was no longer *of* the experience. My conscious, rational reflection on this event has never approached the reality of it. It was as if I were a part of something much larger than what was happening in that room.

Remembering the birth of Janis, in 1943, and my two-week bed rest I was amused to realize that I was up and showering that afternoon and the next day was back at work, running the mimeograph machine and turning out the latest issue of *The Appeal to Reason*, in between sessions of nursing the baby.

Ever since we re-married Gerry had been looking for a house to buy and in the summer of 1957 he found what he wanted, in Southwick, and bought it. I hadn't seen the house until we moved in. It was in a new development and had the extra space Gerry felt we needed with another child.

It also had lots of gimmicks that fascinated Gerry, such as a master switch panel in our bedroom from which we could turn on or off any light in the house or start the coffee pot in the morning. The doorbell was connected to a grandfather clock so every time someone pressed the doorbell we got a concert. It wasn't a house I would have chosen but Gerry had found it and was delighted with it.

He did try to make things work, but he still had terrible migraine headaches and a fierce temper. Often the two coincided and when they did anything could happen. In Southwick, his relationship with Jill again became explosive. He had no patience with her and she had a knack for provoking him. I can never remember what prompted the incidents but they happened. One evening they were shouting at each other, she hurled an insult at him and he chased her up the stairs.

She locked herself in her room and he threatened to break the door down. She climbed out onto the porch roof, jumped to the ground and ran to a neighbor's house. The neighbor kept her overnight to give Gerry time to cool down. When she returned the next day they both acted as if nothing had happened. On another occasion she was running to a neighbor when he caught up with her and dragged her back to the house by her pony tail, as she stumbled along backward, screaming at him.

In the midst of all this he was incredibly gentle with the new baby. When he was feeling mean and wanted to hurt the older children he would say that he had only one child, little Martha, that the rest of them were their mother's. But when he was trying, he did thoughtful things such as buying Jerry a pony, and Jilly the thoroughbred cocker spaniel she wanted in order to start a kennel.

Jan was away at school. She had started attending a Quaker school, The Meeting School in Rindge, New Hampshire, the fall after Martha was born. The Agawam school principal had suggested that we find a school where Janis would be challenged, and the Meeting School offered her a full scholarship. When things were rough at home I often wrote to her but she had little sympathy for me. She had not approved of this second marriage.

One morning when young Jerry failed to do some assigned chore, his father slammed out of the house muttering. That night he came home from work and announced that he had sold the pony, that it was gone, delivered to the new owner. I couldn't believe what I was hearing, then I looked at little Jerry. His face was ashen. He left the dinner table without saying a word, went down to the cellar. My heart was racing and, in order to avoid an outburst in front of the other children, I took a few minutes to calm down. Then I went down cellar to where Jerry was sitting in the old rocking chair, rocking furiously and crying. He turned away from me and shook his head. He didn't want me or anyone else. He was beyond consolation and, although I went down several times during the evening, he refused to come up, and spent the night in the cellar. Throughout the night I would waken to hear the creak of that rocking chair and would quietly weep for my little boy. The incident was never mentioned again.

When Jan came home from school the following summer it was evident that the situation was hopeless. I watched the faces of the youngsters when their father made a cutting or sarcastic remark and knew I had done them no favor by bringing them back into this situation. I had pretty much decided to leave but was feeling a terrible sense of failure. In this marriage he had not been violent with me. But he was cruel to the older children. I also knew that his migraine headaches almost incapacitated him and when he was gripped by one of those I felt enormous compassion for the guy. When I could stand back and look impartially, I suspected Gerry didn't like himself very much—he made no effort to take care of himself. He didn't exercise, ate poorly, and was a chain smoker—a combination of things that led to his death of heart failure at the age of fifty-four.

One day while Gerry was at work I drove to Northampton and looked for an apartment. It had to be done before my resolve weakened because, in spite of everything, I thought I still loved the man. He was the only man with whom I had shared the daily intimacies of marriage, he was the father of my four children. I wanted to believe that, insofar as he was capable, he loved us. The last day, Gerry, smoking one cigarette after another, pleaded with me to stay. He said he was sure we could work it out, he never meant to hurt the kids, it was just his quick temper. He said perhaps if we all took a trip, we could get back together. I knew he believed what he was saying and that he was hurting. I also knew it had been arrogant of me to think that I could make this relationship work and that I was stupid to have jumped back into the marriage a second time. While we talked in the house, Jan and the kids were already in the car out front. Finally Jan honked the horn and yelled, "Come on, Mother, or we'll leave without you!" I went.

An hour later I was standing, holding the baby, on the sloping porch of a two-story plum-colored frame house in Northampton. The older children were peeking in the living room windows of the flat, which was to be our new home. As Jan fitted the key into the front-door lock, I thought, "My God! Here I am again. Back to square one!" Yet almost immediately that thought was followed by another as I looked down at little Martha in my arms: "Another beautiful child!" I was filled with a strange contentment and a knowing that it would all turn out. I didn't need to understand how.

I had no idea how I was going to support the family because I was nursing the baby and was unwilling to go out to work. This was the first of my four babies that I had been able to nurse and I wasn't about to miss the opportunity. Gerry's response to our leaving was to refuse child support until such time as he was ordered by the court to pay it. Thinking back to this time, and to the earlier divorce, I realize that neither time did I ask for alimony. As difficult as it may be to believe today, I didn't even know it was an option.

In the summer of 1958 we were poor. I knew Dad would help if I asked but this time I felt so much guilt that I wouldn't call on him. I managed to pay the rent out of money I had saved but there were days when there simply was no money for food. Our landlady lived in the upstairs apartment and often she came down after they had finished dinner and held out a pan. She would say, "We had more than we could eat tonight and you know how I am about leftovers." I knew that she had cooked more than they would eat so that she could bring some to us. Every time Martha Lopez came to Northampton she brought us vegetables from her garden. I had not told my mother how bad it was but whenever she came up to see us she brought something. One time it was a case of canned tuna. The kids and I laugh even today remembering how often we ate tuna fish that summer and fall. The older three won't eat my tuna casserole even today.

In August, Lawrence Dennis came to the rescue. He was at work on his latest book, *Operational Thinking for Survival*, and asked if I would type for him. I talked the bank into lending me enough money to buy an IBM typewriter and set myself up in the kitchen. Every day Lawrence brought his work to our Northampton apartment. He sat on our couch in the living room with his manuscript, his drink of Scotch in milk, and his pipe that seemed often to need tamping even though he rarely drew on it. He had some very special mixture of tobacco in a leather zipped case that he kept in his vest pocket. He was smitten with Martha. She would crawl all over him and call him "Lala." He kept on writing even when she played with the hair sticking out of his ears. He never scolded her or told her to get down. He seemed delighted to have the attention of this little girl. He said it kept him in touch with why he wanted our country to be true to its promise. I was awash with tenderness as I looked at the two of them on the couch—Martha exploring this big unusual fellow and he pretending to go on with his work while a gentle smile played on his lips. Sometimes when I was nursing her he would set aside his work and just watch. He said he had never seen a woman nursing a child and was moved.

Lawrence was staying at the Northampton Inn and most evenings that we were working he would take me down there for dinner. It was during those dinners that I learned about the Sedition Trial of 1944 and his role in it. As he talked I realized that this man who looked like a big old teddy bear and sat so deeply on my couch that the springs almost touched the floor was really a man of history. In 1938 the House Un-American Activities Committee had been established to investigate Nazi and Communist propaganda, and it was that committee's activities that were responsible for the arrest and trial of the more than thirty Americans charged in the Sedition Trial. Lawrence, his book, *Dynamics of War and*

Revolution, and his newsletter, *Weekly Foreign Letter*, were all included in the indictment as was testimony that he had copies of *Mein Kampf* and the *Communist Manifesto* in his library. The indictment charged the defendants with being part of a conspiracy orchestrated by Adolph Hitler to undermine the morale of the American military during wartime. According to the record, Lawrence stood up in court and spoke for the defense, calling the government's case, "corny, false, fantastic, untrue, unprovable and unsound." He described the trial as a Roosevelt administration fourth-term conspiracy and declared, "Pearl Harbor did not suspend the Bill of Rights." With the death of the Sedition Trial's presiding judge, Judge Eichner, the whole thing ended in a mistrial and was never retried. But the Subversive Activities Control Act and the Communist Control Act (1954) were used by Senator Joseph McCarthy to label many as Communist sympathizers, and continue the harassment of people who were not Communists.

The Communist scare was so great in this country, and the McCarthy witch hunt so virulent that when I wrote a paper on the "First Fifty Years of Communism in China," for a course at Smith College in 1958, and sent it to my Cornell advisor, Knight Biggerstaff, he thanked me and sent it back hurriedly, saying it would be unwise for that paper to be found in his possession.

The people charged in the Sedition Trial never received compensation for their mistreatment and expense, much less any official acknowledgment that the government had made a serious mistake. Lawrence's finances and his reputation were ruined by the litigation, and for the remainder of his life, his newsletter, *The Appeal to Reason* (replacing his *Weekly Foreign Letter*) was read by only the small group who remained loyal to him. He was never vindicated despite the *Washington Post*'s claim that this was "a black mark against American justice," and the federal court's declaration that it was a "travesty upon justice."

When the book we were working on, *Operational Thinking for Survival*, was published, Jim Martin, The Institute for Historical Review's editorial advisor described Lawrence as, "one of the few native Americans who has done any really original political thinking since the time of John C. Calhoun....The book airs the views that led the Roosevelt regime to muzzle Dennis in its infamous 1944 Sedition Trial." As I worked with Lawrence and came to know him I was enraged that our government was responsible for such atrocities as this trial, the earlier assault on Japanese-Americans as represented by Manzanar, and the deportation of Alex Wang among the Chinese students who had been invited here. My association with Lawrence Dennis contributed to my growing social consciousness by teaching me that discrimination and prejudice are not only confined to race but can be applied to anyone whose ideas stray from the accepted.

9

From Hippie Mother to Professor's Wife

My Cornell experience had shown me that I was a whole human being—that I was intelligent, could do college work, could keep up with the eighteen-year olds—so as soon as we were settled in Northampton, I jumped right back into the academic world and enrolled in a class in modern Chinese history at Smith College. By spring I knew that I wanted to go back to school full-time and had to find a way to make that possible. I applied to the University of Massachusetts, where I could attend at the resident-tuition rate. At first it looked as if I might not be accepted because of my "eclectic" background, but I appealed to the Chancellor. He looked over my records, smiled at me and issued a waiver on my behalf, saying, "We need more generalists." I had to make up work because at Cornell I had carried only twelve hours each semester and completed only three semesters. But it didn't matter how much I had to make up. I was studying because I so loved learning. In the fall of 1959 I began full-time study at the University, taking Martha to a woman in town for childcare. (By this time Gerry had been ordered by the court to pay fifty dollars a week in child support so we were a little better off.)

Jan was home from boarding school and also planning to attend the University, so we began looking for a place to live closer to Amherst. One day as we drove along the Connecticut River in Sunderland we spotted a big yellow house with a welcoming front porch, a house that seemed to say, "Come fix me up. I'm a nice old house and I've been empty too long." It had charm, lots of room and a spectacular location, just across Old Sunderland Road from the river and alongside a picturesque waterfall. We inquired around the neighborhood and learned that the house belonged to a family living in New York. The house next door, on the other side of the waterfall, belonged to the owner's brother who said it might be possible to rent the house if we made no demands on the owner to fix it up.

So what if we had only cold water from a single faucet in a black slate sink in the kitchen; so what if it looked as though we could expect no heat in the winter out of that old furnace; so what if the place had obviously been neglected for years. I had been through the renovation process with the Samuel Lane House and was not daunted. It was an adventure and the kids and I all saw it as fun. We rented it, for seventy-five dollars a month, and began immediately to clean it up. It felt more like home than anywhere we had lived since Northfield. If I close my eyes I can still see Janis, with a sledge hammer, banging away to knock down the wall between the kitchen and the pantry. She had plaster in her hair and pieces of lath were flying. The pantry had windows that Jan and I thought should be in the kitchen.

When we cleared the path that led down to the river we discovered a thirty-foot ledge of rock at the shore, a perfect place to picnic, sunbathe and swim. At the bottom of the waterfall, between our house and our neighbor's, a stream ran under a small bridge, down another fall, around some trees and emptied into the river on the back side of the rock ledge.

Jerry was the only one who did much swimming from the rock. The current was so swift that you could be several hundred feet down river by the time you surfaced from a dive and it was a real challenge to swim back. The rest of us were content to sit on the rock and hang our feet in the water. Occasionally we would brave the river by swimming upstream and letting the river carry us back down to the rock. Sometimes three-year-old Martha and I would lie on the rock with our hands in the water, wondering how that water, seemingly so soft, could wear away the rock. Sometimes we sat with our legs dangling in the river and, as we did, I would think back to the days on the breakwater with my father. Along the path to the river were magnificent ferns and we learned that in the spring the emergent ferns, called "fiddleheads," were an edible delicacy. Often we went out with a basket, picked enough for dinner, then steamed and served them with melted butter.

Up the road in back of the house we could walk off into a wooded area and find wild flowers and small animals. Martha and I would walk into the woods and sit on a log waiting for a squirrel or a rabbit to come up and investigate. We learned that if we were really quiet—not talking or moving—these small animals would come closer and closer until it was almost as if we were all wondering about each other. In the late fall we gathered ground pine and red berries to make wreaths and berry bowls for gifts. Our first winter we tapped the giant maple trees in the yard, collected the sap and boiled it down in the kitchen. We all loved pancakes with maple syrup and had never had the fun of making our own syrup.

It was a good thing the kitchen was so primitive, however, because the steam from the hours of boiling sap removed whatever wallpaper was left on the old walls.

It was a time of peace and healing for me. My second failure with Gerry Quigley had left me with a question about my ability to relate as well as grave doubts about my own worth. I was pleased not to have to be in social situations that first year. When I was not in class, I read and listened to music, walked in the woods and sat by the river, and I wrote. Writing had always been a way of expressing myself when I was lonely but in Sunderland it became more. I took photographs of the beauty around us and began writing essays about exploring the area with Martha, intending to eventually create a photo essay of the Connecticut River Valley.

After satisfying the University's requirements for graduation I focused on philosophy courses. I read in phenomenology and existentialism and took courses in logic. I couldn't get enough. Clarence Shute, Chairman of the Philosophy Department, became my adviser. He was a remarkable teacher but one who brooked no nonsense.

The first day in class when he introduced himself and the course he said, "There are only a couple of things you need to know about the way I conduct a class. One is that when I give you a due date for a paper, *that* is the date it is due. It is due in class *that* day, not the next week, not the next day, not the next hour, but in class on the date due. The other thing you need to know is that if you fail to get your paper in when it is due, you will get a zero and there will be no discussion. Are you clear about both of these points? If not, then raise any questions you may have now because this is the last time we'll discuss it."

I approved of this man already and knew I would like working with him. But I was one of the few who felt that way. The room was silent but when class was dismissed, the grumbling and moaning could be heard all the way down the corridor. He was true to his word. After the first paper's due date there were fewer people in the course.

Also I reveled in his method of teaching. He used myths and fables that had been told throughout history to illustrate obscure religious doctrines, he used analogy to help us understand complex philosophical points. There were two kinds of students who dropped out, or were dropped, from his courses—those who were late and those who looked on his myths and fables as storytelling for children and who wanted to argue with his approach. It was the time when academic philosophy was moving into language analysis and scientific philosophy, and students who embraced those approaches did not like addressing the age-old questions to which Clarence Shute was committed. He was a firm believer in the Socratic dictum that "the unexamined life is not worth living" and challenged all of us to see the value in examining our own lives.

My introduction to Asian thought left me with more questions than answers and it stirred up something that had been dormant for almost twenty years—my Christian upbringing. Suddenly I was learning that other religions had quite different views about God—views that were far more acceptable to me than those with which I had been raised. In Hindu texts I read that Brahman is the essence of all we are and all we know—the inner power of all that is. God and Self are one and the same. This was a far cry from the censoring, censuring God of my childhood, the God who was always looking over my shoulder, seeing everything I was doing, knowing my every thought, waiting to punish me at the end of my life. I experienced an enormous relief in letting go of the anthropomorphic God with whom I had grown up. While reading, I also wondered about Satan. Was the Christian God not big enough to accommodate both good and evil so that evil had to be personified and banished to an underworld? I'd always had trouble with the idea of hell as a place. I seemed capable of making my own hell as I went through life. The more I studied and the more I read, the more sense it made and the more freedom I experienced. Then, of course, I wanted to study even more, to use that freedom to continue to explore. It was at this point I decided that religious dogma was a result of people's inability to live with mystery, with not knowing. I neither wanted, nor needed, an explanation for the experience I had during communion, or during Martha's birth, and knew that no explanation would be adequate. I honored the mystery.

Then in the fall of 1960 I took a course called "Mysticism and Philosophy" at Mount Holyoke. The University of Massachusetts was part of a Five-College Consortium which also included Amherst College, Smith College, Mt. Holyoke and Hampshire College. This made it possible for a student at any of the colleges to register for courses at any of the others. The course I took at Mt. Holyoke was being taught by Walter Stace, a visiting professor who had just retired from his position as Stuart Professor of Philosophy at Princeton University. Before joining the faculty at Princeton, in 1932, he had been with the British civil service in Ceylon for twenty-two years. Stace had written books on mysticism. In his lectures he compared reports of mystical experiences to reports of controlled drug experiences. He pointed out that the differences in these two appeared not to be in the experiences themselves, or in the psychological aspects of those experiences, but in the ways they were interpreted. I was fascinated to discover how similar his "introvertive mystical experiences" seemed to my experience during Martha's birth.

This, then, set me off into more study of mysticism. The outcome was my discovery that the common denominator of all mystical experience, however realized, was the feeling of oneness or unity with all of life, or with God where theistic terminology was used to describe the experience. Most mystics, and those who had studied the experience of mystics, said that the experience itself pointed to a momentary illuminating, a powerful sense of identification. It might yield the conviction of something of infinite worth, but most did not insist on that something being "other." It was as if human being was momentarily exploded, and in the brilliance of that explosion saw his/her one-ness with all that is. I knew I'd had such an experience.

Clarence Shute had told us that whereas Western philosophy began with curiosity about the world out there, Eastern philosophy began with a need to understand pain and suffering. I appreciated that because I was struggling to understand myself and my life. I remember a discussion we had about death with one student asking why we were doing that. Mr. Shute said one reason was to rid death of its stigma, another was to allow us to recognize that some of us were the living dead. He said it wasn't death that defeated or destroyed life but rather meaninglessness. If we lived our lives being pushed this way and that, simply reacting to outside influences, then we were allowing the defeat of life. He asked us why we would skim along on the surface of life instead of penetrating, and suggested it might be like the fear of going through doors into dark rooms—we are threatened by not knowing what's there. But if we confronted that fear, by choosing it, we could live authentically and make something of our lives. This experience at the University continued the development of an intellect I didn't know I had until I went to Cornell. It was a time of clear thinking, examining presuppositions, being active in my life and reflecting on that life. It was a sort of coming of age, of knowing myself as a thinking adult.

In the winter of 1960, life in Sunderland was primarily about survival. Every day after school Jerry chopped wood or shoveled snow. Several times during the winter the kitchen water pipes froze, only to flood the kitchen when we succeeded in thawing them. The first time it happened, we all sat down in the middle of the kitchen floor and laughed ourselves silly, then acknowledged that it might have been wise to call the plumber to thaw the pipes for us. And, as we had expected, the one-pipe furnace was not up to heating the whole house, so we spent the winter bundled up in sweaters and extra socks. But it was a beautiful winter for photography and I made the most of it. Some of the best pictures I've ever taken were made in Sunderland that winter.

If there's one thing that most parents recognize and dread, it is the phone call in the middle of the night. My first such call came in the summer of 1961 when the Northampton police phoned to tell me that Jan had been in an accident, that she was in the hospital and her passenger had been killed. I drove to the hospital in a daze, without knowing how seriously hurt she was or who the passenger had been.

Jan had gotten off work at the Northampton A&W late that night and pulled into a station to get some gas. The service station attendant said to her, "Look, this young serviceman is trying to get up north. You're going his way, do you mind giving him a ride?" Jan said, "No, of course not." He got in and they rode off, but as soon as they were out on the road away from town he reached over and began fondling her. She told him to stop and he didn't. It was late at night and the road from Northampton to Sunderland had almost no traffic on it so there was no way of attracting the attention of someone who might have helped. At that point Jan remembered a story I had once told the kids about being in a similar situation. I told them I had said to the guy, "Keep your hands off me! You'd better watch it!" He didn't pay any attention but seemed to figure he had me in a spot where I couldn't resist. My response was to step on the gas and get the car up to eighty or ninety, at which point he pulled away, grabbed the door and cried out, "God, lady, you're going to kill us. Let me out!" I slowed down just enough for him to jump out and then I raced off.

Jan was driving our Volkswagen convertible with the top down. She said she remembered my story and had started to speed up when, on a curve, she met an on-coming trailer truck with its lights on high beam. Momentarily blinded she lost control of the car, went off the road and turned over. She was thrown clear of the car and slid on her back on the highway. Her passenger, the hitchhiker, was killed instantly. My relief at Jan having survived was tempered by the recognition that another mother somewhere had lost a son. It was also tempered by knowing that my story might have been responsible for this tragedy. I had never been so keenly aware of how much influence a parent may have on the actions of a child. Talking with Jan in the hospital I comforted her as best I could, but it was a long time before she was able to rid herself of the guilt of that night.

By my last year at the University, my faith in myself, and others, had been restored and our house was known to be open and welcoming. There was always someone visiting for an evening or crashing for the night. The kids amusedly spoke of having a "hippie" mother. It was that time and the campus abounded with long-haired young men and longer-haired young women. I often went to the campus coffee shop to hear Buffy St. Marie, also a philosophy major, play and sing. Tony Sherrod was one of those who sometimes hung out at our house and I went to hear him read his poetry to jazz. Later, Tony left Amherst to go to San Francisco to be near Ferlinghetti, his role model. Jerry gave me a Miles Davis record for Christmas that year and told me to let go and dance. I took him up on it and when no one was around I would shed my inhibitions and my clothes and just go with the music. At about the same time I got a pair of drumsticks and went around the Sunderland house drumming on the furniture and the windowsills. These were enormously freeing experiences but I couldn't help thinking that my Puritan ancestors must have been turning in their graves.

At the beginning of my senior year, I began to date Milton, a sociology professor. I knew the relationship had no future. I didn't much like him but, in a condescending fashion, I thought of him as a fill-in, a stop-gap measure, someone to go out with until the right one came along. Then, in the 1962 spring semester, the right one did come along.

Janis was enrolled in a Sophomore Honors Colloquium moderated by a Professor Sargent Russell. In February, he started driving her home after class. Although I thought it was generous of him, I disapproved and quietly questioned his motives. She told me that he was recently divorced and had seven children, so I knew he was too old for her. And it seemed odd that he would drive fifteen miles out of his way night after night just to be kind to a student. I could understand his interest in Jan. She was lovely, mature for her age and was a brilliant student but if, as it seemed, he was being more than kind, it was inappropriate and there was no way I was going to let her get into that kind of situation. She assured me I had nothing to worry about, that she was going up to Middlebury to Winter Carnival in a couple of weeks at the invitation of her young man. But I did worry and at the end of the month told her I was going to call her professor at his office and have a talk with him. She asked me not to do that, saying she would introduce us one of these nights.

The next time he brought her home, they arrived to see me trying to help Milton get his car out of the snow. Professor Russell got out of his car and offered to help. Despite the sweater cap he had pulled down over his ears, I couldn't help notice that he was a good looking guy—a little over six feet tall, slender, with a distinguished look about him. When I tried to tell him how to get the car unstuck, he politely but firmly told me he knew what he was doing. And he did. The car was out in less than five minutes. Thanking him, I said, "You must come out and have dinner with us some evening." The invitation was one of those polite gestures we make with no other intention. "When?" he asked. I was caught off balance but then realized it would give me the opportunity I wanted, to tell him he was too old for my daughter, so I said, "How about Sunday night?"

And Sunday it was. He came all shined up, wearing highly pressed slacks and a Harris tweed jacket, and looking most attractive. He was so confident, so sure of himself, so masculine and so good looking—sandy hair above a high forehead, a crooked smile that curved up a little on the left side, that patrician nose, and eyes that bored right through me. We had a pleasant meal and by the time it was over he was no longer "Professor Russell," but "Sarge." Throughout the meal I kept looking at, and admiring his hands which were tanned and well manicured. And he was charming. I was impressed. After dinner we went into the parlor. Sarge sat on the couch, with Jan next to him, and I sat across the room. But it was as if Sarge and I were the only ones in the room. We talked for hours and when he left I knew I was going to marry the guy and I did, three weeks later. It was the same instinctive reaction I'd had when I met Gerry the first time. I might have had some questions for Sarge—about his first marriage, about his seven children, about my plans for graduate study—but they not only were not asked, they didn't even come up for me. It was that intuitive certainty I experience every once in a while. Even though the outcome may not always be what I expect, I believe the outcomes are what I am meant to experience; even my going to jail was what I was meant to do, it had a purpose, whether or not I knew that purpose.

He called on Monday to thank me for the evening and to invite me out to dinner on Wednesday. After accepting the invitation I hung up the phone, jumped up and down and whooped with delight. We went to the Northampton Inn and I sat across the table from him, looking into his eyes and feeling as if I had found my other half. With this man I had all those stirrings in my body but none of the guilt or misgivings I'd had both times with Gerry. This was one my mother would approve of (and she did). By the end of the week we had spent a night together and he had brought to dinner five of his seven kids—Ed, Jon, Timothy, Nancy, Betsy. His eldest son, Pete, was no longer living at home and the oldest daughter, Judy, was in college. I became close to Betsy, Ed, Nancy and Tim while they were growing up and later came to know Judy. Tim and Martha were so near in age and looked so much alike that the next summer when we took them to the park for fireworks, the ticket taker asked if they were twins.

In March of 1962, we were married in Connecticut, as Sarge couldn't legally marry in Massachusetts. He had been adjudged the guilty party in his divorce from Evelyn and wasn't legally allowed to marry in Massachusetts for two years. Mother and Dad were not well enough to attend the ceremony but that ceremony was, after all, only a few words in front of a notary public. I do remember the morning we were to drive to Connecticut. I was afraid it was all a dream, I was sure he wouldn't show up, that I would get a phone call with an excuse. But suddenly there he was, pulling his car into the driveway in Sunderland.

Sarge's mother had flown up from New York to represent the parents (his father had died in 1954). Mother Russell wasn't sure that Sarge had made enough of an effort to reconcile with Evelyn and was a little distant with me, but before long we were good friends. She could see how much happier Sarge was. James and Inez Fuller, my Quaker friends, drove down with us to be our witnesses and two of Sarge's close friends joined us. It was a small but joyful occasion. People who knew Sarge were aware of how unhappy he'd been in his marriage. But, in spite of his unhappiness, he had been terribly dismayed when Evie filed for divorce. Sarge thought she never really wanted to divorce him but only wanted to punish him, teach him a lesson. Knowing he couldn't remarry in Massachusetts for two years, he said, she thought he'd be coming back and pleading with her long before the time was up. But, he met me and that was it.

We had a honeymoon to remember. We drove down to a Rhode Island beach, spent hours walking the shore and getting to know each other. It was like a dream—the dream I'd always had of what a honeymoon would be.

The Amherst newspaper had a field day with the announcement, "University Professor Marries Student," making no mention of the fact that this student was only a few years younger than the professor. When Sarge came, many things changed in Sunderland. Evenings of listening to poetry in the Amherst coffee house were over, drop-ins were less welcome at the house and even when we had invited guests, at a certain point in the evening, Sarge would start unbuttoning his shirt and say, "You're welcome to stay as long as you please but I'm going to bed." The guests rarely stayed on. The light tone of the house changed. One evening when John from my creative writing class came to the house, Sarge invited him to help with crushing berries for elderberry wine and that was the last we saw of John. Sarge was not welcoming to the odd and assorted people who dropped into the house in Sunderland. Sometimes, as with John, he was sarcastic, sometimes just rude. Although it took me a few months to realize it, I was making a transition from being a hippie mother to a professor's wife.

Later I would come to resent some of these changes, but at the time they seemed a small price to pay for marriage to this great guy. Sarge was at the peak of his academic career. He had been nominated several times for a teacher-of-the-year award. His wit and intellect were well known and his colleagues said he sometimes used that wit like a stiletto, particularly with his dean. This may have accounted for the fact that despite his ratings, he remained at the associate professor level for many years, getting his promotion to full professor after twenty-five years on the faculty and nine years after we married. Being at faculty parties was a far cry from being in the student union feeling like an outsider. Sarge was friendly, outgoing, seemed to know everyone, and was a great dancer. I felt quite at home with his colleagues. Being on the campus with Sarge meant meeting for lunch, going bowling, sometimes just walking around the campus. He had been at the University for twenty years and was well known on campus. I liked this change of status.

The first time we went to New York to meet Sarge's family I learned that he had been head of the University of Maine's chapter of Students for a Democratic Society (SDS) and that he had refused to take part in World War II, working in agriculture for the duration of the war. Sarge had six siblings, most of whom lived in or near New York City, and weekends in New York were weekends of drinking whiskey sours, arguing, and playing bridge, all done in great good spirits. The political arguments were only varying shades of left because all of Sarge's siblings were Democrats leaning toward socialism. Martin, Sarge's brother, wrote letters to the *New York Times* which, his wife said, "were so far to the left they would fall off the page." And, for most of them, the Unitarian Church was their bow to religion, although Mother Russell used to laughingly chide Sarge and John as being the only anti-Semites of her children, all the others having married Jews. Learning about Sarge and his family confirmed that I had made a good choice of husband this time.

Three months after our marriage, I received my B.A. from the University, with honors in philosophy. I was accepted for graduate study, with fellowships, at the University of Rochester, at Radcliffe, and at Wesleyan. I was thrilled at receiving these offers of fellowships but immediately realized I wouldn't be able to take advantage of them. Sarge was an associate professor at the University of Massachusetts and I wasn't going anywhere. I applied for admission as a master's degree candidate at the university. The resentment came when I learned that no financial aid was available to me at the university and that, instead of being supported by a fellowship, I would have to continue working in order to study. Sarge had child support to pay, and was not in a position to pay tuition for me. I was determined to go on, however, and applied for a graduate assistantship with the Department of Philosophy.

I liked being married to Sarge. Perhaps it would be more accurate to say that I just liked being married. I loved him and yet always felt that there was a part of him he wasn't sharing, just as there was part of me I wasn't sharing with him.

Once again, sex left me wanting. I loved the intimacy, but was always expecting more. Many nights I was wide awake, staring at the ceiling, when Sarge's snoring told me he was asleep. Both of us had New England backgrounds that got in the way. When it seemed as if we might be expressing ourselves fully, he would withdraw, then laughingly concede that his mother had told him, "Don't be a rooster!" I seemed unable to tell him what I wanted. And we did have other adjustments to make. Martha had been sleeping with me ever since my divorce from Gerry, at which time she was two. It was a comfort for both of us. But when Sarge came he was, understandably, adamant about the privacy of our bedroom and wasn't willing to have me wean her gradually from the practice of sleeping with me. Night after night she would be put into her own bed but then would creep silently back into our bed, only to be carried off kicking and screaming. Often she was not the only one in tears.

Sarge was, at heart, a farmer who earned his living as a professor. We had been married in March and almost immediately he started turning the south yard into a garden. I can still taste the peas we ate without cooking, and the corn that Sarge waited to pick until the cooking water was boiling. He planted fruit trees and berry bushes and we made wine from the dandelions in the front yard and the elderberries from the bushes on the hill in back. His garden was more than his hobby, it was his escape from anything he didn't want to confront. He would go out into his garden for hours, stripped to the waist, working up a sweat, planting or hoeing. By the time he came in from this workout and had taken a shower, he would be his pleasant self again, his moodiness dissipated.

The summer of 1962 was an at-home summer, although we did take a week to go to the Quaker summer conference. Sarge loved the old Sunderland house as much as I did and we spent many evenings and weekends working on restoring it. All of us were comfortable in the old house and were glad when the landlord agreed to sell it to us. Jerry and I began designing what would eventually be a combination kitchen-family room or "great room." It was my first awareness of Jerry's talent for design which would come into play later in his life. We were going to put a fireplace in the corner where the old wood stove had been and a picture window in the back wall of the house that would let us look out onto the bank of wild flowers and stone steps that led up the hill. When the work was finished, I put a small table in front of the window where I might sit shelling peas and watching the squirrels. In the working area of the kitchen I had bins built into some of the drawer space so I could have large quantities of flour and sugar easily ready for baking. In the garage attic, we found some logs that had been there a hundred years or so, since the lumber mill had been torn down, and out of those logs we fashioned a mantel for the fireplace and window sills wide enough to hold plants.

Sarge and I stripped varnish from the banister on the front hall stairs and refinished the beautiful cherry wood underneath. We discovered clear white pine under the painted wood trim around the doors and windows. It was painstakingly slow work but the results were rewarding. I loved that house—the only house I have loved in my life.

In the fall I started my master's degree program. With Clarence Shute as my champion I was given a job as graduate assistant. I had a little office in the basement of one of the buildings on campus and spent hours each week reading and grading papers from introductory philosophy classes. While I pursued my interest in Asian thought and its challenge to my religious tradition, I broadened my study to include Western critics of that tradition—Ludwig Feuerbach and Friedrich Nietzsche. At Professor Shute's suggestion I read Ludwig Feuerbach's *Essence of Christianity* and realized I was not destined for eternal damnation. Suddenly I knew why my Sunday school teachers had insisted on faith and said that doubting was the greatest sin. Through Feuerbach I came to see religion as a useful vehicle, like the ferry boat of Buddhism where the ferryboat represents the practice for reaching the shore of enlightenment. When the ferryboat reaches the far shore, all the distinctions disappear—there is no near shore, no ferryboat, no far shore.

Before starting to work on my thesis, I had to pass an oral examination. That examination was scheduled for a weekday noon. I had been worrying about it for days and on that morning I was almost frantic. Sarge said he would take me to lunch and help me forget but I declined, saying I was too uptight to eat anything. He said we wouldn't have to eat but he did want to meet me at the student union. When I arrived he took me downstairs to the bowling alley. I thought he must be kidding but he said, "No, I'm not kidding. This is the best thing you could be doing right now." And he was right. We bowled several strings and I was so intent on beating him that I almost forgot the exam and had to run across campus to be there on time. And I aced the exam!

My love of, and work with, philosophy was not something I could share with Sarge. His teaching of economics and statistics seemed in a different realm. It was almost as if we spoke a different language and, after a few disappointing attempts, we gave up trying to understand each other's work. My papers came back from Professor Shute with in-depth comments and acknowledgement of my work. The level of communication I had with Professor Shute was something I had been longing for all my life without knowing it. I first had an inkling of it when Gordon Pyper told me his story. It was a dimension of myself that was nurtured at Cornell and at the University of Massachusetts by Professor Clarence Shute, a dimension which, sadly, I was not able to share with Sarge, nor one that I've been able to share with others to whom I've been close throughout my life.

10

Culture Shock and Adventure in Ankara, Turkey

In May of 1964, Jerry turned eighteen, registered for the draft as a conscientious objector and shortly afterward was called into service to train as a paramedic. Our summers with the Quakers at Avon had helped him define himself and although he opposed the Vietnam War, as we all did, he felt he had to do something.

At about the same time, Sarge was appointed a Fulbright professor, assigned to Ankara, Turkey. This was the fulfillment of his dream of traveling which, as the father of seven, had been impossible until his divorce freed him from major responsibility for the children.

I knew nothing about the Fulbright program when he applied for an overseas teaching position. The Fulbright is a program of the U.S. Bureau of Educational and Cultural Affairs which provides grants for graduate students, scholars, professionals, teachers and administrators to work abroad, with the goal of bringing a little more knowledge, a little more reason, and a little more compassion into the American approach to world affairs. When Sarge applied, he had no knowledge of where he might be offered a position but when the offer was for Turkey we were both pleased. This was a part of the world neither of us knew.

We sailed out of New York, with Sarge's sixteen-year-old Betsy and my seven-year-old Martha accompanying us. Betsy was the only one of Sarge's who was interested in going with us and my other kids were grown and on their own. The trip across the Atlantic, on the Cristophero Columbo, was a dream crossing. We had perfect weather and spent most days on deck or in the pool. Betsy and Martha got better acquainted and Sarge and I had hours of relaxing together. It was a good thing because, in Turkey, I was to experience a profound culture shock. I would find myself face to face with who I was by virtue of my rearing, my education, my tradition. Living in another culture would open my mind and broaden my vision in ways that I couldn't anticipate but have come to appreciate.

Istanbul is a fabulously beautiful city to enter by ship. The skyline is all spires and domes and the city climbs the hills. We were met at the pier by a representative of the Fulbright Commission and everything was taken care of for us. It was such a relief, after the struggle we had with porters in Naples and Rome during our stop in Italy, that Sarge just broke down and wept.

In Istanbul we had an orientation that gave us a glimpse into the culture we were about to enter. One morning we had a briefing and were to meet the Fulbright Commission at noon. By noon, we were all slightly tipsy from the *raki* we had imbibed during the briefing. I remember making judgments about drinking so early in the day, but our hosts introduced us to the custom and I must say it made the meeting more enjoyable. By eleven o'clock, Sarge had been belly dancing, aping the performance we had seen the night before in a Turkish night club where, incidentally, the master of ceremonies introduced the performances in five languages.

It seemed to me that the Turks must know how to have fun. I had never been any place where people seemed so relaxed and had such a wonderful time. It certainly wasn't like New England. And I loved the man Sarge was in Turkey. He had wanted to travel all his life and he was like a child on Christmas morning, discovering and delighting in one new thing after another.

The night train trip from Istanbul to Ankara was dreadful, although I may have been the only one who thought so. I was so damned sanitation-conscious that I couldn't relieve myself. I couldn't urinate standing up and, on the train, there was no alternative—just foot treads and a hole in the floor. I swear the train stopped every fifteen minutes. Sarge slept most of the way and the girls dozed as we passed over the dry countryside, but awoke at every stop to see the people getting on and off. Usually they pleaded with me to buy something from the vendors who approached the train at stops, offering sodas and *simits*, a pretzel-like bread, which they carried in flat trays on their heads.

In a country where we would be confronted by the demands of a new culture, the biggest problem Sarge and I had was that he adapted so easily to the culture while I groused and complained about everything. It took me several months to acknowledge that wherever I went I would always take Elizabeth with me. Sarge offered to buy me a one-way ticket home and just as I was about to use it, he took me for lunch at a restaurant he had found. A superb lamb stew and the biggest and most delicious peach I had ever eaten renewed my courage. Lunch for three cost less than two dollars and it was served with courtesy, clean linen and music. Smiling across the table at Sarge, I knew I would stay.

After two days of looking at apartments in Ankara I was dismayed. I thought we would never find a place but just as I was about to give up, our Fulbright representative told us she was moving and offered us her house. After we had moved in I began to wonder if the wrought-iron grillwork, the winding staircase, and the marble terrazzo floors would compensate for the lack of heat, hot water, and dependable electricity. In our first week the electricity was off twice and the water once, for half a day. That is, water for washing. The water for drinking sat in an earthenware jug in the corner of the kitchen.

For the first two weeks it was all too much—too dry, too dirty, too difficult. I wanted to go home and thought to myself that it would certainly be a measure of my character if I were able to turn the year into a fruitful experience. I was surprised by my inflexibility yet encouraged by the fact that occasionally I did laugh at myself. There were times when our adventures were uproariously funny, times they were quite satisfying, and other times when it seemed as if the whole thing had been a terrible mistake.

The oil stove, for example, leaked on the floor. The smokestack had no shutoff and all the heat went up the chimney. The plumber (*usta*), who also took care of stoves and heating problems, came several times to no avail. He was equally unsuccessful in repairing the toilet. It flushed not only when you pulled the chain from the overhead tank but every now and then on its own initiative, startling me awake many nights. If you leaned on the edge of the bathtub while getting in or out, it tipped over. When you emptied it you had to line up the hole in the bottom of the tub with the drain in the floor or there would be bath water all over the house. I couldn't see beyond my intestinal response to strange food and water nor the struggle with inadequate facilities—laundry washed in a bathtub half full of brown, scummy water, drinking water stagnating in a pottery jug, vegetables that were days old before being cooked, bread not wrapped but handled in the market like brooms.

I tried not to notice but it seemed to me that everything was being done the hard way. Our landlord had the house painted for us just before we moved in. Workmen came in with spray equipment and applied whitewash to the walls and woodwork and, at the same time, to the wrought-iron grillwork, windows and marble terrazzo floors, which had been so appealing to me. Then, as the painters finished a room, two women with wire brushes and rags scoured the whitewash off the grillwork, windows and floors. I watched, astounded, but they all sang and laughed while they worked, so I tried to relax and stop judging everything.

When we bought drums to store heating oil, being good Yankees we went to considerable trouble to have right-angle pipes affixed to the hole in the end of the drums so the delivery man would be able to fill them more easily. On the first delivery I heard a great clanking and went out back to see the delivery man banging the right-angle pipe to get it off. Why? We asked him and he showed us his right-angle funnel. Sarge and I looked at each other and laughed.

Our Fulbright representative told us that it was not appropriate for a professor or his wife to do manual labor, that we would lose respect if we did. So we hired a maid, Sultan. When we first met I wasn't sure I could tolerate her and certainly didn't want her too close. She didn't appear to ever wash her clothes or comb her hair.

I knew nothing about her, how old she was, where she lived, if she had a family. One morning, a young girl appeared at the door. She was Sultan's ten-year-old daughter who'd come to get her mother. It was only then I knew that this little girl had full responsibility for three younger children, the youngest six months. We had seen little boys running errands for storekeepers and delivering packages, little boys working in buses and share taxis, little boys walking the streets with huge trays of *simits* on their heads, but we had not seen little girls other than the few fortunate ones who went by our house on the way to school. It now looked as if the others were at home taking care of their mothers' babies.

Sultan's child had a beauty not hidden by dirt. She had exquisite manners. When she came in, she bowed low, took my hand, kissed it then put it to her forehead in a gesture of respect. She had great black eyes in deep sockets and a face that could be twenty or eighty but should not be ten. I could have wept on the spot.

I told Sarge that I would be glad to do my own housework and pay Sultan what we paid her if she would stay home and take care of her children, but I knew she wouldn't—she'd just go out and get another job.

Life in Sunderland, Massachusetts didn't prepare me for Ankara society. At a party at the Embassy, Sarge and I were the only Americans and the manservant was the only Turk. The other guests were assorted West Europeans, from governmental and United Nations agencies and from private enterprise. Much of the discussion that evening focused on the frustration people felt in trying to impact sanitary conditions in the country.

At the beginning of the evening, I was introduced to a fifty-ish woman but heard only part of her name and position. I did hear the words "Danish Embassy" and, to make conversation, asked what she did at the Embassy, as one might address such a question to a clerk or a guide. With an amused smile she answered, "That is a difficult question. The Vice Consul here serves as cultural relations officer, chief administrator, and in various other capacities." I had never felt more like a New England provincial.

Seven-year-old Martha made an amazing adjustment to the new culture. She was enrolled in the third grade in a Turkish school, *Ayse Abla Ilkokulu*, where she made friends and enjoyed school even though her teacher spoke no English. One day she came home and announced that we were to now call her *Marta* instead of *Martha,* her given name, because there is no "th" in the Turkish language and *Martha* was too difficult for her friends to pronounce. She is still called *Marta* to this day. I knew her acculturation was complete the day she came bursting in from school with, "Momma, do you know what those American kids from the Dependents' School did? They threw stones at *our* kids!"

She became remarkably independent for her seven years. I attributed it to her having so much freedom to learn. She went to the store alone and made purchases with Turkish coins; she took the bus to the library. She claimed not to have learned any Turkish but she and Betsy were the interpreters when Sarge and I didn't understand. By simple exposure, she learned Turkish and phonetic spelling.

Marta was allowed to read books in school while her classmates did other things. She also read at night in bed, in the morning before the rest of us were awake and before we knew it she was reading at the rate of fifty to sixty pages a day. When I finished Herman Wouk's *City Boy* I couldn't return it to the library until she, too, had finished it. One night Sarge bought a copy of *Mehmed, My Hawk*, a grim novel of contemporary Turkey by Yasar Kemal, one of the country's radical young writers. Marta read that as soon as Sarge finished it.

Fifteen-year-old Betsy was enrolled as a junior at *Ankara Koleji*, a secondary school. It was not as easy for her. In the States she was an active teenager who was seldom at home. In Turkey, girls were discouraged from being on the streets after dark except with their parents.

Our evenings at home were awkwardly quiet. We had no television or phone and the only English language radio was the Voice of America, which seemed to be all propaganda or static. We played cards until we couldn't bear the sight of them, but when we stopped, Betsy was almost intolerably bored. This was, perhaps, the most difficult time, in terms of family dynamics, but over the course of the year we got to know each other, learned to accommodate, and really became a family—a huge accomplishment!

Betsy's initial boredom was conquered when she began painting and met Yavus, who was in his last year of school. As Betsy said later, it was a first, young love, delightful from start to finish. They could have only a secretive relationship, however, because the mores of the country prohibited an open acknowledgment of their liaison. Although Sarge and I were aware of the relationship, we looked the other way, despite knowing that discovery might jeopardize our stay in Turkey and have serious consequences for Yavus. Sarge's only real concern was that Betsy might get pregnant. She told me much later that she felt many of his questions were inappropriate, intruding as they did into her privacy. Yavus also seemed intent on protecting his privacy. He never came to the house but would stand outside whistling *Singing in the Rain* (their tune) so Betsy would know he was there.

Betsy frequently came home from school upset. Science and mathematics, at *Ankara Koleji*, were taught in English while history and literature were taught in Turkish. The science and math teachers came from Europe or America under contract, and Betsy said most of them exhibited outright contempt for all but a few of the Turkish students. The insult *esek* (donkey) was hurled at slow students, and teachers were generally contemptuous of Turkey as a nation.

Betsy had to deal with her own feelings about the slower Turkish students. She was a bright girl and her previous school life had been in homogeneous learning groups with highly competitive classmates. In a heterogeneous situation, she was disdainful of the slow students and angry with the quick ones who seemed so willing to help them. Over the months she came to appreciate the sense of community and the responsibility felt by brighter students for the learning of the slower.

One day Betsy went with her science class to the Ankara Cancer Hospital for a movie and lecture on the effects of smoking. She said the lecture was dull and the movie old but afterward the students were invited to watch a cancer operation. She couldn't believe the invitation but her friends confirmed it and she accepted.

The students were given white coats and face masks and admitted to the operating room in groups of four. In the operating room they stood on chairs close to the operating table, where a throat cancer operation was in progress. Betsy reported that at one point during surgery, her friend Mehmet was asked to pull his chair back to avoid bumping the doctor. They were told that operating was on a continuous basis and they could come in at any time. Betsy planned to spend her free periods at the hospital. Our initial shock gave way to laughter as Betsy recounted the day to us, but the incident made us appreciate the concern about sanitation we had heard expressed at the Embassy reception.

Sarge and I were taking language lessons at the American Foreign Service Language Institute and it was a good thing we were, because some of the phrases in our Turkish language books were so outdated that we had trouble using them when we first arrived. The phrase *"Aptestane nerede?"* which we were supposed to use to ask for bathroom facilities brought looks of perplexity to the faces of people we approached. Then someone told us that modern Turks use, *"Tuvalet,"* a Turkish adaptation of the French "toilette."

We used our elementary Turkish for getting around, for shopping, and for talking with Sultan who spoke no English. People laughed good-naturedly at our pronunciation but seemed to appreciate our attempts to use their language. Once I was preparing a lesson and, wanting to check my conjugation, turned to Sultan and asked, *"Bugün yabanciyorum, dün, yabanciydim, degil mi?"* (Today I *am* a foreigner, yesterday I *was* a foreigner, right?) Sultan replied, *"Hayir. Dün yabancisin, bugün yabanci degil sin—bugün Türksün."* (No. Yesterday you were a foreigner, today you are not a foreigner, you are a Turk.) I took her hand and squeezed it, surprised, and humbled not only by the warmth of her generosity but by the response I felt and how that response differed from my original reaction to Sultan.

Ankara awakened all at once. First there was the *muezzin*, calling the faithful to prayer. Then, almost simultaneously a morning dove called, a donkey brayed, the neighbors' sheep "baa'd" and the first Ankaran on the streets, the rag man, called out, *"Eskici-i-i"* as he began his trek through the city. Taxis moved through the streets, acknowledging approaching intersections with their horns. There are all sorts of irregular sounds in any city, but city living was new to me and it was the constant sounds that tore at my nerves. On a nearby construction site there was a machine that went "clang clankity clang clang" all day. It was joined by one of the few dogs around who was tied up and barked constantly in a monotone, and by a neighbor's radio playing minor key Turkish music.

I felt isolated. Sarge went off to work early every morning, the girls went off to school, and I was left at home with Sultan, my frustrations, and the outline of the thesis I was supposed to be writing. Some days I sat for what seemed like hours with a pen in my hand and a yellow lined pad on the dining room table in front of me, unable to write. I waited for the dog to stop barking or the neighbor to turn off the music. The noises of the city nearly drove me mad. I looked at the paper in front of me, got up for a drink of water or to go to the bathroom, then came back and looked at that yellow pad again. Eventually I realized that if I was going to get the thesis written I'd have to ignore the noises and start writing.

In *Being and Time*, Heidegger talks about the wish-world humans create for themselves and in which they are often content to dwell. The "wish-world" is the world of the greener grass, the better tomorrow, that blinds us to the possibilities of the here and now. It is the never-realized world, the world in which we go in search of possibilities seeming to offer greater promise. At that moment, trying to write in a noisy city, the wish-world looked most inviting. My wish-world might have been a quiet mountain top, the sun on my back and a breeze brushing the hair back from my face and nothing on my mind but enjoyment of the moment. I knew there were times when dwelling in the wish-world was preferable to being in the present but I also knew dwelling there wouldn't get my thesis written.

I grumbled about not having a typewriter and, because we hadn't brought many books with us, I was always looking for the one we hadn't brought. The American library in Ankara was a minimal collection of books, with none of those I needed. As I got deeper into Heidegger, I didn't like some of the translations and was frustrated by not having access to others. And then there were those moments when I was so engrossed in reading that I was back again in the Cornell library and deep into the historical conversation, this time as a speaker as well as a listener.

One Sunday in the fall we visited the *Yenisehir Pazari* (bazaar) and, as we entered, my first impulse was to flee. It was a huge place, like a circus ground, where farmers came into the city, set up their wagons, and offered their produce for sale; shops and stalls filled the narrow, winding, cobblestone streets, competing for space with carts and donkeys. Going from one shop to another comparing quality and price, you did your own grading—by looking, feeling, smelling, and then bargaining. Bargaining was the rule and was something I'd never done before.

Middle-class Turks with whom we associated daily didn't do their own shopping. The shoppers were their servants, and I felt conspicuous and out of place. But as I began to appreciate the bargains on the wagons, I let go of my self-consciousness. As we made purchases we were discovered by the farmers and porters and suddenly it seemed as if everyone was trying either to sell us something or carry it for us. Muddy, dirty, crowded, indeed a circus, but great fun.

When a man offered me a bunch of parsley I was able to tell him, in Turkish, that we grew parsley in our own garden. He was visibly surprised and smiled at me. The Turks didn't expect Americans to speak Turkish nor did they expect us to grow parsley in our gardens. Sarge carried a string bag filled with oranges, tangerines, lemons, apples, potatoes, onions, and cabbages. At every corner in the market there would be new porters trying to relieve him of his bundle while he repeated his polite Turkish refusal, "*Hayir, tesekkür ederim.*" (No, thank you.)

October 29th is Turkey's Republic Day and we had tickets to the *Cumhuriyet* Parade. People had told us it would be necessary to get there early in the morning if we wanted seats, even though the parade didn't begin until 2:30. We went at noon and couldn't find a seat. We were about to forget the whole thing and go home when we began talking to a young Turkish officer. He seemed interested in helping us but was unable to think of a solution to our problem until I remarked, in Turkish, that we were here for only one year and that my husband was a Fulbright professor at Ankara University. The word "Fulbright" seemed to be the magic one. The young officer went to his superior and in no time at all we were being escorted to seats in a special section under the balcony in which all the government officials, including Prime Minister Inönü, were seated. It was perfect! As troops marched by we could see the white-haired Inönü standing, smiling, and waving.

The parade was an impressive two and a half hours long. Turks in colorful gowns brandished massive swords as they marched behind mechanized army and cavalry divisions; there was Turkish music, whirling dervishes, and Western marching bands. Airplanes dropped parachutists out of the sky like confetti and jet planes soared and swooped in formation. The Turks exhibited great national pride and the spirit of the day was contagious. I had made my peace with being in Turkey.

This was the first time in many years I had been excited by a parade, and it reminded me of my father taking me to the Memorial Day Parade when I was small. I used to sit up on the roof of Dad's store, waving my flag and standing up with my hand over my heart when the flags in the parade went by.

A few weeks after Republic Day there was an anti-American demonstration, this time because of suspicion that the United States was involved in unseating Inönü, the eighty-one-year-old prime minister near whom we'd been sitting at the parade. Inönü was much loved but it was widely believed that the United States disliked his friendliness toward Russia. He resigned after failing to get a vote of confidence, and the pro-Western group took over. It seemed to me, and to Sarge, that our government was pursuing the same questionable course in Turkey that it had pursued in other countries, supporting a faction unresponsive to the needs and wishes of the people. From his visits to the villages, Sarge heard of the neighbor country (the Soviet Union) which was supplying farmers with seed and fertilizer. Whether or not the Soviet Union was dispensing propaganda with their seeds was not the question. The students said all the U.S. seemed to do was talk about "political freedom and democracy" while using Turkey for military purposes. "Containment" had become the cornerstone of U.S. foreign policy, and when Turkey was admitted to NATO in 1952, the United States was granted use of military bases in Turkey as part of building a chain of bases circling the Soviet Union. Those Turks to whom we spoke said they didn't like this policy.

During the American presidential election, we followed the campaign through the *International Herald Tribune,* completed our absentee ballots at the Embassy and, between static and the jamming on the Voice of America, listened to the returns on an old radio. We were elated with the results of the election although our elation had more to do with Goldwater's defeat than with Johnson's victory.

I began to see, on a personal level, those traits that make Americans unpopular wherever they go. I had gone over there as an ambassador of good will, charged with exemplifying what the Fulbright program stood for, yet most of my attention was on criticizing what I saw as unacceptable standards of sanitation. I was disappointed in my own response but even more so with what I saw on the part of those associated with the military.

NATO people and the military in general lived in a style quite beyond that of most Turks. They drove the only private cars (with the exception of a few wealthy Turks and Embassy officials), shopped exclusively at the PX, entertained each other, and made little attempt to know Turks or their language. They acted superior and when they did interact, they were disdainful. There were times when I was sure that the very presence of these people must be an affront to the Turks. I was embarrassed because at this point I had taken to heart my growing appreciation of the Fulbright program and had no idea that we were going to find Americans making asses of themselves and turning the people of the host country against us.

I saw America in a different light than I did in New England. I wanted her to be better than she was and I wanted all of us Americans to be better than we were. I wanted all of us to be worthy of the feeling the Turks expressed for John F. Kennedy, whose assassination, it seemed to me and to them, marked the beginning of our descent from greatness as a nation.

In November I found out that I was going to have a baby. I hadn't had a period since we arrived in Turkey but assumed it was menopause—I was forty-four, after all. By the first of the month, however, I appeared to be putting on weight and was concerned that something might be wrong. Sylvia Kuran, our Fulbright representative in Turkey, referred me to Dr. Necdet Erenus who examined me, grinned and said, "You are going to have a baby, toward the end of April."

At first I couldn't believe him. Sarge and I had been married over two years, I'd had a miscarriage, and we had pretty much accepted that I would not be able to have the child we both wanted. That night, when he heard I was carrying his child, he wept with joy and the family had a celebration unlike any we'd had since we'd been in Turkey. We were going to take a baby home with us! When Sultan heard the news she was elated and repeated over and over, *"Masallah, Masallah"* (God be praised).

Sarge came home from the university every night with some story about what had happened that day. One day after he had been lecturing a week or so, he came home frustrated, saying that he was sure the translator who had been assigned to work with him was not translating. He said he would say three or four paragraphs about something, pause and wait, and the translator would give the students one or two sentences. Sarge said he had no clue as to what was getting across to his students. His frustration resulted from his having spoken to one of his colleagues who shrugged and said, *"Gecmis olsun"* (there's nothing to do about it; may it pass quickly).

Sometimes Sarge went out into the Turkish villages and stayed for a few days. He had great admiration for the Turkish farmers because they were able to grow things in small patches on steep hillsides—places where American farmers would never attempt to grow anything. A couple of times we went with him to a village and were treated as honored guests in the house of the village head man.

One Sunday we rode for three-quarters of an hour in a *dolmus* (share taxi) and then walked a quarter of a mile over a muddy road for tea at the home of Turan Günes, Sarge's colleague at Ankara University.

We were greeted at the door with, *"Hos geldiniz,"* (Welcome) and given slippers to replace our muddy shoes. We were shown into a small formal room with a magnificent rug on the floor, a small prayer rug on the wall, several couches (which, we learned, served as beds at night), elaborately embroidered pillows and pieces of tatting and crocheting everywhere. We were served homemade cherry liqueur and a special candy called "Turkish Delight." Then came chocolates and coffee—strong, hot, and thick.

At about half past five, just as we were thinking it must be time to leave, tea was announced and we were led to the dining room. The table was covered with an assortment of food sufficient for two good meals for a family. There seemed to be no order in eating; I watched our host sampling chocolate cake, salami, and a black olive at the same time. There were sausages, cheeses, breads of all kinds, cake, cookies, olives, *börek* (thin pastry in which meat or cheese is rolled), fresh comb honey, apricot preserves, and tea.

Turan and his wife laughed at our Turkish, they laughed at Sarge, the father of seven with an eighth on the way, talking population control, they laughed at the behavior of the children, making only mild, occasional attempts to keep it under control. The children were loved, fondled, and fed, but seldom reprimanded or restricted. The afternoon was delightfully relaxed, the first such social encounter we'd had.

Christmas—the day everyone had dreaded because of our distance from home—turned out to be a day of unusual closeness. Because it was Friday and Sarge had to work, we rose early, exchanged the simple gifts we had bought each other and had a festive breakfast. The girls didn't go to school and we had a quiet, pleasant day together. We were joined for dinner in the evening by four students from Middle East Technical University and had an evening of good conversation.

A New Year's Eve celebration at the University, for administrators, faculty, and students, was much like a faculty party at the University of Massachusetts except for the presence of students and the interaction between students, faculty, and administrators. At one point while people were standing around the dance floor waiting for music, a young female student darted across the floor, snatched a paper hat from the university president's head, and darted away. He turned, raced after her, caught her, and gave her a resounding slap on her buttocks as he retrieved his hat. They both laughed and he returned to his group. That would never have happened at home. In the classroom in Turkey there was a clear definition of student and teacher roles, but in social situations that definition seemed to be suspended.

After the holidays we left for Adana, on the southern coast, where Sarge was to take his students on a tour of a rich agricultural area. The spectacle of southern Turkey unfolding was almost too much for a single day when one added to it the noise and jovial confusion of the bus, the continual eating, and the public toilets with the demands they made on us.

The next day, Sarge went off with his students, to farms in the Adana area, and Betsy, Marta and I visited the nearby seaport of Mersin, traveling by *dolmus*. On this trip the driver used the horn to clear the road of children, donkeys, sheep, goats, camels, bullocks, and women with loads of fruit on their heads. Alongside the road were orange trees, palm trees, cotton fields, and men sitting in tea houses. Leaving the *dolmus* in Mersin, we became the immediate objects of attention. In Turkish cities, Americans formed a sizable minority, but that was not the case in the countryside. On the streets of Mersin we were acutely aware of being foreigners and women. We wandered along, bought some tangerines from a street vendor, gave money to a beggar and, finally, found our way across a field of dried mud to the sea. We walked out onto a small breakwater and sat down near an old Turk with a small boy. A few minutes later we were joined by a white-aproned *bakkal* (grocer) apparently planning to take his mid-day rest there. Beyond the great new pier and the jetties and the freighters was the Mediterranean. We dangled our feet in the water, talked with and took pictures of the Turks, shared with them our tangerines and our enjoyment of the sea. It was at once strange and yet not strange that I felt so comfortable, so unafraid with them.

In Turkey, there was a wide gap between scholar and worker. The university student enjoyed considerable prestige and exhibited an air of superiority toward anyone who worked with his hands, no matter how capable that person might be. The teacher, the scholar, was held in very high esteem while, at the other end of the spectrum, the unskilled worker was considered—at least it seemed so to us—as not much more than an expendable unit of population. And the prestige enjoyed by the teacher was the prestige bestowed on him or her as a representative of a class of people, rather than on him/her as an individual. I knew it was something I must understand if I were to understand the Turkish people but I also knew it was far from my grasp. The most disturbing implication for Sarge was that these students, with their disdain for manual labor and laborers, would become Turkey's leaders. They would teach, serve in government posts, act as advisers, without ever having actually worked in agriculture. Sarge fraternized with the farm owners, applauded them for what they had done and was dismayed that the students seemed not only to not appreciate what he was doing but to act as if he were lowering himself by being familiar with the workers.

We left Adana, the only foreigners on a bus loaded with oranges, lemons, baggage, furniture, chickens, and a live lamb, in addition to the Turkish passengers. The trip back through the mountains was even more beautiful than the trip down, marred only by the evidence of accidents. Shortly after lunch we saw a bus on its side, off the road. On investigation we learned that the bus driver had swerved to avoid hitting a donkey driver. At the time we arrived, the bus driver was administering Turkish justice. It was swift and simple. The bus driver poked the donkey driver in the nose, hard. There was a rapid and harsh exchange of words, after which the donkey driver turned and left. Everyone helped to right the bus and when it was on its way again, the incident seemed to be over. The girls were upset with the bus driver. We asked them to consider whether this kind of justice might be more fair than the prolonged litigation often involved in accident cases at home.

I arrived back in Ankara feeling as if I had lived a year in the last four days. Home in Ankara looked wonderful. We used a sit-down toilet, ate food from the kitchen we had come to know, drank water from our own dependable jug, and had hot, freshly-baked bread from the corner bakery. It took us a week to recover from the four-day assault on our intestines, but the trip was worth it.

Shortly after our return from Adana we were invited to the 170th annual gathering of Turkey's agricultural engineers. There were folk dancers with knives and swords, belly dancers, musicians with instruments ranging from a set of wooden spoonlike paddles to an electric cello. One of the belly dancers was so provocative that the men in the room began throwing off their coats and ties and joining her on the dance floor. It was marvelous to watch, particularly since we knew no one had been drinking. The party was during *Ramazan*, a fasting period. Everybody was laughing and singing and it was again the difference between straight business men during the day and party men at night. I was reminded of something I had read in college about Chinese businessmen being Confucian bureaucrats by day and Taoist lovers by night.

We were introduced to another cultural difference one evening when we were having dinner with some Turkish friends. I reported having heard of a construction accident in which five men were killed because of poor scaffolding, an accident into which there would be no investigation. The response of Halis, my Turkish friend's husband, was almost cruelly casual: "If five men are killed, there are five more to replace them." That's when I knew that our regard for the importance of the individual was not shared by all cultures. I had known that through reading but had not experienced it before. I had to bite my tongue to keep from making some caustic remark.

I have always loved being pregnant and had never had an easier pregnancy than this one. My friends used to say I glowed and, in Turkey, I was radiant because I was carrying the child of the man I so loved and because Sultan took such good care of me. During the months of my pregnancy, she watched and fussed over me. Each afternoon she brought pillows to the couch, prepared a place for me to nap, put a light cover over me and patted me to let me know that she was there. When I woke, she was right there with a glass of tea and a biscuit or cracker. If I went out to do an errand, she exacted a promise that I wouldn't go too far or do too much. She made sure I got some exercise but not too much. I had never had this kind of relationship with someone who worked for me and wouldn't have known how to respond if I had stopped to think about it. But I didn't stop and think, I just enjoyed it. It wasn't until we were in Izmir, two years later, that I saw my behavior as unusual and understood Sultan's solicitousness. In Izmir, our neighbor in the apartment house was pregnant and was confined to the apartment from the minute she began to show, while I had been out and about—shopping, taking the bus down to the library, not knowing enough to realize that I was flaunting custom.

It was a beautiful pregnancy, marred only by our decision not to share it with people at home. Sarge, the statistician, knew that the probability of a perfect baby went down as the parents aged and he wanted us to delay our announcement until we were sure the baby was all right. Letters home were likely to include some mention of the "surprise" we were going to have for people. It was a good thing we didn't have a telephone or I'd never have been able to keep the secret.

Our daughter, Rebecca, was born at four in the morning on May 1st, 1965 in Ankara Hospital. I had wanted to have the baby at home so Sarge could share the experience with me but, after twenty hours of labor the doctor insisted on taking me to the hospital where Rebecca arrived fifteen minutes later, without Sarge. By nine o'clock that morning I was hungry and asked a passing nurse when I would get some breakfast. She told me I wouldn't unless someone was bringing it from home. I was momentarily stunned, then amused. We were not in Massachusetts; we were in Turkey. I asked to see the doctor. When he came by, he asked me if I would like to go home. Again I was surprised but said I would. He detached the tube from my arm and told me I could get up and dressed. A few minutes later a nurse arrived with the baby and I walked with the nurse and baby out to the doctor's car. Dr. Erenus drove me home, told me to come see him in six weeks, and left. I walked up the front steps and rang the doorbell. Sarge paled when he saw me standing there with the baby, less than six hours after I had left him.

Rebecca slept in her *besik*. The Turkish *besik* is a bassinet hung from an A-frame. It was the best baby bed I'd ever used, because the motion was a perpetual pacifier. During the day I would have it near the table where I worked and would move it gently with my knee. At night a string tied the *besik* to my mattress and when the baby cried I tugged gently on the string until she went back to sleep.

Infant clothing was quite different from anything I had used before and I had to adapt, sometimes the clothing and sometimes myself. I made diapers and receiving blankets for Rebecca and nursing bras for myself. Sultan wanted to wrap the baby in swaddling, as was the custom there. Invariably, if I left the baby for a few hours, I would come back to find her wrapped up tightly in one of the new receiving blankets. Rebecca didn't seem to mind and Sultan was as tender and concerned as if the child were her own, so I let it pass. I sometimes suspected that she might also be nursing Rebecca, when I was away, because she was nursing an infant at home, but I realized that Sultan was going to care for Rebecca in her own way, no matter what I said, so I might as well relax and go along with it.

Life was full for the last few weeks and the closer we came to leaving the more difficult it became. With our departure imminent, we had to secure birth and vaccination certificates so that we could take Rebecca home. She had one birth certificate from the Turkish government and one from the United States Embassy. She was officially named Rebecca by us yet called *Ankarali* by friends who claimed her as a Turk. (She actually does have dual citizenship.) The vaccination certificate attested to the humanitarian flexibility of the Turkish doctor but not to smallpox immunity—he gave us the certificate without the vaccination because, as he put it, "She is too young and pure to be injected with disease!"

Ankara was as green in May as it was gray in September. Days were hot and dry, nights were cool. Spring and the rainy season were just behind us and the flowers were outrageous—tulips the size of teacups, the scent of lilacs everywhere. It was hard to believe that it was the same city we met the previous fall.

Many of the things that made the year meaningful we couldn't take home and wouldn't find there. I wanted the best of both cultures and was torn between wanting to go home and hating to leave. The paradox was that although I didn't feel like an American as I observed other Americans, neither did I identify with the Turks. I was irritated with Turkish lethargy but even more irritated with American bungling and thoughtlessness.

Leaving was especially difficult for Betsy. Her special friend, Yavuz, would graduate that year and go on to become a doctor. With him, Betsy was becoming a woman. She glowed, loved everyone, and couldn't bear to contemplate leaving Turkey. If she had been two or three years older we might have considered her request to stay, but we felt that sixteen was too young for such a decision.

I realized how much I would miss Sultan when we left. I would miss her help, of course, but more important, I would miss Sultan herself—she had become a member of our family. When we first met I wasn't sure I could tolerate her and certainly didn't want her too close with her layers of dirty clothes and matted, uncombed hair. But as we were getting ready to leave I realized that although the clothes and the hair were the same, I no longer saw them. All I saw was a gentle, tender woman of great compassion and unbelievable thoughtfulness—a woman I had come to love. I was deeply grateful for the demands that Turkey made on me. I discovered an openness that I didn't know I had.

Back from Ankara we were at home but, curiously, not at home. A beautiful new baby whom I was nursing, the house we were restoring, the completion of my thesis, *Dasein and the Still Point*, the awarding of my master's degree, yet something was missing.

In my thesis I wrote, "The attempt to communicate is a form of self-affirmation. Insofar as I am able to give expression to my awareness, I lend authenticity to my own existence and give Being a place of unconcealment." My study had led me directly into the question of who I am and I knew I could never abandon the questioning.

The year sped by and before it was over, we had been invited to return to Turkey for the academic year 1967–68. Neither Sarge nor I had any reservations about returning and were even more excited because this time his appointment was to be at Ege University in beautiful Izmir, on the Aegean Sea, and we looked forward to a whole new experience.

11

Guest Lecturer in Izmir, Turkey

Our excitement and anticipation held up through the voyage across the Atlantic but were challenged on the trip from Naples to Istanbul. We'd made the mistake of booking tourist-class passage. The first night on the *Karadeniz* was pure, unadulterated hell, with temperatures that made us perspire although lying perfectly still, the smell of urine assaulting us from washrooms and corridors, dirt everywhere and, of course, diarrhea. It was a disastrous introduction for Jonathan and Timothy, two of Sarge's boys, who were accompanying us for the first time. The three days on the ship were laced with bright spots but for the most part it was an experience one could only wish to be beyond. I again remembered Martin Heidegger's wish-world and suspected there were times when dwelling in the wish-world was the only way of enduring the present.

Our spirits were lifted and our enthusiasm renewed by three weeks in Istanbul before going on to Izmir. The memory of those weeks in Istanbul will stay with me for the rest of my life—the magnificence of the Blue Mosque and *Topkapi* Palace with what must be the most valuable and impressive collection of jewels and porcelain in the world, the beaches on the Black Sea and the Marmara, the Golden Horn at sunset and, most memorable of all, that sense of being present in the meeting place of East and West, of yesterday and today. The views of the Bosphorus and the Black Sea were magnificent, but in the heart of Istanbul cows walked the streets as if they belonged there and I found myself, once again, caught up in that wonderful contradiction that was Turkey.

I was remembering, comparing, wondering. Perhaps meaning eludes those who pursue it—perhaps we can only be open to receive it. Meanwhile we judge ourselves and others. What do all people everywhere have in common? Perhaps the common denominator is that lifelong search for something we'll probably never find but must believe we will. One day we went out into the countryside for a picnic and while we were settling on the grassy slope of a hill, a goatherd came by with his flock. We exchanged smiled greetings and the goatherd continued on to the top of the hill. Soon he began playing his flute. I was enchanted. His playing was at once an extension of himself, a celebration of life, and a gift to us.

Leaving Istanbul we went to Izmir where Sarge had an appointment at Ege University. Izmir is the third largest city in Turkey, with a population of about one million and a half. It is a port city, on the Aegean Sea, and also a center of road and rail transportation. Where Ankara had been somewhat sophisticated—a diplomatic center—Izmir was a bustling business community.

Our first week in Izmir was spent hunting for a place to live while sharing an apartment with another Fulbright family. It was a difficult time and I wondered if we would regret returning. This time we had with us Marta, Rebecca, as well as Jonathan (13) and Timothy (11). Jonathan was miserably unhappy, seemed unable to adjust, and took out his feelings by bullying both Timothy and Rebecca. I took it personally but it may have been that Jonathan was just being a teenager.

One day, nearing the end of that first week, we took the ferry across Izmir Bay to a section of the city called Karsiyaka. The ferry ride in itself was enough to convince Sarge and me that we wanted to live over there, so when we saw an apartment with a sign indicating it was for rent, we took it even though we hadn't looked around, compared prices or done any of those things one is supposed to do before renting. In about the same way, I hired a maid. Zehra came to the door and indicated that someone had told her we needed a maid. I smiled and said, "Yes, and you must be the one." The apartment occupied the sixth floor of a new building on the waterfront boulevard and had floor-to-ceiling glass doors providing access to a balcony and a breathtaking view of the bay and the city to the east. From the bedrooms we had a view of the mountains to the west. Banana palms and conifers lined the boulevard in front of the apartment. The pier for the ferry to downtown Izmir was located less than a block away.

Since my first concert when I was ten, I had been fascinated by the way a symphony builds, one instrument adding its voice to the others until the simple melody grows into a complex and overpowering force. In a strange, distorted way I recall the awakening of Izmir as music. At five o'clock in the morning, the *muezzin* called the faithful to prayer. The call came from every minaret in the city. Before the call was over, the cocks of the city began to crow. During Ramazan, when people fasted from dawn to sunset, a man went through the streets beating a drum, alerting people to arise and eat even before the call of the *muezzin*. Then the first donkey of the morning added a staccato note with his clop, clop, clopping over the cobblestones. People stirred, dogs barked, and somewhere a child cried. Soon one heard all the sounds of the day: "*Eskici-i-i,*" the rag man called out, "*Yumurta, yumurta,*" from the egg man, "*Konak, Konak, Konak*" (the marketplace) from the *dolmus* starter on the boulevard. Then there were the ever-present automobile horns—the Turkish substitute for traffic lights, hand signals and brakes. By eight o'clock on my first evening the sounds had reached such a crescendo that I escaped to the bathtub and lay with my ears under water. The day in Izmir began and ended as did my symphony concert, with the important difference that one set of sounds put me at peace with myself and my world, whereas the other made me simply want to escape.

We had barely settled in when there was an anti-American demonstration in Izmir. Dynamite was thrown into the Commissary and hundreds of Turkish students clashed with American students from the Dependents' High School. The demonstration had been touched off by the hurling of insults at Turkish high-school students by American high-school students. Attitudes at the Dependents' School were almost uniformly negative toward Turkey. We knew we had made a mistake in sending the boys to the Dependents' School but it was their choice. Air Force orientation seemed to do a good job of lousing up what otherwise might have been a great experience for military families. It created an attitude of cultural superiority that insulted the host country and its people. The Turkish group was led by students from Ege University, and because of his affiliation with Ege, Sarge was asked by the U.S. Air Force Security to "talk to those young Turks and set them straight." He agreed to talk with the leaders of the protesting students, met them the next day for lunch and came home convinced that they were justified in demonstrating.

He said the students discussed the U-2 incident in which the Russians shot down an American high-altitude spy plane. The students said that Russia held Turkey responsible for the actions of the American military stationed in Turkey, so the young Turks were most reluctant to have American planes taking off from Turkish soil. Also they resented the Sixth Fleet coming into port, discharging sailors to rampage all over Izmir, insulting women and storekeepers, getting drunk and generally making a nuisance of themselves. They also didn't like Americans living in their midst enjoying special privileges and immunities. Aside from the more obvious manifestations of a military presence, there were things such as the Officers' Club in downtown Izmir, where some Americans spent more money in an evening than many Turks earned in a year (the average annual per capita income, at that time, was about $200). The argument for maintaining the American standard of living abroad made the same impression on me as it did on the Turkish students. Sarge said all of the students with whom he talked were serious and sincere. One of them had a law degree and was studying agriculture in order to work for land reform, needed because large landholders paid no taxes. Another was working on improving food production. By the end of his talk with the students Sarge was convinced that they were not the ones who needed to be "set straight." I'm sure his report to the U.S. Security officer was not what they wanted to hear.

In early November we drove to Ankara for a reception hosted by the American Ambassador. While in Ankara we visited the Hittite Museum; our visit was made much more special by David Owen, an archeologist we first met in Istanbul. He guided us back through some twelve thousand years of the history of Anatolia. All over Turkey archeologists were unearthing treasures and records from early civilizations. The culture of Turkey is overlaid on so many previous cultures that it is hard to grasp, even though there to be seen. It was like standing at the beginning of time. We had passed Sardis on the way from Izmir, had seen an extinct volcano and some fascinating rock formations, explored caves used by early Christian monks. We had picked up some rocks, one of which was hard, creamy-white, fine-grained, with a feeling like talcum powder. At the museum I saw the same kind of rock chipped into stone implements and exhibited in a case with Paleolithic tools and weapons and learned that it was, indeed, talc. The thrill of this recognition was the same thrill I felt each time I saw a Roman road, bridge or aqueduct, or passed a site like Sardis where history was being unearthed. Life here is a constant reminder of the past on which the present is built.

When we returned to Izmir, I was asked if I would be interested in teaching English. I was delighted and was told to report on the 10th of November to Ege University's *Yabanci Diller Okulu* (Foreign Language School). I would teach three classes with different levels of English comprehension and I would meet each group once a week for two hours. There was no syllabus, there were no materials and I was told I was free to do as I wished in the class. In a philosophy class in the United States that freedom would have been welcome but not in an environment where English was a foreign language and my Turkish was barely adequate for the market place.

By the time I entered the first classroom at four o'clock I was paralyzed with fear. My first real class and I had no idea what to do beyond reading the class list and taking attendance. But that was all I needed. My pronunciation of the Turkish names was so bad that students began tittering and soon everyone dissolved in laughter. Then one student, whose name I had mispronounced, corrected me and waited for me to say his name again. I did. Other students followed, correcting my pronunciation of their names, waiting until my pronunciation satisfied them. I finished the attendance check and looked up at the students, wondering where to go next. One boy held up his book and said, "*kitap.*" I repeated the Turkish word and then said, "book." They all repeated "book." We had established a process for the day and, though I didn't know it at the time, for the year. It was a game everybody could play, a game with a pattern we all understood. Class was over before any of us realized what we had invented. A cluster of students walked with me back to the teachers' room and said good night. I almost exploded with excitement. I had not only made it through the two-hour class but had been a success. Two hours before I had been tempted to turn and run. Now I was looking forward to meeting the next group.

My second English-language group was at *Yüksek Ogretmen Okulu,* a government school for training teachers for village schools. All the students were from the village and what a different lot they were! They were eager, spontaneous and, even on the first day, there was little holding back or shyness. The chance to get an education was still a miracle to most of them. There was also little English—this was the first year for most of them—but I wasn't worried about that. The relationship we established in the first ten minutes of class would carry us through. Instead of tittering at my pronunciation of their names, these youngsters laughed boisterously and slapped their thighs. As I read the class list, I noticed from the responses that the students were seated alphabetically. I offered them the option of sitting wherever they liked and they seemed delighted. I knew I'd have to find some other way of remembering names. Once again we played the naming game and when I had difficulty with a Turkish word, someone would go to the blackboard, write it out for me and, with the pointer, show me the phonetic breakdown as it was pronounced. I may have been called "teacher" by these students but learning was certainly a two-way process.

The third group was made up of older and more serious students, most of them in their last year at the University and going on to graduate study. They were intelligent, literate young people with a better command of English than the others, but they also exhibited skepticism toward their new American teacher. They were courteous but didn't give me the open-hearted welcome of my first classes. I respected these capable young men (there was only one woman) and realized I'd have to use a different approach. They didn't accept me in the open, unquestioning manner of the Yuksek students but they seemed willing to let me prove myself. The difference in the students may have been related to the difference in political awareness and sophistication. These were the student rebels who demonstrated against the American military presence in Turkey, while most of the young village students couldn't care less about politics—they were wholly involved in getting an education.

We introduced ourselves to each other and I asked if they had any questions; their response made it clear that they had many. I took advantage of that to establish a *modus operandi*. I told these bright youngsters that I would answer any questions they could ask in correct English and that I would help them with the vocabulary they might need for framing those questions. If I hadn't committed myself to answering I might have hesitated, because they asked very personal questions—about my age, my personal history, my husband's salary in the U.S., about courtship, marriage, whether or not we allowed our children to date. They wanted definitions of "Hippie culture" and "generation gap." They wanted to know if the stories about boy-girl relations and sexual freedom in the United States were fact or myth. They asked about differences between Christianity and Islam, whether or not teacher was an atheist. They wanted to know more about the rationale for American presence and privilege in Turkey. Then there were the inevitable questions about U.S. foreign policy. The atmosphere in the room changed perceptibly when I admitted to sharing their view that U.S. policy in Southeast Asia was wrong. They asked about Robert Kennedy and Lyndon Johnson. As class ended, there were many unanswered questions so I suggested that for our next meeting they write questions in English which we would use for discussion. I agreed to prepare, and they agreed to study, vocabulary lists for those topics.

Early in this teaching experience I depended on intuition and conversation although I soon realized that I would have to prepare my own materials. But I even enjoyed the preparation, which was a monumental job. The only thing the school had was a book designed to teach English to Spanish-speaking elementary children in New York City—hardly suitable for college students in Turkey. I searched local libraries for things I might adapt. Two of the classes needed work in phonics so I developed and mimeographed a series of lessons dealing with specific problem areas of the language. At first I felt handicapped by not having a course outline or materials but then I began to see it as a blessing. It allowed me to design materials appropriate to the needs of each group of students.

It surprised me that I so enjoyed teaching English, but perhaps it was because some of those English classes were also philosophy classes. In the most advanced class, one day the assignment had been to submit a brief written opinion on the question, "Does religion serve as a unifying force in the world or a divisive force?" One opinion submitted was, "Religion is divisive. Because religions are different, they cause arguments between people. The best unifying force in the world is sex." There were several provocative responses.

We had Thanksgiving dinner with Turkish guests in our home, but that night we became acutely aware of being in another country on the verge of war. It wasn't like being involved in a Vietnam war somewhere on the other side of the world, this was a disagreement with a next-door neighbor, a disagreement of long standing. In early 1964, ignoring the 1960 partnership Constitution that was designed to let Turkish and Greek Cypriots share the island, the Greeks murdered hundreds of Turks on Cyprus and Turkey was ready to use military force to protect the Turkish minority but the United States intervened.

"Wait," our Government said. "We'll find some other way to see that Turks are protected." Turkey listened and withdrew but since then had been waiting for the United States or the United Nations to find that other way. When Cyprus was set up as an independent state, in 1960, it was agreed that the Turkish Cypriots could maintain an army of six hundred fifty men and the Greek Cypriots nine hundred fifty; but since that time the Government of Greece continued to send troops into Cyprus until, by the time we were there, they had close to twenty thousand. The Turks were demanding withdrawal of those troops. Recently, thirty-one Turkish Cypriots had been killed in what Greece referred to as a "police action."

The Turks felt that if President Johnson had taken a stand in 1964 there wouldn't be trouble in 1967, so Americans were almost as unpopular as Greeks. An American official flying into Ankara was mobbed by students and not allowed to leave the plane, the U.S. Information Service headquarters in Ankara was stoned and its windows smashed. We were told to stay off the streets unless it was absolutely necessary to go out.

Turkey's planes had been flying over Cyprus nightly and troops were massed on the Greek border. At five o'clock on Thanksgiving afternoon, time ran out for Greece's response to Turkey's ultimatum. We had not heard if there was a response but a blackout was ordered. Sarge pinned up blankets to cover the windows and I reread to the family the evacuation instructions delivered to us the day before by a man from the consulate. Below us, the ferry moved back and forth across the bay like an uneasy shadow on the water and cars gave the streets a burlesque appearance with head lights and tail lights painted blue.

It was difficult not knowing what was really happening. We didn't read Turkish well enough to get much from the newspapers and the U.S. Air Force radio station maintained a news blackout, giving news of Vietnam, Israel, Washington and New York but nothing about Turkey, Greece or Cyprus. I was uneasy and annoyed. I felt that the Turks could ill afford to exhaust their resources in war. There was so much money could do to meet the needs of the people that it seemed a shame to spend any of it on a war. My annoyance was personal as well; I didn't want to be evacuated. I was enjoying myself and even beginning to feel useful. For weeks we didn't know whether we would stay or go. Then the threat of war abated but the anti-American feeling didn't. Once again the United States had sent an envoy—this time Cyrus Vance—to Ankara, saying, "Wait, we'll find some other way." The Turks didn't believe him and were angry.

It was interesting to see the United States as others see it. The *International Herald Tribune*, published in Paris, printed European reactions to U.S. policy. In the eyes of many Europeans, the United States was the greatest threat to world peace and was doubly faulted for masquerading as the guardian of peace. As one commentator wrote, about our presence in Vietnam, it seems contradictory to speak of saving a country while you are systematically destroying it.

In our zeal to protect others against communism we often failed to respect the right of self-determination. For many countries, democracy is too slow. Seriously underdeveloped nations might need a period of centralized control during which the first big steps could be taken without all the political problems posed by democracy. Turkey was a good example. Atatürk was a dictator and, in fifteen years, set Turkey firmly on the road to modernization. In the forty years since he came to power, the country developed a new language, switched from a totally agrarian economy to a mixed economy, developed a program of public education, switched over to the metric system, accomplished the separation of church and state, and switched successfully from a monarchical form of government to a republican form. This could never have been accomplished in so short a time without very strong central control. Atatürk loved Turkey and he was ruthless with those who stood in the way of progress. It seems as if we Americans forget that different situations call for different solutions. What may be good politically in an affluent, highly developed, technological society may be entirely inappropriate in a struggling, underdeveloped, agrarian society.

Marta, Jon, and Tim were all in the American Dependents' School. We were disappointed in not being able to enroll them in Turkish schools as we had done with the girls in Ankara but we didn't have the same options in Izmir. After three months of school, we wished we had tried harder. In the American Dependents' School there was no instruction in the Turkish language so American children learned nothing of the language of the host country and were unable to communicate with Turkish children their own age. Instead of being comfortable with Turkish children in our neighborhood, Jon and Tim associated only with other American children, most of whom did not like Turkey. The boys were clearly unhappy.

My journal at this time read, "This should be a great opportunity for the boys but they have to make their own opportunities to get anything out of them. They couldn't care less about being here. 'It was better in Amherst,' Jon said one day. If they put nothing in, they'll get nothing out. It's a sad waste of time, money, work and hope. At the beginning, several days of extreme tension erupted when I heard Timmy cry out in pain and say, 'No, I won't say it. Why should I?' and then cry out again. I was shaking with an anger that had been building up ever since we left home and when I went into the boys' room I lashed out at Jon about acting like a bully, about his lack of cooperation and about the vile language I'd been hearing him use. I was afraid the year was going to be a fiasco and, perhaps, a year we would come to regret."

Before Christmas the boys had given up and returned to Amherst to their mother. They hadn't adjusted to the cultural change, nor did Sarge and I help them make that adjustment. I seemed to have forgotten how difficult it was for me the first time I was in Turkey and how many months it was before I was willing to stay. I knew the boys felt left out since the rest of us had been there before and were happy to be back. None of us took the time to help the boys through their experience of culture shock. If Betsy had been with us this second time, she might have made the effort on behalf of her brothers, but Jon and I had not developed a relationship before going and Sarge, almost immediately involved in his work at Ege University, seemed not to notice the boys' need of him.

Christmas was again a quiet little affair. We had a tiny tree strung with popcorn and candy. Again Sarge had to work, so we had an early breakfast and exchanged gifts. Zehra was amused by our celebration, which was actually subdued because we were all sad that the boys had left. I had a terrible sense of failure over their leaving. I had hoped they would enjoy the experience as much as Betsy and Marta had enjoyed our first year in Turkey but knew that I hadn't done as much as I might have to insure that. I felt sad that the huge opening Marta and Betsy experienced didn't materialize for the boys. Looking back, I can see that such an opening required acculturation, including learning the Turkish language so as to be able to get around Izmir unaccompanied and to make friends in the neighborhood instead of only at school in the American community. Marta and Rebecca were enjoying themselves. Marta had the advantage of having been in Turkey before and having acquired some Turkish so she got around with little difficulty and made friends easily. Rebecca had the advantage of an unbiased outlook—one place was as good as another as long as all the right people were in it.

The rainy season in Izmir was a series of wild and wonderful spectacles much like the wild September storms I knew as a child growing up on the Connecticut shore. The wind and rain consorted to produce scenes of magnificence on the bay. The sky at one moment was a formidable black, at the next it was a protesting, innocent blue. The water of the bay was a dark blue-gray here and a beautiful green there, and everywhere topped with splashes of white. Gulls glided and swooped past our windows and it was as if all nature was putting on a show for our benefit as we sat in the living room.

On the streets, however, it was quite otherwise. I never went to market without reflecting on the life around us. Turkey is a country of contrasts and nowhere were they more evident than in the covered market area. A European sports car tooted to pass a wagon, or a donkey with baskets slung over its back, or even a camel. A mini-skirted female crossed the cobblestone road and brushed against a woman in an ankle-length black coat with a scarf veiling her face. One five-year-old boy wore shorts, a white shirt, a tie and a V-neck sweater while another wore baggy pantaloons, a dress and a kerchief on his head. There was so much I would like to have had in pictures but would not photograph because the carrying of a camera would set me apart from those with whom I wanted to share the sense of community. The best I could do was put some of it in words.

The first picture I would take would be of a donkey laden with milk cans. The donkey was so much a part of life in Turkey that even we took him for granted, but whenever I encountered one at close range I was attracted by the soft gray fur, the mild eyes, the small frame under the massive load, and the almost sweet expression. One Sunday there was a particularly small and very patient donkey standing in front of a house where his owner was delivering milk. He watched the pedestrian traffic with a quizzical expression and as I thought about him I wondered if he were thinking about us.

On the corner diagonally opposite the donkey sat a beggar, the first of many we passed between the apartment and the market. When we first came to Turkey I was appalled by the number of beggars on the street and was conscience-stricken at the number we simply passed by. But by this time I paid them little more attention than I did the donkeys, except to notice and catalog their differences. The first beggar we met Sunday morning had no legs and sat on the corner with one hand outstretched. Farther down the street stood the blind man who was always there but whose unusual height and dignified bearing set him apart from the others. At the gate to the *pazar* were two more legless beggars, one in a vehicle resembling a baby carriage, the other on a flat cart, the wheels of which he turned by pushing the ground with an implement held in his hands. All of them mumbled supplications and, I was told, hurled curses at those who passed by unheeding. There was one man to whom I gave regularly and, with that gift, made my symbolic gift to all. He sat on a corner between our apartment and the center of Karsiyaka, a man of perhaps eighty years, nearly blind, but with the dignity that characterized the old men of Turkey who, even in blindness and aged dependence, exhibited a nobility which seemed to belong more to history than to the modern world.

There was yet another kind of Turk I wanted to remember. He was called *hamal*, and was the man who worked as beast of burden along with donkey and camel, who walked the streets bent over like his anthropoid forebears, a huge basket of produce or a large piece of furniture tied to his back. I passed him on the streets, took his presence for granted, but was saddened by him.

I had come to love the Turks but loving them was the result of getting to know them and letting them know me. At first I didn't love them—I didn't even like them. I saw them from a different cultural perspective and passed judgment on the way they did things, the way they lived. My reactions were frequently insulting—they were paternalistic and condescending. I saw the Turks as unreflective innocents. I suspect I'm much like Americans everywhere in the world. We are an impatient people and it takes time and effort to appreciate people different from ourselves. With time and effort, however, one begins to appreciate the comment of S. Radhakhrishnan that, "the varied cultures are but dialects of a single speech of the soul—differences being due to accents, historical circumstances and stages of development."

Today I look back on that early period with some embarrassment because I learned so much from these people. I loved the maid, the *dolmus* driver, the students, the *kapici*, everybody! Zehra sang while she worked and turned much of her work into play. One day she had hung the clothes on the balcony to dry when it began to shower. She ran out, pulled the clothes in and no sooner had she finished than the sun came out again. Once more she hung them out. When the second shower came, she pulled the clothes in again and then laughingly collapsed on the couch with the clothes in her lap and said, "Ah, Madam, *gunes oyun oynuyor*!" (the sun is playing).

Rebecca frequently tugged at Zehra's dress when she was washing floors or windows and pled, "Zehra, *gel?*" Zehra would leave whatever she was doing and respond to the child's request. They danced and sang together and sometimes just sat on the balcony watching the activity in the streets below or talking to our canary. Nothing seemed more important to Zehra than Rebecca and the full enjoyment of the moment. As I watched them I wondered why it was that I seemed unable to do that.

When I had begun working at the University I had difficulty commuting because of the connection at Cinarli. At that intersection there was always a crowd of people and little space available in the passing vehicles. One day as I left the apartment to go to work I noticed the *dolmus* starter across the street looking at his watch. I spoke to him and learned that he was trying to judge my time of departure and return, so I told him. That night on the way home I arrived at Cinarli and joined the crowd waiting for a *dolmus*. The first Karsiyaka-bound vehicle that came by was full but the driver stopped anyway, asked his passengers to push over and make room. Then he signaled me to get in. The next night it happened again. It was a week before I realized that they were taking care of me, seeing to it that I got out to the University and back with the least possible inconvenience.

The special consideration I was shown was due largely to my being a teacher. One day a policeman stopped the *dolmus* which had stopped illegally to pick me up. (I had been waiting at a point between stops without realizing it.) The driver apologized but explained that he had stopped to pick up a foreign teacher. Immediately the other passengers in the car began chastising the policeman, calling out, "*Yabanci misafir*" (foreign guest) and "*Ogretmen*" (teacher). These two titles worked magic. The policeman bowed and retreated. Our growing knowledge of Turkish made modest conversation possible with drivers and passengers, and only modest conversation was necessary because so much was a sensed communication. I had developed a real affection and respect for these earnest, struggling *dolmus* drivers on whom we were so dependent.

Zeynep, our neighbor, was the young wife of Mehmet, a successful Turkish businessman, and we became friends soon after we moved into the apartment. The Turks are as forthright about some things as they are evasive about others and on my first visit to her home Zeynep told me about her marriage and showed me her photograph album. Zeynep came from a wealthy and educated (on the male side) family, but had been taken out of high school after two years to study embroidery, knitting, crocheting and tatting, while her father made it known that he was receptive to overtures from families of eligible males.

Mehmet had seen her on the street one day, made judicious inquiries about her character and her family and then asked his father to make the necessary arrangements. Mehmet's father spoke to Zeynep's father and the arrangements were made, conditional upon their acceptance by Zeynep. Zeynep had told her father she would not marry a man she had never seen. Mehmet agreed to make appropriate visits and give her one week in which to make up her mind. That week he visited frequently, accompanied always by his mother or sister, and on those visits told her of his expectations. She would be his wife, bear his children, and grace his home. She would not work, except at fine needlework for her home and family. There would be women to do the housework and cooking, and to care for the children. Zeynep told him she would welcome guests and be willing to visit his parents and hers but hoped that otherwise he would not ask her to go out in the evening. At the end of the week Zeynep signified her willingness and the agreement was sealed by Mehmet's father proffering, and Zeynep's father accepting, a silver tray bearing gifts of finery and jewels, including a diamond ring to be given Zeynep on the wedding day. In the three months that followed there was much entertaining of the betrothed couple but at no time during that period were they alone together.

In Turkey there are two ceremonies for those who want a religious wedding. Because of Atatürk's separation of church and state, the religious ceremony has no legal status and must be preceded or followed by a civil service. During the signing of papers for the civil service it is an old custom for one partner to place a foot on that of the other, signifying the line of authority in the family. If the man puts his foot on the woman's, it means he has assumed the dominant role and she must obey him. If the woman gets her foot on top first, it is supposed to mean that the man will be a *kilibik* (the Turks translate this as "hen-pecked" husband). Zeynep said that in discussing arrangements, Mehmet told her he did not believe in the custom. She was thus quite unprepared when, during the signing of the papers, she felt the gentle but unmistakable pressure of his foot on hers. There was no expression on his face but the gesture spoke for itself.

I visited Zeynep often. In the months of confinement during her pregnancy she was lonely and bored. She didn't enjoy reading nor was she encouraged to read. There was not a book or magazine in evidence in her apartment. Her husband, fifteen years older, was a Yale graduate but she had been carefully insulated against any influence which might be disturbing to her in the role she was expected to assume in life. Although she displayed keen intelligence, she would have little opportunity to use it. She seemed like a delicious confection Mehmet had brought home to enjoy.

In Izmir I read in Camus, Suyin, Malamud and Yevtushenko. In Bernard Malamud's "Suppose a Wedding" a husband and wife lacerate each other in unrelieved vulgarity; even the brief respite that results from the emotional catharsis is colored with defensiveness and small barbs. But where is that lift to the spirit that comes on a beautiful morning, dispelling for a moment all the bleakness, dreariness, meaningless monotony of such drab lives? Where is that appreciation of a first blade of grass forcing its way up alongside the concrete pavement, of the first real spring day and its invitation to relax? These things belong to the most dismal lives and without them, the portraits of despair are unreal. Perhaps that was why I found Yevtushenko so appealing. This young Russian, who grew up in suffering and struggle and even in the kind of discouragement that weaker souls blame for the death of the spirit, found joy and hope to sustain him. He wrote of the nobility of the ordinary human being and found it more important than the sordid garments with which we sometimes dressed our lives. I must thank Turkey and her people for helping me appreciate Yevtushenko, for the mass of Turkish people live in poverty yet are not degraded by it. They wear their mended jackets like robes of purple, they carry themselves proudly, they bestow dignity on the most menial tasks. One day, at the edge of the bay, a team of fishermen each harnessed to a rope, were hauling in a large net of fish. As they came slowly up the beach they swayed in rhythm as they leaned against the rope, muscular bare feet braced on the beach. As one man neared the road, he opened the clamp that bound his shoulder harness to the rope, walked down to the water's edge and fastened on again at the beginning of the line. There was no interruption in the rhythm and the whole performance seemed more like dance than work.

I agree with the Existentialists that we must not expect anything "other"—that this life is all—and this life is what we make it. But I feel that this is cause not for despair bur rather for rejoicing because it gives us to ourselves. A long time ago I discovered that I had to lose the security of belonging in order to find the freedom to search, and had to give up God in order to find myself.

Every two weeks cruise ships docked in Izmir and I was amazed to see American youngsters debarking—in sneakers and blue jeans, carrying knapsacks. I've always thought of Mediterranean cruises as trips that old people take when they are wealthy and retired, but times must have changed because every cruise ship coming in from Istanbul had a cargo of American young people. I had heard of guitar-playing panhandlers in Istanbul who were embarrassing the American Consulate there but I couldn't imagine them being successful enough to embark on a cruise. Never having panhandled I suppose I'm in no position to judge.

Strange, perhaps, but those kids looked good to me. Turkish students had too recently emerged from genuine poverty to care about playing make-believe, so they were almost always dressed up—white shirt, tie, jacket, neat hair, shined shoes. Barefoot, bewhiskered, grubby Americans looked so strange on the streets of Izmir that people turned and stared quite openly, but I felt an emotional tug because, grubby or not, they were from home and, as much as I loved Turkey, I knew I was an American. My impatience with American foreign policy was the impatience of one who wanted America to be a truly great country. My love of such young people was tied up with the hope that they might avoid being seduced by the system and help America realize that greatness.

Arnold Toynbee had been writing in the *International Herald Tribune*, reflecting on his visit to the United States. He said that in most countries of the world young people are clamoring for things they've never had, but in America young people had too many things. He concluded, "These are youngsters who have so much cake they are sick of it." I wondered if they were sick of it because it had been substituted for more important things. Perhaps they were sick of the means that produced it, sick of the callous indifference to the economic inequities of our society, the driving ambition so destructive of human relationships, and the sublimation of everything to the drive for power and money. Toynbee seemed to think these young people were going to be responsible for a value upheaval that might save America. I hoped he was right.

Winter in Izmir began the first of January and ended the first of February. Then spring came. In the narrow street behind the apartment boys rolled metal hoops on the pavement and girls played leapfrog and hopscotch. Across the boulevard in front of the apartment, tea sellers set out the little tables and chairs that had been stored for the month.

One day, riding in a *dolmus,* we saw a little girl carrying a twig of almond blossoms—fragrant, delicate, pink. Rebecca moved closer to her and the little girl held out the blossom. Rebecca sniffed and said, "*Merhaba*" (Hello). They moved closer to each other and were friends. As Rebecca touched the blossom—tiny fingers probing where curiosity directed—I shared in the wonder of learning.

We were raising a little Turk. Rebecca and Marta played with two Turkish girls next door and there was no English spoken between them. When Sarge passed a dish to her at the table, Rebecca thanked him with "*cok merci,*" a frequently used combination of Turkish and French. When she wanted to know what something was, she asked, "*Bu ne?*" instead of "What's this?" When she wanted us to watch her perform she said, "*Gel! Bak!*" (Come! Look!) She used *hayir* (no) and *evet* (yes) and used *cabuk* to make people hurry. It was fascinating to watch her language development because she was learning English and Turkish simultaneously.

In late February we were in an earthquake, my first. It centered in the northern Aegean Sea, killing nineteen people, injuring more than forty and leaving seven hundred homeless on the Greek islands of Hagios Evstratios and Lesvos (the home islands of Aristotle and Epicurus). I became aware of it in the middle of the night when Sarge asked me why I was shaking his bed. When we were fully awake, we both realized that it was not only the beds that were shaking. The doors of the room and the ceiling light were swinging back and forth and we could hear water sloshing out of the toilet. As we looked out the windows to the mountains, I thought the mountains were moving and then realized, with a sinking feeling, that mountains don't move—it was our building that was moving. The whole building was swaying. Sarge and I clung to each other, terrified yet having no idea what to do. We both knew what to do in hurricanes, but earthquakes are not part of the New England scene and we were ignorant. Even common sense didn't suggest anything other than not trying to use the elevator. We did check on the girls but they had slept through the quake and wondered why we were waking them. It seemed hours before the building stopped rocking but we were told it was only a few minutes.

In the morning it seemed unreal but there were cracks in walls and ceiling and everybody was talking about it. The common reaction of Americans was helplessness. In school the next day the children were told that apartment dwellers should sit astride a doorway because the frame of a building may withstand the shock. In all other forms of natural disaster, the earth is there—solid, dependable, perhaps the only really dependable element. In an earthquake the dependable is no longer dependable. It would be a disturbing memory for some time.

One day I was late getting to work, had arrived three minutes before class time and dropped puffing into a chair in the teachers' room. The *odaci* (office man) brought me a glass of tea, and after a few sips I began to relax and smile. As I did, one of the teachers said, "That is why we love you. There is always a sparkle." I couldn't imagine any faculty member at the University of Massachusetts saying that to me. Life in Turkey is much slower and easier and has about it a quality of caring generally lacking at home except in close relationships.

Most of the time I commuted to work by riding the ferry from Karsiyaka to downtown Izmir and then taking a *dolmus* for the balance of the trip out to the college. One day as I was standing on a curb, waiting for a *dolmus*, an inter-city bus pulled up and stopped. I knew that when buses were on a return trip and had few passengers they sometimes offered rides to people waiting for taxis, so I wasn't particularly surprised when the driver opened the door and invited me on. It was after he had closed the door that I saw that there were no other passengers—I was the only one other than the driver. Then I knew I had made a mistake. I sat at the back of the bus and prayed. Before we got to the university the driver took the bus off onto a side road and stopped. Then he motioned for me to come to the front of the bus. Terrified, I did as I was told. When I got to the front I saw that he had unzipped his trousers and wanted me to see what he was offering. Then I discovered how much Turkish I really knew. I told him I was a happily married woman and that I had made a mistake by getting on the bus, and I was sorry if I had given him the wrong message. I called on his courtesy to me as a foreign guest in his country. I told him I was a teacher on my way to a class at the university and that my students would be worried if I didn't show up on time. I had ten minutes of panic but though the bus driver was eager he was not mean or vicious. He heard me and understood what I was saying. He opened the back door of the bus and then chased me to it. As I took the first step down I felt his hand between my legs but I kept going. Later I realized how lucky I was that he had settled for a grab.

When I got to the University I told my fellow teachers what had happened. Their uproarious laughter was unexpected but when they explained, I saw that it was clearly my own fault. They pointed out that I was wearing a sleeveless dress (a sure sign of a loose woman) and that I had gotten on a bus that had no other passengers. The proper move at that point would have been to turn around immediately, thank the bus driver, and get off. When I didn't do that I led him to believe that I wanted the same thing he did.

Kurban Bayram, the Muslim sacrifice holiday, was on the 10th of March the year we were in Izmir. When we had been in Ankara, Betsy and Marta watched with grim fascination the slaughter of lambs by our neighbors, but I saw only the blood that remained to stain the ground. In Izmir I too watched the slaughter, drawn to it with a kind of horrible unbelief. In our apartment there were six branches of a Turkish extended family and so there were six sheep killed, skinned, and butchered in the back yard that morning. The eldest member of the family slit each animal's throat in perpetuation of the ancient ritual and then a professional slaughterer took over. It was a day for reflection. For a week there were sheep in every backyard, sheep tied to telephone poles, sheep being driven to town from all the neighboring communities. This day the backyards of Izmir were red and the odor of death hung in the air. At first I felt carried back to an era in a barbaric past, but then realized that I could not so easily escape. We might not slaughter the lambs in our back yards but we certainly enjoyed the meat on our tables.

I knew it was going to be difficult to leave my students. In one of my classes there were two young people in love but trapped in Turkish tradition. Murat was tall, slender, sensitive, with a wonderful smile and a good mind. Nadide was a quick, restless, searching girl who wanted her independence. The most they could do together was cut classes in the afternoon and go, surreptitiously, to the movies. The very fact that they had chosen each other militated against acceptance of the relationship by their parents. Had Murat's family taken the initiative in selecting Nadide as a daughter-in-law (assuming she was socially eligible) it would have been all right, but having met accidentally made it quite impossible. I talked with Nadide one afternoon and she exhibited a tragic acceptance of the situation. She knew that her relationship with Murat would end when college was over and she would marry someone chosen by her parents.

The situation was changing slowly in places like Ankara where the atmosphere was more cosmopolitan, but there were few signs of change in Izmir. Tradition was strong, yet young people were being exposed to ideas and influences from Europe and America and change was inevitable.

As the end of our year approached, I reflected frequently on the changes my experience in Izmir had wrought in me. I was more alive than I had been in some time, I was more aware of needing others, I was better able to control my tongue, which had always seemed to be in the service of my mind rather than my heart. One day I made a terrible error with that tongue. I was trying to be funny and make a joke (dangerous in another language and culture). Students in law school, medical school and other prestigious places of learning sometimes referred to an eager, hard-working student as an *inek* (cow). One day in class I used this word to refer to Ramazan, a hard-working young man in my class at Yüksek. What I didn't know until later was that the joke is not appropriate for a student from a village background and so my joke inflicted pain on one of whom I was very fond. At least I was becoming aware of the things I said that hurt, but knew that the next step was to become aware before I spoke instead of afterward.

Bülent, one of the students, asked me what would happen to President Johnson after the election. I didn't understand his question so he became more specific. Would Johnson be tried as a war criminal or simply executed without a trial? It was at such times that I appreciated the differences between us. These students believed that Johnson had been condemned by the world and should be shot. Their argument was that if we have, anywhere in our country, a legalized death sentence under which men are condemned to die for crimes of violence, then Lyndon Johnson should be executed. By this time I was sure they were reading of student demonstrations throughout the United States where this chant was being heard: "LBJ, LBJ, how many kids did you kill today?"

Spring is the season of the *sünnet* parades. Every weekend we saw two or three and it was quite a spectacle. The word *sünnet* means circumcision and the parade was part of the ritual celebration of the young male's coming into adulthood. For days, the boy (eleven or twelve) was honored and prepared for the ritual. Vast quantities of food were prepared, the boy was taken to the bath for a thorough cleansing and was outfitted with a suit of elaborately embroidered white satin. On the day of the ritual, the boy was dressed in his new white clothes and a flat, circular blue hat was put on his head. Relatives and friends gathered for a feast at noon, sometimes with music and dancing.

In the middle of the afternoon, the father put the boy on a horse decorated with colorful bits of cloth and a new saddle. The boy then led a parade of relatives and friends through the streets. Afterward he was taken to a room in his home, put on the bed, and subjected to circumcision by the *sunnetci*, a man trained to perform this ritual act. The boy demonstrated his manhood by holding back any outcries or tears. He was then congratulated and praised for his bravery and manliness.

When I first saw a *sunnet* parade and learned of the ritual, I was as horrified as I had been at the sacrificial slaughter of the lambs, but as I thought about it, I couldn't help wondering if it might not be grounded in psychological wisdom. In Turkey, young people, with the exception of those from upper-class families, took on adult responsibility at an early age. The *sunnet* ritual was a rite of passage and the boy was aware of the transition it marked. He did not hover for years in that uncertain, ill-defined period we call adolescence.

Our first end-of-the-year picnic was with some of Sarge's students and I saw cruelty, the kind of cruelty that springs from lack of awareness. One of Sarge's young assistants, Emin, took every opportunity to outwit, outrun, or ridicule Genghis, the other assistant. Emin was the city boy—slim, handsome, confident and brash. Genghis was the country boy—heavy, slow, shy, but sincere and sensitive. Late in the afternoon Genghis Bey's village mother joined us. As she was being presented to us, Marta took the woman's hand, put it to her lips and then to her forehead as she had seen Turkish children do. It was a touchingly beautiful gesture—the first time Marta had made it, to my knowledge, but probably also the last because although Genghis' mother smiled and looked pleased, Emin and his friends laughed. Marta turned to me and pressed her face against my chest to hide her tears. Her tender gesture of respect had been mocked.

Then we had a picnic with my advanced class, at the university's peacock farm. Bülent carried Rebecca around on his shoulders and Sarge discussed politics with Murat. We ate and drank and sang. I wanted to prolong the picnic because I knew it was the last time I would see these young people. My love for the students was only partly because of the ego boost I got from their response to me. There was also the spontaneity, the ready laughter, the obvious caring for one another that characterized their relationships. I watched them grow and flourish and knew that I had contributed to that. All I could think of was, is this what every teacher goes through at the end of the year? I'd been with these young people for seven months, was going away and would probably never see them again. I had a deep sense of loss.

On May 16th I said goodbye to my class at Yüksek. Ramazan stood at the back of the farewell group looking as if he felt like crying but knew he must not. Hamiyet stood near the front, saying, "Teacher, we forget you not." Halis shouted from the crowd, "Socialism or capitalism—which, Teacher?"

That night the bay was particularly beautiful, the balcony doors were open to the sounds of the city, and I felt nostalgic. I remembered other nights, at Abdullah's Restoran with Sarge and the Birnikis, at the Basen with the Fulbright Commission, quiet nights at home. I remembered days at Teos and Pamukkale, days of wandering through history. We had visited Ephesus early one Sunday morning, walking down the Marble Way in a kind of awed silence broken only by the breeze and the occasional calling of a bird. I almost expected to see a child running over the marble pavement, a senator leaning against a column, or a lady of easy virtue idling in the doorway of a brothel. The life that made the city what it was had eternally recorded its presence. Speculating on the people and events that once made the ancient ruins live, I knew that Greek and Roman history would fascinate the most reluctant student if it could be studied in the setting in which it was made.

I went to Turkey searching, as I'd been searching all my life. Preparing to leave I was deeply peaceful. It was as if meaning eluded me when I pursued it and came to me unexpectedly and quietly at moments when I had given up the search.

On May 30th we began the journey back to America. I would have said, "the journey home" but it was no longer that simple—Turkey was also my home. One could not live and work and love in a country for two years without yielding up a part of oneself. I knew that I would never again be wholly American but would be more of a person in America because of Turkey.

12

Troubled Years

The first thing we saw when we walked into our future kitchen in Sunderland was a toilet bowl, with a rose growing out of it, standing in the black slate sink. The Beta Chi fraternity boys, to whom we had rented, had used their imagination on the room. The black-paper-covered insulation walls were covered with graffiti and the white pine subflooring was no longer white. After the shock wore off, we laughed and hired a cleaning company.

When the cleaning people arrived I had my first experience of reverse culture shock. In Turkey anyone coming in to work expected to be invited to have a cup of tea. We would sit down together and inquire about each other's families, sometimes showing pictures. We would talk about the work to be done and then begin negotiations about cost and time. The first figure asked would be too high, with the expectation that we would pay less. The completion date given would be optimistic with the expectation that we would allow at least half again as much time.

In Sunderland, the man supervising the cleaning operation came into the kitchen to speak to me. I began with some polite conversation and asked him if he would like a cup of coffee.

"Lady, I've got three men out there ready to work. The meter's running and it's your dime." I was startled and thoroughly rebuffed. The next day, driving into Amherst, I was looking for a street sign when the car behind me drew up alongside and the driver rolled his window down. "Hey, lady. If you don't know where you're going why don't you get off the road until you find out?" We were back in America and it was going to take some time to adjust.

Once again, however, the Sunderland house and the river helped me to stabilize and appreciate my life. Rebecca and I often walked down to the river, along the path through the ferns, as I had done with Marta when we first moved to Sunderland. One day, as we lay on our stomachs, with our hands in the water, I asked her if she realized that by putting our hands in the water we were changing the flow of the river. She seemed so interested that I went on to ask her if she could believe that every breath she drew and exhaled altered the whole world's atmosphere. She looked at me to see if I were joking. Satisfied that I was not, she nodded. At the age of three, a little girl will believe anything her mommy tells her but I couldn't help wondering how long it would be before she'd recall that moment and wonder if I'd really believed that.

In the fall of 1968 I was hired to teach an introductory philosophy course at Greenfield Community College. I recalled the excitement of my own first course in philosophy and wanted to make this course just as exciting for my students. It was essentially a course in comparative East-West philosophy. Although there was required reading in the appropriate original works, I introduced it by experiential material of my own design. Before having them read Hume I prepared a slide show of objects shown from different perspectives, so they were challenged to recognize that all they could really know about those objects were the sense perceptions they had and even those perceptions depended on how they were viewing the object. Everything else they added to the perception was drawn from the past, from memory. I used things in the classroom to press students back into more and more basic descriptions of what they were seeing. After a session on the idea of paradox, most of the students left with puzzled expressions on their faces. During the next session we talked it out and they began to see that there was little one could know with certainty.

My primary contribution to these students was having them call into question everything they had taken for granted. I suggested that if their beliefs were strong enough they would go back and affirm them. If those beliefs could be undermined by anything I said, or anything they read, then it was better to have questioned them.

For the last fifteen years I had believed I would one day teach. Now I was working as a teacher but not experiencing the satisfaction I had come to expect from my teaching in Turkey. Many of these students came to class looking bored and tired, and I struggled to get through the class period. Philosophy, which for me was so exciting, seemed to die as I tried to pass it on. I felt the emptiness that comes with the awareness that we can't pass it on—any of it—any more than we can pass things on to our own children. The few students who responded were those who really wanted to learn and were using what I offered as a vehicle for that learning.

It was many years later that I saw how I often got in the way. I remembered a student standing up to share something he had realized out of reading the assignment. I was thrilled to see what he had learned but, instead of continuing to listen and letting him finish his thought, I interrupted him, acknowledged him and then went on to elaborate on what he had said, thus robbing him and re-establishing the pecking order so he would know that what he saw was good but, as teacher, I could add to it and make it even better. At the time I remembered this incident I was embarrassed and wondered how many times I had taken away a student's win in order to re-assert my role as teacher.

There were days when life seemed good but there were those days when I felt that life was utterly senseless and that I hadn't even been able to achieve the day-to-day meaning that Sisyphus found. Sarge said I was running away again. Perhaps he was right. But there was something that kept me struggling. Perhaps it was a morbid fascination in seeing how it all turned out. Perhaps it was because, when I came back from my breakdown in 1952, I knew that suicide was no longer an option for me. As I wrote to one of my friends, "The search takes us there and back, back to the understanding that there is no here, no there, no search."

I also began work that fall on my doctorate in philosophy and the first paper I wrote questioned the justifiability of observation claims. The question I asked was whether it might be that "I," instead of being the name of an entity with a continuing existence, was merely a formal indicator pointing to an organizing principle. My professor was impressed with the paper and encouraged me to continue in the department, but early in the program, I discovered that I could not pursue the doctorate without satisfying language requirements in German and French. I had already satisfied language proficiency requirements at Cornell and was unwilling to commit the time necessary to study two more languages.

As I was wondering what to do next, I heard that Dean Allen, from Stanford, had joined the University of Massachusetts faculty and was creating excitement in the School of Education. He was experimenting with a modular curriculum which meant that students could pick and choose from among a host of offerings. I was told I could give major attention to educational philosophy, so in the spring term of 1969, I switched to the School of Education. By spring of 1971, I had completed course work for my doctorate and started work on my dissertation. It was to be about academic recognition of non-academic learning and was based on my experience and the children's experiences of learning in Turkey.

In Sunderland, every weekend and most evenings in the fall of 1969 we worked picking vegetables and preparing them for freezing. By the beginning of November the root cellar held the winter's supply of potatoes, onions, carrots, parsnips and squash and the freezer was filled to capacity with vegetables and fruit. We had jars of strawberry jam and bottles of dandelion and boysenberry wines. I had a glow of satisfaction in having our winter's supply of food prepared. I felt like a squirrel must feel when it has stashed away a supply of nuts for the winter. Our last family Thanksgiving in Sunderland was in 1969. My brother and his family were there, as was my father. Mother was temporarily in a nursing home in Amherst where they were trying to get her to walk again after she had broken her hip. She refused to cooperate and they were unsuccessful. After Christmas, Dad took her back to Stratford but she never walked again.

In the summer of 1970 we entertained and Sarge gardened. Sarge's sister Charlotte and her husband Milton visited often and it was a relaxed, pleasant summer. But by the end of the summer it was evident there were things that needed to be done—things we had done when we first bought the house, such as roof repairs and interior painting. Suddenly it seemed as though all we were doing was working—either on the house, in the garden, or at the University. There was too little time for the relaxation we both enjoyed, and it looked as if this would be a continuing process. We would never be through. That's just the way it was with big, old houses. Sarge acknowledged that although he loved the place, he was tiring more easily and the prospect of always working as hard as we had in the past two years since returning from Turkey was not appealing. That summer someone passing through town saw the house, inquired about it, then came to see us with an offer—an offer that acknowledged the transformation we had effected in the property. We agonized over the decision and finally decided to sell.

Our friends James and Inez Fuller had both died recently and their house on Farview Way in Amherst was vacant. It was just a few blocks from the University, in good condition, and seemed like an ideal solution. We bought it. The house was a traditional Cape Cod cottage with two bedrooms and bath on the first floor, two bedrooms and bath on the second. Rebecca, Sarge and I had rooms on the first floor, Marta and Tim (who had come to live with us) were on the second. Having our teenagers on the second floor meant that most of the noise they called music didn't dominate the house.

One day when Marta was fourteen, she came home from school and asked me, "Momma, will you take me to the doctor for birth control pills or should I run the risk of getting pregnant?"

When I had recovered from the shock of having her ask the question, I made a quick decision and we went to see the doctor. The next question was, "Mom, may I bring Peter home with me some nights? It's dangerous parking out in the woods and here we could listen to music and be with you and Daddy sometimes."

This was even more shocking. All I could think of was my mother. Every time I had a date she would stay up until I came home and then, if I failed to come in from the car fast enough, she would start switching the porch light on and off. If that did not work, she would come out on the porch and call to me. "It's time to come to bed, young lady!" Sarge and I talked about it, he persuaded me that it was okay, and the next weekend Peter had Saturday night supper and Sunday morning pancakes with our family. After that he was with us most weekends and sometimes in the middle of the week. Once I got over the initial shock, it seemed sensible. The relationship between the two was a joy to observe. Marta and Peter were together until 1973 when Marta graduated from high school and went to California, where Jan had moved a few years before.

Although Sarge and I had been residents of Massachusetts since we married in 1962, that marriage was not recognized by the Commonwealth. It had taken place in Connecticut before Sarge was legally permitted to marry in Massachusetts. Sarge's sister, Charlotte, had talked with us several times about having our marriage legalized in Massachusetts. She was concerned that should anything happen to Sarge, Rebecca and I would be unprotected. So, on the 4th of June, 1971, we gathered a few friends in the living room of Farview Way and stood before the Reverend Mr. Bob Hopkins to legalize our marriage. There was an amusing aspect to it. Sarge had not explained our situation to the colleagues he invited and some were left wondering, since Rebecca was a visible acknowledgment of our earlier union. He never did explain, saying it was more fun that way. The vows we took that day were an affirmation of the vows we made to each other in Enfield when we were first married. Sarge did not want an "until death do us part" vow and, since my first such vow had ended in divorce, I was quite agreeable. The vows we exchanged were to remain together, caring for each other and honoring each other, for as long as the relationship was mutually satisfying.

I knew I wasn't being entirely honest about my feelings for Sarge, but part of the problem was not really knowing what those feelings were. At times I was overwhelmed with tenderness toward him. When he was being loving, he appeared extremely vulnerable and I wondered how I could ever be other than tender and loving and considerate of him. But there were other times. Often our communications seemed to slide by each other. It was as if each of us were listening for what we wanted to hear and when we didn't hear that, we tuned out. Also, his sexual needs were much greater than mine and at times I was repelled by the whole damned thing. I put on a cloak of sexuality, at some point in my life, in order to cover up the terrible insecurity which was now so painfully evident. Had I really been a sexual woman or had I put on a good sex act because I couldn't imagine being accepted or loved for any other qualities I might have? How many times had I pretended interest in sex when all I really wanted was to go to sleep? The truth of the matter for me was that, even with Sarge, sex was only occasionally good.

Most of the time during sex I was in my head, thinking about something other than what was going on. I suspect this was a reflection of my upbringing, my thinking it was sinful and perhaps if I separated my mind from what was going on in my body, it would be less sinful. I was never honest enough to tell a partner what I really wanted or what would make it pleasurable for me, yet I always felt cheated by not having gotten it. One thing missing, except with Stanley, my farmer friend and lover, was the man's staying power. I had read, in Indian lore, of Tantric yoga in which the male and female are finally joined in *samadhi*. Ever since studying this with Professor Shute, I had sought to realize, in my life, the perfect union which would yield to both partners that sense of the divine. What had to be done to produce that was for two people to be aroused gradually, over long periods of time, until their union culminated in a simultaneous explosion. I'm sure that was in my mind during sex, especially all those times when I was waiting for what usually came—my partner's satisfaction and withdrawal long before I was there. And, I suspect, my thinking was as much a barrier to that ultimate satisfaction as was my upbringing.

When I tried to be honest with Sarge, he interpreted it as loving him less. How otherwise, since he didn't know of the years of pretending. Why the pretense? I guess that because, since I was twenty or so, men had been attracted to me sexually and I had come to regard sexuality as my primary worth to others. When I wore my hair in a bun and looked mousy, Sarge laughed and said, "If only they knew what kind of woman is hiding beneath that exterior." I was so hung up on the sexy female self-image that I was caught off guard when a male found something else of worth about me. Sometimes I despised my sexuality because it was what I had used all my adult life to get what I really wanted—affection and intimacy.

Sarge and I passed each other in the kitchen, lay next to each other in bed, went through the ritual of lovemaking, and I felt horribly, frighteningly empty. Or was it that my feelings for Sarge were other than I thought they were? At first, our attraction to each other was so great and our day-to-day living so compatible that the difficulty we had in communicating seemed unimportant, but it grew in importance every day.

Once I raised a silly little question about the setup of courses at Amherst High School. He automatically took the other side of the question, as he always did. There was some reason for his doing that because I was being pretty emotional about the issue, but I found myself wishing that just once, sometime when I was upset about something, he would say, "I understand how you feel, Honey." If he then went on to give me a reasonable alternative point of view, I believe I could have listened, but instead what I heard was negative, barbed, and frequently condescending, as if from his pinnacle of wisdom he was stooping to set me straight. I was so infuriated and insulted that for days our relationship was sour. Then we both made a conscious, deliberate effort to smooth things out because our relationship was generally better than anything either of us had known before.

Sarge said the good periods were always fraught with worry about how long they would last. He wanted life to coast along on a nice even plane. He didn't object to the highs but neither did he see their relationship to the lows. I wavered between wanting to please him and wanting to be honest. I read Karen Horney's *Self Analysis* and decided to take a whack at seeing if I could come to an understanding of myself. There had been a few incidents in recent years that were very revealing and I suspected that if I tried to record and understand some of my feelings, I might find that I could function more effectively, and more happily, as a human being.

Horney talked about a "compulsive suppression of feelings and wishes" and I became acutely aware of how much I suppressed my own feelings and wishes. The awareness had been just below the surface for a long time, and on occasions had shown up as I became briefly more assertive, but it never hit me as fully as it did one afternoon when I was remembering something that happened before I married Sarge. It was a little incident but indicative of so much more. A friend stopped in at nine in the evening, apologetically asking if I could type a paper for him, a paper due the next morning. I was studying at the time and it seemed that this friend's dropping in usually conflicted with my need to study or prepare for an exam or do some reading. But there was never any hesitation about dropping my own work and taking on his. I felt slightly martyred, very virtuous and sure that my friend would like me more than he would had I turned him down. Underneath I was disgusted with myself for not having been honest with him about my own work. Acknowledging this suppression of feelings, I had a good talk with Sarge about our relationship. Then we came together in a tender, passionate renewal of our love for each other and began exploring, talking, working through a lot of things.

Seeing Dr. Monroe for a physical, I talked to him about my periods of depression and told him that the most prominent characteristic of those periods was a profound dislike of self. I realized, after hearing myself, that it was only half true, because always battling with the feeling of self-hatred was the struggling, emergent feeling of self-respect that had been growing over the previous ten years. He asked me if I got angry during my periods of depression. The question struck me, because I rarely experienced that cleansing feeling that goes with a good honest burst of anger. I repressed negative feelings before anger got a real chance. The only times I expressed anger were in public situations, such as Town Meeting or a school committee meeting when I encountered sheer stupidity and realized how prevalent it was. Then I lashed out with sharp, cutting remarks that made me feel better at first, then terrible later on. At home I suppressed anger because memories of my mother's anger and Gerry's anger were so vivid and so frightening. And that sentence contains a telling omission—memories of my own anger in the years of my first marriage and the years of being a single mother of three small children.

It took some time between marriages for me to get on my own feet and become independent and I didn't want to relinquish that independence. Rereading *The Prophet*'s words: "Let there be spaces in your togetherness," I thought that perhaps I should create another dimension to my life. Perhaps I could find a sense of self-worth which would then enable me to relate to Sarge as an equal partner rather than as a parasite paying my way with sex and sweetness. If not, then I would return to the aloneness which had been my companion for many years and which was, perhaps, my destiny.

It was about that time that our relationship with Ian and Claudia Scott began to develop. Ian was a brilliant and handsome graduate student of Sarge's. Claudia was a pediatrician practicing in Greenfield. It was with them that we watched the moon landing, a couple of years earlier, since we didn't have television. At first it was just Ian coming to the house frequently for meetings with Sarge, who was his advisor, but then one day he brought his wife and from then on we saw a lot of them socially. Claudia was, at first glance, a strangely unattractive young woman, whose features seemed to be all too large and misplaced, but it took only a few hours with her to forget what she looked like because who she was took over.

Claudia and I said we would like to be next-door neighbors for the rest of our lives—we would like to be able to run in and out to borrow things from each other, to share joy and pain, love and life, to grow alongside each other. In Amherst we had evenings together two or three times a week and it wasn't many months into the relationship before we began discussing the possibility of four-person intimacy. It never came to fruition because although Sarge liked the idea of a liaison with the much-younger Claudia, Ian didn't have the same feeling about such a relationship with a much-older me. That was my first introduction, as an adult, to the double standard. It was okay for Sarge to be twenty years older than Claudia but not for me to be twenty years older than Ian. Our contemplation of such a relationship ended abruptly in late August.

Charlotte and Milton had come to Amherst for a weekend in late August. On Friday night we played bridge. The other three took it so seriously that when I flubbed badly, I felt like the village idiot. I wished we had someone else to make up the foursome. That night, at bedtime, I began lacerating myself and withdrawing from Sarge. His patient, persisting offer to hold me, love me, was enough to help me make an effort on my own behalf. It is marvelous what an orgasm does for me. I relaxed, slept, and woke feeling completely rid of the defensiveness, the self-condemnation. We played again on Saturday evening, and at one point Sarge remarked, "Betty can remember line and verse from one of her thirteenth-century philosophers but she can't remember the last card played in a bridge game." We all laughed and went on, but again, having been the butt of a joke, I was tense and uncomfortable.

It was ten o'clock when Charlotte looked at Sarge and said, "Are you okay?" He was struggling for breath and had a distant look in his eyes. "Shall I call the doctor?" she persisted. Sarge left the bridge table and I guided him to the couch where he lay down. By that time it was evident that he was not well but I seemed paralyzed. Charlotte called for an ambulance which arrived in record time. The paramedics started Sarge on oxygen and put him in the ambulance. I went with him. Charlotte followed in her car. When we got to the hospital our family doctor checked Sarge and then called in a cardiologist. Sarge had suffered a heart attack.

They moved him into a bed in the coronary care unit and I stood by him, holding his hand. Suddenly a violent tremor shook his body and he stiffened. The doctors came running in. He was having a massive one. We had gone into the hospital before midnight and by two o'clock in the morning I thought it was all over, that Sarge was gone. I was paralyzed, not even wanting to be touched by Charlotte, who tried to comfort me. I stood in the hall, dry-eyed and dead inside, sure that the man who had given new meaning to my life was dying. Twice his heart stopped and twice they started it. On one occasion the arrest had been several minutes long and I knew the anesthesiologist was alarmed. I heard him say,

"But it's been too long, there's bound to be damage." The cardiologist's reply was, "Perhaps, but look at that body. This is a young man. We can't let him go!"

The doctor allowed me to stay in the room with Sarge and I tried to direct my consciousness to him, wanting to give him my strength, wanting us to fight this thing together. I was unwilling to lose him. I stayed with him through the night. He was connected to a respirator and a maze of wires and tubes. The doctor had put him on a pacemaker which took over for about three hours until his heart began to function on its own again. By six o'clock Sunday morning he was quiet and stable. The doctor said the situation was extremely grave but at least he had a chance. The unanswered question was how severely had his brain been damaged by oxygen starvation during those periods of cardiac arrest. We had our first indication of that when he regained consciousness Monday morning. He made sounds that were not speech, he moved his arms and legs but the movements were random rather than directed. He seemed not to know me. He did not recognize the names of his children or his siblings. I remember running out to the ladies room and breaking into tears. The doctor told me Sarge had aphasia and had also suffered a stroke which accounted for the partial paralysis of his right side. I was unbelieving. How could this be happening?

By Wednesday he was making progress. He was still incoherent but at least there were occasional recognizable words and he seemed to know me. He was frustrated by his inability to communicate his needs. All day he had been saying "gydadex" and no one understood him. Sitting by him, holding his hand, and listening to him that afternoon I wondered if he might be asking for vitamins. When I asked if that's what he wanted, his face lighted up and he nodded his head. In the midst of all this he remembered his daily vitamins and was worried that he might not be getting them. Charlotte came by his room on Thursday to see if he recognized her but he seemed unable or unwilling to make the effort. It was obvious that he was severely disabled.

On Friday when I went in to see him his heartbeat was irregular and once again I feared I might lose him. When he cried I held him and tried to reassure him but the nurse suggested I let him cry, that the release would be good for him, provided I could control my own emotions. As I was leaving he managed to frame the question of what had happened to him and I told him. He cried again and asked why the doctor had not let him go. Sarge had suffered a terrible loss but, ironically, retained the ability to reflect on that loss. As I was leaving I said, "Goodnight, see you tomorrow," and he replied, "Goodbye, my darling." I cried all the way home and then called the hospital. I was afraid he would take his own life. The nurse monitoring him had heard him and made sure he was heavily sedated for the night.

Saturday morning he was much better. His memory was improving, his speech was better, he was smiling, laughing and occasionally swearing at his handicap. He asked for the children. By Saturday evening he was making an extreme effort to communicate. He obviously had something he wanted to say to me. When I finally realized what it was, I had to fight to maintain my composure. He was saying I would have to find someone else to make love to me because he was going to be a vegetable. I told him that vegetables neither introspect nor analyze, and the fact that he was talking about such a possibility ruled it out. Before I left for the night he told me that the doctor had been honest with him about what was ahead and that he was ready to put up a fight.

By Monday, September 6, I knew he was getting well because he gave me a real kiss for the first time since the attack and was asking questions about possible limitations on his sex life. When I spoke to the doctor later he said it was a good sign, that it indicated Sarge was getting lonely and if he was getting lonely he would make a greater effort to go home. Each evening when I left him I wondered if the phone would ring in the night, but each evening I left with more assurance and hope that we would have a future together.

Charlotte stayed in Amherst for several weeks. I spent most of my waking hours at the hospital and she provided care and companionship for Rebecca and kept the house going. Marta's relationship with Peter sustained her through the autumn.

Rebecca was upset with us for not waking her the night Sarge was taken to the hospital. Milton stayed at the house and, the next morning, told her what had happened. Later in school she wrote, "One night they came and took my father away to the hospital. I didn't see him go, I didn't get to say goodbye. Many weeks later they sent home somebody they said was my Daddy." Sarge looked as if he'd aged twenty years by the time he came home.

It was on the evening of September 27th when Charlotte, who had returned to New York, telephoned to tell me of the death of Sarge's sister, Susan. "Are you sitting down?" she asked and then, without waiting for a reply, "There is no easy way to say this. Susan dropped dead this morning." I did not really hear—it sort of glanced off my consciousness. Susan, Sarge's youngest sister, was only forty-two. How could she be dead? Charlotte said she had simply dropped in her classroom and been pronounced dead on arrival at the hospital. Visiting Sarge that evening I had to keep the news from him. Dr. Berkman asked me to wait until morning, saying that such news is better heard in the morning than at night. I went to sleep that night thinking of how mixed up are life and death.

On the 5th of October, almost six weeks since the night of the attack, Sarge came home from the hospital. Although I was glad to have him home, I worried constantly. I waited to hear the sound of him sleeping before I dared sleep myself and then it was only a half-sleep as I listened for any change in his breathing. By his third week at home there was noticeable progress but his mood swings were dramatic. He said he wanted to be able to read and write again but he had no patience with the process of re-learning things he had done without thinking for so many years. I was housekeeper, cook and constant guardian, but for only about a half hour a day would he let me help him learn to read and write again. Much of the time he was irrational, difficult and complaining. One minute he would be holding a book, tracing words with his finger; the next minute he would throw the book on the floor or at the wall, get up and go into his room, slamming the door behind him.

When he was near death, nothing mattered but his survival and I knew, more acutely than ever before, how much my life was bound up with his. But with him home from the hospital it was different. I could not help wondering how far back he would come, what kind of a life we would have together. By mid-October I was confronting the possibility that the man I married might have disappeared that night in the hospital. I felt enormous compassion for this man but I was in love with the memory of another—a man striding across the campus, tall and straight and smiling, coat thrown open in defiance of the weather, a man tanned and sweating as he cultivated the vegetable garden, a man tender and passionate as we made love, a man confident, sure and outgoing—and that man was gone, perhaps forever. On the 3rd of November Sarge went back into the hospital with an irregular heartbeat. From the time he first came home I had slept with my head near his chest so that I could immediately detect any irregularity, and the night before I had suspected that something was wrong and took him to the doctor in the morning. He stayed in the hospital for two weeks while the doctors made adjustments in medication.

From early December Sarge seemed to make progress. He was working with a speech therapist twice a week, I brought home books so that he could learn to read again and he worked with a calculator to recover the ability to do simple arithmetic. He had difficulty with numbers, being unable to hold more than three digits in memory at one time. This meant that he could read a phone number out of the directory but not remember it long enough to dial it. So he would write out the number, but his writing was illegible, even to him, and he would find that he still could not call the friend he wanted to reach. His frustration was certainly understandable. He knew who he had been, what he had done, and that knowledge made it all the more difficult to accept the person he had become.

Trouble seems to come in bunches. On February 6, 1972, my first husband, Gerry Quigley, died. He had been in the hospital for a week or so with what was called a "minor" heart problem but then slipped away in the night. The suddenness of his death shocked me. There was no opportunity to see him, no chance to say, "I'm sorry," even if it would only have meant, "I'm sorry for whatever hurt and pain you suffered because of me." Our life together had been an open sore, torturing both of us. But with his death, so soon after we had lost Susan and almost lost Sarge, I realized that I was poorer, that his death had, in fact, diminished me. The girls and I went to the funeral but Jerry refused to accompany us. His father had continued to reject him as he grew up, and Jerry said he didn't want to face all those Kaman Aircraft people who had witnessed the rejection.

After our divorce Gerry had been alone until the year before his death when he married the woman who had been his secretary for years at Kaman. He had been financially successful in life and when he died he left everything to his new wife, except for token bequests to his children. Considering how little he had done for the children while he was alive I was bitter and angry. The reading of his will gave me the final chance to be right, the final chance to proclaim what a bastard he was but somehow there was no win in it, only sadness for what might have been.

One evening I had a family meeting with my kids. Jerry had been troubled by unresolved conflicts in his feelings about his father, and Marta confessed that she had felt guilty for years because she had not spoken out when Jan and I were talking about him. He had always been good to her and yet she never spoke up. Listening to them I saw, with painful clarity, how I had influenced their reactions to their father. After talking it out we had a good cry together. I slept better that night.

In mid-February the doctor told Sarge that he would not be able to go back to his job, that he could function all right as a human being but not as a college professor. After his talk with Sarge, the doctor privately told me that I should get busy and get my degree because I would have to contribute to the support of the family. Interestingly, Sarge's first reaction to the doctor's pronouncement seemed to be relief. I knew he had been going to the office but that day he told me all he'd been doing was pushing papers around on his desk, looking at the stuff he had written but could no long read, drinking coffee and hoping one of his colleagues would stop and visit. But then, after that first, honest reaction, he went into a deep depression. He sat in front of the television for hours every day. He would not talk with us except to respond to questions, as briefly as possible, and he had about him a sadness that tore me apart. My frustration at being unable to help him and my sense of having lost the man I loved were almost overwhelming.

Then, on April 7th we had another of those middle-of-the-night phone calls from the police. Jerry was in the hospital. He had been on his way home from the university when a driver, running a stop sign, came speeding out of a side street and hit Jerry's car broadside.

The Amherst police told me that an ambulance had taken my son to Northampton Hospital. I called Claudia and she met me at the hospital where we found Jerry bloody and broken on a gurney in the emergency room corridor, where they were "too busy" to have examined him. Claudia intervened and demanded attention. After examination they said he had a bubble on his heart and would need to be taken to Hartford Hospital which had the equipment and personnel to deal with it. Claudia and I followed the ambulance to Hartford, a distance of about fifty miles. For most of the night we waited to hear whether Jerry would live or die. They finally told us that he had a fractured skull, fractured spine, concussion, internal bleeding and might lose one eye, but that he had a good chance of survival.

For ten days I drove to Hartford every day until he was through the worst of it. The doctors told me the most serious injuries were the skull fracture and the damage to the brain stem. There was no way to predict the long-term outcome. Jerry had planned to be an urban designer when this deadly accident nearly took his life and set him on a different path.

At first I didn't cry at all. There was an unreal quality about everything that was happening, and had happened, over the preceding months. Then the control broke and I cried all the time. If anybody asked about Jerry, the tears flowed, if they asked about Sarge, the tears flowed, if they looked at me sympathetically, the tears flowed. Finally I gave in and went to see the University psychiatrist. He said that when I talked about Gerry's death and his will, it sounded as if I were raging inside. I hadn't thought of that word or emotion but I realized how appropriate it was. All the years the children were growing up, Gerry had contributed the minimal amount to their support and I had expected that he would provide for them generously in his will. When he failed to do that I was left with a strange feeling of impotence. I could no longer even let him know how I felt about what he had done.

The doctor helped me see that I was losing myself in the midst of all the trauma. There were some things I couldn't change but one thing I could do was start building a life of my own. He said that however much I loved Sarge, I would grow to resent him if I waited for him to get well enough to be a real companion again. He made me realize that the best way to get beyond all the trauma of the last year was to get to work.

In July I began hunting for a job and by late August I was working in Dedham, Massachusetts, for an educational research company called Heuristics. It had run an ad in the Boston papers and received hundreds of responses. Someone in the office, however, had pulled out a letter I wrote a few weeks earlier and put it on top of the stack of applications. The head of the company liked the letter, called me in for an interview and hired me. I started at the beginning of the school year.

It was my salvation. Since Dedham, just outside of Boston, was a ninety-mile drive from Amherst, I lived in a motel down there during the week and drove home weekends. Marta and Tim, who was living with us, managed the house and got Rebecca to school during the week. Sarge was on his own. (He'd always been a better cook than I, so I knew he'd be okay.) The motel was near the office and every night I went from the office to a health club where I worked out, swam, used the sauna and showered. Then I went out to eat and back to the motel for television and an early sleep. It was the best medicine I could have had. One of my colleagues at Heuristics was Dwight Smith and we became good friends. He sometimes cooked dinner for me, after which we would sit with coffee, gabbing or just listening to music. Dwight was my first gay friend.

My first few weeks on the job were spent editing and preparing abstracts from reports that had been written on results of the previous school year's research. I got an ego boost when my boss told me that I had been the deciding factor in getting the Worcester School System contract, that they had been impressed with my report on their work and that they liked me when they interviewed me. When school opened I began working with Worcester's Title I and Title III programs. Worcester was halfway between Boston and Amherst so, by the end of September, I had moved back home. I commuted to Worcester three days a week and stayed in Boston only when I had to be there for meetings.

The work was unexpectedly satisfying. I was leading after-school workshops for teachers and following up with classroom observation to support them in using what they learned in the workshop. I was observing in thirty inner-city schools, in all of which the children were socially and economically disadvantaged and where as many as nine languages were spoken. It was here that I noticed children seeming to be losing interest in school by the end of third grade. I also noticed how many fewer children were asking questions. When I asked one teacher about this, she laughed and replied, "If we didn't shut down that questioning we'd never get anything done." I remembered my own questioning, as a child, and was saddened. It seemed to me that honoring those questions was the most important job a teacher had.

Dad was in his early eighties when he had his first stroke. It was barely noticeable except when he seemed to be searching unsuccessfully for a word or when he faltered in his bridge bidding. This was a time when I intervened on behalf of Dad against my brother, who wanted to take over Dad's affairs. Paulie's decision was based on the day he saw Dad give the paperboy a ten dollar tip. Paulie said that if Dad was that irresponsible with money he'd have to take over or there wouldn't be enough money to support them. I retorted that Dad was the one who had earned that money, had invested it and had made sure he and Mother had enough to live on in their old age. I felt that if he wanted to give the paperboy a big tip that was his prerogative. Paulie went to court, however, and was successful. My father was hurt and insulted and I didn't blame him. I was furious with my brother. I had always respected my father for continuing to allow Gram to handle her own finances, even when she had been committed to the state hospital, and I was sad that Paulie failed to extend Dad the same courtesy.

Mother had not walked since she had broken her hip and was confined to a wheelchair. It was as if she'd made the decision that having cooked and cleaned for sixty years of marriage it was her turn to be waited on. Dad did his best but it soon became evident that he wasn't up to the task, particularly since mother had become incontinent and he was confronted with changing and laundering bed sheets every day.

I hadn't forgotten the scene of Gram and her brothers being taken from their home and had resolved that our folks would remain in their home as long as possible. My brother and I hired caregivers and then took turns being in Stratford on weekends. At first the caregivers were there from early morning until Mom and Dad were tucked in bed at night. Dad insisted they'd be okay for the night but one day we heard a story from the morning helper—a story that made it clear day care wasn't quite enough.

As the story went, the caregiver arrived in the morning to find Dad asleep in his twin bed and Mother asleep in a pile of bedding on the floor. Mom's story was that she woke in the night having soiled her bed and called out to Dad to get her cleaned up but, instead of helping her, he simply grabbed the sheets on his side of her bed, lifted them, rolled her out the other side of the bed onto the floor and went back to his own bed and to sleep. She said she yelled at him to get up but he ignored her so when she heard him snoring she gave up, pulled a blanket from the bed to cover herself and went back to sleep. Dad professed to know nothing about what happened but I've always thought that at some level he was remembering all the indignities he had suffered at her hands and was evening the score.

In the winter of 1973 Dad had another stroke, then developed pneumonia and was taken to the hospital. He was eighty-four and the pneumonia was exhausting him. The doctor said he seemed to have neither the strength nor the will to recover. On my last visit, he reached over, took my hand, and squeezed it as he looked at me and then closed his eyes. For several hours I sat by his bed, holding his hand. He did not open his eyes again. When it was time for me to leave, I leaned over, kissed him on the forehead, and said, "Daddy, I love you." He turned his head away but not before I saw the tears. I had never seen my father cry.

I stood by his bed, holding his hand and crying softly. This was my beloved father and he was leaving me. I knew he not only adored me, but that he also respected and admired me. With the self-image problems I had, it was good to know that I had such a father. And now I was going to lose him. I didn't know exactly when but I knew he was going and I also knew I might not be there when he did. "Daddy, I want you to know that you've been the best father a girl could have had. I'll always remember the things we did together, the things you taught me to do, the way you taught me to live. You will be with me always. I love you."

I kissed him again, felt the pressure of his fingers on mine, then said goodbye and left. My father died five hours later that night, February 18, 1973. Although I had known he was going, I was unprepared for the loss and grief. My father was one of the few people in my life who loved me unconditionally. With my father I had experienced a wordless intimacy throughout my life. I had recognized that intimacy in my communications with Norm Stewart and Alex Wang but was saddened because in neither case could it flourish. It had never been present in either of my marriages to Gerry Quigley and in that relationship I realized there was a difference between sex and intimacy. In nursing Marta and Rebecca I experienced the intimacy. With Sarge there had been one or two isolated instances of the kind of communication I sought but they were brief and almost immediately submerged. It was almost as if we were embarrassed by the degree of intimacy, as if we were intruding into each other's soul. Perhaps the closest I came to intimacy in verbal communication was with Clarence Shute, my philosophy advisor at the University of Massachusetts, because I wrote with an intimacy that disclosed who I was and Clarence Shute recognized me. When my father read my philosophy papers he recognized me too. I remember him saying, "I don't understand much of what you write, dear, but it is so beautiful I read it over and over." Going through his things, after his death, I found a collection of letters and papers I had sent him. With his death there was a painful resurgence of longing.

Marta, Rebecca and I spent Easter weekend that year with Mother in Lordship. With Dad gone and Mother so near the end, I knew it might be the last time I stayed in the house. Suddenly it seemed to me that when Mother died I would no longer be anyone's child. Saturday night the child in me wept.

On Easter Sunday Mother told me she wanted to die. The doctor had not allowed her to go to Dad's funeral. He said it might "be too much for her." Too much for what? Mom and Dad had been married for sixty-three years and when he went, she wanted to go also. If she had died at his funeral it would have been perfect. But instead she spent the next few months suffering while doctors tried to prolong her life against her will. She refused to eat so they began feeding her intravenously. She continued to lose weight and they began even more radical interventions. I was aghast at the indignities heaped on this poor woman who was asking nothing more than to be allowed to die. Every time I saw her she pleaded with me to have them let her go. But neither Mother nor I had any say in the matter. Connecticut was a Catholic state and doctors were committed to doing everything in their power to prolong life. My brother and I also clashed over Mother's care. I wanted them to respect her wish to die with dignity. Paul accused me of trying to "push her into the grave." In fairness to him, Paul was still a devout Episcopalian and supported the doctors in what they believed was right.

Mother and I did not have the kind of relationship I had with my father. As her life neared its end, I was saddened by our lack of closeness but didn't know what to do about it. In the last few weeks that she was hospitalized I spent many hours at her bedside. One day, a week before she died, I was visiting her as she struggled with questions about the meaning of life and whether or not her being alive had made any difference. It was then I vowed I would not die wondering if my life had mattered—I'd be damned sure that my being alive *had* made a difference.

At the time of settling our parents' estate, Paul and I went to the lawyer's office together to sign the necessary papers. It had been an amicable settlement but when it was done Paul shook hands with Sarge, then turned to me and said,

"Now, Betty, we can put an end to this brother-sister nonsense. It was necessary as long as they were alive but now it's over." I was stunned, perplexed. What did he mean? But before I could ask, he had turned and left the attorney's office. It was the last time I saw my brother, the last time we spoke, and I have never known the meaning of his cryptic statement. For years I speculated about that meaning. Perhaps I had been adopted; perhaps he had. Perhaps he resented the closeness between Dad and me, or perhaps he thought it unfair that Dad gave me financial help after my first divorce. I knew he was angered by my wanting to let mother die. Perhaps he gave up on me when I left the church. None of these things seemed enough to warrant cutting me completely out of his life, but speculating was just that and nothing more. I wrote letters, made phone calls, but Paul was true to his word and never responded. The answers to my questions went to the grave with him, in 1992.

In mid-April I had gone to the office in Dedham for a series of meetings and, while there, got a call from a colleague of Sarge's who was in the Boston area and wanted to take me to dinner. We had known each other since I first met Sarge and although I was delighted by the invitation, I was also a little afraid because Ted was so attractive. He took me to dinner, we drank, we danced, we listened to music, we walked, we looked out at Boston from the top of the Prudential Building, and then went back to his room. I knew that I was alive and that I was a woman. Only the next morning did I deal with the guilt. There's still a bittersweet quality to the memory.

Later that spring Sarge and I started counseling sessions with one of the University's marriage counselors. Most of the sessions were unproductive, but in late May, I blurted out the story of my night in Boston and, strangely, it became the catalyst for a noticeable change in Sarge. We grew closer and began to plan a future together, something we had both avoided doing. He finally stopped going to the University.

Sarge had been fifty-six when he had his heart attack, one month past the age at which he could have retired on a disability pension which would have been equal to the salary he was earning. As it was, by the time he gave in and acknowledged that he would never be a professor again, the only option he had was to take regular retirement, at the lowest rung on the ladder. This meant that our income was cut by two-thirds. In addition, in choosing his retirement plan, Sarge elected an option that would give us even less income for the remainder of his life but would provide me with two thirds of that income for the remainder of my life, should he predecease me. Had Charlotte not urged us to legalize our marriage, I would not have that protection and am deeply grateful to her.

Marta had graduated from Amherst High School, at sixteen, and had moved to California where Jan was already living. We had been having glowing reports from both of them and, with Mother and Dad gone, began to discuss moving there ourselves. Amherst had too many reminders of what Sarge had once done and could no longer do—the office a block away to which he walked wistfully before finally giving in to the knowledge that there was no longer a place for him there, the garden going to seed because he could no longer labor in it, the snow covering driveway and sidewalks because he could no longer shovel. And there was another factor. Rebecca, who had shown early signs of being a bright and independent learner, was not happy in school, and the school psychologist had suggested transferring her to the special education class. There was no way I would let that happen.

The more we talked about California, the more enthusiastic we became. The warm climate was appealing and Sarge's doctor said it would be easier on his heart than the extremes of heat and cold in Amherst. Sarge had been in much better spirits since his affirmation of life in mid-May. Our relationship was more open and was characterized by greater honesty than had been the case in two years. We could have a new start and we'd begin by driving across the country—something neither of us had done. Our kids, except for Rebecca and Timothy, were grown up and gone from home. I completed my work with Heuristics and resigned at the end of the school year. My doctoral dissertation was submitted to the university and my adviser said I could defend it by phone on a conference call. We sold the Amherst house and most of our furniture, and packed our bags. The money from the sale of the house was invested and on the 15th of July, 1973, Sarge, Rebecca and I left Massachusetts and began the drive across the country.

By the beginning of September we were comfortably settled in Berkeley in a small three-bedroom house with a camellia tree in the back yard and fuchsias all around the foundation.

Sarge had trouble adjusting to a fall with no work. I had found a job at the University Without Walls in Berkeley, Rebecca and Timothy, now living with us, were in school and Sarge was home alone. In planning our move, we hadn't taken into account that Sarge would not have friends or associates in California and would have difficulty making new ones because he was so self-conscious about being handicapped. For a while we accepted social invitations but his pervasive moroseness—which had disappeared for most of the trip but returned as soon as we got to Berkeley—settled down on people and occasions like a blanket and I began looking for excuses to go without him. It was evident he was deeply unhappy but I seemed unable to affect that. Our sexual encounters during this period were invariably followed by tears acknowledging the enormity of our loss.

Just before Thanksgiving, Sarge returned to New York to spend the holiday with Charlotte and Milton and to decide whether or not he would stay in California. At the airport, saying goodbye to him, I felt I was being virtually torn apart. I cried all the way home, but knew that only in part was I crying for the man leaving Oakland that day; I was primarily crying for the man taken from me two years earlier. We didn't know if he would come back—he had not said—but on November 26th we got a call saying he was returning. He seemed like a different person when he arrived. The trip had been good for him and he had spent some time with Claudia, who always bolstered his self-esteem. But within two weeks I was again overwhelmed by his need for reassurance. He seemed not to have the sense of self-worth that would make such constant reassurances unnecessary.

I felt trapped with Sarge but to me this was not an acceptable way to feel about someone who was suffering and down. My feelings about life were too confused even to lend themselves to expression, but of one thing I was sure. I didn't like the person I was becoming.

13

The est Training and Transformation

Early in December while we were waiting for a table at the Jade Pagoda, a little gem of a restaurant we'd discovered in Berkeley, I began a conversation with the woman next in line. When we left the line to go to our table, I thought, "What a shame. I liked that woman and I'll probably never see her again." Throughout dinner I was preoccupied; how could you meet someone and simply have them disappear from your life? Then I did something I'd never done before. I pulled a business card from my purse and wrote on the back of it, "I enjoyed talking with you and would like to get acquainted. If you feel the same, call me." As we were leaving the restaurant, I dropped the card on her table.

The next day Carolie Coffey called and we arranged to meet for lunch. As we talked over lunch, I learned that she was a teacher of sociology at a Bay Area community college and the mother of four grown children. We talked as if we had known each other for years. Then, just as we were leaving, she said, "Someone gave me a couple of tickets for a seminar and I'm not going to use them. It might be a good way for you to get acquainted and I hear the guy is a great lecturer." She handed me two tickets to a special guest seminar about the *est* Training. So it happened that in mid-December of 1973, at the Jack Tarr Hotel in San Francisco, Sarge and I were introduced to the *est* Training.

My first impression was that everyone there looked amazingly healthy. And they were all smiling. My second impression was of the attention to detail, everything was so orderly. On cloth-covered tables, cards and pencils and brochures were laid out as if the distance between them had been measured. A man named George printed name tags for us and we entered a ballroom where there were close to a thousand people.

I was enthralled even before the young Australian seminar leader, Stewart Emery, began to speak. His engaging smile, athletic body, and to-die-for tan made me sit up and take notice. I might have wondered about some of the promises he seemed to be making except that it looked as if most of the people putting on this event had realized those promises. The one that struck me, though I can't pretend to have understood it, was about things clearing up just in the process of life itself. I heard those words as a promise for better things to come and was ready to try anything. We had come to California hoping that it would solve all the problems we'd had since Sarge's heart attack, but hadn't realized that we would bring ourselves to California, or anywhere else we might go. We had learned this on our first trip to Turkey but seemed to have forgotten.

It had been only two years since Sarge's heart attack and my despair when I thought he was dying. Recent months had been full of activity—selling the house, arranging for an auction, packing, then driving across the country and settling into the house in Berkeley. There hadn't been much time to think about ourselves. Settled in Berkeley, the only thing we thought about was ourselves and our relationship. My emotions swung back and forth like a pendulum, one day thinking my husband was back and the next day knowing he was gone. Ever since the heart attack, he'd sat most of the day watching television and, in Berkeley, he got into the same habit. It was almost as if he weren't there. I wanted us to get out as much as we could because the atmosphere at home was so deadening but, when we did go out to dinner, he acted as if we were imposing on him, as if he couldn't wait to go home. He was morose, didn't engage in conversation, or smile or be friendly. I was back in the place I'd been before taking the job in Boston, struggling to find out who I was in the relationship. I felt compelled to stay with this man. Although we hadn't taken "till death do us part" vows, I felt as if we had.

When the guest seminar leader announced a break, Sarge and I were ready to sign up for this two-weekend training without knowing anything more about it than we had just heard. Seated on my left was a young man with long hair, a beard, and ragged jeans who said, "Do it, lady, you'll never regret it." On the other side of him was a dignified woman of perhaps seventy who leaned across and added, "He's absolutely right. You should just go and sign up." We did.

I thought it was wonderful that people from *est* called every few days before we actually did the training—to see how we were and if we were having trouble filling out the forms. It seemed as if they really cared about what we might get out of the experience. We were also invited to a Christmas party for those who had completed the training and those who were registered for it. I had never seen so much enthusiasm and, after the party, couldn't wait for our training.

Even though I was looking forward to the training, I was also anticipating the defense of my doctoral dissertation that was to take place on December 27th in a conference call with members of my committee in Massachusetts. At the end of that call, my committee chairman, Dr. William Lauroesch, said, "On behalf of the examining committee and the University of Massachusetts, congratulations Dr. Russell." I wept as I thanked him. It was the fulfillment of twenty years of work. And, through my tears, I knew that I had finally settled the identity issue that had plagued me since childhood. It was no longer a question if I would be "Betty," or "Liz," or "Paul's daughter or sister." I was Dr. Elizabeth Goodell Russell.

Sarge and I had our first weekend of the *est* Training on the weekend of January 5th and 6th, 1974. Ted Long was the trainer. The whole first day seemed dedicated to giving us rules and telling us about what was going to happen. We were told we couldn't wear watches, we could leave the room only at announced break times and must be back in our seats at the time announced for the break to be over, we couldn't sit next to someone we knew, we couldn't eat or drink anything but water in the training room. We were not to smoke or drink alcohol during the weekend and were encouraged not to do so in the week between training sessions. We were not allowed to take notes. By four o'clock on that first afternoon, I knew we had made a mistake. My back ached from sitting in that straight chair for eight hours and my head ached from listening to what seemed like repetitive nonsense.

The man in the front of the room obviously knew nothing about how people learn. As an educator, I knew that you did not spend most of a day telling people what you were going to do, you just did it. He had spent the whole first day on ground rules, on telling us what was going to happen, and on dealing with questions about, and objections to, the rules and the agenda. I was tempted to get up and leave but had missed the early opportunity to get my money back so decided I would make an attempt to see if I could get things moving. I put my hand up.

"Yes, Elizabeth?" "I am so annoyed with this process I can barely stay in my seat. I was going to get up and leave but I decided to let you know how I'm feeling and ask when this thing is going to get moving." "Thank you," he said, leaving the platform and walking down the aisle to the row where I was seated in an end seat. "Elizabeth, are you a person who is easily annoyed?" "No!" I snapped. "Are you a person who is easily annoyed?" he repeated. "Not without provocation!" "Are you a person who is easily annoyed?" "You've already asked me that and I said no." "Thank you, Elizabeth. Are you a person who is easily annoyed?"

I continued to protest that I was not and the trainer continued to ask the question, the same question, over and over and over again. At first I continued to snap out my automatic response but then, after awhile, I noticed that some of the heat had gone out of my replies and that I was honestly looking into my experience to see if there was any evidence that I was such a person. Suddenly it was as if a film strip were running in front of my eyes and I was on it, tapping a foot impatiently at the super market checkout counter, making caustic remarks to the doctor's secretary about the value of my time, leaning on my horn at a slow driver who wouldn't pull out of the fast lane, snapping at a child asking for a third drink of water before going to sleep. It was true! I was a person who was easily annoyed. But what now?

I'd be damned if I'd let that guy in front of me know what I'd just seen, so I kept on protesting. But there was a difference in my protests because now I knew I was defending a position I had taken and wasn't sure how long I could go on doing that. As long as I had felt that we were arguing about the way the training was being conducted, I could have gone on indefinitely but this was different. I began to feel foolish and started looking down at my shoes. Then, almost against my will, I looked up and a huge grin broke across my face. "You're right, you bastard!" I said, tears of relief streaming down my face. "I guess I am a person who is easily annoyed."

He grinned back at me and turned me around to face the rest of the people in the room. The applause was deafening. People said later they couldn't believe the change in my face from the time I stood up until the moment he turned me around for them to see. And I couldn't remember ever having had as freeing a feeling as I did at that moment. I also felt a wave of love for the man who had put me through the exercise.

The day that had been dragging came alive. I realized there was more to this training than I'd been willing to concede. We were forced to examine things we thought we needed—eight hours sleep, frequent bathroom breaks, regular meals. People complained about the hard chairs, about the room temperature, about everything. Our complaints were heard and nothing changed. It was as if we thought we had a vote on the way the training was run and finally discovered that we didn't. It gave us an opportunity to look at our lives and see where we thought complaining about something would change it and finally understood that's the way it was and all we could do was accept it.

That first weekend we were introduced to something called our "already-always listening." At first I thought it was another confusing use of words but then I saw how well it described the way I had interacted with the students in my

Introductory Philosophy class. I would call on a student who was ready to say something about the reading assigned for the previous night, and before he was finished speaking, I would interrupt and finish whatever he was sharing. Instead of really listening to the student, I had been in my head, preparing a response.

Comparing this with my experience with students in Turkey, I realized that the difference was that in Turkey, I didn't know what I was doing, was willing to let the students know that and help me, whereas in teaching at home I saw myself as the expert at the front of the room, the person with an M.A. in philosophy, the one who knew. Sitting in the training room I saw, with dismay, what I had been doing and wished there were some way of undoing it.

The remainder of that first weekend was a series of highs and lows—highs as I discovered things about myself that had been hidden for fifty-four years, lows as my mind engaged in making judgments and decisions about the trainer, the material being presented, or the support personnel in the room.

Werner Erhard led the second weekend of our training. My first impression of Werner was that he looked remarkably self-assured. He was about six feet tall, a good-looking man with a wonderful laugh, obviously comfortable with a large group of people. He wore fine wool gabardine slacks, a navy sports jacket, highly polished loafers, and argyle socks that showed when he crossed his legs. His clothes must have come from some place like Brooks Brothers, they were surely expensive. Despite his powerful voice, there was also a quiet presence about Werner that made him seem larger than life. I was sure we were in the right place for whatever was going to happen to us next.

After a few reminders—to take our watches to the back of the room and not to sit next to anyone we knew, we were invited to share what had been happening in our lives since the first weekend. By this time, I realized that while I was resistant to being told I couldn't wear a watch, being told when I could go to the bathroom or take a break, having to remain in my seat, those rules were revealing how easily I could be interrupted in my work and justify that interruption. At home, it was a cup of coffee, sharpening pencils, going to the bathroom, making that phone call, checking the mail.

The training supervisor had emphasized confidentiality and there was something about the space of the room, that I felt free to let out the sadness I had in losing the man I married and the resentment I felt at fate or the doctors. It was a wonderful release. I hadn't had any outlet for my feelings because I thought I had to be strong for Sarge. Only twice before, since his illness, had I just let go—once with the University psychiatrist and the other with Ted, during the night we spent together in Boston. In this setting I let it all out—the sadness, the guilt about my feelings, the sense of being trapped.

But what I was experiencing was more than sadness. There was anger and it was not just anger at the doctors or at fate. It was anger at Sarge, yet I knew that was irrational because he was the victim. It was as if I were holding him responsible for that heart attack. It wasn't his fault but that made no difference. This was the first time I'd had the space to acknowledge it. That night at home he thanked me and said it was a relief to have it out in the open rather than hidden. He said he knew I must have such feelings but hadn't expressed them to him before.

The trainer kept asking questions such as, "Who did that?" "Who do you think was responsible for that?" Even as I didn't want to hear those words, I did hear them, and it was the first time I'd felt I had choice in the matter of how I reacted to Sarge. All the talk about responsibility made me uncomfortable. Deep inside I knew I was responsible for the choices I made in my life but wasn't quite ready to acknowledge that responsibility—it would let too many other people off the hook.

I remember little of the content of the second weekend, but I do remember continually being brought up by how little I knew about myself, some of which was revealed each time Werner spoke to us. He said that the philosopher did not impart wisdom but, acting as a midwife, presided over the birth of ideas in other people and, in the *est* Training, the trainer was like a midwife. Nothing could be born which was not already there to be born. I recognized that Werner must be familiar with Heidegger and I had a feeling of being validated. It was as if this man whom I was coming to respect had seen in Heidegger what I had seen that made me focus on him for my master's work.

Werner described compassion as seeing the problem and seeing the person bigger than the problem and said compassion sometimes required being tough with another. Later, when I heard the phrase "ruthless compassion," it seemed to describe perfectly the way Werner interacted with someone who seemed to be stuck or resistant; it was the way Ted Long had interacted with me in the first weekend.

Werner defined ego as the "functioning of one's point of view in the attempt to cause that point of view to survive," and as I heard him I recalled my first weekend attempt to prevail over the trainer and the embarrassment I experienced when I realized what I was doing. When I heard him say that righteousness reinforces positionality, I became very uncomfortable as I recalled the righteousness in that exchange. It was also difficult for me to embrace because this seemed to put a negative connotation on the word "righteousness" which, in my upbringing, was considered a virtue. At one point I tried to argue with Werner. He just listened to me and I understood he wasn't going to do anything with what I was saying. That frustrated me because I wanted him to say I was right or argue with me if I was wrong. Instead all he said was, "Thank you, Elizabeth. I got it."

Sunday afternoon Sarge stood up and went on for so long that someone in the room shouted out, "Sit down, Sarge!" I quietly concurred. When Werner realized that he couldn't interrupt, he had someone escort Sarge out of the room. When he came back, sometime later, he was calm.

I had trouble staying awake in the training. Frequently I would have to go to the back of the room and stand and then, if I continued to nod, I would be given a book to hold over my head. I remember at one moment sitting on the edge of my chair, alert and interested, and in the next, when the subject touched on a painful area, I began to nod. On Sunday night there were two talks. One was about relationships, during which I kept falling asleep. There was obviously something in my relationship with Sarge that I wasn't willing to look at. The other talk, "How it All Began," was a fable from which we learned that life is a game. In order to have a game, something has to be more important than something else, so life is a game in which what isn't is more important than what is.

On the last night of the Training, our "graduation," we were each given a little book, from Werner, entitled, *If God Had Meant Man to Fly, He Would Have Given Him Wings or Up to Your Ass in Aphorisms*. When I took it in my hands, it opened to a page on which were the words, "It's much easier to ride the horse in the direction he's going," and I began to laugh.

That weekend was like being hit by a truck but I didn't have the vaguest idea of what had happened or how it was going to affect the rest of my life. On Monday morning, after a full night's sleep, Sarge and I awoke, looked at each other and began laughing. I felt as if I'd been the butt of a cosmic joke all my life and had just been given the punch line. I was elated. I felt light, almost as if I had shed fifty pounds. It was as if everything in my life had been shaping who I was becoming. Then, in the *est* Training, it all came together and there I was—a whole, complete human being.

People around us noticed immediately that something had changed. A little thing, but one noticed by my daughters, was that I'd stopped smoking. It had been prohibited during the training and when I realized that I had given it up for ten days with no problem, I saw no reason to resume the habit. Sarge, who had been difficult to get along with ever since we got to Berkeley, was suddenly, after these two weekends, ebullient. He hugged everybody, seemingly a different person. I was also beaming and glowing.

Marta, who lived around the corner, came over and said, "My God, what happened? What did they do to you in that training?" It was evident that something dramatic had happened to both of us. During the next week my children observed such marked changes in my behavior and demeanor that those nearby immediately signed up for the training and that produced a domino effect. Marta and Jan's husband enrolled for the following month. Then when Sarge's son, Ed, came home from college for spring break and saw his sister, he enrolled. That summer our youngest daughter, who was nine, took the *est* Children's Training, along with Jan's son, Nicholas, who was two years older.

These two weekends had an enormous impact on me. I knew I had learned more about myself than I had in all my years of formal education. Only later did I realize that the training had given me a profound appreciation of my years of study and I had a greater appreciation of what Werner was talking about because of those years. I knew he was familiar with Asian thought and with the existentialists. Werner acknowledged that he wasn't giving us anything new, that he was a conduit for some of the most influential ideas of history. He said he was just someone who came along at a particular point in time and generated a conversation out of things he'd read and learned along the way. I had always been intrigued by the world in which I lived and, after being with Werner Erhard for that second weekend, I was grateful just for being alive in his time.

It seemed to me that everything in my life had been on a purpose line, whether or not I had any idea of that purpose. I could look back even on my failed marriages, realize that four of my children were the unique gifts of those marriages and know, with certainty, that my choices had somehow been part of a larger plan. Many times in my life it seemed as if I acted impulsively, yet at this time, it looked as if even those actions were prompted by an intuitive certainty. Whenever I questioned my sanity in marrying Gerry a second time, Marta would retort, "I had to get you back together to get born!"

I remember Werner had said that even after experiencing transformation, life would still be a roller coaster—all ups and downs—and knowing we could expect that, we could just notice it and not be disturbed by it. Still I was not prepared when, shortly after the second weekend of our training, Sarge began acting strangely. At first I thought he was just having fun. He said that he and Werner were communicating through extra sensory perception. He put blank pieces of paper in envelopes, addressed them to Werner and sent them off. He said Werner didn't need to have him say anything. He told me that Werner had chosen him to lead a geriatric training. When he tried to convince me that the house had been bugged, I realized he was hallucinating.

On Friday, he said he was just going out for a walk but, actually, he went to the Alameda County Retardation Center to volunteer. Apparently, when he was turned down, he became upset, made threats and brandished an umbrella at the center director. The police were called and he was taken into custody. About noon I received a call from the Psychiatric Emergency Unit at Highland Hospital, where Sarge had been taken in what they called "an acute psychotic state." I rushed to Highland. At the nurses' station I was warned not to go to him. They said he was in restraints and was dangerous. I insisted, "I'm his wife! He's not going to hurt me!" As I went down the corridor to his room, I heard him roaring and was concerned. I had never known him like this and wondered if it might lead to another heart attack. But I also found it strangely exciting. He was tied to the bed with canvas restraints. I leaned over and kissed him. He was glad to see me although he was confused. The nurses told me that when they had first restrained him and left his arms free, he broke off a bed spring, cut the canvas restraints, and threw a urinal at the wall. The strength that must have taken, the rage he must have felt to do that! I could hardly believe it. My mild-mannered professor was suddenly a roaring hunk. Given an invitation and permission I would have jumped into bed with him right there. This was one of those times when I was aware of the back-and-forthness of my feelings about Sarge. Once in a while I saw the man who had excited me from the moment we met and then, at other times, I saw the man he had become, someone I didn't even like.

At home that night I wished I could feel something. I heard Rebecca turning in her sleep, Albert scratching in his kitty litter box and the red-faced clock ticking beside me on the desk. Somewhere on the street, a car was changing gears. Then the refrigerator began to run. At the hospital I was strong as I always was at hospitals, but alone in the quiet house I had to ask how much I had contributed to Sarge's collapse. He and I had talked of separation and had decided to continue together. We still loved each other in the way people do who have suffered and struggled together, but our lives were growing apart as I became more involved in my work while Sarge had no work at all. I found myself wanting the intellectual stimulation of good conversation, no longer possible with Sarge, and often wishing I were not married. I couldn't analyze my feelings—I couldn't feel anything. All I could think about was the ghastly expense, the long ordeal that might be ahead and the prospect of years of uncertainty. I sometimes thought that if we could go back in time I would buy that mobile home we talked of, park it somewhere in the sun and just enjoy living with Sarge for as much time as we might have together. But we couldn't go back and, when I was honest with myself, I knew that wouldn't have been a solution for me.

The next afternoon he was sedated and transferred to a long-term care facility in Walnut Creek. The police had committed him for seventy-two hours. This was the point at which I might have sought the advice of someone who knew something about psychiatry but I didn't, I just went along with what was happening. Talking with me, Sarge seemed unclear about what had happened and what they were doing to him. He said every time he did something they considered unacceptable they increased his medication. He got a cigarette from his roommate, lit up, and was put back in the locked unit.

After the seventy-two-hour commitment by the police, the attending physician asked me to commit him for an additional fourteen days and I refused. He persuaded Sarge to commit himself. At that point I lost patience with Sarge. If it was so bad, why did he sign himself in for more of the same? I had thought when we came to California that we were starting a new chapter in life but here we were with Sarge again in the hospital. I might have been more empathetic if I hadn't had three years of taking care of this man who used to be the man I married. Closing my eyes I could still see him as he was when we were first married, but opening my eyes I saw the gray, thin man he had become, a man who looked twenty years older than he was, a man who seemed to have succumbed to life.

When the fourteen days were up, Sarge continued to be detained "at the doctor's prerogative." It appeared that I no longer had a say in the matter if the doctor himself could keep Sarge there. It seemed, more and more, as if both Sarge and I were being victimized by a system over which we had no control. I was reluctant to call Sarge's siblings and seek advice because I was trying to keep from them the knowledge of his being institutionalized. I was afraid that his sister would think it was the result of his having participated in the *est* Training. Although I could acknowledge that the training had probably been a catalyst for Sarge's breakdown, I was not willing to concede that he had no responsibility for it. I remembered, all too clearly, my own responsibility for the breakdown I had in Northfield ten years earlier. And Sarge had been "losing it" for almost three years. After the training I had been briefly hopeful when it looked as if he'd had as great an experience as I had, but now it appeared that the hospital stay was canceling that out. I was angry at the hospital the whole time because I thought that if Sarge were around Ted or Werner they would have told him to "get off it" and that would have done it. Later, that did happen when he started assisting, but out of the *est* environment, he slipped back into his victim role.

Carolie Coffey, the friend who had given me tickets to the *est* Guest Seminar, was worried about what was happening and asked a psychiatrist friend of hers to talk to me. He seemed interested in what was happening to Sarge and said that what I described sounded like a "constructive psychotic incident," one which had the potential for releasing something that had been locked in for much of Sarge's life. The psychiatrist said it appeared to him that the treatment being given was designed to reinforce control rather than allow for release.

On the 30th of January I was allowed to take Sarge to dinner, outside the hospital. He complained that each time he talked to the doctor about his recent training, the doctor shut him down. Finally, I called Langley Porter, the psychiatric institute in San Francisco, and learned that I could simply discharge the doctor and remove Sarge myself. On the 11th of February I did that, after signing a release form stating that I was taking Sarge out of the hospital "against medical advice." Looking back, I've reflected on how it might have turned out had Sarge been in the care of an enlightened doctor. I've regretted not finding out about other treatment options earlier. I didn't seek such a doctor until the situation looked hopeless. The treatment seemed to be doing nothing and the expense of keeping him at the facility was so great I knew we were in trouble. The cost of the doctor's daily visits astounded me. The insurance covered a major part of it but even the twenty percent remaining was forcing me to dip into the capital we had invested.

At home in Berkeley, life settled down again. Sarge seemed glad to be home, talked with Rebecca about school, asked questions about my job. He was a little pensive but obviously much better than he had been since his hospitalization. Perhaps being in a mental hospital was conducive to behavior appropriate to a mental hospital.

Throughout all of this drama with Sarge I found myself still deeply interested in the training we had both been through and wondering if this might be the work I had referred to in my letter to Cornell, the work I said I would recognize when I was prepared for it. I promised myself that as soon as Sarge seemed stable again I would talk to people at *est* and find out what work there might be for me.

14

Dreams of Being an est Trainer

"Everybody knows it takes at least ten years to reach the top of the mountain of enlightenment but leave it to an American to build a freeway up that mountain!" It may have been at Marta's graduation from the *est* Training that a young Frenchman, who had just completed the Training, uttered these words. The *est* graduates in the room burst into the laughter of recognition but the guests were left wondering.

The next day I phoned the *est* office to ask how one could get to be a trainer. I was sure this was the work for which I'd been preparing. I was directed to Randy McNamara who, at that time, was in charge of the training division. I gave him my credentials, half expecting him to welcome me immediately into the program for training trainers. I was surprised and a little taken aback when he told me that the first thing to do was to begin assisting. In speaking to me, Randy's voice had been stern and I suspected I should do as he said, so I immediately made an assisting agreement and began work at the *est* office. I had completed my work with the University Without Walls at the end of 1973 and was eager to get started at *est*.

At that time the office was three rooms on Kearny Street, off Broadway, in back of Finocchio's Restaurant in San Francisco. The staff was small, perhaps forty people, reflecting the beginnings of the new organization. All those on staff and those assisting had completed the *est* Training, which had started in October 1971, so it was an unusual environment, an environment which I soon realized was an extension of that training. Although I was doing clerical work, I learned something new about myself each day.

One time I was given a project of typing letters for Werner. The first hour I did quite well, turning out several perfect letters, then I made a mistake. I took some Liquid Paper, dotted it on the error and waited for it to dry. My supervisor, whose desk faced mine, looked up and shook her head. "We don't use correction fluid on Werner's letters." "Okay, thanks," I responded, removed the letter and put in another piece of paper. The next time I made a mistake, I tore the paper out of the machine, crumpled it up and threw it in the wastebasket. Again my supervisor shook her head, "We don't do that either. It's a waste of stationery." "Well, what *do* I do when I make a mistake?" I asked.

She just looked at me, saying nothing. For a few minutes I sat in front of the typewriter, paralyzed. Then I got defensive. She couldn't have been expecting me to type without making an error. Everybody knows that to err is human. Was this woman really expecting me to work without making an error? Then I got angry. This was ridiculous! Then I felt hopeless. I couldn't do this simple job. I wasn't the good typist I'd thought I was. If this was one of the requirements, I'd never be a trainer.

I finally recovered and began typing, this time with a focus so complete that the time seemed to fly by. For three days I typed letters without an error. I wouldn't have imagined it possible, but because of my supervisor's commitment to my continued training, I discovered a capability I didn't know I had. And each time something like this happened I realized that I was capable of much more than I knew. What a gift! I had been in a number of work environments in my life but had never before been in one that demanded so much of me or that gave me so much in return. I began to understand our assisting agreement which was that we would get more out of our assisting than we put in.

Ever since my year in North Carolina I had been a civil rights advocate—demonstrating, writing letters to the editor and making sure my children grew up in an environment free of bias or prejudice—but my advocacy was challenged, that spring, when Marta was raped by a black man in Berkeley. He held a knife to her throat, subjected her to four hours of assault, then threatened to kill her if she reported it to the police. This also marked the end of my pacifism. As I held and comforted Marta that morning I knew I could kill the man if I had access to him. Having completed the *est* Training just a month or so before the rape, Marta was better able to handle it than she might otherwise have been but, for months, she lived in fear. The rape triggered our move from Berkeley to El Cerrito, a middle-class suburban community to the north.

That summer Rebecca took the *est* Children's Training. I was so elated with what happened to her in that training that I observed her growth and then wrote it up, two years later, for the *Graduate Review*, a newsletter distributed to graduates of the *est* Training. Almost immediately, however, there were behavioral changes that astounded me. This child, who two years earlier had not been reading and had been referred to in a psychologist's report as "passively dependent and in need of constant support and reassurance" was now reading and was dramatically demonstrating her independence and self-sufficiency. One evening I was telephoning to locate a sitter for Rebecca and was becoming increasingly frustrated by my failure to find one available. When my frustration expressed itself as irritation with Rebecca, she looked up from her book and said, "Mommy, I think you ought to get clear that if you insist on having a sitter, it is for your sake, not for mine—I don't need one." At ten, she was ready and willing to stay home alone in the evening and I had to admit that the sitter was for my peace of mind.

When my first assisting agreement ended, I began assisting in *est*'s Educator Project. The organization was just beginning to respond to requests being made by teachers who had taken the *est* Training. While I was assisting in the Educator Project I was offered a job at Massachusetts' University Without Walls in Amherst, at an attractive salary, but turned it down. I thought about what it might mean to be on the faculty of the University and about what that salary would mean to our family, but we had just come to California, were enjoying it and I thought I was on my way to a career as an *est* trainer.

After assisting for three months, I was interviewed by Laurel Scheaf who asked me if I would like to join the *est* staff. Laurel had learned about my background and, in consultation with Werner, decided I might be the one to take on the Educator Project in a staff position. My job in Berkeley had been less than fulfilling and would end in June, I had just received my doctorate in education, my work in Massachusetts had been in teacher training, so this seemed like a perfect fit. I accepted the invitation and began work in The Educator Project, reporting to Laurel Scheaf. Laurel was a strikingly handsome young woman, perhaps thirty years of age. She was close to six feet tall, slender, with wavy, short brown hair and piercing eyes. The way she carried herself was almost as if she dared anyone to comment on her height. I had been intimidated by her since our first meeting and the prospect of working for her was both exciting and terrifying.

Soon after joining the staff I was invited to meet with Werner. The idea of a private meeting with Werner so thrilled me that I changed my clothes over and over to be sure they were right and I drove into the city ahead of time to be certain I wouldn't be late. Because I arrived early and was evidently nervous, Werner's aide led me to a settee in the hall and brought me a drink of water, saying it would be just a few minutes. It seemed like hours although it couldn't have been more than fifteen minutes when he said, "C'mon, Elizabeth. I'll take you in now." My knees were shaking, my palms so sweaty I wiped them on my slacks as we walked in so they wouldn't be damp when Werner greeted me.

He was standing in front of a fireplace, in which a low fire was burning. The room looked like a small library, with books lining the walls and a leather-topped table on which stood two stemmed glasses and an open bottle of wine. Werner was looking at the fire and he turned to me, holding out both hands for mine. The setting was so perfect it felt like one I might have seen on the pages of *Esquire* magazine. Werner was wearing a smoking jacket over his sharply-pressed gabardine slacks. He was even more handsome at close range than he was in front of the training room. His dark eyes seemed to penetrate, as if he could read my mind, and his hands, beautifully manicured, were alive and expressive. It was the first time I had noticed the cleft in his chin.

Almost as soon as he took my hands and spoke my name, the fear vanished and I felt amazingly comfortable. We sipped wine and talked, for perhaps two hours, about the work *est* was doing in the field of education. He told me about the training that had been done in the Watts district of Los Angeles and said one was planned for a school in Contra Costa County. He said that *est* was moving into the field of education and was moving so fast that within six months the Project would become a division. He asked me about the work I had done in education which, thus far, had been mostly in teacher training. He told me he had been leading the educator workshops and he believed that, with my background, I could take on that job and do well with it. Did I think I could? Well, yes, of course! He said I could go with him, observe what he did and then take over. He also told me that they were planning a dinner with the *est* Advisory Board to introduce me and that I would join the Education Committee of the Board.

As we talked, my sense of self grew larger by the minute. I saw myself in the front of hotel ballrooms, leading workshops for hundreds of teachers. Werner seemed to have no doubt that I could do the job and I was sure that his faith in me was warranted. By the time our meeting was over I knew that this man, like Gordon Pyper at Mt. Hermon, saw something in me and was providing an opportunity for that something to flourish.

Being on staff was like a continuation of the training program. There were things Werner said that have stayed with me through my life. "You can never have enough of what you don't really want," and, "If you have to ask if it's good enough, it isn't." Every time I'm doing a job and asking myself that question, I hear his answer. One morning, Werner stood up in front of the staff and held up a paper clip. "How many of you saw this on the stairs as you came up this morning?"

There was an embarrassed hush acknowledging that most of us had either seen it and ignored it or hadn't seen it at all. I knew I had seen it but thought Werner was being silly until that night when I got back home. As I opened the door I saw a shoe of Rebecca's on the floor and realized that it had been in that spot for days but this was the first time I'd really seen it. It was as if I had stolen a little consciousness to wrap around that shoe so I wouldn't have to do anything about it, just as I had with the paper clip on the stairs. And that was like pulling a thread in a knit piece—suddenly it all unraveled and I saw dozens of situations in which I had seen something peripherally, but took no action, like seeing a crumb on the floor under the dining room table and ignoring it rather than getting out the vacuum cleaner but then seeing that crumb over and over and over. Because I didn't act, that crumb stayed in my consciousness as a sort of grayed-out reminder. That staff meeting and paper clip have stayed in my memory for thirty years, coming to life every time I pass over something. I have some old photographic equipment I've been meaning to get rid of for years but it is still in a drawer in my bedroom. Every time I open that drawer, I see the photo equipment and experience a little discomfort but, each time, ignore the discomfort so I won't have to take action at that time.

In August Sarge started assisting in the *est* office and it was a life-renewing experience for him. Ever since his training and subsequent hospitalization, he had been subject to rapid and extreme mood changes. But we were taking a seminar and he decided to assist. In his first assisting agreement, he worked on the incoming phone calls. Sarge's speech had been slow ever since his illness and when a call came in he would start by explaining to people that he was slow because he had been sick. People calling from across the country were more interested in getting their money's worth on the phone than they were in hearing about Sarge's illness and they were often short with him. As he realized these people were not interested in his problems or explanations he began to speed up. In a few weeks he had given up explaining, was speaking at an almost normal rate, and was looking like a different person.

His next assisting job was for the Accounting Department. They offered him a job as cashier at seminars in the evening. He explained that his ability to do arithmetic had been damaged and he might have difficulty counting and keeping track. The person whom he was assisting told him they were sure he could do it. They also told him, with a touch of humor, that at the end of each evening he would have an opportunity to reconcile money and receipts. If any shortages showed up, it was no problem, he could simply make them up out of his own pocket. Given Sarge's pecuniary bent (he hung paper towels over the edge of the sink to dry for re-use), his arithmetic skills improved rapidly. I was delighted that Sarge was assisting. It gave him some hope for a future he'd thought he didn't have.

In September of that year, Sarge decided to take a room in San Francisco rather than coordinate transportation with me. The freedom to set his own schedule for coming and going seemed important to him and, given my long hours, it was difficult for us to travel together. I was so engrossed in my job that I barely noticed his leaving except for feeling relief and sadness. At this time my feelings for him were mostly empathy and impatience. And I was making comparisons—comparisons with the man he had been before and comparisons with the men I associated with on a daily basis.

I had been working for two months at the *est* office when I realized that the demands being made on me were forcing me to expand beyond what I ever thought was possible. It was as if my life were an expression of a whole and complete person who broke down now and then, made mistakes. There was a shift from being totally self absorbed to a sense that something else was emerging. I was learning about myself at such a pace that I felt stretched almost to breaking yet, despite the long hours, I was going home each night with more energy than I had in the morning. I was no longer simply glowing with the sense of what had happened to me—I was feeding it back into everything I did. It was an amazing thing. I wondered if I would ever stand off, look at it and understand. I must confess, today, that I paid little attention to how my intensive work schedule affected my family. Rebecca seemed so independent that I didn't worry about her and when Sarge was grumpy, I just assumed it was Sarge. It didn't occur to me to prioritize or to balance my schedule to include time with family.

In November, I took part in the first meeting of the policy-making group involved with the Educator Project. The group was impressed by the requests coming in and felt it was time for a name and status change for the program. The program would become a division of *est*, would be called "*est* in Education," and I would manage it. I could barely suppress my elation. This was exactly what Werner had predicted in my first meeting with him after I joined the staff.

It was during this time that a seminar leader—and I was always taking an *est* seminar—talked about getting rid of the baggage of our past that we carried around with us and likened it to peeling off the layers of an onion. As I contemplated this I was almost paralyzed by the realization that there was no core or center to an onion, that when I had peeled off the last layer there would be nothing. Until that moment I had expected that there was a self, underneath the layers, a self at the center, but suddenly I was confronted with Nothing.

I enrolled in the Guest Seminar Leaders Program (GSLP) which was the next step in my preparation for being a trainer. I was at the first national meeting of this training program designed to prepare people to lead introductory seminars on the *est* Training and it was a major confrontation for me. I was being asked to demonstrate excitement in what I saw as ridiculous ways. The exercise I remember most vividly was one in which I had to stand on the stage in front of several hundred people and, at the top of my lungs, shout out, "Don't you ever, ever, ever let me catch you brushing that dog's teeth with my toothbrush!" Because it wasn't done with enough fervor the first time, I had to repeat it until the audience was satisfied. They said the point was for us to notice where we were stopped and to choose to get beyond that. No matter how hard I tried I was never able to overcome all of the restraint, never able to silence the little voice telling me that it was all nonsense. Later I heard that there was a distinction between excitement and enthusiasm—excitement being considered a high-energy state whereas enthusiasm was seen as an inspired state—and what we were really cultivating was the ability to distinguish between the two. We could know that we inspired people by our speaking if it was evident that they were moved. I had an example of this, some years later, when I heard myself on the radio, aware that it was I, yet somehow moved to tears by that person speaking.

Just before Christmas of 1974, Werner took the staff and their families to Mexico on vacation. Sarge was no longer living with us, so just Rebecca and I went. We had a few days in Mexico City, staying at the Queen Isabella Hotel, touring the city and going to a bullfight. I didn't see much of the bullfight because most of the time I had my eyes closed, opening them and cheering only when cries of the crowd indicated that the bull had scored a point. For the balance of the two weeks we were in Puerta Vallarta. I had never been to Mexico and this coastal resort made me think I'd died and gone to heaven. Werner had seen to it that everything was arranged so that we would have a carefree, fun-filled vacation. We played donkey polo on the beach, parasailed over the ocean, swam and danced until three in the morning, had great food and hours of languishing on the beach. It was the first time I had been in a play situation with Werner and was delighted to see that he played as hard as he worked. I have a picture of him taken at two or three in the morning when he had been dancing for several hours. His shirt was open and he was perspiring but so intent on the dancing that he seemed not to notice the picture being taken.

I recall a time, years later, when Rebecca and I were in the *est* parking garage on California Street and Werner came down to the garage. She leapt out of the car and ran over to hug him. And this is who Werner was for Rebecca. I was envious because I felt the same way about this man but couldn't express it so openly—there was always something holding me back. I was stiff and tense when

Werner hugged me, without knowing why. Today I realize that my hesitation was grounded in upbringing. As a child I had almost no hugging. If my father wanted to kiss me goodnight, he would put his hands on my shoulders, to be sure there was no body contact, then lean over and give me a peck on the cheek. I grew up thinking there must be something wrong with hugging. Today I feel a little cheated. If Werner were to hug me now I think I'd be content to be hugged forever, but maybe not. Underneath, that Puritan girl's still alive.

As important as Werner was for me in 1974, it was only a hint of how important he would be throughout my life. Everything he said resonated, for me, with that sense I'd had as a child—that "something" I couldn't identify. It related to my experience at Marta's birth but I couldn't say how. At that point in my experience of him, it was more like an intuitive grasp that this man would validate everything I held as a child, he would validate me for having clung to that childhood certainty somewhere deep inside. It had been buried for years at a time but was never completely lost and in this situation, was coming back to life. I felt privileged to be working for Werner and was sure that someday history would record him as one of the greatest men of our time and my grandchildren would be able to say, "My grandmother worked for him."

In February of 1975 Don Cox became president of the organization, in a move toward professionalizing the management of the rapidly-growing organization which was then using *est* as an acronym for Erhard Seminars Training. Don was a big man, physically, and I was a little afraid of him. I certainly didn't have the kind of relationship with him that I'd had with Werner. The trainers were relieved of some of the day-to-day management for which they had been accountable and were, instead, working to expand the Trainer Body by introducing the Trainer Candidate Program. At this point *est* began to be an organization delivering a wide range of programs in cities around the country.

During spring vacation that year Timothy came home and did the *est* Training. I attended his graduation and he was blooming. I'd always loved him but that night he was so radiant I wept. Unfortunately, the training had a similar effect on him as it had on Sarge. Shortly after the training, Timothy had a psychotic break. He dropped out of U.C.L.A. and, for years, depended on Lithium to maintain his equilibrium. I was sad and wondered if the Training could really have had that kind of impact on people. I didn't want to believe it could, so kept Timothy's story to myself. Later, when I was leading guest seminars it was always in the back of my mind that two members of my family had suffered ill effects after taking the *est* Training and I wasn't sharing that with people. I was sharing only the great things that had happened to us. I never acknowledged that I was withholding the downside because of not wanting it to reflect badly on Werner and the organization.

One day in early 1975 a young man named Frank Siccone came into the office. He had just received his doctorate in education from the University of Massachusetts, having worked with some of the same faculty members as I had. He came to California hoping to work for Werner and joined the staff at about the same time that we became the *est* in Education division. Frank was slight of stature—about 5'6" and 140 pounds. He had dark, curly hair, a Mediterranean-type complexion and eyes that seemed to promise a wonderful surprise. He was sharp and had a good sense of humor. He and I became good friends and he often supported me in the workshops. A few months later, Joan Holmes also joined the staff of *est* in Education. She had been instrumental in setting up the Children's *est* Training in the Castro Valley School where she was principal. Joan was a tall, stately woman, with a slender body and blonde-brown hair. She always seemed too big for our little office and I was too naive to realize that the job was only a stepping stone for her, that she had greater ambitions.

Shortly after Frank arrived, we planned a workday for educational administrators from the Bay Area. It was to be held at a wooded estate in Marin and Werner was to lead it. I was thrilled by the opportunity to have Werner meet with these educators but my thrill was short-lived. I had neglected to ask for support from the logistics department until it was too late, so on the morning of the event, Frank and I were at the facility, vacuuming the rug, setting up chairs, and struggling to close the draperies so we could videotape the workshop. The room was in a state of total disarray when Werner came in, accompanied by his aide. They greeted us courteously, Werner sat down, said nothing else and waited until we were through. Then I discovered we had failed to bring blank tapes so wouldn't be able to tape the event. For me, it was the last straw and I was near tears, holding back only because I was too embarrassed to cry in front of Werner. The educators came, Frank said Werner was brilliant, and the day went off perfectly but I wasn't there to see it because I had left the facility as soon as Laurel Scheaf arrived. I knew I had failed miserably and was sure I would be fired. For days I waited for the axe to fall but nothing happened.

Today I remember Heidegger talking about our "thrown way of being" and realized my thrown way of being was to doubt myself, to prove that my mother knew what she was talking about when she said I never did anything right. My "thrown way of being" allowed me to go only so far; it wouldn't allow me to really succeed, because underneath all the pretense I knew I was that bad little girl. Since the training, I had been working at letting go of my past, but it seemed that my past was not letting go of me. A year or so later I set up an event in Castro Valley, where Werner spoke. I had almost forgotten the earlier incident but at the end of this session, Werner asked me to join him in his car for a few minutes. When I did, he took my hand, smiled at me and said, simply, "I felt supported this time, Elizabeth." We both knew to what he was referring. I could have wept for the generosity of this man.

Being on the *est* staff also meant having a busy social calendar. In July we all went to Ringling Brothers Circus—fifty adults behaving like kids with popcorn and balloons. At first I felt silly, as if we were too adult for this, but then I let go, ate cotton candy and behaved like the child I had been at the circus years before. In August, there was a brunch on the grounds of Golden Gate Park following a visit to the Chinese archeological exhibit. In September the staff hosted a birthday party for Werner, renting a bay ferry for the day, and in October we were all together at the wedding of two *est* trainers. Since I didn't have much social life at home, this was all a bonus.

For the Christmas party that year Werner rented the Kabuki Theater in Japantown. There was music and dancing and a staggering array of food. One huge table had nothing but oysters on the half shell, another had cracked crab, another had *sushi* and *sashimi*, and then there were all the more usual *hors d'oeuvres*, wine and champagne. Affairs such as this were almost overwhelming for me. Only at the Embassy party in Ankara had I encountered such hospitality, such opulence, and even then there was no array of food such as at this party. On New Year's Eve there was a church service for the staff and their families at the Episcopal Church on Gough Street. The service was led by the Episcopal priest, assisted by a rabbi and a gospel choir from Oakland. For me it was deeply moving and took me back to the years when the church had meaning for me.

It was at the brunch in Golden Gate Park that I first met Bob Fuller. My meeting with him had been preceded by a strange happening. The week before, I dreamed of meeting the President of Oberlin College. It was so real for me that I went into the office and asked Frank to search our records to see if he could find such a man. Frank found nothing and I dropped it. On that Sunday morning in Golden Gate Park I was standing with a cup of coffee in one hand, and a pastry in the other, when Julia Dederer, a staff member in the Consulting Services Group, came up to me with a great-looking man—well over six feet tall, slender and forty-ish—dressed in blue jeans, a turtle-neck T-shirt and running shoes.

"Elizabeth, I think you two should get to know each other," Julia said. "This is Bob Fuller. Bob, Elizabeth Russell is the head of *est* in Education. You should ask her to tell you about it." With that, Julia walked away. I grinned at him and said, "So, you know what I do. Now why don't you tell me what you do." He grinned back. "Well, to start with, I did the *est* Training in October of 1974. I'm doing research right now and I've been in education awhile. I used to be President of Oberlin College."

It was remarkable that I dropped neither the coffee nor the pastry but my face must have reflected the shock. When he asked me if I were okay, I assured him I was and then told him of my dream. He laughingly conceded that the dream must have meant we were to work together. We exchanged phone numbers and he said he would call me for lunch one day the following week. He did, and we lunched and talked. He was interested in what we were doing and wanted to know more about it. I told Bob about the training in a fifth-grade classroom in a troubled area of Los Angeles, a training that had made a huge impact in that community. I also told him about the work we were currently doing. I also told him that, in September, I was to begin leading educator workshops across the country and that he'd be welcome at any of those he'd like to attend.

Werner had been leading the workshops and was turning that over to me. He was providing teachers a place to share what had been happening in their teaching since they had taken the *est* Training. This was all new for me. In my previous work in education I had seen myself as the center of the action, as the bearer of good ideas and advice, but in this situation I realized I would be a facilitator, the person who supported others in being present in their speaking. I accompanied and observed Werner on a number of occasions and then began leading (the first time with him observing me). Thinking back to this time I realize that I thought I was being hired because of my doctorate, and that may have been true. The doctorate lent some credibility to this new venture into education. But seeing Werner leading, I realized who he was for the teachers and saw that the challenge for me was to empower them while remaining invisible.

It was during this time that Werner was acknowledged by Karmapa and Muktananda, as a great teacher who had achieved enlightenment. When Swami Muktananda publicly recognized him as an enlightened one, I felt validated. He was everything I'd ever read about "masters" and I felt fortunate, indeed, to be working with him. Later, when it seemed to me that Werner made mistakes, I recalled having read that even enlightened people made mistakes—it wasn't that they were perfect but that they had a glimpse of the way things really were.

William Bartley, in his biography of Werner, compared him to Wittgenstein, who had an intense personal interest in the transformation of his students and insisted that philosophical encounter with him produced moral change. That

Werner had such an interest is as true for me today as it was when I read it. I loved that man and, three decades later, love him still. Whenever I was around him, life took on more immediacy, more color. The world looked more beautiful and I liked the Elizabeth who showed up in those circumstances. Werner has always been to me a reminder of what is possible for a human being. I knew that he knew who I was even if, most of the time, I didn't. In loving Werner I came to see the love I'd had for Gordon Pyper, for my professors at Cornell and Clarence Shute at the University of Massachusetts. I would have been embarrassed then to think that what I felt was love for them, because I had a notion that love was either that chemical reaction I had with my husbands when we first met or the love I had for my children; this was a different kind. The love for Werner, Clarence Shute and Gordon Pyper was a love that made me feel better about myself—a love that made me feel as if I could do and be anything I chose to do or be.

It may have been about this time that Werner asked me why I wanted to be a trainer, saying that there were many other things I could be in life. But I couldn't hear him. I had identified this job as the one I was intended to do. I couldn't just go with the flow but had to try and force it to go the way I wanted it to go. Writing this is even more difficult than acknowledging it quietly to myself. I see it as the story of my life.

As the head of *est* in Education, I was interviewed by *Psychology Today* and remember being upset and angry over the way my responses to the interviewer's questions were taken out of context, twisted and used to serve that interviewer's investigative reporting agenda. When I registered my upset with Werner's office, I was told that even lousy PR was better than no PR at all and I shouldn't worry. This was only one of many inflammatory and inaccurate reports that appeared in the media, most of them written by people who had not participated in the *est* Training and didn't know what they were talking about.

I traveled from San Francisco to New York to Boston to Washington, back to Los Angeles and over to Honolulu, leading workshops. Sarge and Rebecca accompanied me to the first Honolulu workshop. We stayed in a make-believe Hawai'ian village in Waikiki and our delight increased each day with wonderful food, ukulele music and the swaying bodies of hula dancers—both male and female. I had seen female hula dancers in movies but had not seen males, and was impressed to see men with tanned, muscular bodies swaying to the music. To me, it was far more seductive than the strutting, macho behavior many men seemed to think made them irresistible. Before this visit was complete, I knew that one day I would live in Hawai'i.

Bob Fuller attended several of the workshops with me, listening to speakers, questioning people in the audience, talking with me afterward. At the conclusion of one evening workshop he proposed we let him write up the work that *est* was doing in the field of education. I discussed Bob's proposal with appropriate people on staff and we signed a formal agreement for a book. As a member of the National Humanities Faculty, Bob had visited dozens of elementary and secondary schools in all parts of the country and I felt we were privileged to have him interested in *est* in Education.

In the summer of 1975 I assisted in the *est* Children's Training. My first reaction when I heard the trainer talking to the children was, "For heaven's sake, doesn't she realize she is talking to children? They're not going to understand what she's talking about!" Then I watched, with amazement, as one child after another stood up to ask a question or make a comment that proved conclusively that they understood. And then, almost before I had time to let this in, I had become a child myself. Pictures of my childhood flashed before my eyes and I was in tears. I was back in touch with the sad little girl who showed up on the pages of the photograph album. My supervisor suggested I sit on the sidelines and said she would replace me because I obviously was not going to be any good as an assistant in that training. In between the times when I was overwhelmed with memories, I watched these children interacting with the trainer, just as had the adults in my own training. And the material being presented was the same material presented in my training—not watered down for the children, not making concessions to the age of the participants, other than making the days shorter because the children caught on so much faster than the adults.

Alongside my own emotional response to all this was an embarrassment at having considered children as lesser beings—cherished, yes, but treated as if they needed to be coaxed or manipulated into adulthood. Then I thought of my educational training and how it fostered the idea of children as being "less than"—human beings who needed socializing to make them fit into our society and needed educating according to what we adults thought they should know. These were full-fledged human beings, not just kids. And, as I reflected on what I was seeing, I realized that I, too, was a full-fledged human being and had been all my life. When I thought of Werner saying that the trainer acts as midwife—presiding over the birth of ideas in people, ideas which were already there to be born—I had to confront the next step, which was that children were not empty vessels into which we poured, or blank sheets on which we wrote, but human beings with ideas ready to be born. The training was allowing those ideas to be born at nine or ten instead of at thirty or forty.

At the end of the training in which I assisted, there was an exercise in which the children got up in the front of the room and shared their "act," or persona, or whatever it was that they used to get along in life. The child I'll always remember was a Japanese boy, of ten or eleven, who had been sober-faced and quiet throughout the weekend. He stood on the stage in front of the entire group and said, slowly and dramatically, "My act is inscrutable Oriental," then grinned from ear to ear as the audience laughed and applauded.

The training had affected many areas of my life but one I particularly noticed was how much less critical I was of my children. Rebecca and I were out Christmas shopping together one day, using the third-level plaza that made it possible for residents of Golden Gateway, where we were then living, to shop and bank and dine without having to go down to the street. Rebecca, then ten, had run on ahead of me and I was watching her with the tenderness I always experienced when observing her. This day, one of her knee socks was slipping down her leg and as I looked at her I realized that, in the past, I would have run to her, pulled up the sock, and then given her a hug. But on this particular occasion I didn't have to adjust anything, she was perfect the way she was, slipping sock and all. With a little regret for the things one cannot change, I recalled all the times I had almost given my approval of a child's appearance but then had adjusted a collar, smoothed the just combed hair, looked behind an ear, or examined fingernails. My approval was always conditional—the child would be okay when that little thing was corrected or adjusted. I thought of my father and of what it meant knowing that he loved me unconditionally. I suspect there's a logical extension of this, which my mind has always resisted, that I should be able to accept myself in the same way—just as I am, without adjustment, correction or addition.

In January of 1976 Sarge left again, this time to live in Berkeley with a woman he met in a seminar. It seemed to me that his efforts to make peace with himself, the world, and life required him to leave me periodically. His leaving was not a personal affront. I had greater freedom than I'd ever known in my life and that freedom didn't depend on whether or not Sarge and I were living together. I worried less about him each time but knew the time would come when we would have to face the reality of our marriage.

In the holiday staff meeting just prior to Sarge's leaving, Werner delivered an ultimatum to those of us who were in relationships that were not working. He said we had three choices—we could clean up the relationship and make it work, we could sever the relationship, we could leave staff. He said it didn't work for people to be on staff with half their attention on relationships that didn't support them. Although Werner's remarks were addressed to the whole staff (and I knew there were several of us in relationships not working), I felt he was speaking directly to me. As our second weekend trainer, Werner had become aware of the circumstances of our marriage and knew that I had expressed feeling trapped. I suspect he also recognized that the basic principle of my life was the need for approval and, out of that need, I would find it difficult to leave a husband who was handicapped. He would have been right about that. I might grouse and complain about Sarge but to leave him would have been unthinkable—what would others say? I would have to make it all work. Looking back on the time it appears that, instead of making the decision for myself, I was covertly setting myself up to have the circumstances make that decision for me.

Near the end of 1975, the *est* in Education office was moved out of the Union Street *est* headquarters into a second-floor office down the street. When they moved us, it felt like being kicked out of the family. I was in a small private office and Joan and Frank were located in the outer office. I could hear them talking and laughing, sometimes with the assistants who were working. I was sure they were gossiping about me. It's difficult to write about this because I'm aware of how petty I was being at the time. I was becoming more and more paranoid about being left out. My work suffered.

It was during this time that I had a phone call from my son, Jerry, who had just flown in from Cape Cod, was in San Francisco for the night, and wanted to take me to dinner. I'm embarrassed today when I remember telling him I couldn't get away because of my job and the work I had to do. I seemed to ignore his having flown cross the country and taken time out of his trip to be nice to his mother. I had hoped that all my children would do the *est* Training but that night I blew it as far as Jerry was concerned. He's never even been willing to talk with me about it since, except on the few occasions when we've had nasty verbal exchanges after I asked him to do the training or the Landmark Forum and he refused. It was two or three years after our training that Jan, my oldest daughter, did the training but, when she did, she hugged me and said, "Why did you let me wait so long?" I knew Jerry would benefit but I had made it just about impossible for him.

Shortly after the first of the year, our offices were consolidated and moved to a much larger building on California Street and I had forgotten my pettishness. There was plenty of work for all three of us and I was excited about what was ahead. But then, one day in a staff meeting in early March, Laurel Scheaf, without saying anything to me, announced that Joan Holmes was moving to the Graduate Division and would be reporting to her. I couldn't believe my ears! No one had consulted me about this. Joan was an *est* in Education staff member!

How could she simply be transferred out of my division without my knowing anything about it? I knew, of course, that Joan had known ahead of time and that Frank may have known as well.

I left the staff meeting in a rage, went directly to Laurel's office, waited for her to return and told her what I thought of what she had done. I accused her of not having the decency to discuss it with me before announcing it in the staff meeting. I was furious and shaking all over. Anger was such an unused emotion for me that when I succumbed to it I was almost out of control. I told Laurel I was quitting and went home. The day was shot. By the next morning I had cooled off. I knew that I had over-reacted, and had resigned out of righteousness. I really loved my job. But Laurel had already talked to Don Cox, my boss and *est*'s Chief Executive Officer, and when I went to see him, he said, "Elizabeth, when I worked at Coca Cola and someone said, 'I quit,' I said, 'Here's your hat.'"

That was it! I was out. Unbelieving, and in tears, I raced out of the building. At home I shut myself in my room and sobbed. If it were happening today I think I would go back, demand a hearing and re-apply for the job, but at that time I had no sense of responsibility for having lost my job. I thought Don should have known I didn't mean it and should have taken into consideration what I had achieved, but he didn't and no matter how I looked at it, I was the one who said, "I quit."

We had been on the verge of something big, of having the training accredited, of being able to do more work in schools, of working with Stanford's School of Education, and suddenly it all came to an abrupt stop. All the work that went into building up the contacts and establishing a division in *est* that could work with other institutions was wasted. The program simply died and Frank Siccone left the staff. I was overwhelmed with guilt and furious that neither Joan nor Laurel picked up and followed through on what had been started. It was not only anger at them but anger at myself, for having failed those people who were counting on me to have *est* support them in making a contribution to education.

Bob Fuller's book, *A Look at est in Education,* which he wrote with his associate Zara Wallace, was published in 1976. The book included not only the report on the workshops but also reports on the in-school trainings we had done in Los Angeles and Castro Valley. He concluded the book with, "Since research on the effects of the *est* Training on academic achievement is just beginning, it is too early to form any judgments on this important question. However, there can be little doubt that the great majority of *est* graduate educators share the feeling that the *est* experience has transforming power, in both their personal and professional lives." In the Introduction to his book, Bob Fuller also wrote, "It is one of the apparent paradoxes of the *est* experience…that the deeply personal experience of self that people have in the training functions to strengthen their connection to the world and their fellow human beings." Today I see this connection evidenced in the many programs authored by *est* graduates all over the world, whether or not the source of that connection is overtly acknowledged.

Even though I was no longer on staff, I was elated with the book, and grateful for Bob's effort to make our work in the field of education visible, until I saw that Joan Holmes was named as "Manager of *est* in Education" in the acknowledgments, even though I had been in that position during the time the material was being gathered and I was the one who got the contract for Bob to write the book. Once again, the anger took over and, with it, that incredible loneliness. Only as I write today can I fully acknowledge my responsibility for the lost opportunity, and apologize to those who felt betrayed when the program was abruptly terminated. Only today can I recognize that I seemed more willing to let the program die than fight to keep it alive. Also today, however, I know that I have been a stand for the transformation of education ever since.

15

LSD, Awakening and Hawai'i

Suddenly I was home alone. Rebecca was in school and Sarge was still not living with us. As long as I had been working, his leaving had not much affected me, but with the loss of my job, I saw that I'd been hiding in my work to avoid confronting the problems at home. I felt confused and alone. I confided in a friend who suggested that I talk about my upset and confusion with Leo Zeff, a psychiatrist friend of hers.

I made an appointment with Leo, intending only to talk with him about my problems but suddenly he was asking me if I would be willing to use a psychedelic medicine to help me sort things out. I knew that Leo, as an associate of Timothy Leary, had made a considerable study of psychedelic drugs. I hesitated, only momentarily shocked by the term "psychedelic medicine" and what I thought it meant. We had lived in a university community in the '60s, after all, and I'd heard of people "dropping acid" but never thought I'd be one of them. It didn't take me long, however, to let go of the shock and replace it with excitement and anticipation. I'd lost my job, my relationship with Sarge was a mess and I knew I needed help, so I agreed.

During two preparatory meetings in Leo's office we talked about my children, my work, my relationship with Sarge, my childhood. He asked me about my religious practices. When I told him I'd left the church, he wanted to know about my early relationship with the church and why I had left. He asked me what kind of music I liked. He asked if I had any concerns about what we were planning. I lied and told him I had none but that I was hoping it might be a cure-all for my problems. My lie was to cover the fear that my trip might be one of those I'd heard referred to as "bummers."

On March 20th, Leo came to the apartment, gave me some tabs and a drink of water and told me he would be guiding me on an LSD trip that might last as long as fourteen hours. Almost as soon as I swallowed the tabs I began worrying. What was I doing? Was I out of my mind? Then, as Leo and I talked while I was waiting for the drug to take effect I relaxed, opened up and told him I was a little afraid of the proposed trip but beyond that I was devastated by losing my job. It seemed like a validation of my arrogance and looked as if I had set up the situation to fail so I could prove to myself how incapable I was. That let me off the hook for being responsible for the failure.

I spent the day in my waterbed, under an electric blanket, with a mask covering my eyes and headphones providing the music Leo had planned. I was feeling pampered and almost obscenely comfortable except for wondering what my mother would have said if she could have seen me. By the time the drug had really taken hold, I was no longer thinking.

The trip first took me out of my body; it took me to a level of consciousness where I could look down and see Elizabeth lying on the bed, without having any sense of identification with her. Then that picture dissolved and there was nobody in it—there was no bed, no room, none of the familiar surroundings. My rational consciousness was suspended. There was only light—lots of light and color but it wasn't as if I were observing that—it was more like being bathed in it, floating in it, turning over and over in a warm soothing bath of color and light. Then what had seemed like a cocoon opened up into a dimensionless space with more color and light but with those colors changing, mingling and then alternating with dark shadows. Thinking back to the experience I'd say that the colors were synchronized with the music, so that when the music was subdued or slowed down, the colors deepened and the dark shadows appeared. The dimensionless space seemed like the universe and it was as if I were being absorbed by that universe in one moment and then, in the next moment, I was absorbing all into myself. As a unique, bounded individual I gave way to a sense of being one with the universe, just as I had experienced during the birth of Marta, when the universe contracted and expanded with each contraction of labor. In this experience, however, the universe was flowing, shifting, changing color, changing perspective. At one moment I was the vortex and everything was whirling around me; in the next moment I was the whirling, shifting and there was no vortex. Then, without any awareness of time change, the universal became the particular and, in those moments I was Jesus being nailed to the cross, dying and being reborn, I was a baby in the birth canal struggling to be born. Sometimes when I was being Jesus on the cross I was also a little girl in tears on her knees in church on Good Friday. There was no separation of the experience of that little girl from the experience of the man on the cross. The baby had died and been reborn over and over again. Toward the end of the experience I had just been born and was crying almost uncontrollably.

As soon as I was fully conscious, Leo led me to the bathroom where I looked in the mirror and saw the face of a new-born, an infant with eyes almost closed, cheeks swollen and red, the whole face giving evidence of trauma. I cried out, "Leo! That can't be me!" But as I stood looking, it was almost as if that reflection in the mirror was a newborn adjusting to light and noise.

Later, as I rested, consciousness sharpened and my sense of individuality returned, albeit reluctantly. I was silent for maybe a half hour as I thought about what had happened, but soon realized that thinking about it was all I could do. I was no longer of the experience and my conscious, rational reflection on the event would never approach the reality of it. Many times since that day, however, I have been reminded of the experience by hearing Gounod's *Ave Maria*, one of the pieces of music listened to during the trip. The experience was so powerful and encompassing that when I was fully awake I wanted to embrace all those I loved and somehow share it with them. Leo sat with me for hours while I looked at old family photographs and let flow all the feelings associated with those photographs. When he finally left, I returned to bed to a sleep undisturbed by dreams or even by the sounds of the city.

The next day I shared with Rebecca simply by being with her—the space I was in seemed to reach out and wrap people in it. I spoke with other loved ones but soon realized I could communicate nothing of what had happened to me the day before. In addition to experiencing that enormous love for people, I had come to "know" something never before available to me—something I suspected was never available to the discursive intellect, something that was gone before I was able to speak it. All I was able to do was to tell people how much I loved them and let them see that something had impacted me powerfully.

It seemed to me that the darkness in which I had been dwelling, just prior to the trip, was the necessary condition for the experiencing of the light and this seemed contradictory only when I viewed it without reference to the paradoxical nature of reality. I could accept myself with my weaknesses and strengths, accept my finiteness, accept the pain of hurting and being hurt, the joy of living fully. Through self affirmation, I could watch God disappear and not cry out. When I was willing to be honest about the impact of the experience, I saw that it had broken down my defenses, it had blown my past to pieces. I had never been more vulnerable and I would forever be grateful to Leo.

Sarge came back home in April, life seemed to settle down again, and in early summer we talked about moving to Hawai'i. I remembered when I had first flown into Honolulu and been overwhelmed by the green of the ocean, the dark mountains, the scent of flowers and coconut that greeted me when I stepped off the plane. I was in an appropriate mood to surrender to the beauty of the islands, so in August of 1976, we packed and moved. Our first weeks in Hawai'i we lived at the Kaimana Beach Hotel, where we had a small housekeeping unit and spent most of our days on the beach. Then we learned of a condominium for rent at the Mauna Luan in Hawai'i Kai. We had a spacious apartment on the ninth floor but the thing that made the Mauna Luan special was the setting. There were beautiful gardens and a free-form swimming pool set in the midst of those gardens. The pool had a long, curved slide into it and I can still see the three of us clowning and laughing as we took turns on that slide. I also recall sitting with Sarge in the Jacuzzi at sundown, drinks in our hands, watching the clouds slip down between the mountains as the sky darkened. At such moments, I felt complete, whole and totally at peace.

The problem with living in Hawai'i was that instead of getting up every day and looking for work, we woke up, looked at the sky and said to each other, "What a beautiful day to go to the beach!" And, living only five minutes from Hanauma Bay, we often did. During the first six months in Hawai'i, Sarge walked and swam and I looked up people I knew in an attempt to find work. We had been drawing on our invested funds ever since Sarge went into the Walnut Creek Hospital. With no money coming in, other than Sarge's modest pension, we were fast depleting those funds.

By spring of 1977, I was working. I had a consulting contract with Med-Assist, a school that trained medical and dental assistants. The director told me that the school had never been accredited, they had financial problems and the faculty and staff seemed unwilling to support him. I worked with the director for a year and we succeeded in getting the school accredited and on a sound financial basis. We were never able to get the support of the staff, but I helped the director to see that perhaps he was not in the right job. He found someone to replace himself and went back to the things he enjoyed—practicing dentistry and riding the surf.

Then I met Mike Manos in a seminar and he invited me to work with him when he took on directing the Variety Club School. Many of the teachers there had been in the first *est* Training in Hawai'i. My job was primarily administrative, helping Mike set up filing systems and the structures that would help him in getting his job done. I also led an in-service workshop on communication for the teachers. I had a few speaking engagements, ran some workshops for students in education classes at the University of Hawai'i and then began working with Carrigan, Hoffmann & Associates, financial advisers. My job was conducting small group sessions designed to have people identify attitudes they had about money, and locate those attitudes in their early lives or in the attitudes of their parents. Though I seemed to be good at what I was doing, I didn't fail to appreciate the irony of it. My own financial situation was in utter disarray.

When my mother and father died, leaving a house but not much else, my brother bought out my interest in the house for $28,000. I put that into a money market account along with the roughly $25,000 we had made on our sale of the Sunderland house. The money from the sale of the Amherst house bought us a modest little cottage in Berkeley, California. We had decided to leave the rest of the money in the bank in Amherst until we got to California and had given some thought to investing. As we crossed the country we stopped to visit a gold mine and both Sarge and I were impressed by what we saw and heard. When we were settled in Berkeley, we went to a brokerage firm in San Francisco and told them we wanted to invest half of our money in gold and the other half in Levi Strauss stock. Sarge's nephew was part of a management team charged with turning around Levi Strauss International and we both thought Dick was going to do wonderful things for the company. But the broker essentially told us we were crazy, that we should invest in something solid that would serve us for "the long haul." Since neither Sarge nor I knew anything about handling large sums of money we took the advice of the broker, investing a few thousand dollars in Levi Strauss and the rest in the conservative investments recommended. Had I really insisted, we could have invested as we'd wanted and eventually benefited from both our chosen investments—gold went sky high and so did Levi Strauss—but, instead, I complained about the broker to anyone who would listen.

The agreement Sarge and I had made when we moved to California was that I could use the interest from the invested money to live on as I needed it, and Sarge would have his pension. We would share the cost of raising Rebecca. When Sarge was in the hospital, after the training, we had to draw money from the invested funds because the doctor's and hospital charges exceeded our insurance coverage. Sarge had taken early retirement, so his pension was about $9,400 a year and, in Hawai'i, that just about covered our rent so until I began to work, we were again drawing on our investments. The bottom line of this whole story is that from 1973, when we crossed the country, to 1978 when we went to India, that investment, which could be providing for me today, had been used up. Instead, I have two-thirds of Sarge's pension, now a little under $12,000 a year, plus another $10,000 from Social Security.

In April of 1977 Sarge left again, this time to go back to the mainland, and I suspected it would be for good. In my journal I wrote, "To hell with it. I'm constantly striving to make something beautiful out of a relationship which now is only occasionally nurturing. So what if once a year we experience that marvelous closeness that brought us together, that's not enough to compensate for the days and weeks of living together in a silent mutual survival pact. There's no right or wrong in it, it's simply that the relationship no longer nurtures either of us."

Shortly after Sarge left I filed my application for *est* trainer candidacy. Whatever loss I felt about my job, whatever my feeling of being shafted by the organization, these dimmed in comparison to what I felt could be my contribution as an *est* trainer—being a catalyst for the kind of change that had taken place in my life following those two weekends in 1974. I had taken all of the preparatory trainings and programs, had led the required guest seminars, and had started the graduate seminar program. One of the requirements of the application process was having a letter of recommendation from one of my children. This letter was written by my son, Jerry, and I confess to being teary-eyed as I read it today.

> "In the thirty-one years of my life I have watched [my mother] struggle through good times and bad, with a partner and on her own, and always with the same or near end result: things worked out well. I used to think that we were lucky but gradually, I realized that things worked out well on a regular basis because Mom got out and worked hard to see that that was how they came out. In everything that she has attempted she has not only succeeded but has done so with honors. I suspect that some might point at her marriage record and say, not so! I maintain that she is simply ahead of her generation or, from a different point of view, one of the forerunners of today's society. Her ability to rethink her moral position when new factors come to light has been a model to me, my sisters, and to many others who have turned to her for advice.
>
> "Since I gather from her request that she is extremely excited about the possibility of the position for which she is a candidate, I can only assume that if she is selected, she will perform in that position beyond the expectations of the selection committee. She is my mother and I love her and I know that she always does things better than she needs to do them because that *is* the way she does things."

Having sent in my trainer application I began cleaning up the apartment, completing things, communicating with people but, all the while, feeling alternately excited and threatened by the prospect of trainer training. Rebecca gave me a surprise party for my 57th birthday, but it wasn't nearly as big a surprise as the letter I received the day before, from the *est* Training Division, accepting me into the pre-trainer candidate program. Randy McNamara also gave me an assignment, at that time, which was to write the story of my life in order, he said "to complete your past." What he meant by that I didn't know but I was ready to do anything he asked. He said that each time I sat down to write I should go back to the beginning rather than picking up where I had left off. That assignment was the beginning of this book.

Rebecca had invited Roger and Claudia Whitlock and Stephanie Feeney to celebrate my birthday with us. Both Roger and Stephanie were on the faculty of the University of Hawai'i and I had met them when leading educator workshops for *est*. Claudia, Roger's wife, was in the training department of Liberty House, at that time the only department store in Hawai'i. They were all delighted with my acceptance into the pre-trainer candidate program. As the guests were leaving, Rebecca and I stood at the window waving to them, blowing bubbles out into the night and watching them ride on the winds or drop into the pool nine stories below. I experienced a little sadness that Sarge wasn't there to celebrate with us.

It was during this time that Rebecca and I discovered that we were so attuned to each other that one of us would sometimes voice what the other was thinking. One night we were with friends, playing Charades. She and I were on different teams. When I stood up and said I was thinking of a song, the title of which had seven words, Rebecca spoke right up, "Mares Eat Oats and Does Eat Oats." After another turn and another similar response the group decided to let us play only on the same team. We were less surprised than the others but had often wondered about this synchronicity. Because Roger was at the University and was intrigued, he arranged for us to be interviewed by a researcher interested in electro-magnetic theories of communication. The researcher asked us questions such as, "Does this happen when you are in different rooms or only when you are in the same room? Are you aware of who initiates the exchange?" We were amused, feeling a little like experimental animals, but were also aware that there was an unusual and, to us, unexplainable quality in our relationship. Later, I learned that in some Mahayana Buddhist traditions such events are seen as expressions of "non-local consciousness." That explanation seemed perfect to me.

Sarge had settled into his life in San Francisco and had taken a job as a messenger at the Bank of America. He wrote to us regularly and each letter reminded me that I loved him but was relieved not to be living with him. On the 16th of September he suffered another heart incident, in San Francisco. He was delivering a package in the Bank of America building, blacked out and fell. Apparently there was a malfunction in a heart valve, cutting off the blood supply to his brain. My initial impulse was to take the first flight to San Francisco but when I talked with him on the phone, he was in good spirits and told me to stay where I was. Before Christmas he decided to return to Hawai'i. Seeing him again I was sure I was committed to our marriage and willing to let the ups and downs be contained in that commitment. I was sure I loved him deeply. It would be a few weeks before I acknowledged to myself that nothing had changed. He looked like the man I had loved and married, but he was not.

Sometime that winter I had breast augmentation surgery. Although I wanted to look like a boy when I was young, I disliked my flat, boy-like figure as I grew up. In Hawai'i, many of the women I knew were having implants. Sarge kidded me about what I was doing, but it was evident that he liked my newly-acquired breasts. And it made quite a difference in my feelings about myself. I remember being taken out by friends for a celebration dinner and feeling like a different person, as I viewed myself in every mirror we passed. Had I known how much trouble these implants would give me later on, I would have had second thoughts about giving in to my vanity, but at the time I was delighted with the outcome.

Early in 1978 I signed a contract to lead a course at Chaminade University, a course for "displaced homemakers." Sponsored by NOW (National Organization for Women.) the course was actually a ten-week series of seminars, modeled on the *est* seminars in which I had participated over the years. There were sixty-five women in the course, women who had been divorced by their husbands who, under the Hawai'i legal system, were required to pay only one year's "rehabilitation alimony." That was supposed to be enough to enable these women—many of whom had never worked outside the home—to support themselves. My challenge was to help them see how they might do that. The course was successful and, as it neared the end, one of the participants who lived in Kailua asked me to come there and lead one for women of the Catholic Church. This recognition gave a much-needed boost to my ego and I began that second series in May.

The thing I remember most about these courses was the work we did in having people appreciate who they were and what they had to offer. Throughout the course we did exercises designed to make people more aware of themselves and their abilities and then, as a project for the course, we assembled a book of "Hawai'i Resources," including places that could be resources for the women to use, places to which they could contribute time, and the skills these women themselves had to offer others. As they began to see that they had abilities they might share, the women opened up in class. One woman stood up and proudly announced that she could teach people to make pies, that she made the best pie crust in Hawai'i. Another said that she could teach hula classes. Another said that many years earlier she had completed law school but had never taken the bar exam and had never practiced. She realized that she would need to study but was now committed to passing the Hawai'i bar exam. For many of these women the end of the course signaled a new beginning in life. For me, it meant a new direction for work. I realized I had the ability to reach and inspire people about what was possible in their lives. Obviously, communication should have a role in my future, whether or not that future was as an *est* trainer.

Since moving to Hawai'i, I had been assisting in the *est* office in Honolulu and participating in seminars. In August, I learned about, and decided to join, a group of Hawai'i *est* graduates who were going back to California for the Six-Day course at Tahoe. The Six-Day was partly a physical challenge and partly an awareness course, focusing on our "acts" in life—the way we present ourselves to others. Every day we were in the classroom and every morning we did setting up exercises and ran a mile, all of this before a seven o'clock breakfast. One morning we were out in the mountains taking part in a "ropes course."

The ropes course had three main events: the zip line, rappelling down the mountainside, and the Tyrolean traverse which involved crossing a ravine hand-over-hand on a rope. The zip line was pure thrill—better than a roller coaster ride—and I scratched my legs only a little in rappelling, once I had conquered the fear of stepping backward off the mountain with only a rope to guide me to the bottom. But the Tyrolean traverse was a nightmare. Later I learned that the trick is to push off and glide to the middle of the rope, letting the weight of your body take you there. But I like to manage things, so as soon as I stepped off the edge I took charge and began pulling, hand over hand. By the time I got to the middle I was utterly exhausted and looking to the other side could see that it was all uphill. Trying to do it my way wasn't working. I was sure I couldn't do it. I would have to just hang there in the middle until one of two things happened—either the rope would break and I would crash to the ground or my body would break in half. Then someone on the ground shouted up at me, "Hey, Elizabeth, don't run your old lady number here!" Old lady, indeed! I was only fifty-eight! My fury at being called an old lady set the adrenaline flowing. I grabbed the rope and, hand over hand, pulled myself to the other side where people helped me up on the rock. I was barely conscious when I collapsed on the other side but I heard cheers and clapping and knew I had done it. It was another of those times when I had a new experience of myself, an experience of going beyond what I thought of as my limits, discovering a dimension I hadn't known existed.

Another of the exercises we did in the Six-Day was designed to help us get rid of any anger or resentment we had from the past. It was in this program that I finally let out all the rage that had gripped me since Gerry Quigley died. When he and I were divorced the first time, I got thirty dollars a week in child support. Our divorce was granted on the grounds of "cruel and abusive treatment," but I didn't have sense enough to realize that I was entitled to alimony. Gerry took the house, the furnishings, two cars and whatever was in our bank accounts, including money from the sale of the Samuel Lane House and the summer business which I had run. I had not retained a lawyer at the time of the divorce nor had my father suggested that I do so. The real impact of this decision didn't hit me until Gerry's death, in 1972, when I learned that he had died leaving a significant estate to his wife of one year, and realized that one reason he had such an estate to leave was his investment of the money from the sale of the Samuel Lane House and the miserly contribution he'd made to the raising of his children over the years. In the exercise we were given a padded club and asked to beat it on a padded saw horse, making that saw horse someone we wanted to punish. This gave me permission to vent all my pent-up rage with Gerry, not only for his decision to leave everything to his new wife instead of to his children, but also for the years when I wanted to hit him but didn't dare because he was so much stronger than I. When the exercise was over I felt drained, emotionally exhausted, but at the same time, felt an enormous sense of relief and a kind of freedom. My anger toward Gerry had been a monkey on my back for years and suddenly it was gone. I literally felt pounds lighter. When I went outside after the exercise everything looked brighter and crisper, as if I had been through a cleansing process that removed the filter through which I usually saw the world.

Near the end of the Six-Day course, Jinendra Jain, one of the trainers, announced that we were going to take the *est* Training to India and he was seeking volunteers. Jinendra had been a Hindu monk and an interpreter for Swami Muktananda before meeting Werner and joining the *est* staff. He had been a lecturer in English at Delhi University before joining Muktananda. He was a slight man. My mother would have said he looked as if a good wind would blow him away. I was not aware of standing up when he put out the request for volunteers but suddenly there I was, on my feet with my arm in the air, volunteering to go to India. I was as surprised as the people around me. What on earth was I thinking!

On getting back to Honolulu, I realized that I hadn't consulted either Sarge or Rebecca before volunteering, but when I told them what I had done, I was surprised at the reactions. I had assumed I would go alone but Sarge seemed eager and willing to accompany me. His lifelong yearning to travel had only been stimulated by our years in Turkey, and he agreed with me that the opportunity was too good to pass up. Rebecca said she'd think about it but it didn't take her long to get into the spirit of the moment and choose to go with us. She would miss a year of school but we all agreed that the year of living abroad would be sufficiently educational to make up for the year of school. Sarge and I remembered Marta's years in Turkey.

In order to bear the cost of transportation and the cost of living in India for six months, we sold everything, including the car. The sale helped make the trip possible, but this adventure dealt the final blow to our finances. In my zeal, I did many things that I have since regretted, such as selling Grandma Randall's sterling silver flatware and discarding all my files, including years of writing and the Connecticut River Valley photo-essays, which were almost complete. The only thing I didn't sell was the three-dollar gold piece Uncle Will had given me for a wedding gift, and I have it still. Three weeks later, in the middle of a September night, we found ourselves in Bombay, still wondering how on earth it had all happened.

16

Supporting est of India

Sarge, Rebecca and I arrived in Bombay in the middle of a September night in 1978. We walked carefully through the airport lobby to avoid stepping on people sleeping on the floor. A dozen little boys wanted to carry our bags for us and taxi drivers argued loudly over who would take us to the hotel. Riding through the streets of Bombay I realized that it was not only in the airport that people were sleeping, they were sleeping on the sidewalks and in the doorways. The trip from Hawai'i had been tiring but we had a comfortable room and a good night's sleep at the Oberoi Intercontinental Hotel. The next day we had lunch with Jinendra Jain and Mina Krishnan in the hotel coffee shop and I felt immediately at home.

Mina was the Bombayan who had volunteered to host the training in India. She was a fortyish matronly woman with a huge smile, a handsome husband, and a little girl of nine or ten. Mina's brother had taken the *est* Training in the United States and had been so impressed with what he learned about himself that he asked Mina to do what she could to start the program in India. Mina had been talking with friends before we arrived, had generated considerable interest and had a core group of people ready to work, in addition to the volunteers coming from the United States. One of those volunteers was Rabi Pradhan, a young Nepalese whom I'd met in the Hawai'i *est* office. There was also a doctor and his wife from Florida, an aspiring actress from Los Angeles, a writer from Washington, D.C. and several others.

After leaving the Oberoi Hotel (which was too expensive for a prolonged stay) we tried two other hotels, then gave up and took an apartment in Atur Terraces on Cuffe Parade. Rabi, also looking for a place to live, moved in with us. My sense of humor was adequate to see me through the limited amount of time we spent in the Bombay apartment. I was able to look at the surroundings in which we would be living, remember our first year in Turkey, and relax. We were on the tenth floor of an apartment building considered one of the better places to live in Bombay; we had a living room, kitchen, two bedrooms, a bathroom and a windowless storage room which we gave to our part-time cleaning man for his use. The kitchen was a sliver of a room, equipped with a two-burner gas hot plate and a sink with a drainage pipe aimed at a hole in the floor. We brought in a water-filter system and set it on one of the small counter areas. The refrigerator was in the living room because there was no space for it in the kitchen. Looking out the living room window to the field across the street we could see families living, cooking and sleeping in newspaper huts. Even though our apartment would have been unacceptable for a professional family in America, the disparity in living accommodations between us and the people across the street was so shocking that we were humbled.

Most of the time I was either at the office in Mina Krishnan's home, out in the community introducing people to the *est* Training, or visiting schools and talking about education. Sarge and Rebecca were sometimes assisting and sometimes just getting acquainted with Bombay. Mina's husband, Mohan, was an architect who viewed our operation, and our presence in his home, with amused tolerance. He had little interest in what we were doing but was willing to be supportive of Mina, to whom it seemed important. We sometimes saw him in the mornings as we were arriving and he was leaving for his office.

One weekend morning, shortly after we arrived in Bombay, we woke up and remembered it was the day Mina and Mohan had arranged to meet us for a celebration that was to take place at Chowpatty Beach. As we looked out the windows of the apartment it looked as if all of Bombay was going to the celebration. The streets were filled with people, all going in the same direction. Some of the children carried streamers cut from newspapers and there was a steady and expectant hum of voices. Not wanting to miss out, we hurriedly ate our breakfast and went down to the street to join the crowd. Almost immediately we were swept up and carried along. Sarge and I each grabbed one of Rebecca's hands to keep from losing her. Looking at each other, we wondered if this had been such a good idea but, by that time, there was no turning back, we were simply propelled along by the mass of people moving toward the beach. As we neared the corner where we would have turned off to get to Mina's house, we saw them waving a banner at us and shouting laughingly, "It's okay, You're going in the right direction. See you there." We didn't get on the beach but we were close enough to see that people had erected a huge, perhaps three-story high, paper-mâché figure, which had been ignited and, as we watched, was being devoured by flames. Before the flames died down, and while we were still wondering what the figure had been, the crowd had reversed and we were being pushed in the other direction. Hastily turning around to keep from being knocked down, we once again became part of that massive crowd, this time heading back toward our part of the city. When we finally got back to the apartment, we sat down on the front steps, looked at each other and began laughing. We hadn't known what we had gone to see and didn't know what we actually did see, but had been part of a riotously jubilant mass of people who had taken us there and brought us back. And we'd had fun!

Each day, as we walked from our apartment to Mina's, we passed an old man begging. The first morning, as we passed, he put his hand out and made a plea for money and I gave him a few coins. The second morning I was embarrassed but sort of pretended he was not there. I knew I wouldn't give him money every time we passed. The third morning, instead of pretending he wasn't there, I looked into his eyes and greeted him with, "Namastee." He pulled back his extended hand, pressed it to the other hand in a reverential gesture and replied, "Namastee." From then on, we greeted each other every morning but he no longer asked me for money.

I adapted to India much more readily than I had to Turkey, even though the poverty was more evident and widespread and the lack of sanitation greater. Turkey had taught me that it was the people who make a country and I loved the people I met in India right from the start.

As soon as we had established the office in Mina's home, we began enrollment activity. Mina, however, had been telling her friends about the *est* Training for months and as soon as we arrived with supplies, including enrollment cards, people came knocking at the door, money in hand, to register. The number of "walk-in" registrations reminded me of my first days in the *est* office on Union Street where we had a bank of five phones dedicated to incoming calls, phones which were busy all day. In Bombay, it was not phone calls but people knocking on Mina's door.

Najma and Sultan Loynmoon were among the Bombay volunteers with whom we worked and became friends, often dining with them in their home. Neither of them had done the training but both were looking forward to it. Sultan became the most important member of the logistics team, often locating substitutes for things we didn't bring and couldn't find. We relied on him for his imaginative improvising. There was nothing resembling a podium for the front of the room so Sultan had one built. Instead of the smooth stones normally used in one of the training processes, Sultan provided us with metal balls made in a friend's factory. Trying to maintain American standards for a program being conducted in India was a challenge. We prepared class lists on a Smith-Corona portable manual typewriter, but because there was no copying machine and the training manual called for six copies, we used carbon paper and made six corrections for each mistake. Working with Indian volunteers was quite different from working with volunteers in the United States in that none of these people had done the training and were working simply on the recommendation of Mina's brother.

Sometimes Jinendra and I co-led guest seminars, sometimes they were led by Dianne Hammond, another *est* staff person and assistant to Jinendra, and occasionally I led one alone. As soon as we had trained Bombay enrollment volunteers, we Americans pulled back and let them do the enrolling. We wanted it to be an Indian production. One of the first whom we trained to lead introductions was a young woman named Sushma who opened her home for the purpose. These were very informal affairs as Sushma had a three-year-old child who wanted to be in the midst of the group and knew, as children do, how to be distracting.

As a spokesperson for the training I was invited to address Rotarians, corporate boards of directors, and private social groups. The first corporate group I addressed was the board of directors of a large manufacturing company and the meeting was held in their board room. I was seated around the table with eight men. At first I thought I might not be able to speak, I was so intimidated, but the men sensed my discomfort, had tea brought in, and began chatting informally. Within a few minutes I was over my fright and started speaking. "The first thing I want to do this afternoon is acknowledge the arrogance of being an American woman coming to India to talk to you about enlightenment and transformation." There was gentle laughter and the group was ready to listen. I spoke about my study of India at Cornell and my appreciation of its history and tradition. I suggested that much of that tradition had been buried under the westernization of India and the training might put people back in touch with that tradition. This time there was a general murmur of approval. Most of the directors were older men saddened by what appeared to be a forgetting of the roots of Indian culture. All of them registered for the November training in Bombay.

Another time I visited the All India Women's Federation, a group lobbying for women's rights. On this visit I talked about the *est* Training and answered questions about the education of women in America. Several members enrolled in the training, the first among them being Kamala, a married woman, perhaps forty years old. Kamala showed up early for the first day of the training, excited to be a part of this new thing. I didn't see her during the day but at about five o'clock in the evening I noticed her going, with the training supervisor, to the back of the room where she began talking to a man. The man was her husband who had shown up at the door demanding to see her. The training supervisor had escorted her to the back of the room. There were several minutes of quiet argument between husband and wife, then the woman turned to the supervisor and said, "I must go home now." The supervisor responded, "If you leave now, you will not be allowed to return for the balance of the training." "Yes," she said softly.

"I'm not sure you understand. You will not be able to attend tomorrow's session nor next week's sessions. Do you realize that?" "Yes," she said and quietly left.

The next morning Kamala was one of the first to show up, ready to go into the room. She'd not believed that she really could not return. She was visibly upset, pleaded at length with the supervisor and left in tears. About two years later I received a letter from Kamala, thanking me for having introduced her to the training. She said that not being allowed to return on that second day had forced her to look at the disparity between what she professed, in her work with the All India Women's Federation, and the way she allowed her husband to dictate to her in all phases of life. She said the experience had a major impact on her life and her work.

In that first training I did a lot of hovering, watching the Indians we had trained doing registration, logistics, trainer support, all of it. It was sometimes amusing, often gratifying. The cultural differences had interesting ramifications. On one occasion Landon Carter, the trainer, dropped a book on the floor to illustrate a point. People in the group gasped. Only later did we learn that to drop or throw a book on the floor was a cultural taboo in India. As I listened to the people who stood up and talked, I realized how universal are the basics of our lives and problems—wives and husbands, parents and children having trouble relating, people having trouble with money, jobs. The setting was different, the details were different, but underneath, it was the same as in the trainings in San Francisco or New York. In the week after completion of the first *est* Training in Bombay, book stores in that city reported running out of copies of the *Bhagavad Gita*, the demand for them was so great. There had been, indeed, a forgetting of tradition.

One day recently Rebecca and I were reminiscing and she reminded me of Christmas Eve in Bombay. Werner had given instructions that the volunteers were to be taken out for a great dinner. The restaurant had the kind of atmosphere one expects for a New Year's Eve party, with hats and streamers and noisemakers, but we were open to whatever might happen. There was fine food and dancing and then, on the stroke of midnight, the band struck up and people began to sing, "Happy birthday to you, happy birthday to you, happy birthday, dear Jesus, happy birthday to you!" We nearly collapsed in laughter. Rebecca still says that Christmas Eve was the best New Year's party she's ever attended.

Right after Christmas Sarge, Rebecca and I left Bombay and took a twenty-four-hour train trip to New Delhi where we were to set up an office and prepare for the first training there, in January. We found and rented a two-bedroom first-floor flat in a section of New Delhi called the Defence Colony. My family occupied one of the bedrooms; Jinendra Jain, his wife and two young children joined us later and occupied the other. The dining room became the office and the living room was the site of our introductory events. We had a cook, two maids and a gardener. It seemed absurd, given the size of the house and the yard, yet it seemed to be expected. The two maids were sisters and shortly after they came to work they asked if they and their families could live in our garage. I was aghast. Although we did have a cold water tap in the courtyard, there were no sanitary facilities and I could not see how a family could possibly live in the garage. But my New Delhi friends told me it was commonplace and that the maids were fortunate to have found a job in a house that had a garage.

The cook was a gaunt man, about fifty years old, although he looked seventy. He was a good cook—too good—and I gained twenty pounds during our stay in India. After the first time I saw the maid helping the cook prepare vegetables for salad by chopping them up on the marble kitchen floor, I decided it would be best if I stayed away from the kitchen. Our cook had a persistent cough, and when Sarge got sick two months into our stay, we were all tested for tuberculosis. The results showed negative for Sarge but positive for the cook, so we had to let him go and one of the maids took over cooking. Although Sarge didn't have TB, he did have a staph infection which kept him in the hospital for a couple of weeks. Briefly I thought he shouldn't have come but then I became so engrossed in getting the training going that it overtook my concern for him. It wasn't until we got back to Hawai'i that he discovered he had also picked up some intestinal parasites.

One of the first people we met in New Delhi was Indira Higham, a striking young woman with black hair, black eyes and a sharp tongue. Indira became an invaluable aid. She was a writer and illustrator who managed a publishing house in New Delhi. She introduced us to the great little restaurants tucked away in corners of the city, and to people who made our stay easier and more pleasant. We became good friends. Indira had previously taken the *est* Training in the United States and was going to be a major player in this first New Delhi training.

One day we went to her apartment to have tea and make plans. Talking about our experience of the *est* Training, Indira said she had taken it in San Francisco in 1974. We asked her what month and when she said January, Sarge and I looked at each other, then at her and acknowledged that we too had taken it in San Francisco in January. Suddenly she threw her head back and laughed. "Oh, my God, you were that old couple who monopolized the training with your problems!" Sarge and I looked at each other and grinned abashedly. Until that moment I hadn't realized that both he and I had been trying to enroll people in how hard it had been—he from his point of view and me from mine. Each of us had seen ourselves as victim, caught in a hopeless situation. Another person to whom we became close in New Delhi was Man Mohan Roi, a history professor at the University of New Delhi. He was a gentle, soft-spoken man and frequently came to the Defence Colony house to assist Rebecca, who was serving as registrar for the New Delhi training. Some years later I saw Man Mohan at the first Hunger Project Africa Prize Dinner in New York and both of us cried at seeing each other again.

For guest events in New Delhi we set up a regular schedule of teas, at our house, to which anyone could come to find out about the training. There was a guest tea every Wednesday evening and every Saturday afternoon. We served tea, *pekora* and cookies. These events were quite different from those in San Francisco and I have never ceased comparing them. A person might come to the first one, register, and then return to every tea until the time of the training. Another person might come to five or six teas before registering. Students came back with friends from their dormitory, wanting to engage in intellectual debates about the premises of the training. Some of them had listened to a KQED taped interview with Werner and had probing questions. It was sometimes hard to bring the afternoon or the evening to a close. These events were lively, participatory affairs and all seemed to feel welcome, whatever their purpose in coming. There were no follow-up calls not only because telephone service was so poor at the time but because such calls were not necessary. If people heard anything that interested them, they came back, usually bringing friends.

We hosted a total of nineteen guest teas in our house in Defence Colony and seventy-five percent of people in the first Delhi training were people who had attended one of those teas. Dianne Hammond encouraged us to hire a hall on a couple of occasions to try and replicate the special guest seminars in the States and to attract influential persons, but it didn't work. Nobody came. Dianne said she hired the halls and tried to make the enrollment process more closely approximate that in America because that is what Werner wanted. I'm sure it was difficult for her, being in India, seeing what worked and what didn't, yet being accountable to Werner who wanted it done the way he thought it should be done.

There was one very noticeable difference in enrollment in India. The culture is such that if a relative or close friend recommended the training to another, that other would invariably register, out of trust in the friend's judgment. That happens much less frequently in America where there is often resistance to, rather than acceptance of, such a recommendation. This puzzled me at first but I suspect it reflects the difference between our societies. In India, as in most of Asia, the family or group is more important than the individual and in the United States the emphasis is reversed.

On one occasion I was invited to address a class at the School of Business at New Delhi University. The invitation stated specifically that it was an informational session at which there could be no enrollment. There were about twenty-five students and they wanted to know everything about this training that was coming to New Delhi. They asked great questions and I was actually relieved because I could talk about the training without having to think about handling registration and money. I passed out copies of the *est* brochure, in the back of which were registration cards, but told the students I could not accept enrollments. If they wanted to register for the training, I told them, they could come to the address on the back of the brochure. The students were eager and the fifty minute period was much too short. I thanked them for their attention and their questions. As the students left the classroom, they filed by the podium where I was standing and quietly handed back the brochures. At first I was disappointed that they hadn't taken the brochures with them, but then I opened one and noticed that there was a check with it and that the registration card in the back had been completed. I hastily put the rest of the brochures in my briefcase and left. When I got home I found that a majority of the students in the class had completed registration cards and enclosed checks!

As registrar for the New Delhi training, Rebecca did a remarkable job of keeping the records straight—no easy task in a city where few had telephones and where the service was so poor that it was difficult to talk to those who did. She also assisted with logistics and developed a crush on Suneil, a delightful young Indian who became the logistics team manager for the training.

In New Delhi I continued to speak to groups at schools and colleges and to answer questions about differences in our educational system and philosophy. The teachers I met exhibited an openness that was delightful. It was also during our stay in New Delhi that I had my pre-Trainer candidate interview with

Landon Carter. I felt acknowledged by Landon and was sure I was finally on the path to becoming an *est* Trainer.

The introduction of the *est* Training in India was surprisingly successful. Within five months three trainings were completed, six hundred people had participated and there was a demand for trainings in Madras, Calcutta, Bangalore and Puna. The New Delhi training had been an interfaith, international event. There were Christians, Sikhs, Hindus, Muslims and Jains; there were people from different parts of India—Bombay, Coimbatore, Chandigarh, Rohtake and Delhi—and different parts of the world—Ireland, Germany, Africa, Afghanistan, Nepal and the United States.

At the end of six months we had to leave India. We had been there on tourist visas which were expiring. But before we left, we made a quick trip to see the Taj Mahal and were glad we did. I was awe struck by the realization that this magnificent structure had started out as an idea in the mind of a human being who was able to translate that idea into this thing of beauty. Had that person wondered whether or not his life had made a difference? Though we were leaving I had a sense of having created something out of nothing, nurturing its development, and then experiencing its completion. It had been a rewarding six months. In March I wrote, in a memo to Jinendra:

> "This whole experience has been of inestimable value to me. The people I've worked with have served as mirrors and I've had an opportunity to see my pettiness, my ego-centeredness, my stuckness and, also, my capabilities, my intentionality, and my magnificence. I have owned this training!"

Unable to get a flight directly home, we extended our stay by going to Nepal for a week, then on to Bangkok for another few days before flying to Hong Kong and home. Our first night in Hong Kong we ate in a Japanese restaurant near the hotel. The food was delicious but the serving size was obviously designed with Japanese people in mind. We were as hungry when we left as we had been when we entered, and perhaps that was why all of us spied the familiar golden arches across the street. It was the most welcome sight we had seen in weeks. We ate Big Macs and drank chocolate shakes and knew we were ready to go home. On April 3rd, 1979, we flew from Hong Kong back to Hawai'i.

I had not thought about where we would live when we returned from India, and so we arrived in Honolulu with no idea of where we would sleep that night. I made some phone calls and learned that our friend John Connolly was leaving town for a week. I talked to him and he said he would be pleased to have us use his house while he was gone, so within a few hours of arrival, we were comfortably settled in John's house on Kilauae Avenue, getting ready for bed. Returning to Hawai'i we had nothing but the suitcases with our clothes so it was easy to move from one place to another. I have always been pretty much at home wherever I am but it became evident that was not so for Rebecca. One night at John's, I was tucking her in bed when I noticed she was trying to hold back tears. She had been such a great sport on the whole trip I could not imagine what was wrong, but on pressing her, I learned that she was feeling homeless. When I thought back to her room in Amherst and the care she gave her things, I realized how much more important stability was to her than to me. With no consideration of that, I had uprooted her and taken her half way round the world, and then brought her back to a place where we had no home and very little money. For me it was all part of the adventure, but looking at Rebecca that night, I realized it was ceasing to be an adventure for her.

A friend of John's had been told of our situation and before John returned the friend found us a house-sitting opportunity up on Waialae Ridge. It was a beautiful house, with a swimming pool and a magnificent view. We packed our bags, moved up to the Ridge and, for a couple of weeks, relaxed while taking care of cats and plants. Before the time was up at Waialae Ridge, Dan Seveland, who had been a neighbor at the Mauna Luan, approached us and asked if we would be willing to live in a house he was trying to sell in Koko Kai. He said that, for insurance coverage, he had to have someone living in the house. There was no furniture in the house but there was good padding under the carpet and Dan thought we could sleep comfortably on the floor. We moved in as soon as our agreement ended on the Ridge. The house on Koko Kai was new, had never been lived in, and had a magnificent view of the bay and the ocean. Dan had been right, and with the help of foam rubber mats, we were quite comfortable sleeping on the floor. We bought pillows, borrowed some canvas lawn chairs for the living room and a card table and chairs for the dining area, bought a few disposable aluminum foil pans for the kitchen and were all set.

After we moved into the new house, Sarge became increasingly silent and morose, sometimes sitting on the front porch for hours just staring off at the ocean and other times wandering around the neighborhood with a bag picking up aluminum cans and debris that he found on the road. He had not been well in India, and his lack of energy was not surprising. The love and compassion I felt for Sarge in 1979 were not the feelings I had for him when I married him in 1962. Every once in a while I would look at him and be overcome with sadness for both of us. Had I known what a loss it would be when we finally separated and he remarried, I might have made more of an effort to find the man I had married, but I was convinced that man was gone forever. I felt that life had played a dirty trick on both of us. Then, one morning during our stay in Koko Kai, Sarge wakened and turned to me, saying, "I think we should get a divorce. I want a woman who didn't know me before." As he went on, he also said I was too attached to Werner and I could understand how he would feel that way. Sarge communicated cleanly and clearly what was so for him. He was winding down, wanting to simplify his life while I was still intent on being an *est* trainer. He wasn't interested in hanging around playing second fiddle to me. Also, he wanted a woman who wouldn't always be making comparisons with the man he had been before his heart attack and stroke.

We filed papers in May, the hearing was on June 18th, and the divorce became final on July 1st. This was not at all the kind of divorce I had from Gerry Quigley. It was not an angry, "I can't take it any more" divorce. The step Sarge took released us both. Before he left, we threw a divorce party—a brunch at the Halekulani Hotel's beachside restaurant—for all those in Hawai'i who were close to us. People were amused, many of them complimenting us and saying it was the first such party they'd ever attended and they thought it was a great idea. Before the guests had disbanded, Sarge said goodbye and left for the airport.

With Sarge gone, Dan Seveland assumed a caregiving role. Dan had been a friend since we first moved to Hawai'i in 1976. He was forty-five or fifty years old, tall, straight with an enviable tan, sandy hair bleached almost white by the sun. I believed him to be gay but sometimes, as when he took me out to dinner at Michel's, he was dressed so beautifully and treated me so tenderly, I couldn't help wondering if I were mistaken. Dan had been disturbed about Sarge's moroseness since we returned from India and when he left, Dan stayed in close touch with Rebecca and me. Sometimes it was for breakfast at the Yum Yum Tree, sometimes dinner at Michel's. One night he came to the house with a basket of strawberries, a pint of sour cream and a box of brown sugar, and the three of us sat on the floor dipping and slurping. Then the day came that Dan brought some people to view the house and they bought it. While I was pleased for Dan and I knew it was inevitable that Rebecca and I would return to the mainland, I was sad. Hawai'i felt like home. Rebecca and I left Hawai'i on June 28th, again not knowing where we were going except back to San Francisco.

Almost as soon as we arrived in the Bay Area we heard that Sheila Babbie, a friend of mine from Hawai'i, was looking for me. I contacted her and learned that she was assembling a team to revise *est* graduate seminar materials and wanted me to work with her. Rebecca and I would get room and meals at the Six-Day site in Kirkwood (near Lake Tahoe) in exchange for working with Sheila and the *est* trainers in charge of the project. Rebecca and I talked about it. Because the project was to be for almost four months Rebecca would miss more school. She was unconcerned about that and I was sure she had benefited more from her time in India than she would have from a year of school so I raised no objection. The work was being done at Kirkwood because that was the site of the Six-Day course and many of the trainers were involved with that course and visited frequently. We lived in *Cabin G*, as our lodge was called, along with seven others including Sheila and her nine-year-old son Aaron. At Kirkwood it was like being in training all the time. We all knew the standards to which we would be held by the trainers.

There were three full-time typists and it was my responsibility to see that the typed work was of the quality expected. At first I spent most of my evenings red penciling typed pages, then I decided that was a waste of time. One morning after breakfast I met with the typists and said, "I'm unwilling to spend so much time proofreading your work. From now on, the first time I find an error I will return the work to you. You may give it back to me when you think it's perfect. When I read it that time I'll be following the same procedure so I suggest you have it right before you give it to me the first time." There was some grumbling but my job became much easier as people became more responsible for the quality of their work.

After a couple of weeks Sheila asked Rebecca if she would be willing to be cabin manager. 'Becca was delighted at the opportunity. She was good at the job and commended by the trainers. She knew what needed to be done and was politely firm about getting it done. Only one person had a problem with it—a middle-aged volunteer who objected to being managed by a fourteen-year-old girl. The woman did not stay long. Working in such close proximity to the Six-Day site had some interesting side effects. Whatever was happening in the course on a particular day would be reflected by the people in *Cabin G*, even though we usually did not know what had been happening in the course room until the end of the day. On the day the course was dealing with resentment, we all seemed to have something to gripe about; on the day of the sex talk all of us in the cabin were itchy, wishing to be someplace else, talking about our men friends. Once again, that phrase, "non-local consciousness" came to my mind.

Saturday nights we went into Tahoe for dinner and gambling. One night I got lucky, won several hundred dollars and took Rebecca—who had to sit in the lobby with a book while I gambled—to the South Shore Room to have dinner and hear Judy Collins sing. I'm embarrassed to admit how we got in to that sold-out event but since I'm being candid here...I told Rebecca to follow me and not say anything. We got in the "Reservations Only" line and when we reached the desk I said simply, but with dignity, "Dr. Elizabeth Russell, party of two." The man at the desk checked his list twice then, without betraying anything, said, "Yes, of course, Dr. Russell. This way please." I assumed they must leave a few tables for just such unexpected brazenness. Once we were seated I forgot all about the deception and enjoyed the evening.

We left Kirkwood on October 15th to go to Santa Clara for Marta's wedding to Stephen Weinstein. The wedding was lovely and Marta was radiant in a gown made from a white and gold *sari* Najma Loynmoon sent me from India. It was an emotional day for me. Every time I looked at Marta I was overwhelmed with love and started crying. In marrying Stephen, Marta became step-mother to an eight-year-old half black daughter, Maisha, and as I saw them together I recognized that my reaction to Marta's rape had not been racially motivated but was a response to the violence and invasion. Maisha became a dearly-loved grand-daughter. Sarge was at the wedding with a new woman and for the first time I knew how his first wife must have felt, in 1962, when she heard that Sarge was seeing me. He and I were married less than three months after his divorce from Evelyn and now here he was, with another woman, three months after our divorce. I was confused. While I was living with Sarge I didn't want to be, but when he was gone I missed him. While we were at Kirkwood he wrote me seeking another reconciliation but it made no sense to me and I told him that. We had been on and off for several years and in those years he left us half a dozen times, each time to seek the comfort of another woman. Clearly, the relationship was no longer viable. In mid-November he wrote, saying he was going to marry. I knew that it was finally over and I experienced an emptiness beyond anything I had ever known. It was as it had been when Mother and Dad died, except then I had Sarge to turn to. This time I had to deal with my grief alone and it was a grief I hadn't expected. I thought our divorce was going to make it better for both of us, yet I was grieving. Sarge went on to marry a woman who hadn't known him before and to live a good life for another ten years. For a time after his remarriage I felt bereft and wondered if I had been released, or condemned to more loneliness.

Leaving Kirkwood, I had no job and no place to live and felt lost and irresponsible. It seemed to me that I should have more to show for fifty-nine years of living. But there was no time for recriminations. Rebecca still needed parenting and

I needed a job. Sarge's sister, Charlotte, had recently moved to California, we discussed the possibility of living together and, in the spring of 1980, rented a house in Cupertino. It worked out well for us because I had no household furnishings, having disposed of all of them before going to India, and Charlotte had everything we would need. The house was a small, one-story frame house on a *cul-de-sac*, with three bedrooms and a tiny garden in back. In early March, Charlotte entertained some family members, including Sarge and his new wife. After they left I went to my room, acknowledging to myself that I hadn't cried all of my tears, that I was still caught in the trap of loving the man I had married eighteen years before and not wanting to live with the man he had become. I knew that on one of my tomorrows I would pass out of this phase but at the moment knowing that was of no help.

When we had settled, I began working for Marta and Stephen in what was then an advertising specialty company called Logo. It didn't take me long to discover that making "cold calls" to prospective customers was not up my alley but I have always been able to get secretarial work, so I pocketed my pride, forgot about my doctorate, and applied for work as a temp at Memorex. After a few weeks I was transferred to Memorex Finance Corporation where I filled in for the president's secretary who was on leave of absence. I enjoyed the work, and my boss gave me much latitude in the job. I worked with him preparing speeches, I ran interference for him, I read and highlighted material for him, I handled routine correspondence. In addition, I watered his plants, served his coffee and made sure his office was immaculate, with none of the resentment I had experienced when I was a twenty-two-year-old secretary at General Electric. The decision I made back then was that I was never going to be anybody's secretary again, I was never again going to be subservient to anybody, particularly to a man, in the work environment. I realized that with this man I was doing many of the same things I had done in 1942 but, instead of hating them, was discovering what it was like to be performing those services so this man could get his work done. I was always looking to see what I could take on that would free him and the more I found to do, the more fulfilling the job became. He said he had never felt more supported in getting his job done. As I reflected on my experience of thirty-eight years before I realized that while I could remember the things I found so distasteful about the job, I couldn't put myself in that girl's place. I had grown into a person who knew how to support someone else. I knew what was possible for human beings and knew I was free to choose. When my boss's regular secretary returned in the middle of the summer, my job was finished, and I was, once again, wondering what was next when I was offered the job of heading a new non-profit corporation that was just in formulation.

17

"It Will Happen by Christmas"—The Holiday Project

For close to ten years, the *est* Holiday Hospital Project had organized volunteers for holiday visits to people confined to institutions—hospitals, nursing homes, prisons. Groups of volunteers made or purchased gifts, held gift-wrap parties and, with personnel at the institutions, made arrangements for visits. In early 1980 the project was incorporated, as a non-profit public benefit corporation in California, and named The Holiday Project. When it came time to formally launch the new program, the board of directors invited me to head it. I was thrilled at the opportunity to be back in the *est* environment and, on September 8th, I became National Coordinator of The Holiday Project. Shortly after I accepted the position I had a note from Werner. He wrote: "How thrilled I am that you, *you*, are doing this project. I know it will be handled and it's good to have you home. I love you."

When Werner said, "I love you," he made me feel as if I were someone worth loving. It took me back to Uncle Will who was the first adult who loved me in that way. I always knew with Uncle Will that I was whole and complete exactly the way I was, even though at that time I was a little girl whom almost everyone else thought needed fixing. When I realized that Werner loved me, it was the same thing. He saw me whole and complete exactly as I was, without any fixing, and in that love, I was able to see myself.

I expected The Holiday Project to be a challenging task but I had no idea how challenging until I realized that I had less than four months until the Christmas/Chanukah season began. From September to December, I was engaged in getting this new non-profit venture incorporated in thirty states across the country. In every state where we incorporated, volunteers were being asked to take on considerably more responsibility than they'd had when it was operated by *est*. Whereas volunteers in the past had only to organize visits and visitors, they now would also be responsible for accepting donations, keeping financial records and contributing to support of the national office. My job was to see that it was done in such a way that we maintained the financial integrity and viability of the whole, while allowing it to expand. It was as if the project had moved through adolescence into adulthood and I felt much the same about myself. At sixty years of age I was taking on a job for which I'd had little training and which would make huge demands on me. It was at this point that I acknowledged the power of speaking—the power of communication—because the only way this could be accomplished was by saying, "It will happen by Christmas," and communicating that to the people with whom I was working across the country.

My vision for the project was that the name, "The Holiday Project," would someday be as easily recognized as "The Salvation Army." My experience of the volunteers was such that the goal seemed not unrealistic. Many had full-time jobs yet gave hours each holiday season to organizing the project in their communities. In the fall of that first year I spent most of my time on the telephone—supporting, encouraging, acknowledging, and doing all the legal stuff that accompanied incorporating.

One of the first local volunteers I had spoken with, after taking the job, was Victor Ozeri in New York. He had been involved in the Holiday Hospital Project since its beginning, had chaired the New York committee and had offered to coordinate the Northeast Region. He was recommended by people in New York who had worked with him and I accepted his offer. Victor and I were on the phone several times a week between September and December and each time we talked I was more at ease with him. One day we were talking and laughing and he said, "Elizabeth, are you married?"

I was surprised by the question but answered, "No, but I have been." "Do you have children?" "Yes." "How many?" "Five." "Five!" There was a long pause, "How old are you?" "Sixty." Silence, then, "I'm twenty-five."

It was my turn to be shocked. When he asked the first question I was amused but excited. He had a deep and powerful voice and sounded as though he might be fifty or sixty years old. My mind had immediately started entertaining possibilities. Suddenly I began to grin and then to laugh. Victor joined me and in a few minutes we were both laughing uproariously. He confessed that he too had been entertaining possibilities. Victor and I met in person at the Project's first annual conference in San Francisco the next summer and I realized that had I first met him in person, I would never have come to know him as I did. He was young—looking even younger than he said he was—and shorter than I. He was dark-haired, sort of a stocky build, and was wearing a flashy sport jacket and wing-tipped shoes. As I looked at him I realized how many people I had passed by, simply because there was something about their appearance, or their age, that made it seem unlikely we would have anything in common. And I am sure the same was true for Victor. While he had the kind of upbringing that would have made him courteous to this older, white-haired woman, had he seen me first he certainly wouldn't have engaged in the kind of repartee we'd had over the months. To this day I am grateful that we did not meet earlier because Victor is still one of the joys of my life.

One of the most valuable lessons I've learned from Werner is that as self-awareness expands, it takes in others and, eventually, expands to see the self's relationship to, and responsibility for, the whole. And that explains something about my relationship with him. It wasn't that he didn't see me, the individual called Elizabeth, but he always saw more, he saw the possibility that this individual represented. And that was the way he viewed all of us. It was as if he could see into us, see more than we could see of ourselves and that was why, in an event such as "Celebrating Your Relationships" he could stand on the stage in the Oakland Coliseum, read love poetry to thousands of people and have them all aware of their love for everyone in the Coliseum, have each one aware of being larger than the individual sitting in a particular chair. The only way any of us could express that awareness was through the emotive outburst that followed the event—roaring, cheers, whistles, tears, hugging. I was there with members of my family, all of us crying together in the love and recognition of being part of a huge extended family. At that time, the extended family was just beginning to include people across the country but today, as I write, it includes people all around the world, with the Landmark Forum being offered in more than eighteen countries and six languages.

My memories of Werner and my times on staff are disjointed; they come up at odd moments often unaccompanied by a framework of dates or associated events. But I do remember that Werner, at events such as the Peter Senge course, "Leadership and Mastery," was like a student with lots of questions, eager to learn, ready to respond every time Peter asked a question. He was the same way when Hubert Dreyfus came from U.C. Berkeley to give some of us a short course on Heidegger. It was a rare and wonderful opportunity to participate with Werner that way. At times he was brilliant and hard, at other moments so compassionate and tender that just to look at him produced overwhelming feelings of love. At such times my experience of Werner was that he was an exemplar of that innate desire to learn which characterized my life as well.

One morning, during Leadership and Mastery, he came into the course room, greeted me by standing beside my chair and putting his arm across my shoulders. For several minutes I just rested my head against him and experienced greater peace than I had ever known. When the course concluded, I again reflected on the level at which I was participating in life, and on the people with whom I was playing. I was in a big game. I realized that it was not an accident that I was in a big game with big people. I had one of those rare glimpses of myself as a big person. The following day I was in a strange place of not knowing—not knowing anything specific, just a space of not knowing. And, at the same time I was beginning to experience myself as trustworthy. It was a kind of emergence, as if there were someone who had been locked up inside, or had been in hiding, and was finally ready to come out but didn't know how. I felt a little tentative, a little shy, awkward, and experienced an unaccustomed tenderness toward the people with whom I lived and worked, and toward the person Elizabeth.

When Werner had first offered me the opportunity to join staff and head the Educator Project, back in 1974, I was thrilled and excited but always held that job as a stepping stone on the way to being an *est* trainer. When, in India, I had my pre-trainer candidate interview with Landon, I thought I was coming close, and the months at Kirkwood fed my dream. Instead of following up, however, to see that my file had reached Elaine Cronin, *est* of Hawai'i's Center Manager, to see that it had been signed and forwarded to the training division at headquarters, I waited. Most of my life I had been "waiting"—waiting to be invited, waiting to be discovered—and then complaining when nothing happened. In this case I waited several years before inquiring of the training division and learning that Elaine had never forwarded my file to headquarters, that she was no longer with the company and that my file had, apparently, been lost. They had no application, no notice of my acceptance into the pre-trainer candidacy program, no letters of recommendation, no report of Landon's interview, nothing. It was as if the years of preparation had not existed. Again, I was stunned and unbelieving.

The thing about being an *est* trainer was so big, it was to be my supreme accomplishment in life but, obviously, it wasn't an accomplishment I could let myself have. It would have required giving up all the stuff I'd had since childhood about not being good enough. That early pronouncement had imprinted itself so deeply that I couldn't deny it, even though I couldn't acknowledge it either. I thought I was doing everything I needed to do to reach my goal but it was as if there were an undertow, a current that was always pulling me under. Looking back on this period I thought being an *est* trainer was my goal, yet I went off on several different tracks, assuming they were all related, all part of the necessary training. As I write this, I know that had I really intended to be a trainer or a Landmark Forum leader, I would be that today.

As head of The Holiday Project I had some rare opportunities. In late November I was invited to the Franklin House for a reception honoring Valentine Bereshkov, First Secretary of the Soviet Embassy in Washington. It was the beginning of Werner's effort to learn about the Soviet Union and its people. Also at the reception were Bill Davidson, a psychiatrist who worked on the Presidential staff as an expert in the way nations perceive one another and who had brought about the meeting at the Franklin House. Among the other guests were Robert Balzar, wine editor of *Holiday* magazine and the *Los Angeles Times*, and actor Burgess Meredith who was a lifelong supporter of the Human-Dolphin Foundation. During the evening I talked at length with Burgess about dolphins, was fascinated, but left with more questions than answers.

One could see how eager Werner was to learn, yet when Bereshkov asked him what he wanted, Werner's response was that he didn't want anything. Hearing this, I wanted to ask, "Nothing?" It seemed to me that what he wanted was an opening for friendship between the American and Soviet peoples. This relationship developed with Werner being invited to Bereshkov's home in Washington and Bereshkov coming out for a tour of the wine country with Werner. The point of the relationship was simply to be related and it was the beginning of a real friendship. In consultation with the U.S. State Department and Soviet Ambassador, Anatoly Dobrynin, an agreement was reached between Werner Erhard & Associates and the Znanya Association, Soviet Academy of Adult Education, out of which came a long association with the Znanya Society and Werner's work with Soviet managers. Dr. Olin Robison, then President of Middlebury College and Senior Consultant to the U.S. State Department on matters pertaining to the Soviet Union acted, at that time, as adviser to Werner on his work with the Soviet Union.

One of the programs that started during this period was World Runners which organized the Moscow Marathon. The Moscow Marathon had two intended results: 1) the raising of at least one million dollars for The Hunger Project and 2) to have at least one specific collaborative initiative jointly run by the United States and the Soviet Union for the developing world. The second Goodwill Games in Seattle in 2000 completed the project which, by that time had raised two million dollars for The Hunger Project and had three pieces of legislation, dealing with the developing world, signed by Bush and Gorbachev.

World Runners has since joined an organization called Global Partners which is now making significant contributions to the people of east Africa.

All of this developed out of the possibility of being related and Werner's commitment to being better informed, trying to understand, making our society and its leaders more accountable to answering the hard questions. It always amazed me that when Werner wanted to learn something, he didn't just go to a class or read a book (though he did those too) but he sought out the experts, the people who might know the most about the subject in which he was interested. So it was that he was learning from Valentine Bereshkov and from Olin Robison, whom he credited with our success in relating to the Soviet Union.

By mid-December The Holiday Project was well established. We had put together a network of seventy committees across the country and had raised eighty-five thousand dollars. I'd had a separate phone line temporarily installed in Jill's house, where we were spending Christmas that year, and before I went to bed Christmas night I had received a phoned-in report from every Holiday Project committee in the country. The volunteers had visited a hundred forty-two thousand people on Christmas Day and raised more than a hundred and thirty thousand dollars. It was a job well done and as I acknowledged people on the calls I found myself in tears over and over again. And that emotion seemed to include everyone around me. I could never remember a Christmas of more family closeness. We had fires on the hearth and, at night, sat around—drinking, reminiscing, and admiring Marta's new baby. There was snow in the woods and the day after Christmas we went cross-country skiing. I felt truly blessed.

In April, I was promoted to Executive Director of The Holiday Project and Victor Ozeri and Fran Alexander, in New York, became National Coordinators. Fran was an executive on loan from IBM. In June, David Norris (an *est* trainer) and I led the first Holiday Project National Conference, at Fort Mason in San Francisco. Many of the people attending that first conference were unsophisticated travelers. One young woman came from Vermont with the baby she was still nursing and said it was her first time out of Vermont and first time on an airplane. The conference established the Holiday Project volunteers as family and, initially, David had a problem breaking into that family. About noon of the first day a participant stood up and said that when he came into the room and saw David sitting at the front he was annoyed. He said it was as if the mother of the family had brought home a stepfather without telling the kids. Everybody laughed and David was accepted.

People from all over the country shared stories of happenings in their communities, happenings that brought laughter and tears to the room, happenings that gave reality to the word *miracle*. Someone told of a volunteer visiting a hospital in New York City, walking into a ward and standing beside the bed of a teenage girl who had overdosed on drugs Christmas Eve. Suddenly the man bent down to look more closely, then cried out and took the girl in his arms. He'd recognized the sister who had run away from home two years earlier. Another told of a man, totally paralyzed by a stroke, who had been denied the financial help needed for equipment that would allow him to communicate, on the grounds that being able to communicate was not "medically necessary." For months he had been locked into a lonely world by himself. The group raised money, bought a computer and equipment that utilized the man's ability to slightly raise and lower his head (the only movement of which he was capable). A month after Christmas we received a letter—a letter that had been tapped out one key at a time on a computer, by a man with a wand attached to a headband. The letter said, "Thank you. I'm back in touch with the world."

When the conference was over I reflected on the work I was doing and on the place it had in my life. From the time I was a little girl I had wanted the world to be a place that was safe for love, for laughter, for tears, for joy, to be a place without wars and killing, poverty and suffering. The adults in my world always called that idealistic or unrealistic and somewhere along the way I allowed their pronouncements to alter my belief that it could be that way. Now and again I would press through and reassert my conviction because at some level I knew it had to be possible. On another level, however, I doubted myself because there was so much agreement that I was wrong. In the work I did with *est* and The Holiday Project I felt as if I were being true to myself, that the work we were doing had the possibility of making the world a better place for everyone, and although it would not happen in my lifetime I would know that I had contributed to the ultimate realization of the vision.

At the next year's Holiday Project conference, in June of 1982, the Project was turned over to the volunteers, under the management of Fran Alexander, supported by Micki Goldberg, who had been active for years in the Project. The board of directors wanted to see if the project could be run on an all-volunteer basis. Although I had reservations about the idea, I didn't voice those reservations, at least partly because I had such confidence in Fran. At the end of the conference, I was acknowledged for the work I had done and was asked to continue my participation on the board of directors. The 1981 project had more than doubled the results of the previous year, the volunteers having raised well over half a million dollars in cash, goods and services, and having visited twice as many people. With his acknowledgment of me, Werner also gave me a check in recognition of my work in India—a check that compensated for the personal funds spent in making that trip.

The following year, Jim Durgin and Barbara Knox, two other old-time Project people, took over management of the Project, and by the end of that year it was evident that the organization could not be completely run by volunteers. Both Jim and Barbara spent so much time on the project that they jeopardized their jobs. They urged the board to reconsider and, before the beginning of the 1984 season, Rita Saenz was hired as Executive Director. She came from Governor Jerry Brown's office in Sacramento and had management experience with charitable organizations. I was disappointed in not being asked to return to that job but was still willing to remain on the board of directors. And I was being asked to use my Holiday Project experience as a consultant to two other non-profits that had just been formed under the umbrella of the new Werner Erhard & Associates.

In July of 1982 I began working as a consultant to the Education Network, a group of educators who stayed in touch after the demise of *est* in Education, and to the Growing Older group, a group of older *est* graduates. Within a year, it was evident that the Growing Older group was not going anywhere and the Education Network had appointed an Executive Director, so once again, I was looking for a job. My original application to be an *est* trainer had been lost in the machinery of the organization and my re-submitted application was rejected. I was angry, hopeless and wanted an explanation but didn't ask for one. Had I thought it was age discrimination I would have made a fuss but the closest they came to that was suggesting that I might not have the stamina for the long days in the training room.

My proposal for a public information office was turned down as was a proposal I had submitted to Hermenet, another of the associated entities. In the meantime I was transcribing tapes of Werner events and being continually challenged to look at myself as being responsible for everything that was happening. While I could accept that responsibility intellectually, it still felt as if I'd been the victim of a hell of a lot of stuff in my life. And when I owned the responsibility, it seemed hopeless. At that point, my life appeared to be one of struggle and effort. There were moments of happiness, months of success and acknowledgment but the thread that tied it all together was one of struggle and loneliness. The vision that had been reawakened by my *est* participation seemed to be clouded over. As long as I was busy and involved, my life was good, but when things turned sour, I began to feel old, useless, and sorry for myself. At such times I forgot all about responsibility.

But then I'd attend some *est* event and be back in touch with myself. It was in the event, "A World that Works for Everyone" that I realized I hadn't answered the questions Werner was asking. He asked us to look at the question: "Does my life really matter?" Then he went on to suggest that, in the way we ordinarily live, the only possible answer to that question is, "I doubt it." That's exactly where I was. But then he went on to say that acknowledging that answer made a new domain possible—a domain in which things could show up, in which the future could be created. He said the purpose of the evening was to open up the question, "Does my life matter? Do I really matter? Do I make a difference? Does anything make a difference?" and to ask those questions in a way that would make a difference in the world. Since I had been asking these questions since my mother's death (and probably before) the evening had a tremendous impact on me. He said that to be able to make a difference we must create a new context. In that context I make a difference because everybody makes a difference. The rule of that context is that everybody makes a difference or nobody makes a difference. It is a world of "you and me" rather than "you or me." If my basic principle is that who I am makes a difference, life becomes an adventure. He went on to say, "I wish I could take you back to your childhood, back to when you had visions, dreams, when you were naïve, and I wish I could then move you forward to see when it was you decided you didn't make any difference. You watched that early enthusiasm become blunted, you learned not to be totally invested in anything, you learned not to care so much." Listening to him I found myself in tears. Those words were for me. It was if he had known about my childhood. This is what I mean when I tell people, "He gave me my life."

In March of 1983 I was hired by the Babbie Enterprises Research Group to work with them on gathering data on the new Youth at Risk program, a program of the Breakthrough Foundation. Part of their work was designing instruments for assessing that data on a longitudinal basis. One of my jobs was interviewing kids in Oakland who were applying for admission to the Youth at Risk ten-day course. Being interviewed were leather-jacketed eighteen-year-olds whom I would not have wanted to meet on the street at night. There was a black girl of fifteen, a hundred pounds overweight, with an "I don't give a damn" expression on her face and a cigarette dangling from the corner of her mouth. We knew she did give a damn or she would not have been trying to get into the course. Sitting across the table from another applicant, a baby-faced fourteen-year-old, I had the shock of my life when, in response to my question, "What did you do?" he replied, "Killed a guy."

The course consisted of ten days in the mountains with, as in the Six-Day course I'd done in 1978, a strenuous physical activity program combined with classroom work designed to have the kids confront and acknowledge responsibility for their own lives. Werner led this first one. At the time, I questioned whether or not the course could do anything for these kids but I wanted to see, so at the end of the ten days Rebecca and I went to Fort Mason to meet the bus when they returned to San Francisco. The parking lot was filled with parents, social workers and people like 'Becca and me who were just interested in seeing what, if anything, had happened.

It was hard to believe that the youngsters getting off that bus were the same kids I had talked with in Oakland. The fat black girl had opened up like a flower. She jumped off the bus singing and ran to hug her mother. Some of the toughest-looking kids had turned into pussycats with grins. There was laughter and tears and the boys picked Werner up on their shoulders and carried him around the parking lot. I was in tears, then looked at Rebecca, hugged her and began laughing. It was nothing short of miraculous!

The Babbies had been contacted by Joanne Black, a renowned marketing expert, who had been hired to review all previous research on the *est* Training. The Babbies organized focus groups to discuss the pros and cons of the *est* Training. The outcome of questions about the guest program was a report that fifty-one percent of the respondents felt pressured to bring guests and resented that pressure. One person reported that her desire to share the results of the training in her life was stolen from her by the seminar leader telling her she had to bring guests. Another part of the research, into guest seminar effectiveness, showed that it had declined dramatically from the outset. Joanne presented a range of options for addressing the situation but she was rebuffed. It was almost as if Werner took, as a personal affront, any mention of guests or graduates feeling pressured. My understanding was that he didn't like the findings so he shut down the research project and fired Joanne Black. This was when I began to acknowledge that my idol had feet of clay, that he was human, after all. It's interesting to me that twenty years later the organization was still grappling with the issue of pressure.

Before I had finished my work with the Babbie Research group, I received a job offer from The Health Resource Network in Baltimore. A Holiday Project friend, B. J. Sobus, had recommended me to the doctor who started the program and incorporated it as a non-profit, educational corporation. I flew to Washington, was interviewed, and received a job offer. At about the same time I was offered a contract to write a book about computer camps.

I had been wanting to learn how to use the computer and had been intrigued by the phenomenon that would soon be called "the computer culture." I had listened in on conversations, looked over the shoulders of people at work, attended computer fairs and listened as others asked the questions I didn't even know how to ask. I visited computer stores and pretended to be in the market. I got more and more interested but still wasn't doing anything about learning to use the computer. Then one morning my friend, Jim Durgin, told me the best way to learn would be to go to a computer camp so I immediately made inquiries about computer camps in the area, then contacted a friend at Sybex publishers and asked if they would be interested in the story of a grandmother going to computer camp. They were, and offered me a four thousand dollar advance to write the book, "Grandma Goes to Computer Camp." I contacted the Baltimore people, agreed to their offer on condition that I could start my work in the fall. So, the summer of 1983 was spent making arrangements, attending, and writing about computer camp.

18

The Last Man

In late August Rebecca boarded a plane for Ithaca, New York, to begin studying at Cornell, and with her leaving another phase of my life ended. I suddenly felt unnecessary, finished, as if my purpose in life had been to raise the children and it was over. Once again, I experienced that pervasive loneliness. I could stand up, at a Holiday Project conference, speak of the illusion of separateness and know whereof I spoke, but confronted with something as personal as letting go of my last child, the words sounded like trivia. I knew that I separated myself by choice, largely by listening to the chatter of my mind, but there seemed to be a forgetting, a forgetfulness of who I was and in that forgetfulness I saw myself as small, unable, the victim of circumstances. The irony of the situation was that even recognizing what was happening, I seemed unable (or was it unwilling) to bring about the shift that would take me out of the mood. But there was work to be done, commitments to be met.

By early September I had submitted the first draft of "Grandma Goes to Computer Camp" to the publisher and by the first of October it was rejected. I was disappointed but accepted the judgment of the editors. I left for Baltimore having sublet the San Francisco apartment and arranged to live temporarily in the home of one of the executives of the Health Resource Network. In mid-December I moved into an apartment of my own in Lutherville, just outside of Baltimore.

Almost from the beginning I had misgivings about the job. The organization had been incorporated as a non-profit charitable corporation and I had been hired by the board of directors because of my success in launching The Holiday Project. It was almost immediately evident, however, that the doctor who had agreed to incorporation either had no idea of the rules governing non-profits, or no intention of abiding by those rules. It was also evident that he had no intention of turning over the management of the corporation to this woman from San Francisco. It became increasingly clear that he really wanted an executive secretary, not an executive director, and had acquiesced with my being hired simply to please the board. But I had a one-year contract and was determined to make it work.

If emasculate were a word one applied to females it would be appropriate. I was accountable to the board but had no leverage in managing the doctor or his spending of the corporation's money. I tried to make him understand that we were open to public scrutiny and some of the things he was doing with the money would not bear such scrutiny. But he considered it his organization and it was obvious that he would run it as he wanted. The vice president of the corporation knew what the doctor was doing, knew it was the reason that the board had hired me, but he was unable to influence the situation.

On February 22, 1984, I was fired after a series of explosive exchanges. It started with me reminding the doctor of the need to operate with integrity. "You can't do that! We've talked about this before. Our books are open to the public; the money we receive is a public trust."

"I know we've talked about it. And you can't tell me what I can and cannot do. I'm paying your salary. This is my organization and if you don't like the way I run it you can leave." "I was hired to run it so that you could go back to being a doctor. If you're trying to make it difficult enough so that I'll leave, you're making a mistake. I intend to honor my contract with the corporation and to see that you do also." "I am the president and if you won't quit I can fire you!" "We have a contract." No matter how angry I was, I would not quit. I was acutely aware of my experience with *est* and was determined that I would not quit no matter what. "To hell with the contract! You're fired!"

At that, I picked up a notepad from my desk and threw it at him. I asked him later to note that I chose to throw the paper notepad rather than the stapler though one was as close as the other. Obviously I didn't want to hurt him but did want to express my anger and frustration. And it may have been that my throwing something at him was symbolic because I'd not felt I had that option when confronting Don Cox at *est*. Here I was, only a few months into the new job and already I was out. On the 18th of March there was a meeting with the board of directors and I had to confront defeat. My determination to have it be successful was not enough, given the shaky foundation, the doctor's apparent unwillingness to face the financial situation, and my abrasiveness toward him. During the meeting one of the directors said to me, "I haven't heard you take any responsibility for what happened, Elizabeth."

He was right, he hadn't, and I hadn't. But in the privacy of my own thoughts I had gone around and around about what went wrong, what I could have done. I knew that, at some level, I was responsible but knowing that contributed nothing except to add evidence to a massive sense of failure. The thoughts running over and over were, "What's the matter with you? Don't you know how to get along with people? Couldn't you have let him do what he wanted to do instead of assuming that you were responsible for his actions as well as your own? When are you going to learn?"

I knew that the doctor had started the organization, it was his baby and I would have made more progress if I had used diplomacy instead of head-on confrontation. I could not direct the organization because the doctor had never given up directing it himself. I knew and respected the board members, valued their opinion, and was sad that I had not justified their confidence in hiring me. By myself, at home, my life looked like one long series of failures. But even as I thought about giving up, quitting, the voice of sanity, or perhaps authenticity, said, "You don't get to quit. Your job is to clean up your messes and contribute to your children and to the world."

My contract with The Health Resource Network was for one year, with relocation expenses to be paid both directions. Regardless of my other feelings about the doctor I have always respected him for honoring our contract by paying my moving expenses and my salary throughout the year.

It seemed as if each time I hit bottom, there was something that pulled me back up. This time I had taken Cristy Bokovoy, the young woman sharing my Lutherville apartment, to an *est* guest seminar, where she registered for the training. I had no hesitation in encouraging her to register. Besides being fond of her, I knew she was struggling with a life-threatening health issue. Not a day went by that I didn't think of Werner and thank him for the training. At the end of her first weekend, Cristy and I talked for hours. I asked myself how I could ever withhold that gift from another and yet, as soon as the thought appeared, I was reminded that I had done something to get in the way of either my Jerry or Jill doing the training.

Shortly after arriving in Baltimore, I had attended a Washington reception and met John Hannon, a successful businessman with an interest in education and money to invest. Mutual friends had told him he should ask me to work with him. One day, shortly after I lost my job, he invited me to lunch. We met at a restaurant in Lutherville and spent two hours getting acquainted and talking about what we would like to see happening in education. By the end of the two hours I was sure we would work together and was also uncomfortably aware that I found this man enormously attractive. After lunch he walked me to my car and kissed me soundly by way of saying goodbye. I was taken aback and stood by the car for a few minutes to recover.

John had told me he was married and that his wife Chris was terminally ill with diabetes. He said caring for her was his highest priority in life. I later learned from friends that he had been caring for her at home for many years, in the last two of which he had been performing heroically by managing her dialysis treatment himself so that she could remain at home with her family. It wasn't long before he called and invited me to have dinner at his home and meet his wife and their two children. I accepted the invitation immediately and then wondered at myself. At some level I knew I should not let this relationship develop because I was so powerfully attracted to him and not at all sure I could keep it on a professional basis. But I did let it develop and we saw each other frequently during the next few months. Sometimes we worked together on an educational plan, sometimes we would meet for lunch and sit talking over coffee, sometimes he would take me out for a drink at the end of the afternoon. It seemed to me that I had been growing up as a woman in order to be able to relate to somebody like John. I couldn't have related to him twenty years earlier. The biggest thing I had with him was the ability to communicate—almost as if our thinking was so attuned that one of us frequently voiced what the other was thinking—but this communication was most often on an intellectual level, seldom personal. Also, there was something I admired but which also scared me and that was his wildness. He talked of many things I couldn't imagine doing, such as going hang gliding while stoned!

In an April journal entry I confessed, "I'm in love with John Hannon or it may be that I'm in love with love, but I'm so engulfed with love and the need to be loved that I'm in tears at some time every day. I'm afraid and unsure of myself. He is everything I have ever wanted in a man. I'm not willing to be involved in something where I'm waiting for another person to die, yet I feel like the moth being drawn to the flame. I'm clear that if I want to be in a relationship with this man, it will be as one of John's women. He speaks of long-term intimacy—women he's known and loved for twenty years and continues to know and love. He speaks of the way they've made his life richer and of the tacit understanding he has with Chris, that he will live and love as he does and will not burden her with knowing the 'who' and 'when' of it. And I'm not turning away. I think it is quite possible for a man (or a woman) to love more than one person at a time. And when we walk into a restaurant with his arm around me, I feel like the most beautiful, the most desirable woman in the place. I'm experiencing a love so big it continually surprises me. I listen to his stories about the wild things he does in life and think, 'Why would I want to get involved with someone who lives as this guy does?' but then I look over there and see him and see through all the story, all the talk, and into him and into all that is so lovable."

One night I went to see the movie, "Greystoke," the movie about the legend of Tarzan, and shared my reaction with John. He, too, had seen it and called it a beautiful and moving film. But my reaction went beyond moving. I was reduced to sobbing and left the theater with swollen eyes. I knew that I had in me the wildness Tarzan exhibited in letting out his pain but also knew that, in me, the wildness was harnessed. I seemed not to have the freedom to roar when the pain was too great. I must have the ability to sing, to roar, to run, to leap but it was as if those capabilities were somehow locked up. Part of John's attraction was that his wildness was not locked up. He could be dangerous for the person I thought myself to be. It was as if each love of my life prepared me for the next and my capacity for loving seemed to grow. My love for John was more "other" oriented than in any previous male relationship. I knew I would have to expand.

Rebecca and I had planned that as soon as she finished the school year we would return to San Francisco, and I was torn. Perhaps I should stay in the area and be there for John when, and if, he needed me. The doctors had said his wife could go any time. But I could not square that with my conscience—it would have been like hanging around waiting for Chris to die. John's last words to me before I left, however, were that he had no intention of letting me get away.

I remained in Baltimore until May 19th, then drove to Cornell, picked up Rebecca and started back across the country. Rebecca had completed her freshman year at Cornell and realized that she could not make it financially without taking a year off to work full-time, so she was going back to San Francisco to find a job. I had to look hard at my willingness to let her interrupt her studying. I knew there were financial problems but was I really honoring her decision or was it that I'd made such a poor adjustment to the empty-nest syndrome that I wanted her home for a year? After waiting all those years for my children to be grown up, I'd made the remarkable discovery that they were my real, lasting friends.

I remember little about the trip across the country except that we made it in record time and I do remember that driving across the country I kept thinking I was crazy to leave John. I loved him so very much. We didn't do much sightseeing but we did have a couple of adventures. One night—I believe it was in Wyoming—we stayed in a motel where they turned off the power at nine o'clock. Suddenly the lights and the TV just went off, with no warning. We were petrified, slept in our clothes and left at sunup. On our last morning we had breakfast in a place with slot machines and I lost what little I had in my purse at the time. Somewhere on the trip I had decided to ease the job of driving by teaching Rebecca how to drive a car with a manual transmission. We went around and around a parking lot, with gears grinding and the car jumping and jerking before I gave up and decided it would be easier to drive than to teach her how to stick shift.

Back in San Francisco, I was achingly lonely. I had children whom I loved and who loved me, yet the loneliness was like the place I came from. It was almost as if I wanted to keep it that way. Having found a man whom I could love with all of me, that man was married to someone else and deeply committed to her. Then, during the night of July 11th I had a call from one of my Baltimore friends who knew of my relationship with John. She called to tell me that Chris had died. I called the next day and spoke briefly with John, simply to let him know I knew. I had to hold onto knowing that I would not have done her harm intentionally even though I may have done so by loving John. Or, if he loved me as I loved him and Chris knew that, it might have freed her to let go.

At this point I would have done anything John asked and was afraid he wouldn't ask. He was a man of enormous power and energy, in the prime of life. I was sixteen years older than he. Given the way I'd set things up in my life, I knew I could be setting myself up for rejection, simply out of the prospect of it being too good with John. Aware of the influence of conversation in shaping the future, I could only wonder about the way I spoke of a possible future with John.

Ever since taking the training I had seen "riding the horse in the direction it's going" as a kind of fatalism. It seemed to me that my life was like a giant road map and if I were omniscient I'd be able to see the whole thing laid out, but as it was I suffered from a kind of tunnel vision. "Riding the horse..." seemed to mean that I could flow with it, let it happen, wait to see what was next. Suddenly I saw something different. All the words such as "taking a stand", "living as your word," etc. seemed to imply that I had something to say about the direction in which that horse was going. The two views seemed incompatible yet, given my understanding of paradox, that shouldn't have surprised me. Then I began sorting out my feelings. I could no longer deny that I loved this man but I couldn't see a feasible form for a relationship with him. I'd never been straight with him about my age considerations. I knew he was coming out to San Francisco in September and I resolved that I'd be honest with him then.

John called on the 20th of September to tell me when he'd be arriving, and he ended the call with, "I love you, Lady," and I was in heaven. Whenever he ended a call that way, my reaction was more like that of a sixteen-year-old girl than a sixty-four-year-old woman. We'd never had more than a few hours together at one time and suddenly we were going to have nine days!

We drove down to Carmel and Big Sur, stayed in Monterey, walked the beaches, poked in tide pools looking for starfish and sea anemones, sat on a wall watching the sun set, drank wine, smoked a little pot and talked endlessly. He told me about the years of his marriage to Chris, about his children, his work. I mostly listened but did answer his questions about my marriages, my children and my years with Werner. On the way home we stopped at Fort Funston to watch the hang gliders while he told me of his own hang gliding adventures. This man was so much more than anyone I'd ever known that I couldn't imagine not having him intimately involved in my life for the rest of it.

The following week he shared with me the wonder and awe of his first personal encounter with Werner. In the evenings, John included me in the dinner groups of people from the Landmark Forum (which was replacing the *est* Training). Were I an ardent feminist I might have been offended by his proprietary ways but I am not and I was not. He was thoughtful, generous, considerate, and I loved being with him in that setting.

When he returned to Annapolis, we talked regularly on the phone but I still had not told him of my concern about the difference in our ages. It may have been because I was afraid he shared that concern. The months flew by and on April 25th, John drove to New York City to be my guest at the Holiday Project banquet in "Windows on the World," the restaurant on the hundred and sixth floor of the World Trade Center. The banquet was the culmination of the Project annual conference, being held in New York that year. I introduced John to my friends, I danced with him and, as always when I was with him, felt like a beautiful and loved woman. I knew that I was glowing and people commented on it afterward. The party was over at one in the morning and we drove back to Annapolis, arriving at four thirty.

John had arranged a party for me at his home on Sunday night. The evening was a delightful renewal with friends I had made during my stay in Baltimore. John was a marvelous host. The next day he took me to an oyster bar and I ate oysters for the first time in my life. I'd grown up in New England and would never touch oysters but with John I would have tried anything and did, discovering what I'd missed over the years. When I got back to San Francisco I discovered that he had tucked a set of wind chimes in my suitcase. I had admired them in a store one day when we were shopping together and he had bought them for me without my knowing. It was the kind of thing he did.

On June 16th I turned sixty five. I had been dreading this birthday but Marta and Rebecca invited friends to join us for dinner on Fisherman's Wharf and gave me a delightful evening. It was as if the love that filled me reached back in time and colored all my earlier birthdays and the people around them. Waves of tenderness washed over me. The next day I rode the cable car and paid my five-cent fare with delight and amusement. Suddenly being sixty-five became a celebration of being "grown up" and of being able to ride the cable car for a nickel and go to the movies for half price. The word "Senior" lost its pejorative tone and took on stature.

Four days after my birthday I flew to Washington for a week with John and his kids in their Annapolis home. They were days of quiet contentment—walking the beach hand in hand on the Eastern shore, watching the children racing ahead to play in the sand, having them teach me how to catch crabs, visiting museums, eating lobster and oysters on the half shell. One night John gave a party and invited our special friends. We cooked out, drank too much, sang and gabbed until early morning. He was such a wonderful host that people seemed reluctant to leave. It felt as if John and I were acknowledging our couple-ness.

In mid-August Werner did an event on relationship, at Davies Symphony Hall, which was telecast to Washington. The theme was relationship as possibility. All I could think of was what the possibility might be in my relationship with John. Because the event was telecast, John participated in Washington, asking himself the same question, and we talked for hours the next morning. He too was wondering and we speculated about what we two could do, as a team, if we were empowering each other. There were two dimensions to our questioning. One was about the personal relationship but the other related to the work in education that had drawn us together in the first place. John had the means to finance the program we were dreaming up and I think he saw that as what we could do together. While I also felt that, my hormones were raging and my wanting a personal relationship with him took over. Hanging up the phone that morning, I had a deep sadness, almost as if I knew it would not happen. John occasionally talked of wanting to have more children.

That fall, I began work with Transformational Technologies, an organization that had grown out of the demand, by corporations, for the *est* work. Transformational Technologies had its central office in Sausalito but had affiliates all over the country. Jim Selman was President and Michael Reed, an *est* trainer, was Vice President. Jim was an enormously powerful man with a deep voice and a way of speaking that held people's attention and inspired confidence. Our staff meetings were like mini trainings but Jim was good at what he did and I thoroughly enjoyed working with him. I listened to him as he coached the affiliates and saw no way they could fail to be empowered by him.

It wasn't long before I was once again confronted with a negative financial situation. I thought about bankruptcy but knew I could not do it, it was incompatible with my upbringing. I had credit card bills so large that my monthly payments covered only the finance charges, I had a car loan, was making modest contributions to Rebecca's tuition fund and had a loan to be repaid to Sarge's brother Martin. And worse, I had taken money out of an account that I had set up for a Turkish friend, and she was asking for that money. My courage seemed to be crumbling. Here I was, sixty-five years old, in debt, and with no provision for a future in which I might no longer be able to work. I felt hopeless but almost as soon as I acknowledged the feeling it vanished. Feeling hopeless wasn't going to remedy the situation. I asked Jim Selman for a loan and he refused. Although annoyed at the time, I was later grateful. I asked Marta, and I asked Jan, and both of them said they thought a loan was not the answer and that we should talk about it.

So, the next Saturday Jan and Marta came to San Francisco and the three of us sprawled on the living room floor of my apartment with my financial records, yellow pads, pencils, and erasers. Jan acted as recorder, taking down information about my income and expenses while Marta asked questions and probed to be sure they were getting all the information. Then we looked at the alternatives to borrowing more money and getting even deeper in debt. By midafternoon we had a plan and went out to dinner to celebrate. The plan involved selling my car and committing the money from that sale, and the attendant expenses of owning a car, to paying off my debt. Additionally I committed a part of each pay check. As soon as the car had been delivered to its new owner I felt a sense of relief and knew that our plan would work. It did. Within four years, I had not only paid off all my debts but had a small savings account. I took the bus to work in Sausalito, walked wherever I needed to go in the city and rented a car when I wanted to go away for a weekend. The exercise I got from walking contributed to a sense of well-being and I was grateful to my daughters.

My work at Transformational Technologies was essentially office administrative work, and evolved into my working as an assistant to Jim Selman. The job had been set up with flexible scheduling so I could pursue other options such as setting up "Writing to Read" centers for IBM. But, within a couple of months I was feeling like part of a team, thoroughly enjoying my work at Transformational Technologies and not looking for anything else.

One Sunday morning in April of 1986 I phoned John. We had been planning to take the children to Hawai'i in the summer, I hadn't spoken with him for several weeks and knew it was time to make reservations. The phone rang and a sleepy-sounding female answered it. "Oh, Elizabeth. How good to hear from you. John has been meaning to call you." John came on the line. "Hi, Lady! How are you?" Without waiting for a response he went on, "We want you to come to Annapolis week after next, to our wedding."

After a gasp and a moment's silence I blurted out, "John! You can't mean it!" then hung up without waiting for an answer. The words were for myself. For about three hours I wept—furious, torn, empty, raging—and then, for the remainder of that Sunday, I was numb and unbelieving. I had thought this relationship was the one that would end the longing. How could I have been so stupid, so blind.

I talked with Shellie, my Baltimore attorney friend, and learned that John was marrying a woman as much younger than he as I was older and that he would have his wish for more children—the woman he was marrying was pregnant. He had spoken of wanting more children but I had not listened, had not wanted to hear. The sense of betrayal was so great I was lost in it but suspected that I had been lying to myself. John had persisted in saying we were good friends but his actions, even though we'd not had a sexual relationship, spoke of more than friendship. Then there was the embarrassment of thinking I had acted inappropriately for my age and of wondering who else out there was being embarrassed for me.

With John married I again experienced an aching loneliness. Whether or not there had been anything real going on for him I held it as if there were. I could feel loved and wanted and feminine just by conjuring up a picture of us walking into a restaurant together, his arm around me, or hearing him close a phone conversation with, "I love you, Lady." This was the end of another era in my life, the man era. The net of my experience with men had been pain and heartache and, regardless of whose responsibility it was, that was the way it had been and I wanted no more.

In the days that followed I had little space for others. I was consumed by loss and grief. I was deeply morose and kept wondering how I could have been so naive. In June of 1986 I did the Landmark Forum in order to take a look at the way I seemed to create my life, and to get ready for whatever was next.

19

Mrs. Santa Claus: Another Year of The Holiday Project

That fall, Robert Chester called me to discuss the possibility of my returning as Executive Director of The Holiday Project, starting in January 1987. I enjoyed my work at Transformational Technologies and debated with myself about leaving but was thrilled to be asked to again take on the Holiday Project job so accepted the offer. In late October I received a letter from Werner:

> "I will not be able to attend the Holiday Project Ball this year, I will miss having the chance to be with you; however, I wanted to take this opportunity to express my sincere appreciation for who you are and for what you make possible.
>
> "Thank you for the leadership you provide. You have moved hundreds of people across the country to participate in the work of The Holiday Project. Your commitment has been an opening for people to take on the management of The Holiday Project as well as participate in the events surrounding the holidays. Your actions and your spirit have moved people to contribute not only with their heart and their time, but financially as well. You have also given San Francisco a memorable and magnificent yearly event, The Holiday Project Ball.
>
> "Thank you for your generosity and support. I love and appreciate you."

At the 1986 Holiday Project ball, I was introduced as the new Executive Director. For many in San Francisco I had always been identified with The Holiday Project and the applause at the announcement reassured me that I had made the right choice. Shellie Frankfurt came from Baltimore, Richard Carpenter from Houston, and Ray Castleberry from Atlanta. (Ray later died of AIDS.) Marta was my guest and it delighted me to have her share the evening. John Denver was our guest of honor at that ball. I'd always had a special fondness for John and recalled the night, at a North Beach Restaurant dinner hosted by Werner, when John introduced his latest song, *Calypso*, before it was released to the public.

The upset I had been experiencing since the loss of John was buried beneath the excitement of once again heading the Project, and I was looking forward to realizing the goal we had set years ago, of having "The Holiday Project" a common household term around the holidays. In December, B. J. Sobus and I appeared on Willard Scott's *Today* show in Washington, D.C. It was fun and Willard was generous with his acknowledgment of our work. B. J. was our public relations man in Washington but he was much more than that to me. He was a dear friend and I was dismayed when I learned, shortly after the first of the year, that he had AIDS. I had been unwilling to confront that possibility earlier, even though he had been ill intermittently for months.

I spent most of 1987 traveling and raising money for the Project. During the year I made visits to Detroit, Los Angeles, Miami, Washington D.C., Boston, Ithaca, Philadelphia, New Jersey, New York, Sacramento, Denver, Houston, Baltimore, Atlanta, Chicago and Portland, Oregon. In Atlanta I was met at the airport by a representative of the Ford Motor Company who gave me the keys to a Mercury Sable they were making available to me for my stay. I talked with people at Delta Airlines and Coca Cola, where I learned that employees were supported in gathering in the company's cafeteria for gift-wrapping parties. On the day I visited AT&T, I was treated royally with a luncheon in their board room and the promise of a substantial donation. Carole Ashkinaze, who had hosted me and been responsible for setting up the meetings, also introduced me to people at *The Atlanta Constitution* and Cox Communications.

During one of my meetings in Baltimore, a volunteer handed me a note. It was a message from John Hannon, asking me to call him and saying that if he didn't hear from me he would be at the airport before my flight. I had no intention of calling him, or of seeing him, and thought he had a nerve to suggest such a thing. I waited until the last minute before going to the airport. But as I was getting out of the car, he came out of the terminal, a baby under each arm and the most sheepish look I'd ever seen on the face of a man and I burst out laughing. He said he hoped that if he brought the twins along I might forgive him, and I did. When I got back home I wrote to him:

> "For two years I nurtured a dream. Like most dreams it bore little relation to reality. And I'm clear that it was solely my dream, you didn't encourage it or feed it. Actually, you often and honestly discouraged my attempts to give the dream reality. I thank you for that.

> "I guess we always have to waken from our dream even though the temptation is to linger a little longer in the hope that it will turn out right. At some level I know it has turned out right and that this is what turning out right looks like.
>
> "Thank you for the dream, John Hannon. I will always treasure my memories of you and your children. Have a good life."

With this letter I let go of the experience of loss I'd had since that morning in April of 1986. I have not heard from nor seen John Hannon since writing that letter but, looking back, am grateful for having known and loved him.

In Washington on the twentieth of May, I spent the afternoon in the hospital with my friend, B. J.—who was comatose—holding his hand and talking to him. I couldn't believe he was going. It was almost as if I thought I could keep him by holding his hand. At five o'clock that day his mother made the decision to remove the life support system that had been keeping him alive despite damaged and failing liver and kidneys. The next day he died. His death was inappropriate—he was a good man, a talented man, a young man, and he was contributing much to the world—but then, I guess we really don't get to decide whose death is inappropriate, do we? B. J.'s memorial service was on the thirty-first of May. Many of his friends spoke at the service and, at the end, we released a thousand balloons into the air outside the church. It was as if we had released him with them.

The 1987 national conference of The Holiday Project was in Houston. It was as spectacular as one might expect such an affair to be in Texas. One hundred forty-seven people attended, representing ninety-six percent of the committees. One of the Denver committee people told us that the employees of Coors, with the blessing of management, were knitting lap robes for people in the nursing homes that The Holiday Project would be visiting during the holidays.

While in New York in September I attended the first Hunger Project Africa Prize Dinner at the New York Hilton. There were twelve hundred people attending, including some of my friends from India. I wore a dress for which I had paid too much, but seated at a table with African dignitaries and an assistant to President Reagan I was glad to look as I did. John Denver was Master of Ceremonies and Robert McNamara gave the keynote address and awarded the prizes. I had mixed feelings as I looked at Joan Holmes on the platform. There was pride in her accomplishment but that was tinged by something I couldn't identify—perhaps sadness—related to *est* in Education.

In October I again went to Washington for a Holiday Project national committee meeting and to appear, once more, with Willard Scott on the *Today* show. It was not the same without B. J. While in Washington, I had a radio interview with Marion Barry's wife and was amused to learn that the interview aired at 6:00 a.m. the following Sunday morning, but even more amused when I heard from viewers. From Washington I went to Burlington, Vermont, for three radio interviews and a television interview. One of the radio interviews in Vermont was taped and I listened to it on the radio in my hotel the next day. It was a strange experience. I listened to that person on the radio as if she were someone else and, as that person talked about The Holiday Project and shared some of the stories, I was so moved that I found myself in tears. I knew I had recorded the day before but as I listened, there was me hearing and that other speaking and although I knew they were the same, they were not the same.

On Thanksgiving Day I was interviewed on CNN, and we had five Holiday Project cities on the NBC nightly news on Christmas Day. For the holiday ball that year our guest of honor was the actor, Hugh O'Brian.

It was the outstanding year of The Holiday Project. The Project was acknowledged by President Reagan and was written up in *Good Housekeeping* magazine. We raised more money and had more participation than at any time in the Project's history. And we were networking. The publicity brought an enormous volume of letters and calls from people who had never heard of *est* or Werner Erhard, people in small towns all over the country, people who were elated to know that such a project existed and wanted to know how they could take part. We were preparing information packets to help people set up committees in new areas and give them guidelines about raising money and visiting. The Project was taking off as I had dreamed and I wanted to expand the staff. I knew it would be a financial strain for the first year or so but was sure it would be worth it. The board didn't want the project to expand that way. Although they spoke of networking, they said they wanted to keep it small enough for quality control, as if quality could be guaranteed only by people who had done Werner's work. I knew that any such control would be the antithesis of networking, in which one community reaches out to neighboring communities and the thing spreads with a life of its own. Certainly it presented a challenge to us. We knew we would have to prepare materials that embodied the purpose and intention of the Project, that established rules for those who elected to use the name "Holiday Project" and consequences for failing to operate by those rules. It was a challenge but not an impossible one. I knew it could be done and was sure it was the only way to really have the program expand into the world, as Werner was always urging us to do.

The directors, however, were unwilling to have us expand our staff, accept funding from outside sources or take up the offer we'd had of a direct mail campaign, and absolutely unwilling to have the project go in the red, even for one year. It wasn't until a few years later that I recognized that I had been "micro-managed" by the board instead of being supported in winning on the job. I had not met my fund-raising target for the year, but realized later that part of that failure was due to my covert assumption that fund-raising was the responsibility of the board. On the twentieth of January, 1988, I was fired. In fairness to the board, I must add that they invited me to stay on as fund-raiser but I knew that my ability to raise funds was directly related to my work with the volunteers, and that was what I wanted to continue doing. I didn't take this gracefully—screaming at the directors, stamping out of the room heedless of the curious stares of people in the outer office and, once again, going home in tears to rail at the unfairness of the world.

I suspect that if you heard this story from the then-chairman of the board you might hear a different version but the way I've related it is the way it was for me. After being fired I stopped participating with Landmark (the organization replacing *est*) and engaged in the self righteous game of blaming those I held responsible. I had so identified with the project, inappropriately perhaps, that loss of the job included a loss of identity as well as a shattering blow to my self-worth. Almost literally I didn't know who I was. For two months I was in pain, anger and despair. Volunteers across the country had called me "Mrs. Santa Claus" and I had come to believe that's who I was.

Looking for my own responsibility in the matter I began asking questions: Was I afraid of success? Was I willing to be a typist in Werner's office but unwilling to succeed on a big job? Was it possible that when I saw myself doing great things, I started muddling around, creating confusion so that I'd get fired? Was it that I was good in the start-up stage of a project and no good in the sustaining period? Was it possible that I had an investment in, a commitment to, failure? And, if the answer to any of these questions was "Yes," then the next question was, "Why?" The only voice I could hear was that of my mother saying, "You can't do anything right!" Why not, instead, my father saying, "I'm so proud of you!" or my Uncle Will assuring me that I was on the way to having greatness show up in my life. At some level, I knew that making any of them responsible for my life was copping out.

But life is paradoxical. Early in March I learned that I was to be honored with an award which, coming at the time it did, both embarrassed and delighted me.

Each year four San Francisco women were honored as "Women of Wisdom" by the Professional Women's Network of San Francisco and in 1988 I was one of the four. The others were Louise Renne, San Francisco City Attorney, Ann Hammer, Education & Corporate Relations Director, Golden Gate University, and Irene Manning, movie actress and teacher of voice, dancing and modeling. The awards were made at a dinner in the ballroom of the Portman Hotel. Marta and Jan were there, along with several hundred others and, as honored as I was, what moved me most was having my daughters share the honor with me.

Each of us receiving an award had been asked to prepare a talk about her life, and that challenge gave me the outline for this book, as I had to look and see not only what my life had been but what I wanted my future to be.

As I related the story of my life to the audience at that event, I wasn't just telling a story, I was loving that little girl who so craved to be loved. I was going back to the years when she needed to be understood and forgiven, back to the years when she struggled to raise her children and keep from taking her own life. I was also realizing that my mother loved me in the only way she knew how and that she did the best she could. When I was through speaking and looked out at the people who had been listening, I saw the emotion in the room and realized that in my sharing there was something universal—something that touched almost everyone in the room—and in that moment I was humbled.

20

Expect the Unexpected

I was once again wondering what was next when my daughter, Marta, offered me a job with her and her husband, Stephen, in their company in Silicon Valley. I started in March of 1988 and, by October, Marta had discovered that we worked well together and she had decided to take advantage of my background by putting me in charge of training and education for the company. I loved working for my daughter and realized I was not the only one. When she went out onto the production floor, workers turned to greet her with warmth and affection. Part of this, I knew, was because she was interested in their well being and in their families and often provided assistance for employees needing it.

Fifty-eight percent of the work force at Logistix were of Hispanic origin so one of the first things I did was to begin teaching ESL (English as a Second Language). This work was not unlike my teaching in Turkey in that the students and I had no common language and that seemed to make it doubly rewarding for all of us—as they were learning English, I was learning Spanish. Through 1989 we continued ESL classes, encouraged employees to take off-site courses, and began the study and implementation of World Class Manufacturing principles. Executives gathered to listen to tapes of W. Edwards Deming, and assembly workers had classes in total quality control.

On October 17, I was completing work for the day when our building began to shake. Earthquake! My memories from Izmir were vivid. I scrambled from my desk and stood in the doorway into the hall. Again, it lasted only a few minutes but they were minutes that felt like hours. The only damage to my office was caused by the file cabinet tipping over onto my desk, making me glad I was not still sitting there. We closed the building and sent everyone home. When I reached my apartment building, in Cupertino, I found that we were not being allowed in—all gas and electricity had been turned off and would stay off until they'd determined the extent of structural damage. The managers of the building were well prepared, however, and by the time I arrived they had set up tables on the lawn by the pool and were serving snacks and drinks. They had a radio and speakers so we could all hear what was going on elsewhere. By seven o'clock in the evening we were all quite mellow—full of wine and food, visiting with people we had never spoken to before, relaxing on the grass with blankets and pillows provided by the building management. I couldn't help reflecting on the fact that we were suddenly a family—a family made so by the threat of disaster. I had not known any of my neighbors, yet here we all were sipping wine and listening to the radio together as if we'd known each other for years. But that radio was telling us about horrendous things happening in neighboring communities. A freeway had collapsed in Oakland, a section of the Bay Bridge had collapsed, and there was devastation in the Marina district of San Francisco.

People from our building were spreading blankets and preparing to spend the night on the lawn but I wanted to be with my own family, so I left and drove across town to Marta's. Over the next few days we were aghast as we watched news broadcasts of workers finding bodies in the wreckage of the East Bay freeway, of people standing outside their homes in the Marina district watching helplessly as barricades were erected to keep them from entering their homes. There was a deep sadness for all those who had suffered and died and a sobering recognition of the power of nature. Those few days together with family were a reminder of how precious life is and how lucky we were to be alive and together.

A few months later, during a routine visit to my dermatologist, the doctor noticed a spot on my face that had not healed. He did a biopsy, discovered that the little spot under my right eye was a basal cell carcinoma, and recommended immediate surgery. This should have been a warning that I had a predisposition for cancer but I thought of it as a minor inconvenience. I'd been having pre-cancerous lesions removed from my face for several years and thought of this as one of those. That little cell, however, had put out tendrils into my cheek and it took thirty-one stitches to close the incision, from the inside corner of my right eye to the corner of my mouth. I was horrified by the bandaged face I saw as we were leaving the hospital. The first day I went back to work after the surgery, someone in the shop gasped and asked, "What happened to you?" I suspect it was a question many people had but were reluctant to ask.

My friend Alex Wang was arriving at the San Francisco Airport just a few days after the surgery and I had agreed to pick him up, so in spite of being acutely aware of my appearance, I drove up to the airport to greet him. By this time Alex had become internationally known and traveled widely, and whenever his travels took him through San Francisco he made time for a visit with me. My appearance mattered not at all to Alex. We had a quiet evening of conversation at my apartment and the next morning he came into my room, sat on the edge of my bed, touched my face lightly and said, "It doesn't matter. All I see is the beautiful woman I loved thirty-eight years ago." For a moment I was back in Northfield, dreaming of the future I might have with him, before he told me he was promised. Even as I looked at him that morning, I barely saw the gray hair and other signs of aging. This was my Alex.

There was a gentleness about him that I had known only in my gay friends, and I was reminded of that a few days later by a letter from Dwight Smith, my friend from Heuristics days in Boston. He was losing his battle with AIDS and writing goodbye letters to those he loved. His letter reminded me of the tenuous hold we have on life. Dwight had been a dear friend for eighteen years.

One night that spring I went to the Flint Center, in Cupertino, to hear Kitaro in concert. It was magnificent and, in the middle of "The Silk Road" I felt tears on my cheeks and realized the last time I'd heard it was with John Hannon. In that moment, I realized that my relationship with John was another area of my life that I could just let be the way it was, without thinking it should be some other way. I could also acknowledge that I have always been an achingly lonely human being without thinking I should be some other way.

This was also the year I went up to Grace Cathedral in San Francisco for Easter, not having been in an Episcopal Church for years. The whole service was moving, as was being part of the huge crowed that gathered. At the end of the service I went forward to take communion and, as I was kneeling at the altar rail, having taken the sacraments, I was suddenly overwhelmed by a sense of being all of it. I *was* the music, the flowers, the rafters overhead, the stained-glass windows, the white vestments of the servers—all of it—including the person kneeling. I didn't want to get up and leave. Recognizing paradox as the underlying principle of life, I knew that this experience of "oneness" belonged inseparably to the loneliness.

It was when I was doing a routine breast examination in December of 1990 that I felt a small lump in my left breast. I was not particularly alarmed, sure that it was not serious, but called and made an appointment with my doctor. We agreed that, after the holidays, he would remove the lump and do a biopsy. On January third, Marta drove me to the hospital. The doctor used a local anesthesia, removed the lump and sent tissue to the lab for examination. As they were preparing to take me to a recovery room, he came back. "The good news is the operation's over," the doctor said, as he returned from the lab. The tone of his voice, and the pause, made it clear that there was also some bad news which he didn't want to deliver. "The bad news is that the biopsy shows cancer cells in your breast. Let them take you into the recovery room and I'll come in and talk with you and your daughter in a few minutes."

I just stared at him, unbelieving. I'd been certain it was nothing more than a harmless tumor. As they wheeled me back, the word *cancer* kept repeating in my head, always followed by, how could it be? There had never been cancer in our family. My mother died at ninety-one and then only because my father had died three months earlier and she no longer wanted to live. Mother did not exercise, she ate butter, drank strong coffee with heavy cream, ate thick steaks and made her chocolate cake with lard. Until the last years of her life she was much overweight. I had thought I would surely outlive her, given that I ate wisely, exercised regularly, and kept my weight under control. I thought I might even live to be a hundred, so the pronouncement didn't fully register. How could I possibly have cancer?

The doctor came in and talked with us. Marta and I listened because neither of us knew much about cancer, but both of us were too stunned to grasp what had happened. On the way home we stopped at Winchell's and had doughnuts and coffee. It was an "Oh, what the hell!" gesture since eating doughnuts at Winchell's was not something either of us normally did.

Then it began—X-rays, blood tests, a bone scan, and a mammogram of the other breast. The mammogram was my first and when they told me the tumor might have been discovered a year earlier with a mammogram, I realized the cost and foolishness of not having had the tests regularly. The chest X-ray was negative, as was the mammogram, but the bone scan showed a gray spot on my right thighbone. The following day I went back for another X-ray, of the femur, which confirmed the findings of the scan—there was an abnormality in my leg. My dreams these nights were filled with awful scenarios of what might happen.

It was suddenly becoming real. On January twenty-first I entered the Good Samaritan Hospital in San Jose for surgery to remove the rest of the lump, to biopsy my leg and the thyroid gland, in which they had also found a lump. When it was over and I had come out of the anesthesia, the surgeon came to my room. "I wish I had good news but the fact is the cancer is an invasive carcinoma which means that we should do a mastectomy. And the lump in your thyroid is also malignant. The findings on the leg are inconclusive."

I heard him but could make no response. What could I say? Now they were talking about removing a breast! I had lots of plans, but everything had changed in one minute, with that word, *cancer*, and my mortality looked back at me every time I looked in the mirror.

A few days later, Marta and I had meetings with the doctors. I asked the oncologist to be honest with me about my chances for recovery. I was seventy years old and did not want to go through extensive treatment if the probability was that it would not extend my life appreciably.

The doctor was straightforward with me, "Today we have a pretty good record with breast cancer, if it's caught soon enough, and I think we caught yours in time. However, there are no guarantees with cancer and we still don't know about your leg. I would suggest that if there's anything you've wanted to do and have been putting off, you not put it off any longer. Get through this surgery and then go do it!"

Surgery was scheduled for February 14th. (I found something darkly amusing about have a breast removed on Saint Valentine's Day.) When I woke up in the recovery room, the pain was so intense I didn't even notice the missing breast. For almost two weeks I was possessed by that pain. Staying in Marta's home, I moved from the bed to the recliner in the living room and watched soap operas to take my mind off my body. Marta's boys, Alex and Remy (seven and eleven) were more considerate than I could have imagined possible. One evening, at the dinner table, I was apologizing for being so much trouble when Remy looked at me and said, "It's okay, Gram. If it weren't for you, we wouldn't even be here." I squeezed his hand, being too moved to speak.

The one thing that took me out of my self-absorption during this period was the *60 Minutes* show attacking Werner Erhard. I didn't actually see the show but hearing about it, I was convinced that it was a frame up. I knew this man and had no doubt that it was a smear job. I wrote a strong letter to Mike Wallace because Werner had hosted Mike at one of the Community Workshops in San Francisco, and treated him with the greatest courtesy and respect, yet Mike didn't have the guts to stand up to David Gerber, producer of *60 Minutes*, and say, "No, we shouldn't do this. It would be sewer journalism." I didn't have long to focus my rage on this, however, because I was still recovering from the mastectomy, as well as preparing for thyroid surgery, and the body has a way of taking over when it's hurting.

By the end of March I was feeling better but was jumpy and irritable—snapping at Remy and Alex and miserable with myself. I knew I had to do something. I asked the doctor when I would be able to travel and how soon I could swim. He said that by the middle of April both would be okay. On the tenth of April I was on a plane headed for Florida to visit my cousin Herb and his wife in Vero Beach. For a week I lay on the shaded deck of their condo, watched boats on the canal, watched the Masters Golf Tournament on television, read, and slept. Each day

Herb and I would go to his club pool and each day I was able to do a little more. On my last day Herb took me to the ocean. Although he had to grab and steady me, I felt invigorated and alive for the first time in three months. On that last day in Florida I knew that whatever plans I made for the future would have to include being able to swim in the ocean. This was the beginning of real recuperation. I was a candidate for estrogen-blocking medication so instead of having to undergo the rigorous chemotherapy I had so dreaded, I would be taking oral medication—Tamoxifen as an estrogen blocker and Synthroid to compensate for the lost thyroid function.

I was back at work in early May—going into the Logistix office on a "now and then" basis, to see how it was. Increasingly, I became aware that I was not up to returning to that job. For one thing, it had become big enough for two people, and for another, whether it was the anesthesia, the strain of surgery, or age creeping up, my memory suddenly had great black holes in it. I would open a file drawer to look for something and discover that I had no idea where it was or even what I was looking for. Someone would come to the office and stand in front of my desk and, although I knew the face and had worked with them for three years, the name was not available. I would pick up the phone to place a call and forget the number I'd just looked up. Was it, perhaps, time to quit?

On my last day at work, June 27, 1991, friends and co-workers gave me a farewell party. I felt appreciated and loved. The following day Marta and I drove to Sacramento for the presentation of a State grant for the company. We had submitted a training grant proposal the previous fall and it had been accepted. It was the perfect culmination of my three years at Logistix. For weeks I had been thinking about the future and remembering the doctor's words, "If there's anything you've been wanting to do and have been putting off..." One of the things I had been putting off, for eleven years, was a return to Hawai'i so, without much forethought, I packed up and returned to Honolulu.

Every time I looked out the window I felt as if I'd hit the jackpot. I was living in a condo on the fifteenth floor of Mt. Terrace, a building in Hawai'i Kai, with a view over the marina and out to the ocean. Having met a woman looking for someone to share her condominium, I moved in. I had a beautifully furnished room with a computer desk, lots of bookshelves, my own television, and a bathroom and dressing room. A bus at the corner would take me to Hanauma Bay for swimming and snorkeling and it was a fifteen-minute walk to a shopping center. I swam every day, ate conscientiously, slept soundly. Every time I returned to the mainland for a checkup, my doctor said, "Whatever you're doing seems to be working. Keep it up."

In the spring of 1992, Sarge and my brother died, within two weeks of each other. In April I flew to San Francisco for Sarge's memorial. His children and his remaining siblings were there and we had hours of sharing memories. My grief over Sarge had been spread out over many years and his death provided a kind of release. I had lost the man I knew and loved many years earlier, yet every time I saw Sarge it was a painful reminder of that man. With Paul's death I realized that my questions about his severance of our relationship would never be answered but knowing that provided a kind of finality in itself. With his death it seemed as if the earlier memories of my beloved brother were restored. In saying goodbye, I knew how much each of these men had enriched my life.

I was back in Hawai'i when Hurricane Iniki hit the islands in September. There was some damage on Oahu but nothing like the destruction when Iniki hit Kaua'i. The next day a call came out for volunteers to go to Kaua'i and I responded. I spent three weeks on that island, as a volunteer in the Office of the Mayor of Kaua'i, helping with the overload her office was experiencing. One day I took a car and a camera and started driving around the island to take pictures. Within an hour I was so devastated by what I saw that I turned around and went back. The camera was unnecessary and seemed intrusive. What I had seen was etched on my mind. Houses were turned over on their sides with furniture and clothes spilling out of them onto the ground. Families were wandering around the wreckage looking stunned, almost as if asking what had happened. Giant trees had been uprooted and lay across fields and roads, intermingled with electric wires that were snarled up and broken. Small animals looked dazed as if they didn't remember where they belonged. Once again, I was sobered by the power of nature.

At the end of my three weeks I had observed enough about the workings of the office of the mayor that I thought I could make an impact if I could stay on longer. I suggested to the Mayor that she hire me to come back and do some training with her staff. She invited me to submit a proposal; I did, and in late June of 1993 began working as a consultant, on a one-year contract, spending a few days each month on the island.

As I was preparing to begin working on Kauai, I got a call from Marta saying she was working in Tokyo, would be there for several weeks and suggested that I come to visit. She said she had an apartment and I could stay with her. I didn't think long before I realized I might never again have such an opportunity. I made phone calls to postpone a few things and called her back to say, "Whoopee, I've made plans and will be coming into Narita Airport at two o'clock on Friday afternoon and will be able to stay for ten days."

Marta had a studio on the sixth floor of Ark Tower East, part of the Ark Hills complex of offices, restaurants, symphony hall and hotel, in a section of Tokyo called Roppongi. The apartment looked out at Tokyo Tower and the city. Thus it was that on the night of June 11th, 1993, I was lying in bed looking out at the lights of the city of Tokyo and wondering at the unexpected ways of life. Two days later, Marta and I left Tokyo, on the Bullet Train, for a weekend in Kyoto where we stayed in a small Japanese inn, visited Buddhist temples and ceramic shops, sampled unknown food and took pictures of everything.

When Marta went back to work, I joined a guided tour of Tokyo and saw all the tourist sites. The next day was my birthday and also my first experience on my own in a city where I didn't know the language. Not encountering many Japanese with a command of English made my outing even more exciting. In a restaurant in Ueno Park, confronted with a menu in Japanese and a waitress who smiled but shook her head when I spoke, I looked around at the other diners and finally resorted to pointing to another diner's plate. The waitress smiled her understanding. She was obviously used to tourists. In the station, for my return, I bought a ticket, but it was a wrong ticket—one for a train rather than a subway—and the subway entrance gate refused it. I could find no one to tell me how to exchange that ticket for the right one so I put it in my pocket, found the correct window and bought a subway ticket. Back in Roppongi I exited the subway station and began walking home. I had walked well over a mile when I realized I wasn't seeing anything familiar and began to suspect that I had walked in the wrong direction. That suspicion was confirmed when I hailed a taxi. The driver turned the cab around and started back in the direction from which I had come.

As soon as I got back to the apartment I flopped into a chair, laughing at my misadventures. After a few minutes I shed my clothes, sponged myself, sat in the deep luxury of a Japanese bath for a half hour, then read for a couple of hours until Marta came home. So it was that on my birthday in 1993 I was in Tokyo, having dinner and sharing a bottle of *saké* with Marta, not at all ready to give in and quit. I remember glowing and thinking it wasn't bad to be turning seventy-three if I could celebrate it like that. I knew I was as eager as ever to see what was next.

After my return from Japan I began my year of working with the staff of the Mayor of Kaua'i. I did a needs assessment, interviewing each staff member to see if I could locate the source of the many problems that plagued that office. Mayor JoAnn Yukimura was the most dedicated, hard working civil servant I could imagine, yet it seemed as if she were always trying to catch up with the job. Hurricane Iniki had been a major disaster, with a near-total communication breakdown that left people without emergency information and those on the western part of the island feeling isolated. That hurricane was not one that any amount of preparedness could have tamed or made less tragic for the people of Kaua'i, but, as with any major disaster, there had to be a scapegoat. Though it was disappointing, it was not surprising when Mayor Yukimura failed to win re-election in 1994.

My contract with Kaua'i fulfilled, I left Hawai'i in the early summer of 1994, to return to the mainland to live. Exactly where I would live was uncertain but again I knew that would be resolved. With my health back, the most important thing seemed being near my family once again. One of the first events of my return was a mid-June reunion of the Russell family, held on the campus of Haverford College in Pennsylvania. There were more than sixty people, many of whom I hadn't seen in decades, some adults who had been toddlers when I saw them last. I'm thankful for having been there, because my beloved brother-in-law, Martin, died shortly after the reunion. I realized that as long I continued writing, Martin would always be with me. After the reunion, I visited friends and relatives in New England, then returned to California for Rebecca's engagement party and a trip to Alaska to visit friends in Anchorage.

It was my first visit to Alaska and I was stunned by the magnificence of glaciers and mountains. We were surrounded by such majesty that I was silenced. Gary, my host, seemed to remember enough of his first impressions to simply let me absorb it all. From Gary's backyard I could see snow-capped mountains in the distance and I could see a bear catching a salmon with his paw in the Turnagain Arm (Cook Inlet). Another day we hiked along Eagle River to a reindeer farm where I saw my first live reindeer.

At the end of July I was back in San Francisco, thinking about where to live, when I got a call from Tom Strickland, a friend of mine from Hawai'i. Tom was living in Chile for a year studying Spanish and invited me to come for a visit. I didn't even have to think about it. Of course I would go!

On the second of August, I boarded a plane for a flight to Santiago, via Miami, for a month's visit to Chile. I arrived in Santiago at 8:50 in the morning, having flown sixteen hours and looking forward to falling into bed, but Tom met me at the plane, saying, "How perfect! It's a beautiful day and I've got the whole day to show you around Santiago." So much for falling into bed!

During the first part of the visit I stayed with Tom in a small apartment he had rented in Reñaca, a coastal resort town. Tom had a car and we drove up the coast to near the border of Peru, then across the Andes to Argentina and down south to Villarrica and the lake region. The best part of the visit to Chile was the people I met—the Gonzalez family in Viña del Mar, at whose home we twice had dinner, the people who served us at the *Hosteria de Colina*, in Villarrica, and our hosts in Santiago, Antonio Saldivia and his wife, Anita, with whom we had meals and played games while living in their little guest cottage. And the whole trip would have been worth taking just to see the *Tentación de San Antonio*, a painting by Claudio Bravo which left me gasping as it conveyed three-dimensionality in a two-dimensional work. I have never been educated to appreciate art but I stood in front of that painting mesmerized, much as I did in front of the Taj Mahal in India.

The previous two years had been so full, that instead of looking for a place to live in San Francisco, on my return from Chile, I decided to take up my daughter Jill's offer. She and her husband, John, were compiling a bibliography and had invited me to come and work with them for a few months. They had, for many years, been collecting the work of Tasha Tudor, a Vermont author and illustrator of children's books, and were in the final stages of completing the bibliography. They had the most extensive collection of her work in the United States, which they sold through their on-line book business, *CellarDoorBooks.com*. (The bibliography was published in the fall of 1998.)

My work for Cellar Door Books was primarily entering book descriptions into the computer and taking book orders over the phone when neither Jill nor John was there. John had a full-time job as Director of Learning Resources at the New Hampshire Technical Institute Library, so work on the bibliography was his evening and weekend work and it was slow.

Jill and John offered me the beautiful little apartment they had just finished over the garage. It had a bedroom, a bath, a kitchenette and small living room with a wall of windows looking out onto a spacious back lawn. There were bird feeders, little stone walls, and it was all bordered by a large growth of deciduous trees. When I was not working, I read, listened to music and sometimes just sat on the couch by the windows, watching the squirrels and birds in the backyard and reflecting on my summer. I felt quite pampered, with the luxury of the apartment and John bringing me the Concord newspaper every morning for me to read with my breakfast.

In Concord I began singing with the "Songweavers," a one-hundred-eighty-member chorus led by a woman who had been a friend of Pete Seeger and the Weavers. It was a gratifying experience since I thought the thyroid surgery had damaged my vocal cords and found it was not so. The Songweavers' Christmas concert that year, "Pax in Terra Nostra" was performed in Concord, Manchester and Boston. The Boston reception was terrific, the only disappointment being an encounter with a young black woman in the women's room during the break.

"I'm enjoying your music but how come there are no people of color in your chorus?" Those of us in the restroom looked sheepishly at each other, then one local Concord member spoke up. "I'm sorry to have to say it but it's only because there are no people of color in Concord." I hadn't realized it until that moment, but as I reflected on the people on the streets and in the stores, I knew she was right. It surprised me that I hadn't noticed it until this young woman spoke.

Early in the new year I became absorbed in watching the O. J. Simpson trial. On the afternoon of February 23rd, I hadn't tuned in but Jill, who had the TV on in her living room at the other end of the house, phoned me and said, "Mom, come on down and watch the trial with me. Marcia Clark and Judge Ito are having a fight!" I leapt off the couch and started down the stairs. I must have missed the first step because I flew, headfirst, down that flight of stairs, hitting my head on the wall at the landing, then flipping over and tumbling down the last three steps to the hall floor. Although I hadn't lost consciousness, I knew I was badly hurt and needed help. But with the television on in the living room, Jill had not heard my fall. I crawled into the kitchen where Jill's Yorkshire terrier, who had come to greet me, saw that something was wrong and ran barking into the living room to get Jill's attention.

Jill called for an ambulance that arrived almost immediately and took me to the Concord Hospital Emergency Room. After making a quick examination, the doctor said, "You've broken your neck, you've got a fracture in that right arm and probably some broken ribs." He put me in a halo—one of those monstrous things they screw into your skull—and set my arm by yanking it, with accompanying pain more excruciating than any I'd ever known.

Jan and Marta flew from California and, with Jill, visited every day. After a week in Concord Hospital there seemed little agreement about what should be done and the girls decided to send me to Massachusetts General Hospital in Boston. The next day I was transported, by ambulance, to Boston and put under the care of a team made up of a neurosurgeon and an orthopedic surgeon, a team that had been recommended by a renowned doctor friend of Jill's. After examining me and looking at X-rays, the doctors told me that they would not recommend surgery because, at my age, the chances were only fifty-fifty that I would survive the operation. They said that by allowing the fracture to heal, with the help of a halo and then a collar, I should have pretty good use of my neck, needing only to be careful of shocks such as sudden stops. It sounded as if they were talking about a life of looking over my shoulder, so I asked, "What would you recommend if I were twenty-five instead of seventy-five?"

The neurosurgeon smiled and said, "Surgery."

It didn't take me long to make a decision. I wasn't willing to settle for limited mobility if there was a chance of full recovery. I responded, "Then pretend I'm twenty-five and do that surgery."

The doctor heard the certainty in my voice and scheduled surgery for the next day. They removed a piece of bone from my left hip and affixed it to the vertebra near the top of my spinal column. When I awoke in the recovery room I was aware of only one thing—I was alive—and I knew that by how much I hurt. But, by the next day I was in a pleasant hospital room, with a soft collar supporting my head and relatively little discomfort. I also, however, had little use of my upper arms which the doctor explained by saying there had also been some spinal cord injury. As I became more aware, that translated into being unable to raise my hand to my face—to feed myself, brush my teeth, wash my face or comb my hair. Asking how long it would be before the use of my arms returned I was told, "We'll just have to wait and see but we will start physical therapy right away."

In addition to working with my arms, the therapist helped me regain use of my left leg, which had been temporarily assaulted by the removal of a piece of bone from that hip. She walked with me—first with a walker, then with a cane. After a week or so we began to climb stairs and I felt as if we were making great progress. Everybody was astounded because I came back so rapidly. I knew I had a choice—I could resist what was happening or I could just be with it. Every night I went to sleep listening to sounds of the ocean with earphones connected to my CD player. At some point, the night nurse would remove the earphones and turn off the player. They joked with me a little about lulling myself to sleep but their joking had a quality of tenderness in it.

Jill, Jan, Marta and Jerry were with me before and after the surgery; they made sure I was okay, then Marta and Jan returned to California. Jill and Jerry visited every two or three days. Jill brought me clothes that could be worn without having to go over my head and a mobile of flying geese which she hung in the corner of my hospital room. Jerry walked up and down the corridors with me, sometimes staying to help me eat lunch and play *Rummikub*. Judy Hanscom, my eldest stepdaughter, drove down from Maine to see me and her visits gave me the opportunity we'd never really had to get acquainted. This love of, and for, my family was a major factor in my healing.

It was seven weeks from the time I fell, to the day I returned from Boston to my apartment at Jill's. Physical therapy continued on a daily basis. I still remember sitting on the floor having a ball rolled for me to roll back, and feeling utterly frustrated at being unable to catch or throw a Frisbee. At night, before going to sleep, I often thought about why I seemed to cling so tenaciously to life. I saw the cancer and the broken neck as nothing more than stumbling blocks—things to get beyond to go wherever I was going, even if I didn't know where that was. I did know, however that there was still something for me to do in life and I wasn't ready to be taken out of the game.

Along with the impatience to get to that "somewhere," however, there was the occasional fear of being overtaken by the years. Sometimes the conversation with my children turned to "What if…? What then?" But I've never been willing to entertain those questions. They give more power to the circumstances of my life than I am willing to give. I know I am responsible for my experience of these last years—I can listen to the chatter in my mind, and the chatter of others about aging, or I can be present to my life, regarding every day as a gift, relegating that chatter to the background.

In my last visit to the doctor, he said he was pleased with the results of the surgery, was confident that I would regain use of my arms and had only one caution—no more body surfing and no bunjee jumping! I laughed with him about the bunjee jumping—something I've never had a desire to do—but was actually a little disappointed about the body surfing because that was one of my favorite things to do in Hawaii.

I had been determined to be well in time for Rebecca's wedding to Jacob Notowitz, scheduled for June 11, and I returned to San Francisco just a week before the wedding. Wearing a soft collar on my neck, I flew first class and was pampered by a flight attendant, who escorted me to the ladies room, cut my food and helped me to eat. In San Francisco I stayed with Rebecca. Jacob's family had supported the kids—both emotionally and financially—and the entire wedding was planned without my having to do a thing except show up. And show up I did. On the wedding day Rebecca was radiant and before the ceremony Jacob came to where I was sitting, knelt down beside me and said softly into my ear, "I will always love her and take care of her." The tears that had been held back for weeks threatened to ruin my makeup.

The doctor had said I could take the collar off for the wedding but when Jan saw me dancing, she came out and whispered in my ear that if I didn't sit down she would bring the collar out and put it on me on the dance floor, right there in front of everybody. I gave in and returned to my table. The day went beautifully and my only sadness was that Sarge couldn't have been there to walk his little girl down the aisle. Marta was her matron of honor, Jan and Jerry were there, as was Susan, Jill's daughter. Nancy, Betsy, and cousin Barry, represented Sarge's side of the family, along with his remaining siblings.

While I was staying at Rebecca's, before the wedding, Margaret Baker, with whom I lived in Hawai'i from 1991 to 1994, called and invited me to return and stay with her for the summer. Since Hawai'i and healing were synonymous in my mind I accepted the offer and, on the 28th of June, boarded a plane for Honolulu. When I got to Hawai'i and went into the pool at Mt. Terrace, I was dismayed because the most I could do was a sort of dog paddle on my back. The arms didn't work well enough to swim! I went for physical therapy twice a week and did exercises at home night and morning, both in and out of the pool. By mid-summer I was able to swim the sidestroke and felt as if I had won the Olympics. At the end of September, when I was ready to return to California, I was swimming ten laps of the pool in the crawl—something I had thought, a few months earlier, I might never do again. The first time I succeeded in swimming from one end of the pool to the other, I stood up, clapped my hands and said out loud, "By God, I've made it again!"

When I returned, Pauline Proschan, a San Francisco friend, offered me hospitality while I looked for an apartment in the city. Pauline and I had been friends since we were both in the Growing Older group in 1982. I was with Pauline for a month and then moved to the Cathedral Hill Plaza, where I had lived in the eighties. This time there was a beautiful corner apartment available, with two windows facing west and floor-to-ceiling windows opening onto a balcony along the north side of the living room. Because it had two bedrooms and two baths I knew I could rent out a room and thus be able to afford it. By the middle of November, however, I was again worrying. Planning for retirement was not something I had ever done and here I was, with an income of eighteen thousand dollars a year, living in an apartment for which the rent was almost seventeen thousand and I hadn't yet rented out the extra room.

I thought back on all the financial mistakes I had made in my life, all the "what-ifs." Ever since leaving my job at Logistix, I had managed on Social Security supplemented by part-time work and, after Sarge's death, by a small pension, but furnishing an apartment in San Francisco had put me back in debt. I tried telling myself that as soon as I was established and back in touch with people in the Bay Area, I would have someone with whom to share the apartment, I would have work, but all I could see were the bills.

My sister-in-law, Charlotte, had asked me, a few weeks before, "Who do you think will hire you?" In my bravado I laughed, while quietly wondering if she might not be right, but then I told myself that I was in transition, that it looked hopeless only because I couldn't see what was ahead or what would pull me out of the financial morass. Before the holidays, things began looking up. I was tutoring older people who wanted to learn to use the computer, and a young Japanese student would move in at the beginning of the new year. Suddenly I knew everything would work out. It always had, but occasionally I forgot to trust the process. Motoko Komatsu moved in and by the middle of February, 1996, I was thoroughly enjoying her. She was a beautiful, highly educated (M.D.) woman who thought she wanted to do something other than work in medicine. Her father was supporting her so she was attending City College to improve her English and was experimenting with this and that, including ballroom dancing. I was able to overlook the mess in her room given that she honored my request to keep the mess there and not in the living room or kitchen. It was like having a daughter at home again—I helped her with homework, corrected her English pronunciation, cautioned her about the guy who wanted to sleep with her but wouldn't use condoms. She did little things like wash and wax the kitchen floor without being asked and went through the apartment gathering and emptying all the wastebaskets. She was really sweet when not involved with that man who treated her so badly, but when he was around she acted like a naughty child and was a pain in the neck. I hoped she would find a nice guy.

In the following year she did, and late in the fall of 1998, I witnessed her marriage to Todd Porter at the city clerk's office. She moved out and I was once again looking for someone to share the apartment. A note on an Internet bulletin board prompted lots of inquiries. It was amusing to get a call from a young man who wanted to see the room, have him knock on the door and then suddenly change his mind when he saw his prospective landlady, but it all worked out perfectly. One day I had a call from a young woman student who had seen the ad. When she called she pronounced her name and then spelled it for me. I recognized immediately that the difference between spelling and pronunciation could mean she was Turkish and asked her if that was the case. She was delighted that I had recognized it and even more pleased to learn that I had lived in Turkey. Ahu Kiciman came to see the available room, took it, and was with me until the middle of August 2002, when she completed her study and returned to Turkey.

21

The Prodigal Returns

I hadn't participated with Landmark since leaving the Holiday Project in 1988, except for reviewing the Landmark Forum in Hawai'i in 1994. At that time I cried for most of two days afterward as I confronted the fact that it had been twenty years since I declared my intention to be an *est* trainer and I had not succeeded. I was overwhelmed by sadness as I realized the dream was over. I felt almost as if I were recovering from a beating, a physical pummeling, in the midst of which there were moments of lightness when I realized that acknowledging the end of the dream left a clearing, an opening, for something else to show up. I had no idea what that something else would be but the opening allowed for possibility, for creation. Perhaps it was up to me?

Then, in early 1997, I accepted an invitation to watch the video tape of an event that had been held in Los Angeles—an event declaring Landmark Education's commitment to the future, to its goals for the year 2020. I was moved by watching the tape, even though I was sitting in front of a VCR in San Francisco. One of the speakers in Los Angeles was a 13-year-old girl who spoke of having grown up in a Landmark family and being unable to imagine growing up any other way. I knew I wanted it to be possible for all children to feel that way about their parents and their upbringing. Hearing her also took me back to what I had thought I might accomplish with *est* in Education in 1974–76.

I was back in the game! The prodigal daughter was returning to the fold. Recognizing that I would be a hundred years old in 2020, I vowed to be around to celebrate both events. Almost immediately I registered for the Wisdom Unlimited Course—one of the extended programs of Landmark—and for the Introduction to the Landmark Forum Leader Program (IFLP). It was almost as if, having been away from the work for so long, I couldn't get enough. During the fourth weekend of the Wisdom course I recognized that whether or not I'd become a Landmark Forum Leader, everything that had happened along the way had been on purpose. I wouldn't have been exactly where I was by any other route and I was mightily pleased with my life right then.

During the second weekend of the IFLP I had a disconcerting insight. I knew that ever since returning to Landmark, I had been using my history in the organization to criticize today's Landmark. The supply room in the office was not the orderly one that I remembered from my staff experience, the guest events didn't have the level of impeccability which I was sure was responsible for the spectacular results of our guest events back then, assistants weren't managed in a way that insured they would get more out of assisting than they put in. And on and on. Every time I was in an event I found something to criticize. Looking from this into my life allowed me to see how frequently I listened for "something's wrong." Having the opportunity to speak about this in the weekend allowed me to see what I had been doing and also to see the opportunity I had to use my years of experience to support and empower today's organization instead of criticizing everything. It was a wonderfully freeing shift.

In the third weekend of the IFLP I had another breakthrough—one that enabled me to see how I had been interacting with Jill for years, being stuck in judgments that kept me from seeing and appreciating the person she is today. I knew, even as I saw this, that I would forget, from time to time, and slip back into the old ways but I also realized that I would never slip back without being aware of doing so and knowing I'd have to suffer the consequences.

On Mothers' Day of 1999 I had gift I could never have foreseen. Thirty-four years before, Sarge's eldest son, Pete, had fathered a child who was given up for adoption at birth. That child had been born around the same time as Rebecca, and both Sarge and I, as well as other members of the Russell family, had made pleas to be allowed to adopt him and raise him as our own, but the birth mother refused and put him out for adoption. The child, now a young man, had just found his birth family and I received a call on Mother's day giving me the news. I was elated. For thirty years, as I watched Rebecca grow up, I had wondered about this nephew of hers. The news, though wonderful, was tinged by sadness because Pete, the boy's father, had died the year before, alone and in tragic circumstances. In New Hampshire for my birthday that year I drove down to Needham, Massachusetts, to meet this long-lost step grandson. As I approached the house, Ward Slocum Caswell came out of the kitchen door, his arms open to welcome me. We embraced and I turned my head aside to hide the tears that had come unbidden.

The year 2000—my eightieth—was a highlight, with a fabulous birthday celebration, another Russell family reunion, a Holiday Project reunion for early players, an acknowledgement party in New York just before Christmas and the holiday itself with my East Coast family. Marta had planned a week's worth of activities for my birthday. She said that a day wasn't long enough to celebrate eighty years of living. The Russell family reunion that year was held at Asilomar, on the California coast near Monterey, and the Holiday Project gathering, organized by a team of old players led by Sidney Weimer, was in the mountains of Colorado.

In Colorado, we hiked, fished, took tours, played billiards, went on hayrides and danced, but mostly we shared with each other what we had been up to in the years since we worked together. Earl Babbie, a former member of the board of directors, joined us. Victor Ozeri brought an RV, which he parked on the campgrounds and provided late night parties where we reminisced and, with the help of vodka, told jokes that got more and more colorful as the night went on. Richard Carpenter provided logistics support, as he had for the first annual Holiday Project conference in San Francisco. Richard had, for years, acknowledged me for seeing beyond his history into the person he was and some years ago sent me a holiday card with this message: "I am always inspired and empowered from your caring for me. Thank you for seeing the me inside, thank you for your love and respect. Enclosed is a picture of the marble floor tile with your name on it. It will be part of the floor in one of the temples of the Emerald and Reclining Buddha complex in Cambodia. I'll show it to you in person one day soon and give you a personal guided tour." (I'm still looking forward to that Cambodian tour with Richard.). On our last evening, we had dinner together and people shared what had been happening in their lives in the years since we'd worked together. There were many whose sharing bore testimony to the impact their lives had had on their communities and by the end of the evening we were all in love with each other again. Victor Ozeri's life had been such a miracle of transformation from those days that I asked him to share the story, a part of which follows:

> "As a child, I was told quite often by both educator and parent not to hope for much, as I didn't have the capacity to amount to much. So you can imagine what a gift The Holiday Project was to me. To discover, at the age of 29, that you are more than you've been told, was a contribution of immeasurable value. With that thought, I began to look for gainful employment that would raise the bar of what I had been doing with The Holiday Project. In very little time I was offered a position to go to the People's Republic of China to work for a handbag company....The next ten years in Asia were a grand adventure, with one success after another and, at the same time, being afforded the privilege of making a contribution to the People's Republic of China. In 1991 I returned to America and started my own company. Today I operate Interasia

Bag Manufacturers, Ltd. in Hong Kong and China with a staff of 150 in our three offices and several thousand factory workers in Quong Dong Province."

Victor went on to amaze us with an account of all the community service he is contributing in the city of New York. Those of us who had known him "back when" were overwhelmed by what we heard. We had always loved Victor but had only glimpses of what he had become in the years since we last worked together. I was in tears as he finished speaking.

I stayed in touch with Victor after the reunion and when I told him that I was planning to have Christmas with my daughter in New Hampshire, he asked me to stop in New York City. He had reserved a hotel room for me and the next day took me for lunch at the Tavern on the Green in Central Park, then to Harlem to visit the Children's Storefront school, which he supports. Meeting with the headmaster of the school, I had an experience of being "more than" Elizabeth in our conversation. It was almost as if our thoughts about education were so compatible they took on a life of their own. It was one of those times when the connection was so powerful and the communication so good that the conversation seemed almost independent of the people conversing. Friday night Victor hosted a dinner at the Russian Tea Room, and again on Saturday night in the Jazz Room of the Blue Water Café. Both nights there was a surfeit of food and drink and acknowledgment, making me again aware of how much I value my relationship with this young man. Sunday morning, after a leisurely breakfast at the hotel, I rented a car and drove to New Hampshire for Christmas with the family.

It was a hectic, fun-filled time including a first meeting with my new great-granddaughter, Taylor, and an hour of watching *Lady and the Tramp* with Amanda, another great-granddaughter. After Christmas I had a couple of falls, cut short my stay in New Hampshire and returned to San Francisco. There were more doctor visits, more tests. A neurosurgeon said it looked as if there was pressure on the spinal cord but suggested waiting a few months to see if it would take care of itself before doing a surgical correction. Marta suggested I go back to Hawai'i for recuperation and that was all I needed. I made arrangements and, on the first of March, left San Francisco on a United Airlines flight for three months in Honolulu. I came back to San Francisco on May 29th, having shed the problems that sent me to Hawai'i, wondering only why I didn't pack my belongings and make it my permanent home. Back in my apartment, looking at all the family pictures, I had my answer.

Today, the whole group that I call "family" includes five children, six stepchildren, twenty-three grandchildren and, as of this writing, twenty great-grandchildren. Since they are spread from Maine to California. I doubt that I will ever see them all together but have no doubt at all about them enriching my life. Although my children were seldom consulted, or considered, when I was making decisions, they were good sports and complained only infrequently. Rebecca was in nine schools in her twelve school years and says it taught her adaptability and that she took our way of life as an opportunity to invent herself time and again.

Jan, my eldest, "mothered" her two younger siblings when we were at Cornell and has continued mothering me as we grow older together. She attended The Meeting School on a full scholarship, as did Jerry. Both she and Jerry graduated from the University of Massachusetts. Jan is now a teacher and a subsistence farmer in northern California and is married to Michael McDonald. She has a son, Nicholas, two adopted daughters, and is raising her granddaughter. Jill was awarded an R.N. and B.S. in 1978. She has three children—Susan, Jeff and Stott—and is married to John Hare, with whom she runs an online book business and with whom she co-authored the bibliography, *Tasha Tudor: The Direction of Her Dreams*. Jerry has spent most of his adult life as a lobsterman and boat designer on Cape Cod although he is currently working for FEMA. He has never married and we laughingly chide him for being the family bachelor. Marta has two children—Remy and Alex—and a step daughter, Maisha. With her husband, Stephen, she started a business and became a highly successful businesswoman, appearing for many years, in *Working Woman* magazine's list of "Top 50 Women Business Owners." Rebecca graduated from Lowell High School in San Francisco, as a National Merit Scholar, and from Cornell with a degree in linguistics. She is married to Jacob Notowitz and is a full-time mother of two—Joshua and Tamara. Betsy, probably because of her year with us in Turkey, has been the one of Sarge's children with whom I've had a close and continuing relationship. She is a pathologist in Salt Lake City, is married to Victor Pollak, and has two grown children—Rachel and Ben. I regret not having made the effort to nurture the relationships with my other step children although I do treasure my visits with Judy whenever I'm on the east coast and I usually hear from Ed at Christmas.

Soon after my return to California I had a phone call from Alex Wang's brother-in-law telling me that Alex had died, on April 8th, but because I was away they didn't know how to reach me. Alex had been ill only a short time, having been diagnosed early that year with pancreatic cancer. All I could think of was why hadn't I gone to Beijing for a visit as Alex had been asking me to do for years. I had been putting it off and suddenly it was too late. I was heartbroken. Alex was one of the most important men in my life. Our relationship never depended on physical proximity but was kept alive by letters and an occasional visit when he was on a lecture tour. After hearing the news of his death I called and spoke to his daughter, who lives in Chicago, and to whom I had always been "Aunt Betty." Then I wrote my farewell letter to Alex, simply for myself.

> "I learned yesterday of your death. I find it difficult even to write that word because I can't grasp the enormity of it. I have loved you for fifty years and even though we were both married to others I thought of you as my friend, my lover, my soul mate.
> "The flood of memories that washed over me last night was almost enough to drown me except that they were all so beautiful. You teaching my children games that encouraged cooperation instead of competition. When they were squabbling you found ways to distract them until they forgot what they had been squabbling about. And when I got upset about the way people treated you, you were the one who pleaded with me to forgive them. You said they didn't have the power to hurt you and were only hurting themselves. You taught me lessons in living that I'd never had from my parents, my church or my teachers.
> "We were separated, during our lifetime, by a culture and half a world, yet our love and friendship survived that separation. Why then now, dear friend, should it be any different? You will always be a part of my life and I will always be grateful for having known and loved you. So this is not goodbye, it is only bon voyage."

As I write, Alex is as much alive to me as he was fifty years ago. My relationship with him is outside of space and time. We connected immediately at the Quaker conference and maintained that connection over our lives. He married Lillian and when he brought her to San Francisco to meet me I knew that she knew what our relationship was. Even without a common language, she and I became close very quickly. We both loved the same man.

In June of 2001 I started the year-long *Partnership Explorations* course, one of the senior courses of Landmark Education Corporation. The course was led by Brian Regnier. Of all the people who worked with Werner, I see Brian as the closest to Werner. Yet there is a comic element about that because Werner is a tall, good looking man over whom women swoon, and Brian is short, skinny, not very handsome, has a sort of pixie expression and wears glasses. Also Brian is irreverent in speech and has a quirky sense of humor. But, for all the difference of style and form, these two men have made the most difference for me of all the people I've worked with in *est*/Landmark and I love them both.

The *Partnership* course was the closest I'd come to a philosophy course in many years. It was essentially a program researching the capacity of the human being to remake the world through language—a remaking that starts with relationship rather than individual. At the beginning of the course we were told that if we were willing to be deeply, profoundly confused, there would be enormous benefits, that "already knowing" would get in the way. The course called for a shift from approaching the world through myself, as individual, to approaching it through relationship and I discovered that trying to understand that put me squarely into the confusion which the course promised would benefit me. But there was something about the idea of approaching the world through relationship that gave me a hint of what had happened with Mark in my meeting at the Children's Storefront School in Harlem. There it seemed as if the conversation was the product of our relatedness and Mark and I, as individuals, showed up out of that conversation. And then Ken Ireland appeared, saying he would like to work with me in editing this book. It wasn't long after starting to work with him that I realized our relationship was producing something I'd been unable to produce alone. This was the beginning of the conscious awareness of a shift from focus on Elizabeth as identity to Elizabeth as belonging to family, community, society, world—a shift that doesn't stay in place but moves in and out with, I must admit, the focus mostly on Elizabeth as identity.

After completing *Partnership* I enrolled in the next course, *Power and Contribution*. In that course I made an impossible promise—one that I do not expect to live to see fulfilled but a promise that will form the context for the rest of my life. That promise is that by the year 2030 all children in the world will have their innate desire to learn nurtured and supported. I saw that this promise brought me full circle back to the beginning of my life. As a child I had passion for learning but that passion was denigrated, "You ask too many questions," so it went underground but has been like a spark that has burst into flame from time to time throughout my life. It was the spark that prompted my questions to Uncle Will about the universe; it was that which Gordon Pyper recognized when he encouraged me to apply to college, that which kept me sitting on a stool in the stacks of the Cornell library. It was that which had me take flying lessons and have a baby unaided at home, so I could really find out what childbirth was. It was that which made me opt for an LSD trip, rush off to India without a second thought. It is that which fills each day with possibility. It explains many of the things that seemed impulsive, unreasonable but were actually in the service of that innate desire to learn.

Once again enrolling in the Landmark Forum, in February of 2004, I had a quest. It was to see if I could find out what it was that I didn't know I didn't know about myself. I realized this was a question that arose out of the *Partnership* course and still had not been answered. I had a notion that there was something profound that was hidden, something which, if I knew it, would allow me to experience myself as whole and complete—that self I had glimpsed over the years but which, as an on-going state, eluded me. From the time I was a little girl I had been trying to get somewhere, to get better, get smarter, get more beautiful, be more loved. This translated into always feeling "less than"—less than the other girls in school, less than my teachers and, much later, less than Werner. I was talking to a friend one day after completing the Landmark Forum and was suddenly aware of being senior to the experience I was relating. This led to recognizing myself as senior to the Landmark Forum, senior to the Landmark Forum leader. It was as if I were holding it all. Briefly I knew myself as context. There was no place to go, nothing to get. I had it all, yet there wasn't any "I." This was the space, the clearing, the context in which everything occurred. This was what I had been seeking throughout my life—the place I had glimpsed during Marta's birth, during my LSD trip and, momentarily, when I was lost in the symphony or in a sunset.

Looking back over what I had written I had that same sense of being senior to all of it—all the details of my life—of actually holding it all, being able to turn it this way and that to look at it, recognizing that the acute loneliness and the experience of oneness were merely ways of describing what was being experienced at the time and that experience was part of a whole that rendered itself available to division, to description, only by abstraction, only by standing off, looking at the experience and giving it some kind of interpretation, giving it a name. My life as a whole is just that—my life as a whole—and as such it is senior to the details; it is the place in which everything happened. In that space, the details take on different shapes, different hues. I look back on that little Puritan girl and look at her with tenderness. I look at my mother with compassion and see someone other than I thought I knew. The memories of my brother as the adored one return full blown. For the men I loved there is gratitude for whether or not such relationships realized the potential I thought they had, each one helped shape the person I've become.

Epilogue

Now there is this business of growing older. I'm not fully at peace with it yet. As I look in the mirror, the reflection I see there is incompatible with my sense of self. I'm sixteen or forty, in love, walking the beach with my father, driving a car too fast, nursing a child, teaching a class—but I'm not that reflection in the mirror. And I'm closer to acceptance. I notice that when I look away from the mirror I'm still wondering what else and who else may be out there for me.

And life goes on. I've had a hip replacement, a stroke, another spinal surgery and the loss of my beloved sister-in-law, Charlotte. I may have a year or ten years left or I may make it to a hundred, but I know there are no guarantees and I am living every day as if it were the only one. I wake each morning with curiosity about what the day may bring and go to sleep each night with gratitude for loving, for being loved and for being alive.

As I get older, I have all the aches and pains of an aging body, but they are in the background while what is in the foreground is that elusive something of which I've been aware most of my life, that thing that kept me reading under the covers at night when reading was forbidden. When I looked up at the night sky and wondered, it was that curiosity, that innate wanting to learn. It has been alive ever since I was a child and, today, wanting to nurture that desire in myself and others is what keeps me going. Keeping that spark alive is the not-so-secret secret of living full out up to the end of life.

Today I know Elizabeth as the totality of all she has lived through, as a whole human being nearing the end of her life—freed of judgment about how she might have lived, what she might have done. This place of acceptance is a place of freedom because it allows me to love the particular human being I am; it is a space of openness because, although I may be "nearing the end," I'm not there yet and tomorrow looks like an invitation to adventure.

In pursuit of the question of who I am, I have finally come to see that I am nothing apart from everything else, but I show up in my speaking and listening. I am a clearing for conversation to show up in the world. Only as an identity—only when I think all I am is Elizabeth—am I separate. I really know who I am in those rare moments when the question, and I, cease to exist, as when Marta was born or when I am overpowered by the music of the symphony, the beauty of a sunset. At those times I literally experience a dissolving of the barriers that keep me separate. Fleeting though they may be, these moments tell me I am not alone, that I'm one with all that is. Today, though I certainly don't dwell in that space of *oneness,* I have more frequent glimpses of it. There are moments when I know that I am connected to everything, but I also know that, in my everydayness, I will forget and return to seeing myself as less than, separate from and, sometimes, as victim.

As a human being I am a unity of experience in which recalling the past and anticipating the future join to increase awareness, thus endowing the present with authenticity. The past lives in the present as memory but the authentic experience of the present, which assumes memorable quality as it passes, is out of time. It is consciousness without being consciousness *of,* it is understanding that does not take an object but simply enjoys itself. It is reaching the age of 85 still wondering because, for me, what's next has no definition and is still the greatest secret of all.

For many years I asked myself the same questions as had my mother. Surely she had asked them out of the same sense of loneliness, that recognition that each of us is, basically, alone. We are born alone and will die alone but in between birth and death we may experience that sense of "oneness" that links us to everything else in our world. If we are willing to honor paradox and confusion in our lives, we may have a glimpse of the truth and know that, no matter who we are or what we have done, our being alive has made a difference.

Now, struggling for what it is that's trying to be said as I bring this to an end, I realize that if you have read this far, you have listened, you have honored my expression, and you may also have heard the one who is as close to you as your Self.

978-0-595-36168-7
0-595-36168-4

Printed in the United States
94903LV00003B/157-177/A

Reading Under the Covers

◆

An Autobiography

Elizabeth Goodell Russell

iUniverse, Inc.
New York Lincoln Shanghai

Reading Under the Covers
An Autobiography

Copyright © 2005 by Elizabeth Goodell Russell

All rights reserved. No part of this book may be used or reproduced by any means, graphic, electronic, or mechanical, including photocopying, recording, taping or by any information storage retrieval system without the written permission of the publisher except in the case of brief quotations embodied in critical articles and reviews.

iUniverse books may be ordered through booksellers or by contacting:

iUniverse
2021 Pine Lake Road, Suite 100
Lincoln, NE 68512
www.iuniverse.com
1-800-Authors (1-800-288-4677)

ISBN-13: 978-0-595-36168-7 (pbk)
ISBN-13: 978-0-595-80613-3 (ebk)
ISBN-10: 0-595-36168-4 (pbk)
ISBN-10: 0-595-80613-9 (ebk)

Printed in the United States of America